NO.6 #8

Story by: Atsuko Asano
Art by: Hinoki Kino

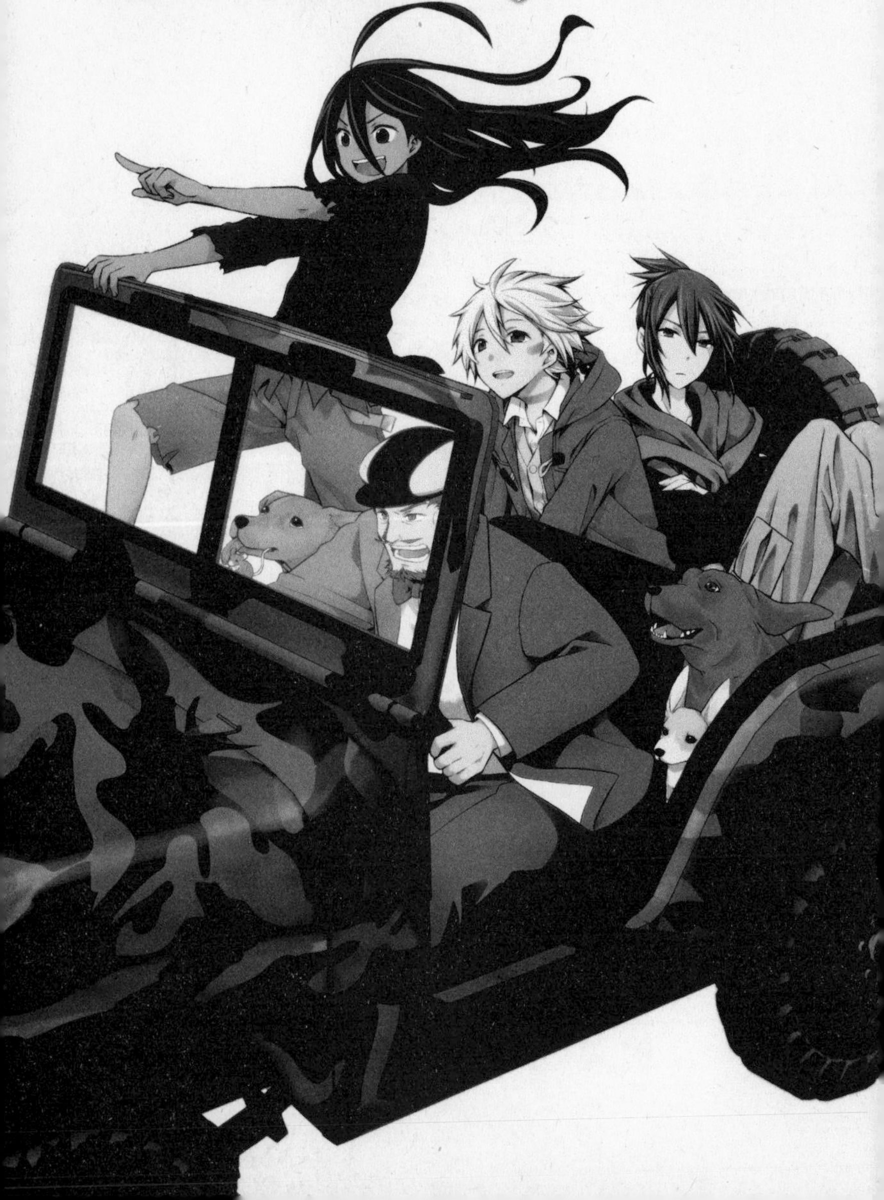

A Kodansha Comics Trade Paperback Original.

NO. 6 volume 8 copyright © 2013 Atsuko Asano, Hinoki Kino
English translation copyright © 2014 Atsuko Asano, Hinoki Kino

All rights reserved.

Published in the United States by Kodansha Comics, an imprint of Kodansha USA Publishing, LLC, New York.

Publication rights for this English edition arranged through Kodansha Ltd., Tokyo.

First published in Japan in 2013 by Kodansha Ltd., Tokyo
ISBN 978-1-61262-578-2

Printed in the United States of America.

www.kodanshacomics.com

9 8 7 6 5 4 3 2 1

Translation: Jonathan Tarbox/Arashi Productions
Lettering: Christy Sawyer
Editing: Ben Applegate

NO.6

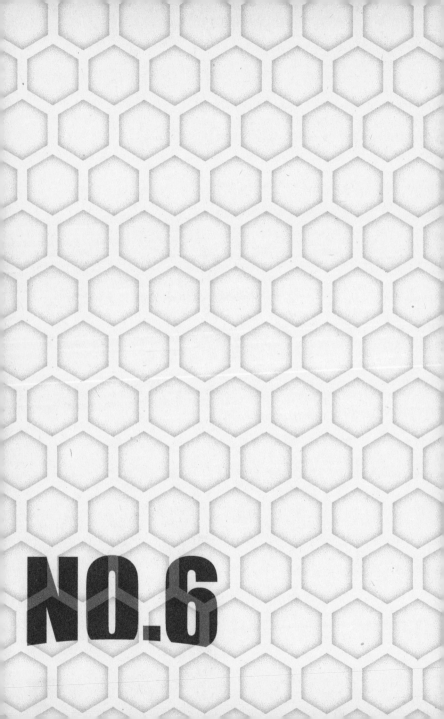

NO.6

#8

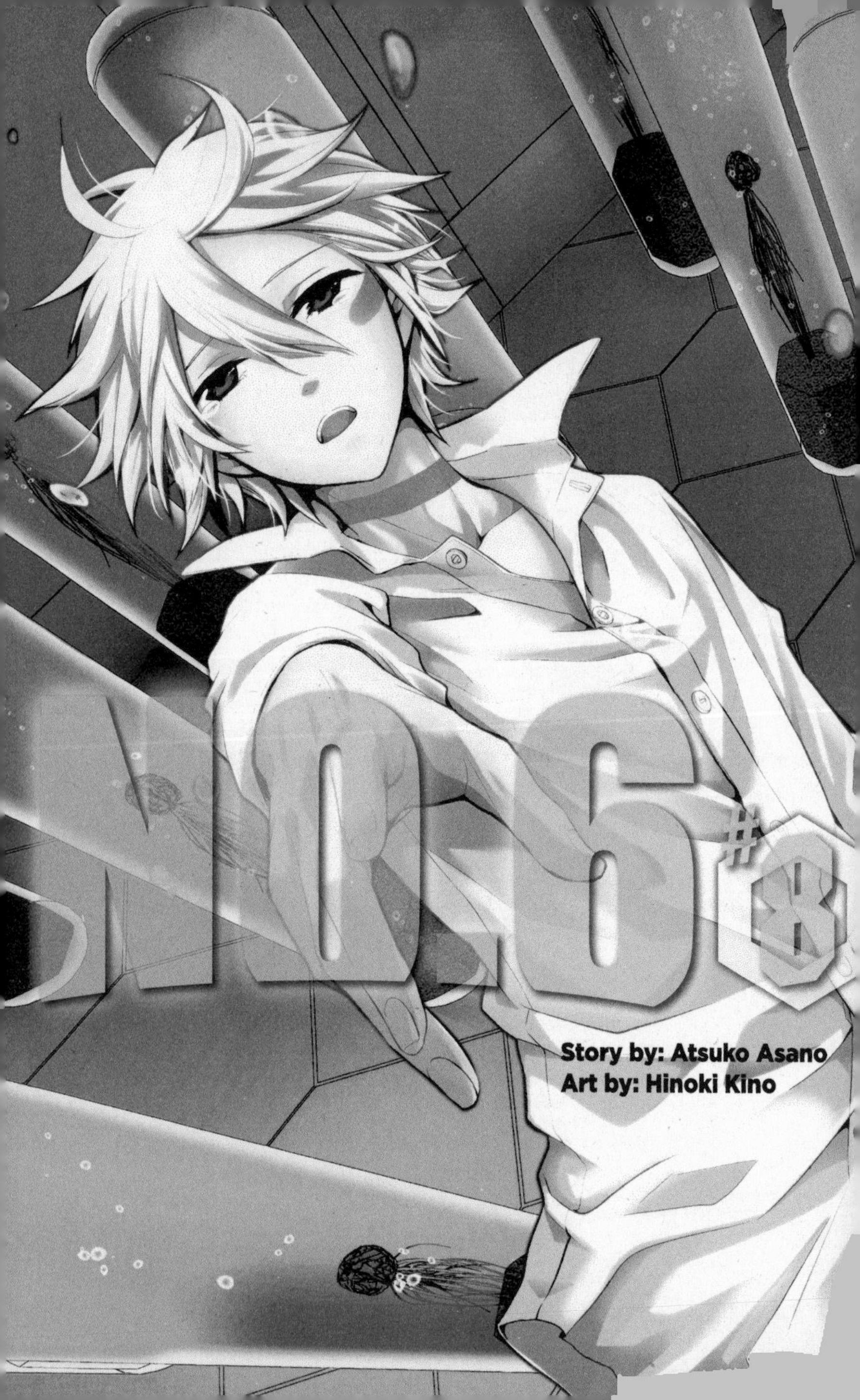
NO.6
#8
Story by: Atsuko Asano
Art by: Hinoki Kino

STORY and CHARACTERS

Shion was raised as a privileged elite in the holy city of NO. 6. As the Public Security Bureau was arresting him on charges of murder, a boy named Rat, whom Shion helped during a storm four years earlier, stepped in to save him. Together they escaped NO. 6 and fled to West Block, a place of violence and chaos. Shion was infected by a mysterious parasitic bee, but survived, living together with Rat in West Block. After hearing that his childhood friend Safu had been detained and taken to the Correctional Facility, Shion decided to go free her. With assistance from Dogkeeper and Rikiga, Shion and Rat snuck into the Correctional Facility. Inside, the two of them found piles of corpses with their brains removed. A security officer ran them down, and just as Rat had given up, Shion suddenly shot their pursuer. Cracking under the weight of having taken a life, Shion reached the top floor, where he suddenly encountered Safu...

Chronos

The top-class residential area, open only to special elite citizens.

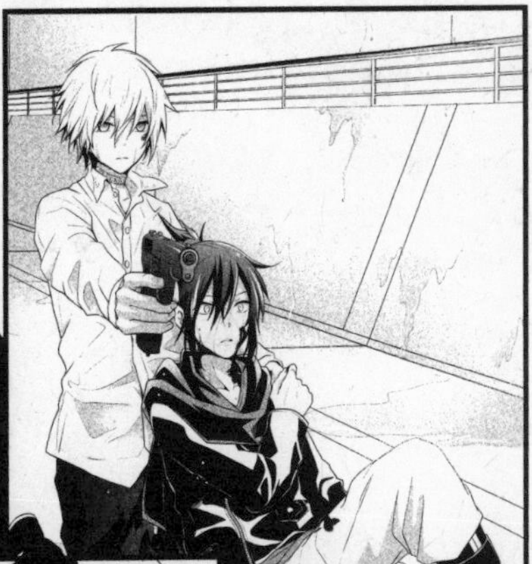

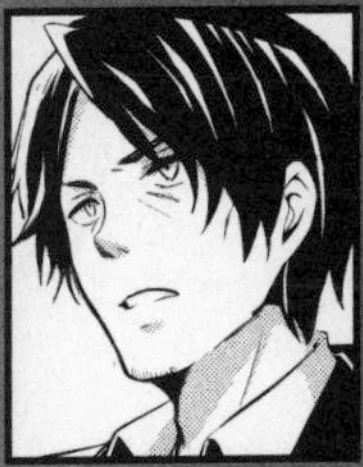

YOMIN

He's doubted NO. 6 since his wife and child died.

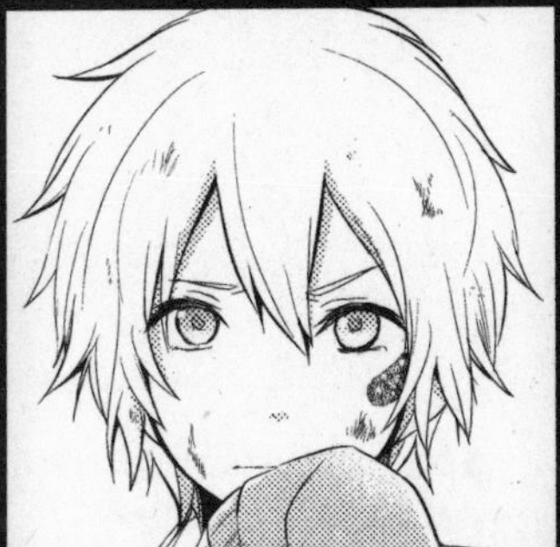

SHION

A former elite candidate, he was a kind, gentle youth, but as his life has grown harsher, he has begun to change.

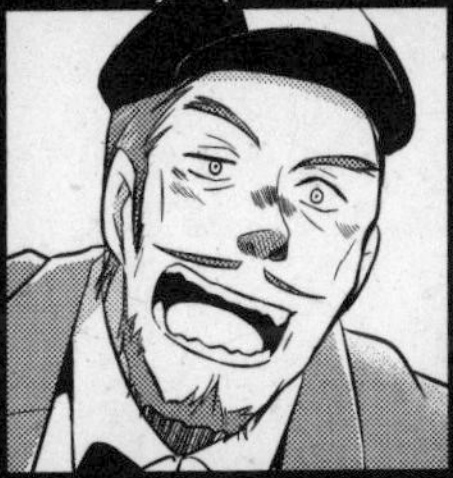

RIKIGA

A former journalist who now publishes a porno magazine in West Block. An old friend of Karan.

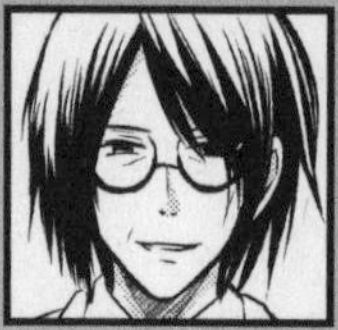

The Man in White

An ambitious research scientist.

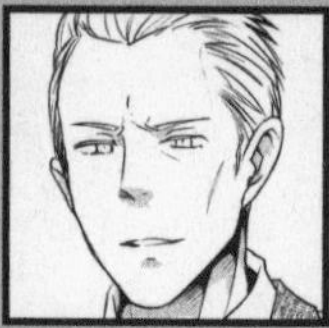

The Mayor

The most powerful man in NO. 6.

Inside NO. 6

Upper Class

The center of the city, with the Moondrop (City Hall) at its apex.

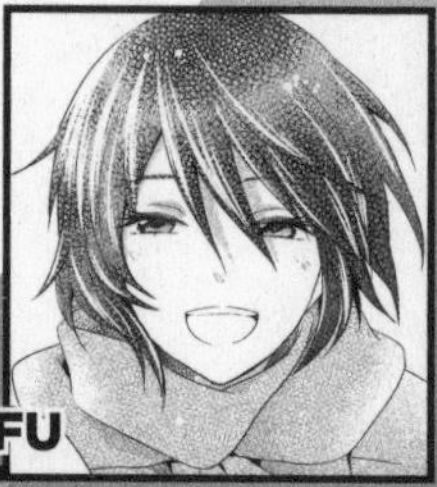

SAFU

A childhood friend who loves Shion. An elite researcher who specializes in neuroscience.

Arrested

The Correctional Facility

The prison for criminals from NO. 6. Located in West Block.

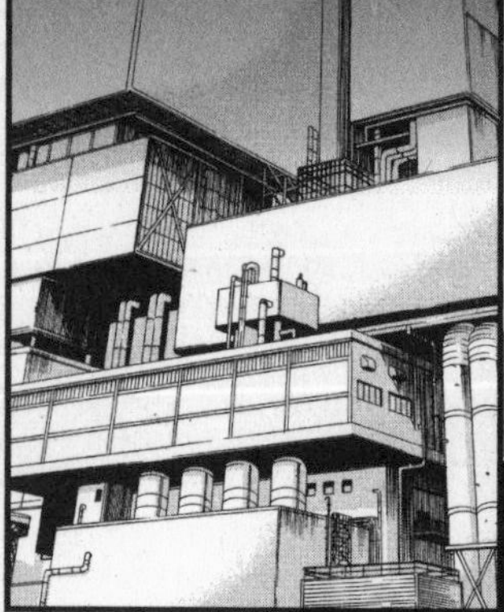

Lost Town

The lower-class residential area for the city's disenfranchised.

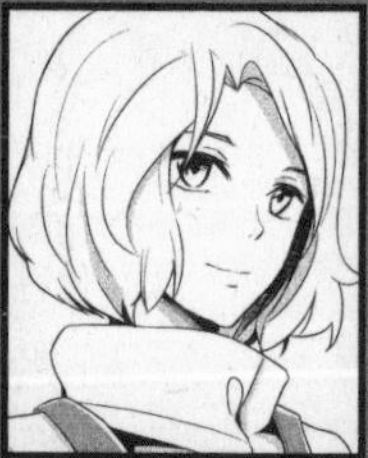

KARAN

Shion's mother. Operates a bakery in Lost Town.

The Outskirts

West Block

The dangerous special zone outside the walls of the city.

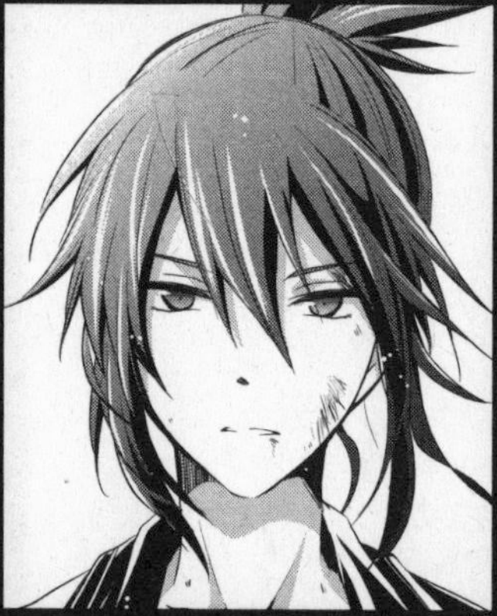

RAT

A youth who despises NO. 6. The sole survivor of the massacred "Forest People."

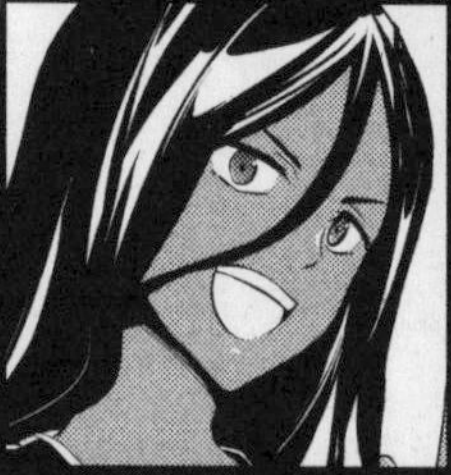

DOGKEEPER

Lives with dogs and operates a dilapidated hotel. Also gathers information for a price.

NO.6

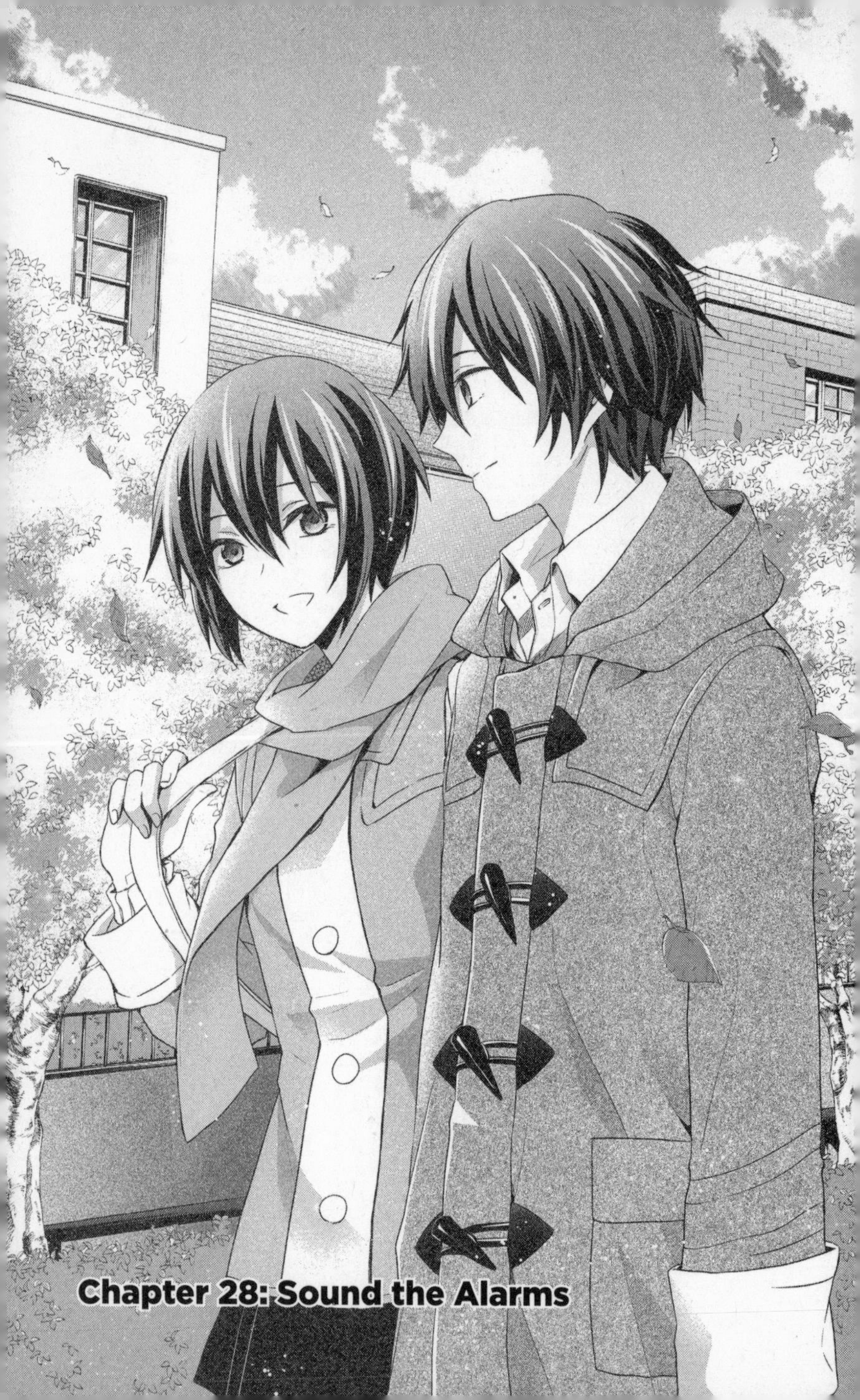
Chapter 28: Sound the Alarms

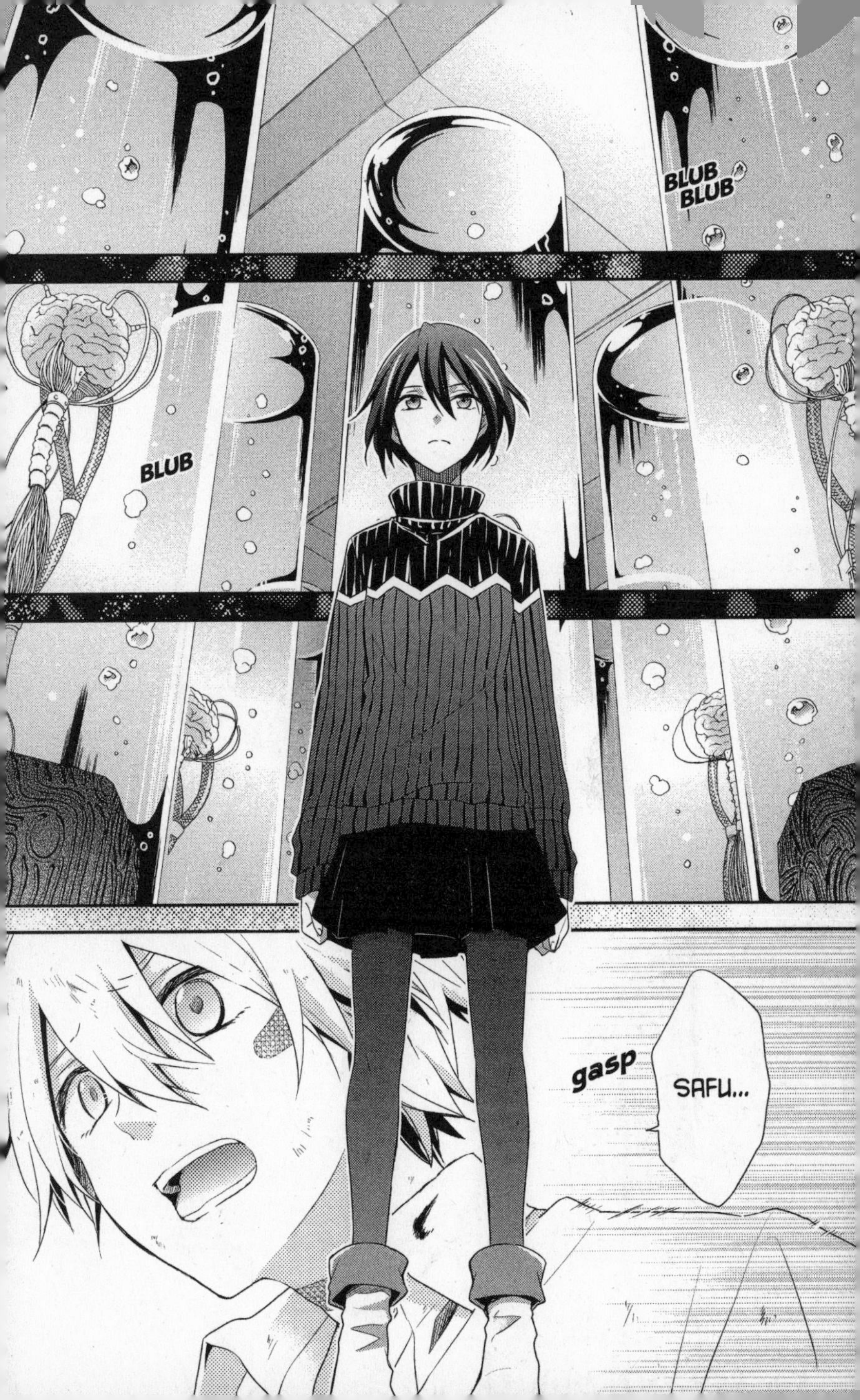
BLUB BLUB
BLUB
SAFU...
gasp

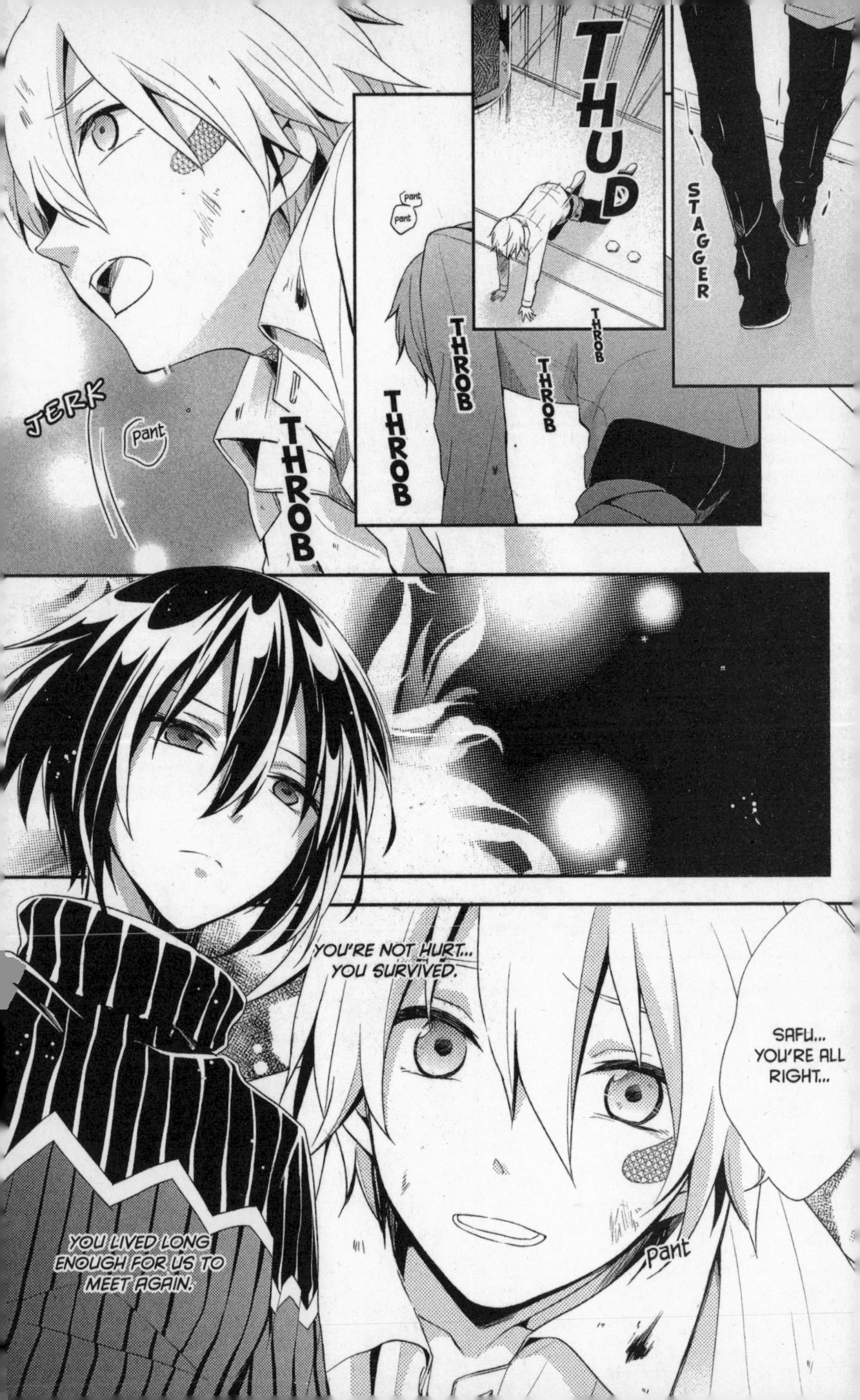

STAGGER
THUD
pant
pant
THROB
THROB
THROB
THROB
THROB
pant
JERK
SAFU... YOU'RE ALL RIGHT...
YOU'RE NOT HURT... YOU SURVIVED.
Pant
YOU LIVED LONG ENOUGH FOR US TO MEET AGAIN.

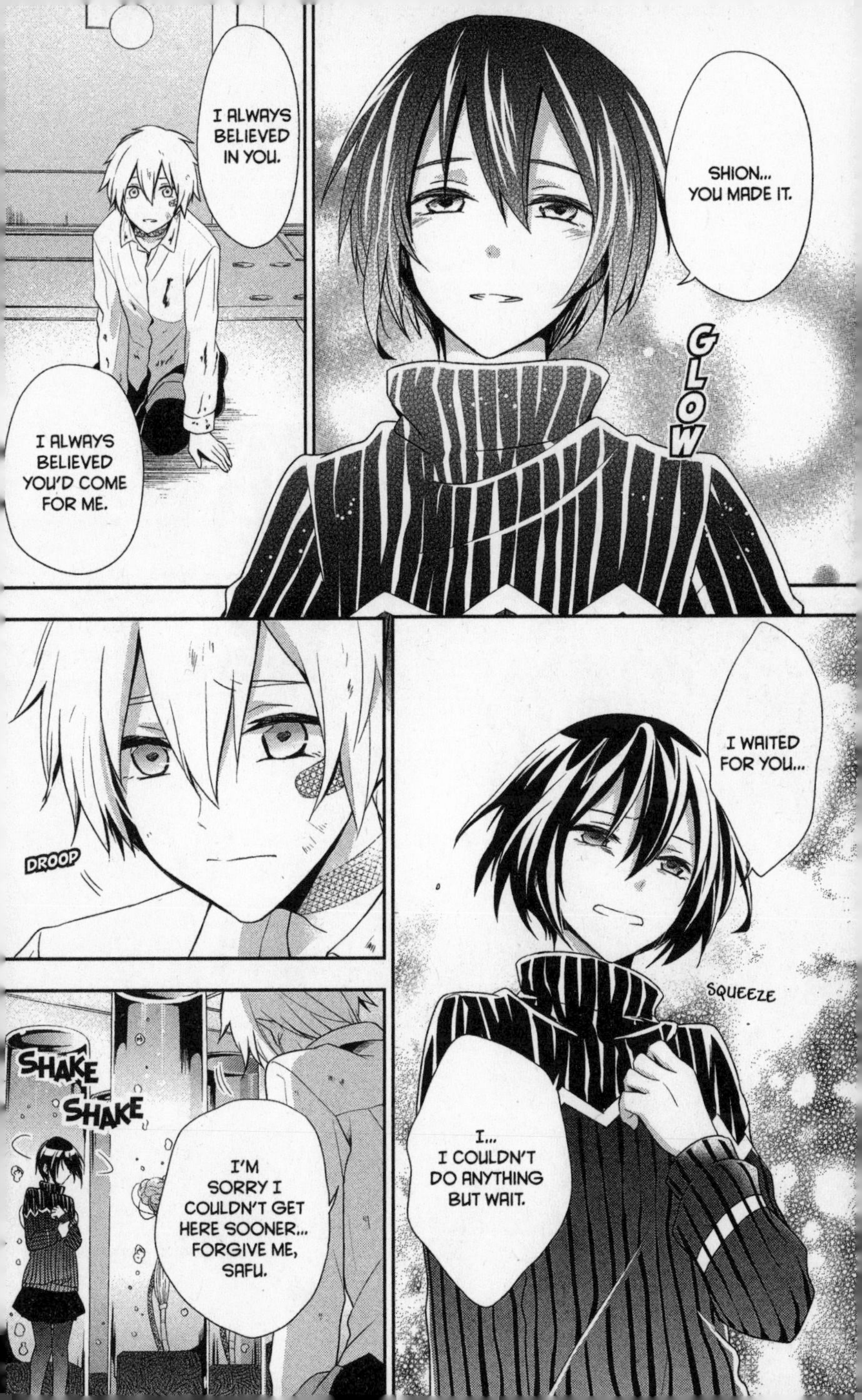
SHION... YOU MADE IT.
GLOW
I ALWAYS BELIEVED IN YOU.
I ALWAYS BELIEVED YOU'D COME FOR ME.
I WAITED FOR YOU...
SQUEEZE
I... I COULDN'T DO ANYTHING BUT WAIT.
DROOP
SHAKE SHAKE
I'M SORRY I COULDN'T GET HERE SOONER... FORGIVE ME, SAFU.

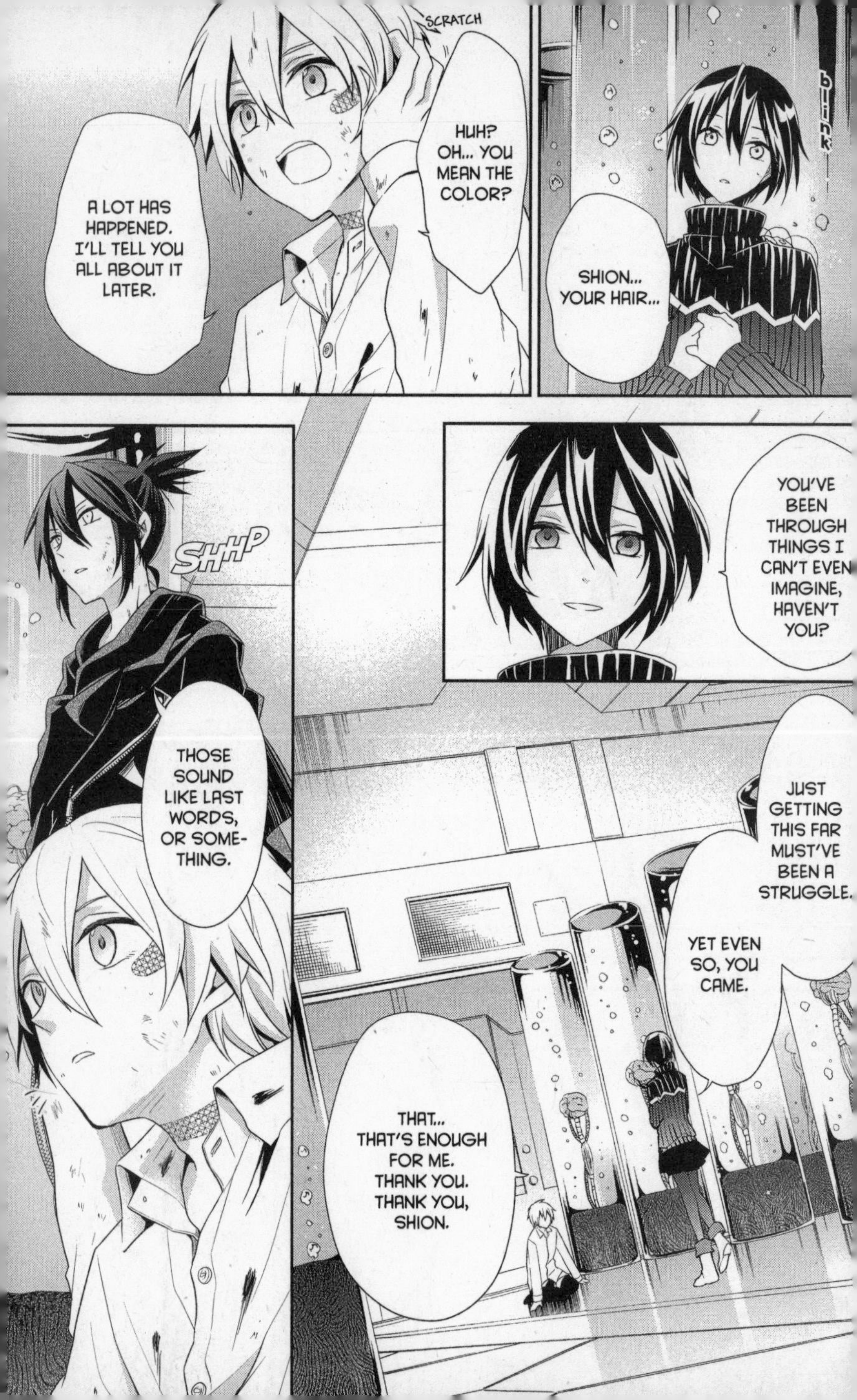
blink
SHION... YOUR HAIR...
SCRATCH
HUH? OH... YOU MEAN THE COLOR?
A LOT HAS HAPPENED. I'LL TELL YOU ALL ABOUT IT LATER.
YOU'VE BEEN THROUGH THINGS I CAN'T EVEN IMAGINE, HAVEN'T YOU?
JUST GETTING THIS FAR MUST'VE BEEN A STRUGGLE.
YET EVEN SO, YOU CAME.
THAT... THAT'S ENOUGH FOR ME. THANK YOU. THANK YOU, SHION.
SHHP
THOSE SOUND LIKE LAST WORDS, OR SOME-THING.

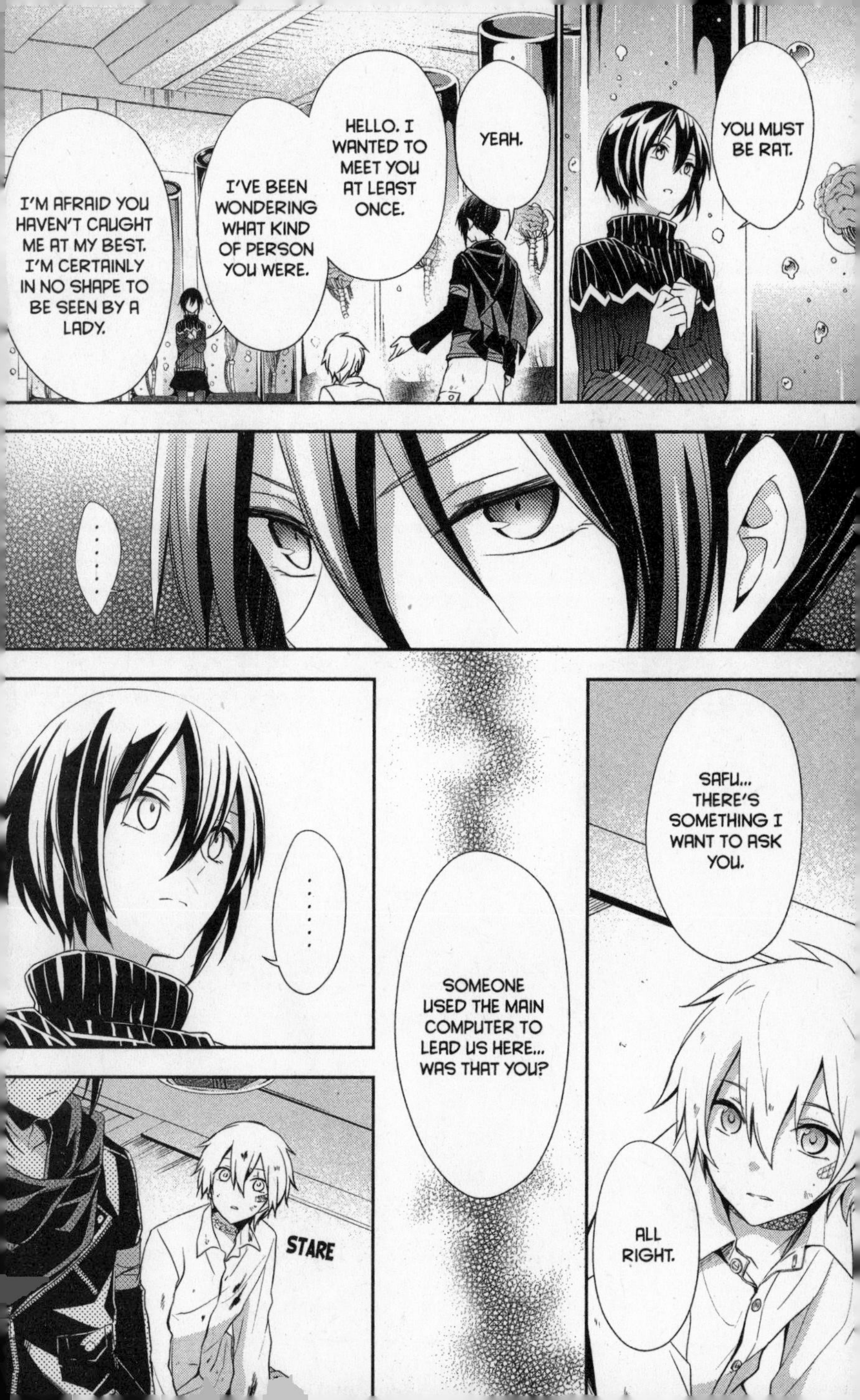

YOU MUST BE RAT.
YEAH.
HELLO. I WANTED TO MEET YOU AT LEAST ONCE.
I'VE BEEN WONDERING WHAT KIND OF PERSON YOU WERE.
I'M AFRAID YOU HAVEN'T CAUGHT ME AT MY BEST. I'M CERTAINLY IN NO SHAPE TO BE SEEN BY A LADY.
......
SAFU... THERE'S SOMETHING I WANT TO ASK YOU.
ALL RIGHT.
SOMEONE USED THE MAIN COMPUTER TO LEAD US HERE... WAS THAT YOU?
......
STARE

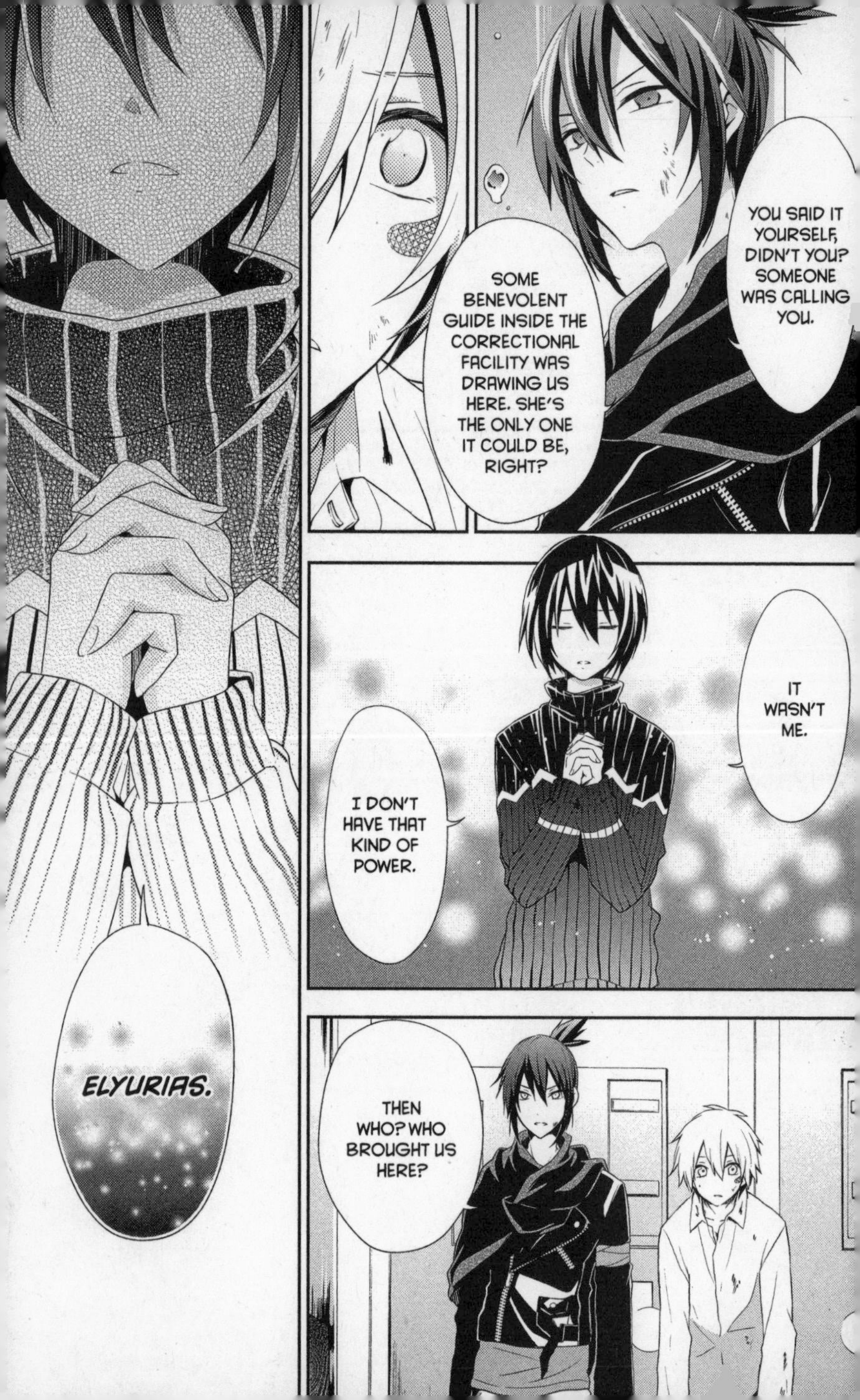
YOU SAID IT YOURSELF, DIDN'T YOU? SOMEONE WAS CALLING YOU.
SOME BENEVOLENT GUIDE INSIDE THE CORRECTIONAL FACILITY WAS DRAWING US HERE. SHE'S THE ONLY ONE IT COULD BE, RIGHT?
IT WASN'T ME.
I DON'T HAVE THAT KIND OF POWER.
THEN WHO? WHO BROUGHT US HERE?
ELYURIAS.

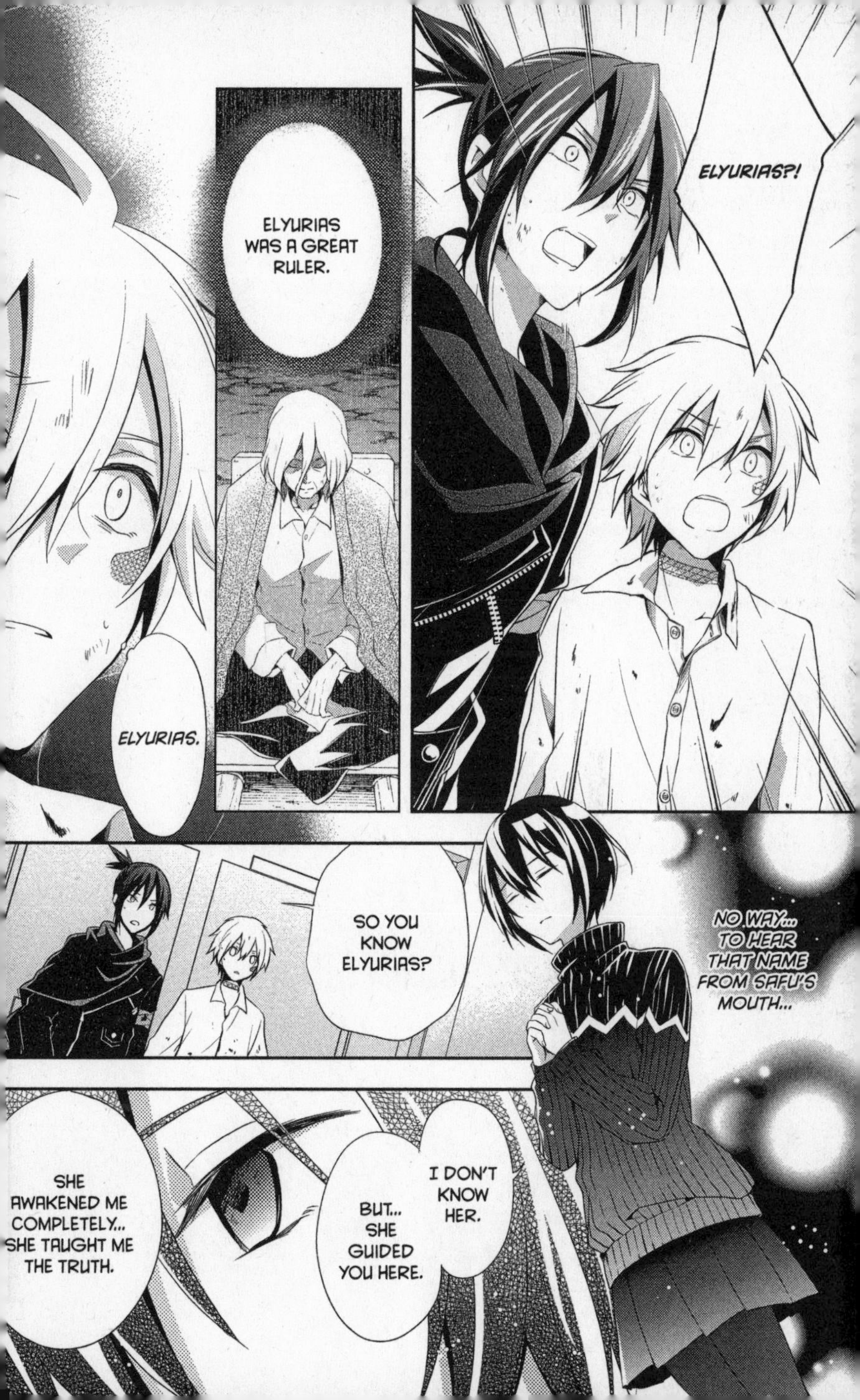
ELYURIAS?!
ELYURIAS WAS A GREAT RULER.
ELYURIAS.
NO WAY... TO HEAR THAT NAME FROM SAFU'S MOUTH...
SO YOU KNOW ELYURIAS?
I DON'T KNOW HER.
BUT... SHE GUIDED YOU HERE.
SHE AWAKENED ME COMPLETELY... SHE TAUGHT ME THE TRUTH.

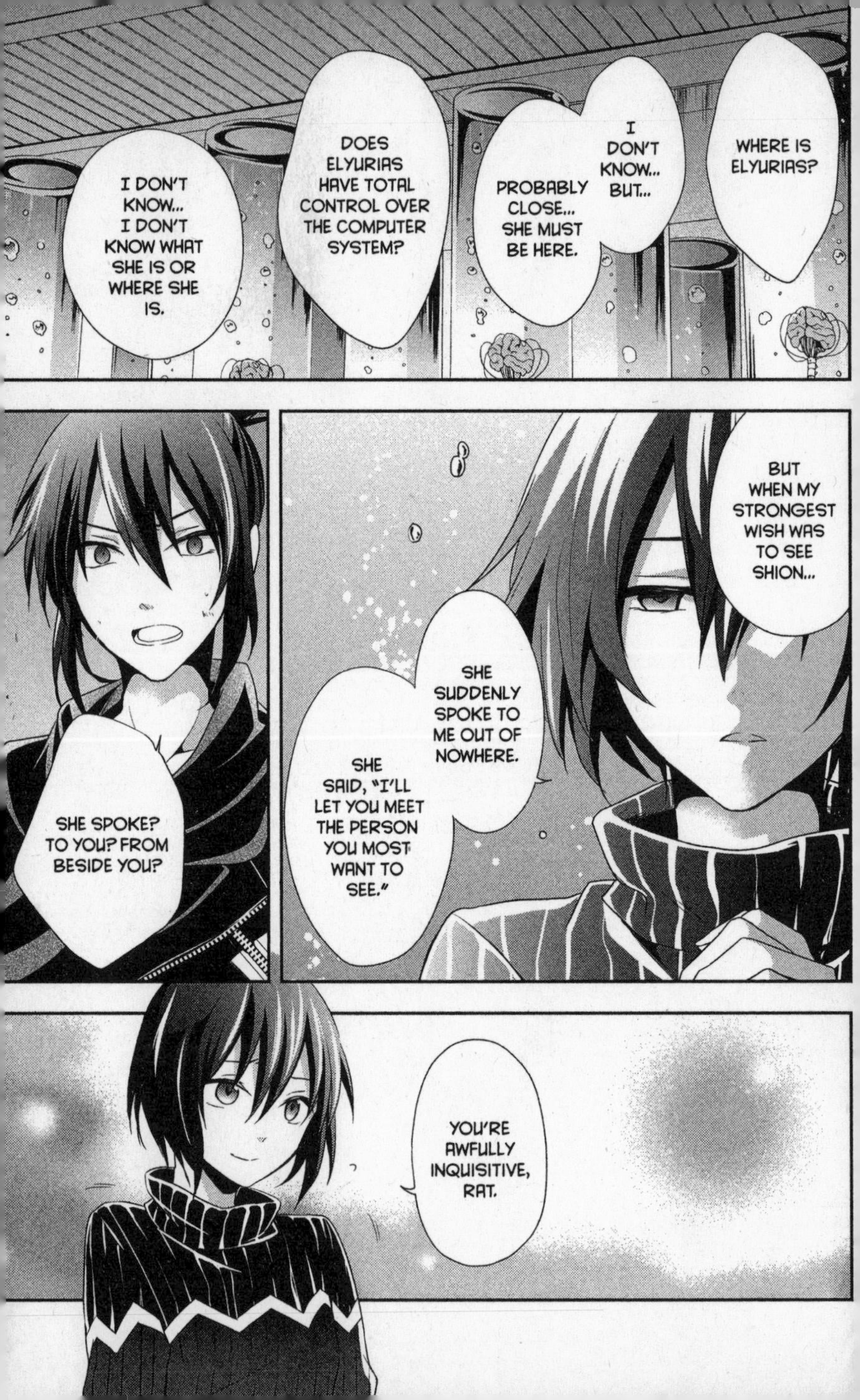
WHERE IS ELYURIAS?
I DON'T KNOW... BUT...
PROBABLY CLOSE... SHE MUST BE HERE.
DOES ELYURIAS HAVE TOTAL CONTROL OVER THE COMPUTER SYSTEM?
I DON'T KNOW... I DON'T KNOW WHAT SHE IS OR WHERE SHE IS.
BUT WHEN MY STRONGEST WISH WAS TO SEE SHION...
SHE SUDDENLY SPOKE TO ME OUT OF NOWHERE.
SHE SAID, "I'LL LET YOU MEET THE PERSON YOU MOST WANT TO SEE."
SHE SPOKE? TO YOU? FROM BESIDE YOU?
YOU'RE AWFULLY INQUISITIVE, RAT.

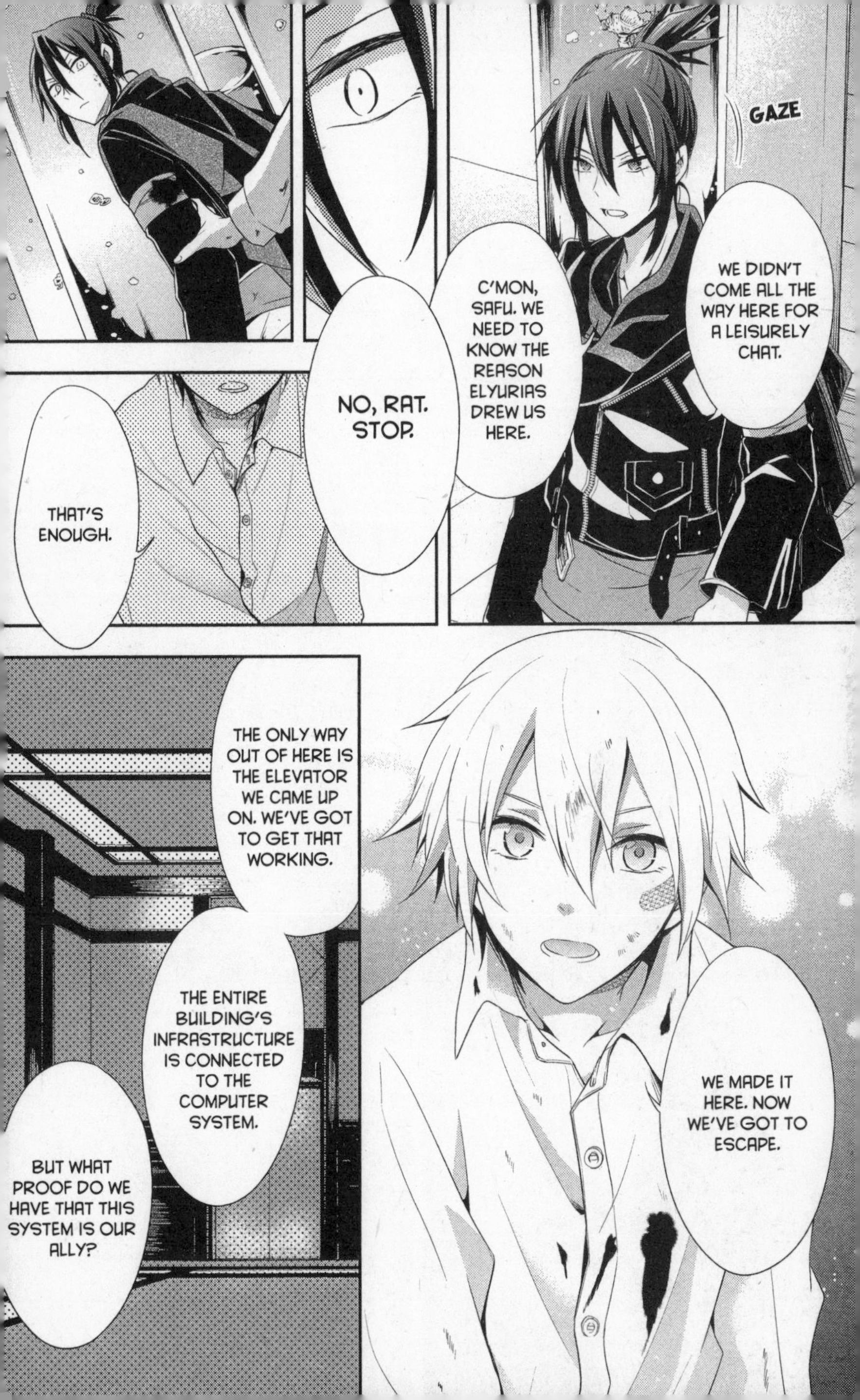
GAZE
WE DIDN'T COME ALL THE WAY HERE FOR A LEISURELY CHAT.
C'MON, SAFU. WE NEED TO KNOW THE REASON ELYURIAS DREW US HERE.
NO, RAT. STOP.
THAT'S ENOUGH.
WE MADE IT HERE. NOW WE'VE GOT TO ESCAPE.
THE ONLY WAY OUT OF HERE IS THE ELEVATOR WE CAME UP ON. WE'VE GOT TO GET THAT WORKING.
THE ENTIRE BUILDING'S INFRASTRUCTURE IS CONNECTED TO THE COMPUTER SYSTEM.
BUT WHAT PROOF DO WE HAVE THAT THIS SYSTEM IS OUR ALLY?

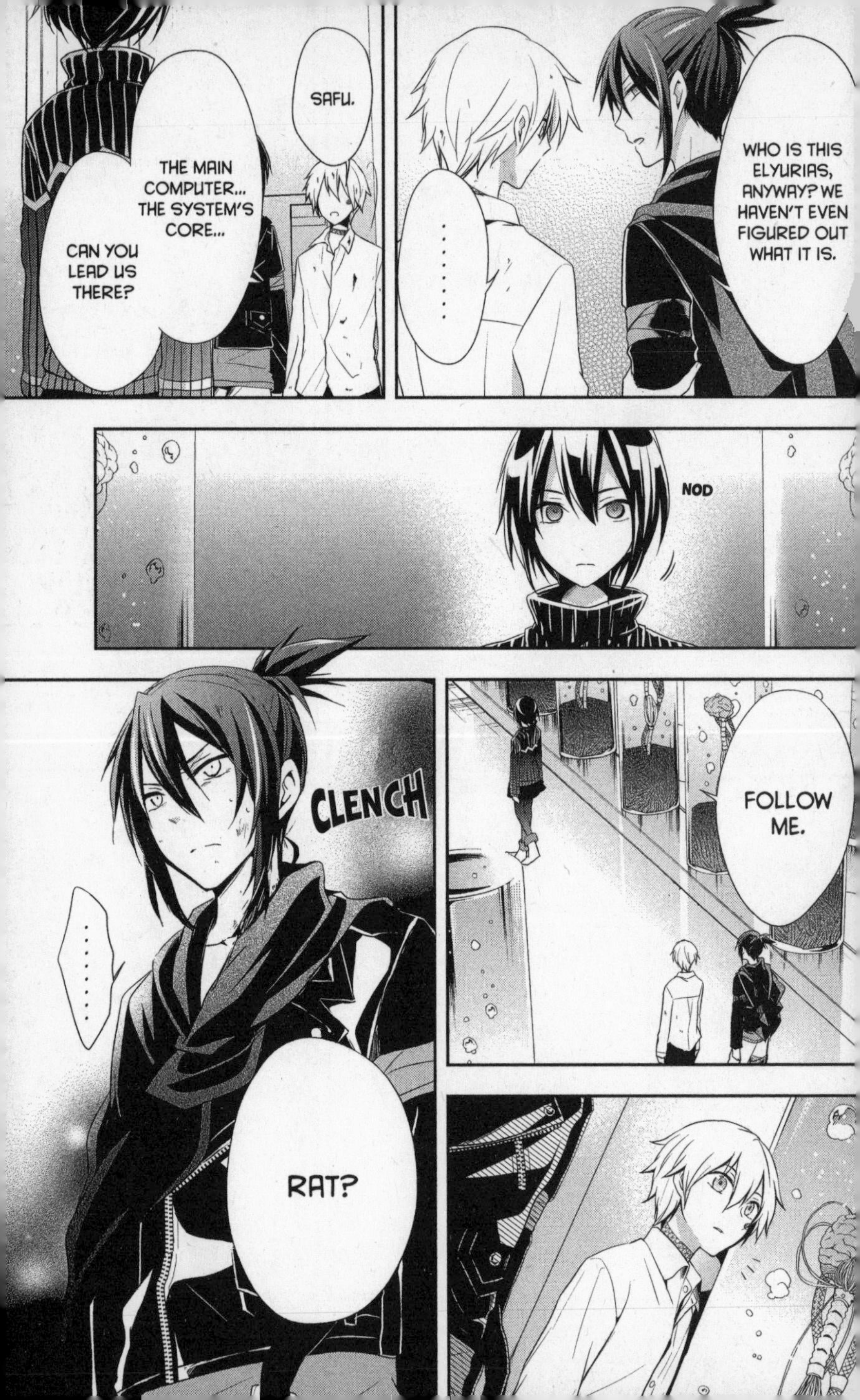

WHO IS THIS ELYURIAS, ANYWAY? WE HAVEN'T EVEN FIGURED OUT WHAT IT IS.
......
SAFU.
THE MAIN COMPUTER... THE SYSTEM'S CORE...
CAN YOU LEAD US THERE?
NOD
FOLLOW ME.
CLENCH
......
RAT?

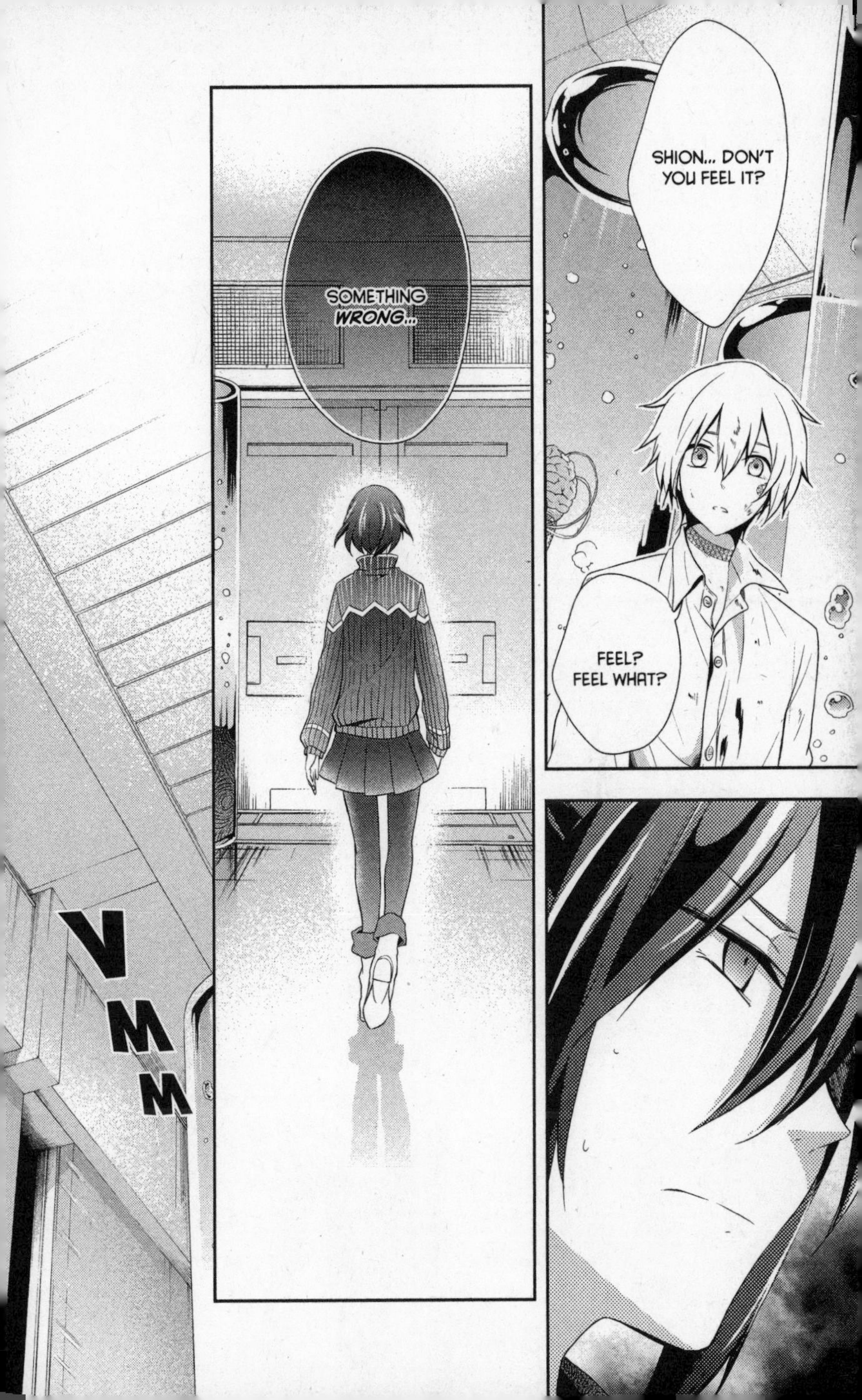
SHION... DON'T YOU FEEL IT?
FEEL? FEEL WHAT?
SOMETHING *WRONG*...
VMM

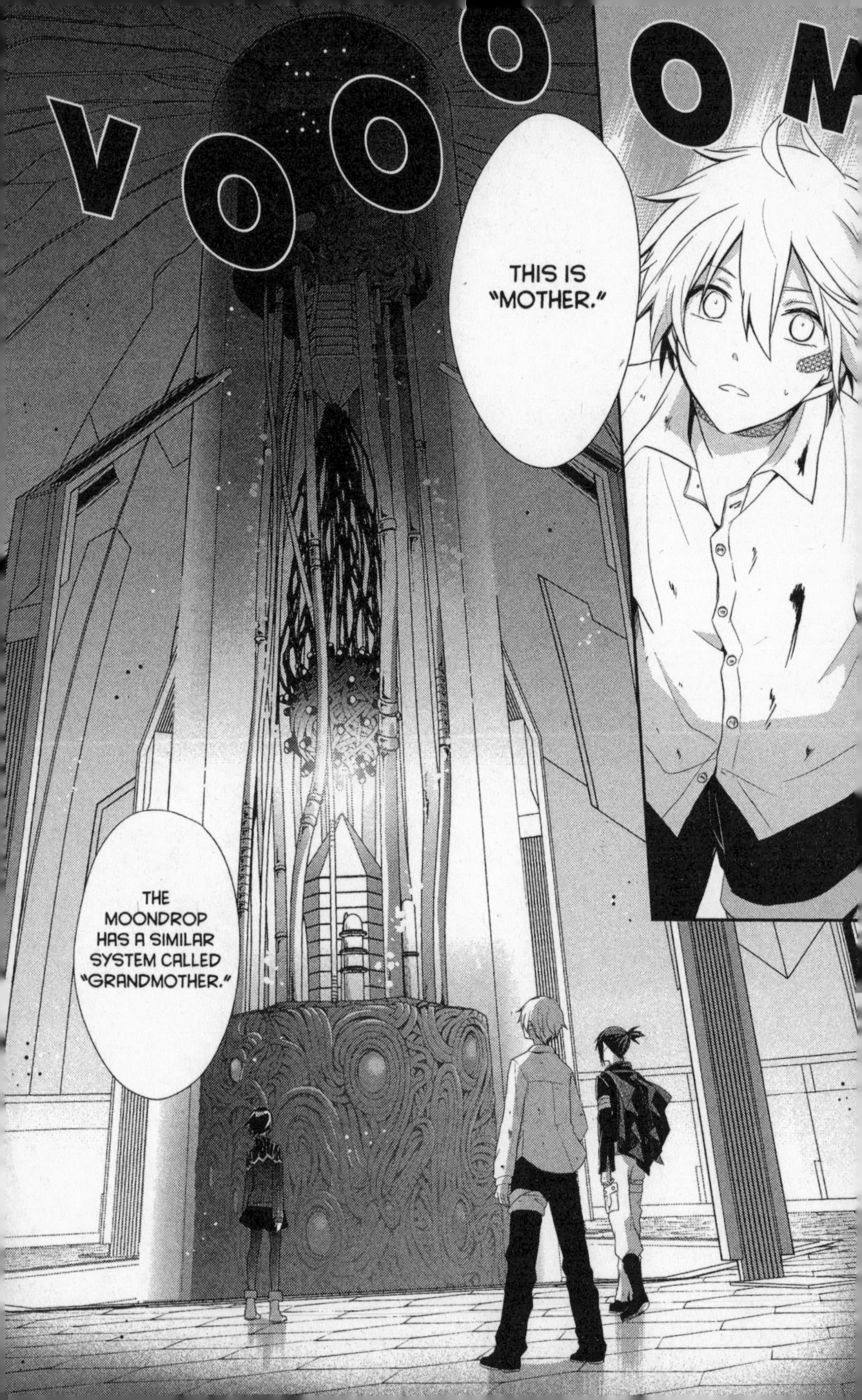
VOOOOM
THIS IS "MOTHER."
THE MOONDROP HAS A SIMILAR SYSTEM CALLED "GRANDMOTHER."

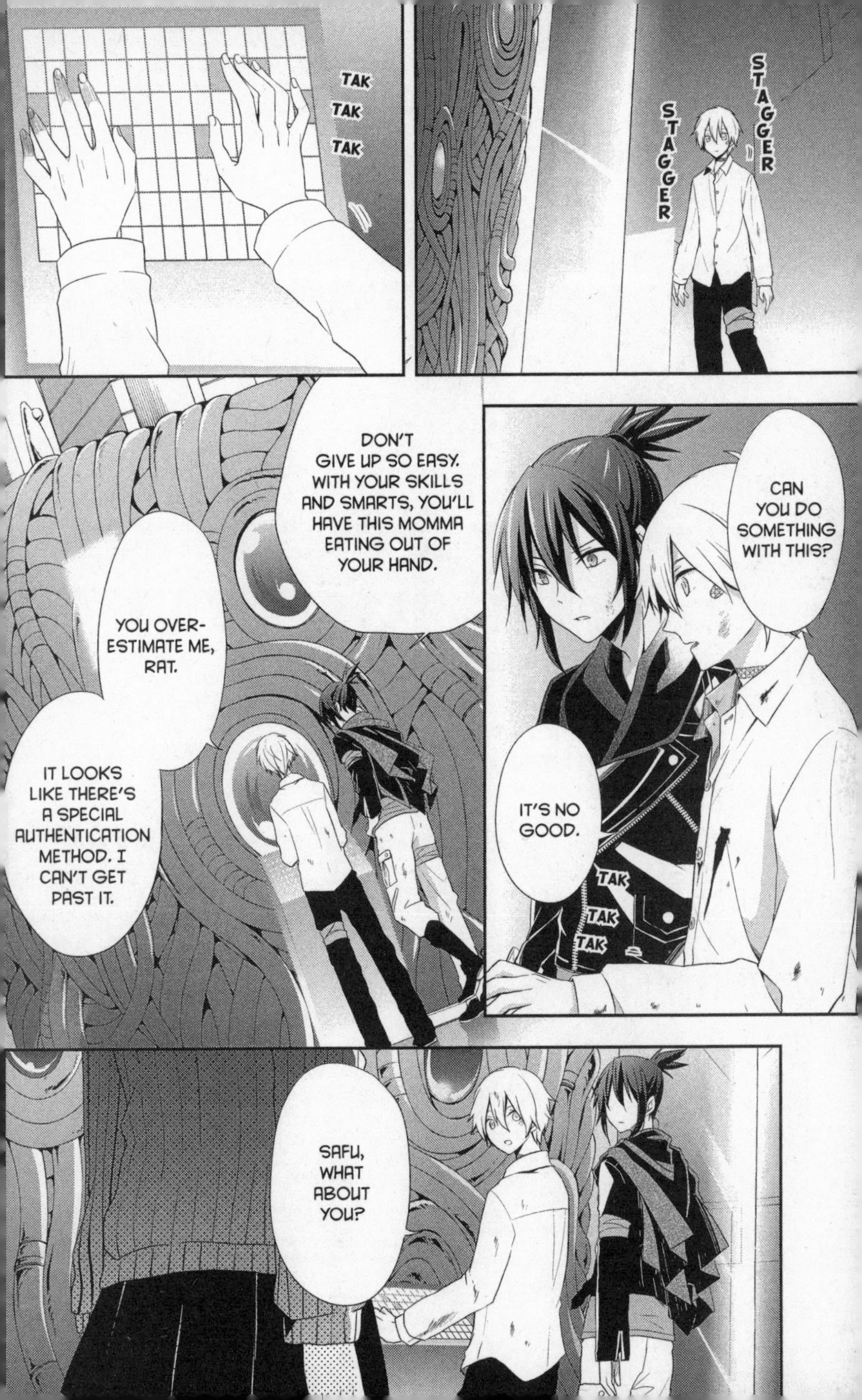
STAGGER
STAGGER
TAK
TAK
TAK
CAN YOU DO SOMETHING WITH THIS?
IT'S NO GOOD.
TAK
TAK
TAK
DON'T GIVE UP SO EASY. WITH YOUR SKILLS AND SMARTS, YOU'LL HAVE THIS MOMMA EATING OUT OF YOUR HAND.
YOU OVER-ESTIMATE ME, RAT.
IT LOOKS LIKE THERE'S A SPECIAL AUTHENTICATION METHOD. I CAN'T GET PAST IT.
SAFU, WHAT ABOUT YOU?

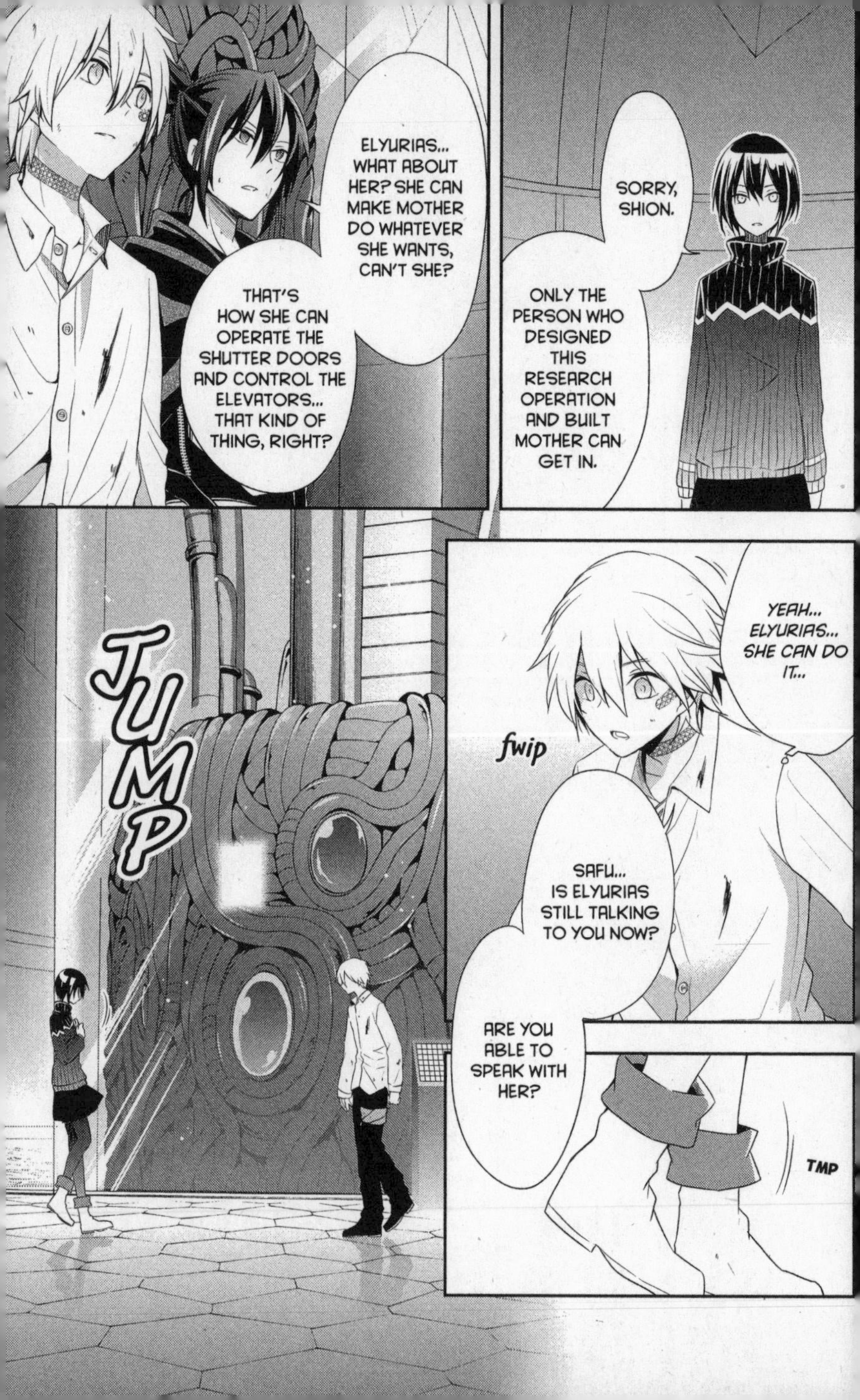
SORRY, SHION.
ONLY THE PERSON WHO DESIGNED THIS RESEARCH OPERATION AND BUILT MOTHER CAN GET IN.
ELYURIAS... WHAT ABOUT HER? SHE CAN MAKE MOTHER DO WHATEVER SHE WANTS, CAN'T SHE?
THAT'S HOW SHE CAN OPERATE THE SHUTTER DOORS AND CONTROL THE ELEVATORS... THAT KIND OF THING, RIGHT?
YEAH... ELYURIAS... SHE CAN DO IT...
fwip
SAFU... IS ELYURIAS STILL TALKING TO YOU NOW?
ARE YOU ABLE TO SPEAK WITH HER?
TMP
JUMP

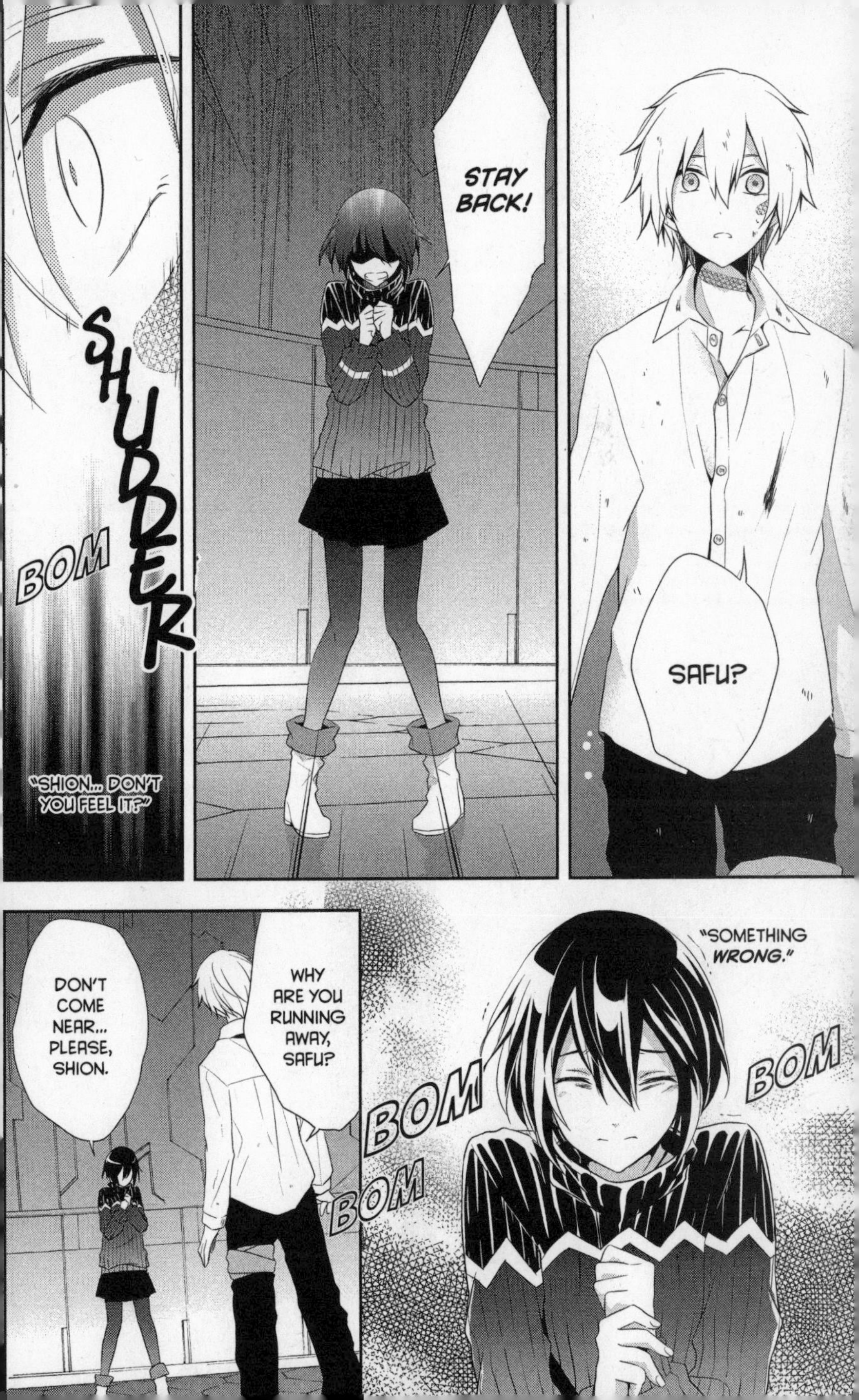
SAFU?
STAY BACK!
SHUDDER
BOM
"SHION... DON'T YOU FEEL IT?"
"SOMETHING WRONG."
BOM
BOM
BOM
BOM
WHY ARE YOU RUNNING AWAY, SAFU?
DON'T COME NEAR... PLEASE, SHION.

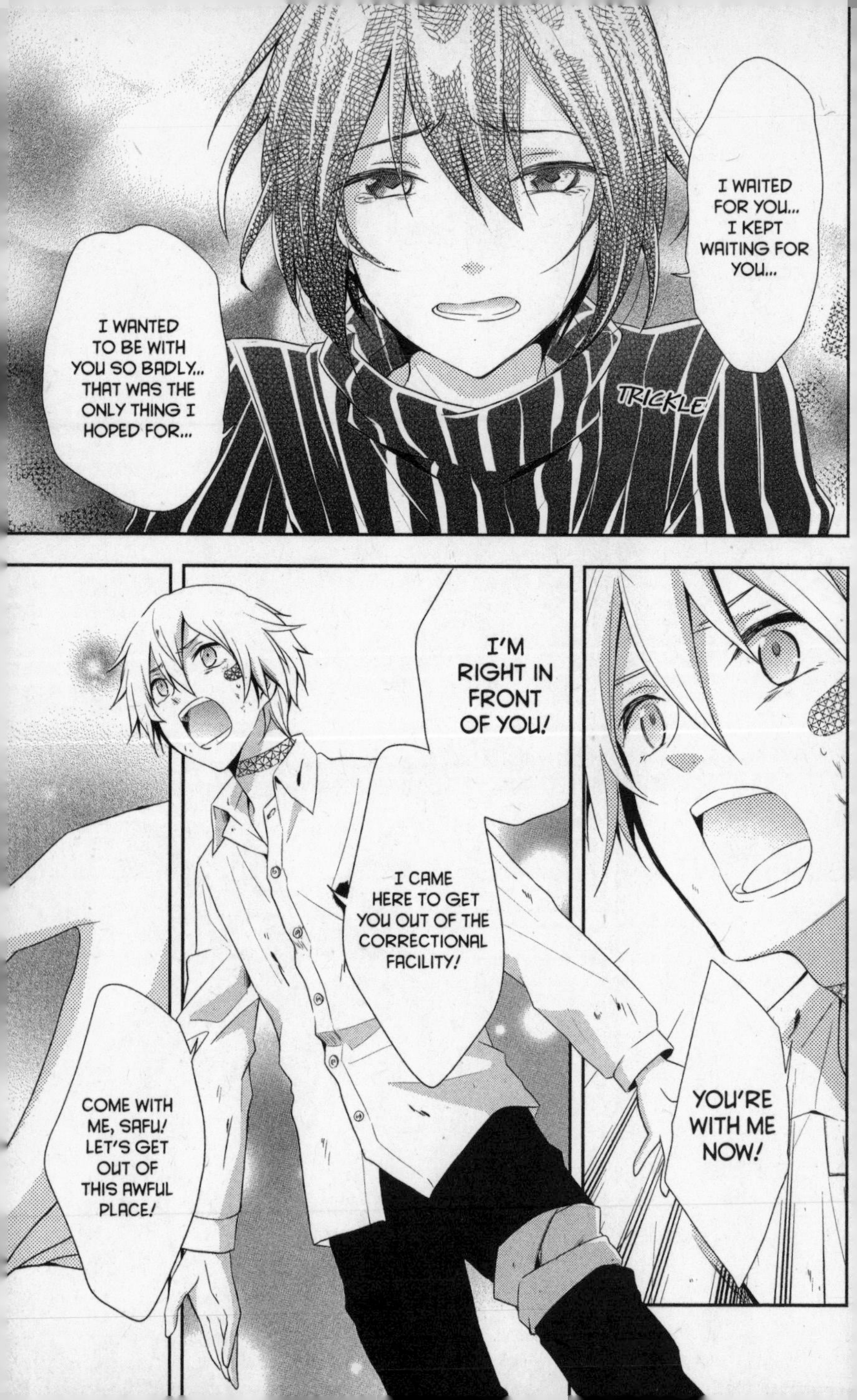
I WAITED FOR YOU... I KEPT WAITING FOR YOU...
TRICKLE
I WANTED TO BE WITH YOU SO BADLY... THAT WAS THE ONLY THING I HOPED FOR...
YOU'RE WITH ME NOW!
I'M RIGHT IN FRONT OF YOU!
I CAME HERE TO GET YOU OUT OF THE CORRECTIONAL FACILITY!
COME WITH ME, SAFU! LET'S GET OUT OF THIS AWFUL PLACE!

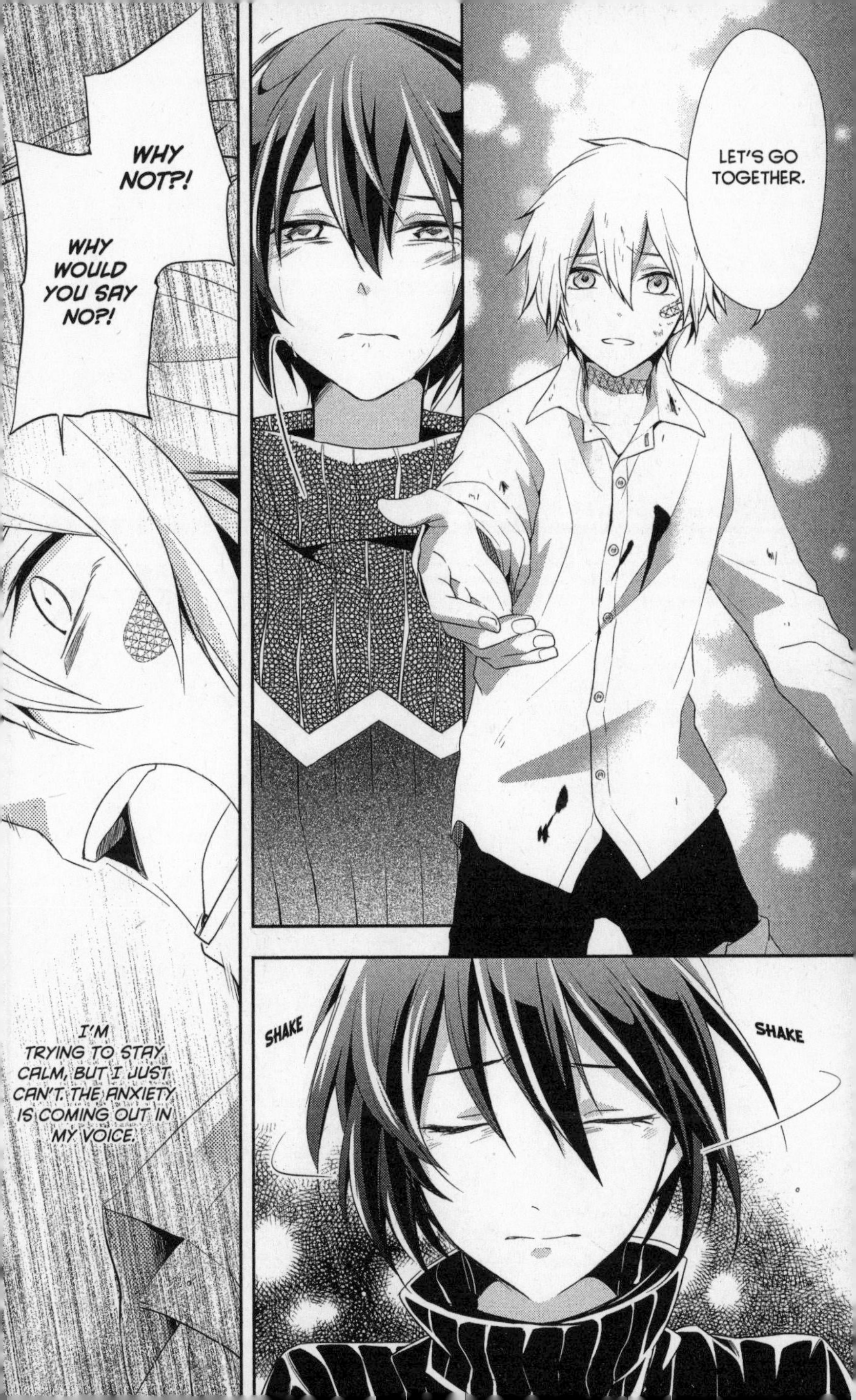
LET'S GO TOGETHER.
SHAKE
SHAKE
WHY NOT?!
WHY WOULD YOU SAY NO?!
I'M TRYING TO STAY CALM, BUT I JUST CAN'T. THE ANXIETY IS COMING OUT IN MY VOICE.

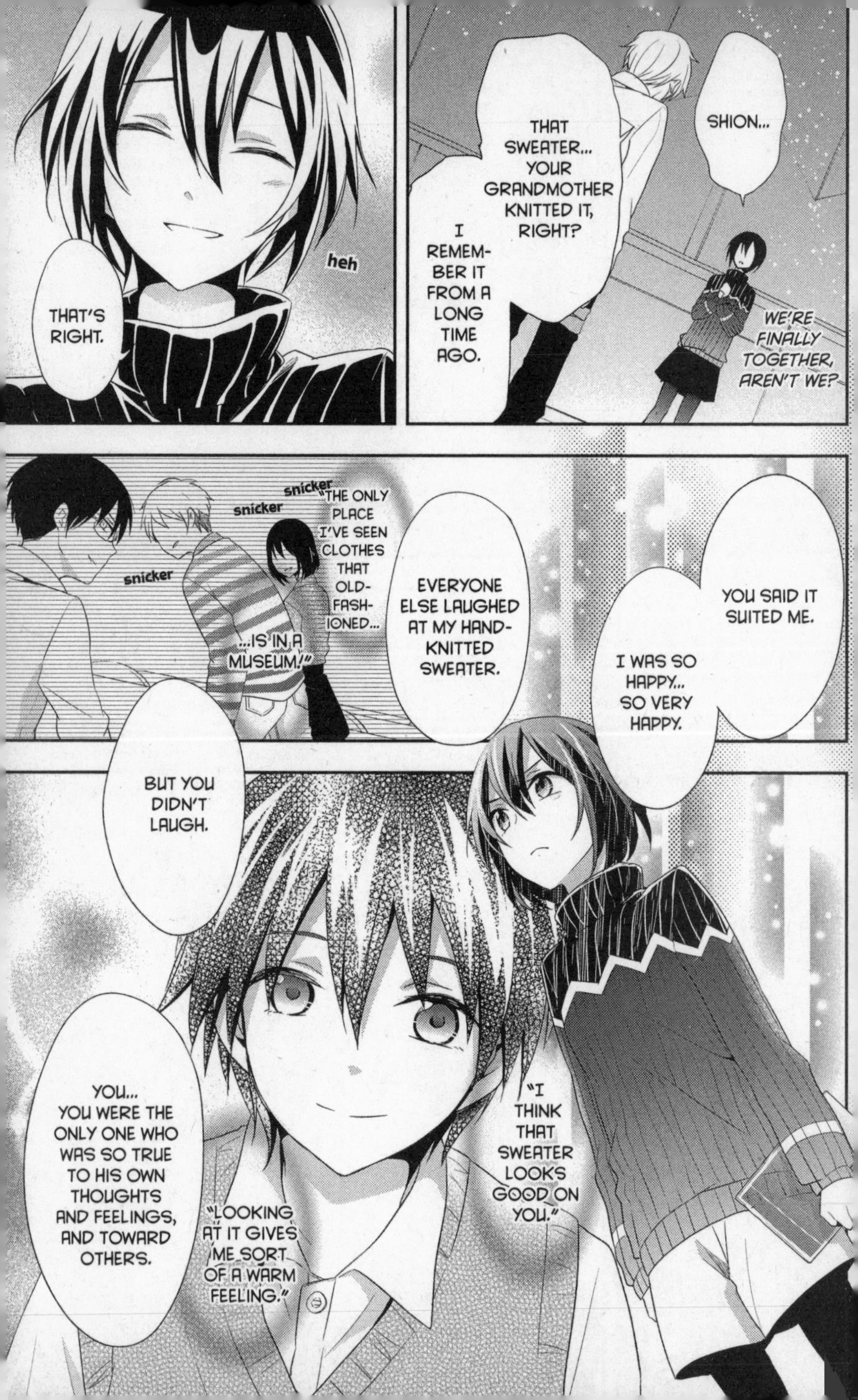
SHION...
THAT SWEATER... YOUR GRANDMOTHER KNITTED IT, RIGHT?
I REMEMBER IT FROM A LONG TIME AGO.
WE'RE FINALLY TOGETHER, AREN'T WE?
heh
THAT'S RIGHT.
EVERYONE ELSE LAUGHED AT MY HAND-KNITTED SWEATER.
snicker
snicker
snicker
"THE ONLY PLACE I'VE SEEN CLOTHES THAT OLD-FASHIONED...
...IS IN A MUSEUM!"
BUT YOU DIDN'T LAUGH.
"I THINK THAT SWEATER LOOKS GOOD ON YOU."
"LOOKING AT IT GIVES ME SORT OF A WARM FEELING."
YOU SAID IT SUITED ME.
I WAS SO HAPPY... SO VERY HAPPY.
YOU... YOU WERE THE ONLY ONE WHO WAS SO TRUE TO HIS OWN THOUGHTS AND FEELINGS, AND TOWARD OTHERS.

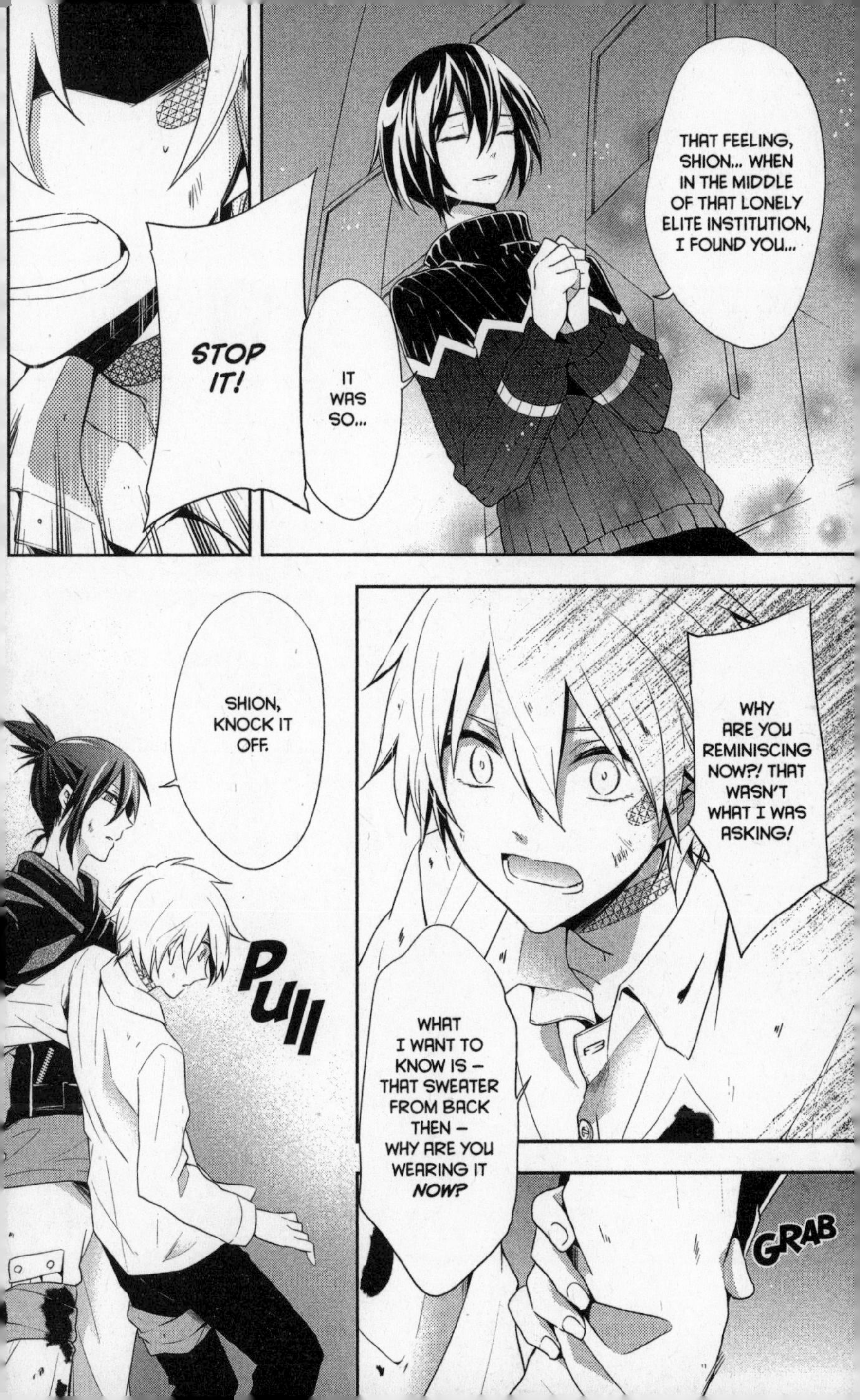
THAT FEELING, SHION... WHEN IN THE MIDDLE OF THAT LONELY ELITE INSTITUTION, I FOUND YOU...
IT WAS SO...
STOP IT!
WHY ARE YOU REMINISCING NOW?! THAT WASN'T WHAT I WAS ASKING!
WHAT I WANT TO KNOW IS — THAT SWEATER FROM BACK THEN — WHY ARE YOU WEARING IT NOW?
GRAB
SHION, KNOCK IT OFF.
PULL

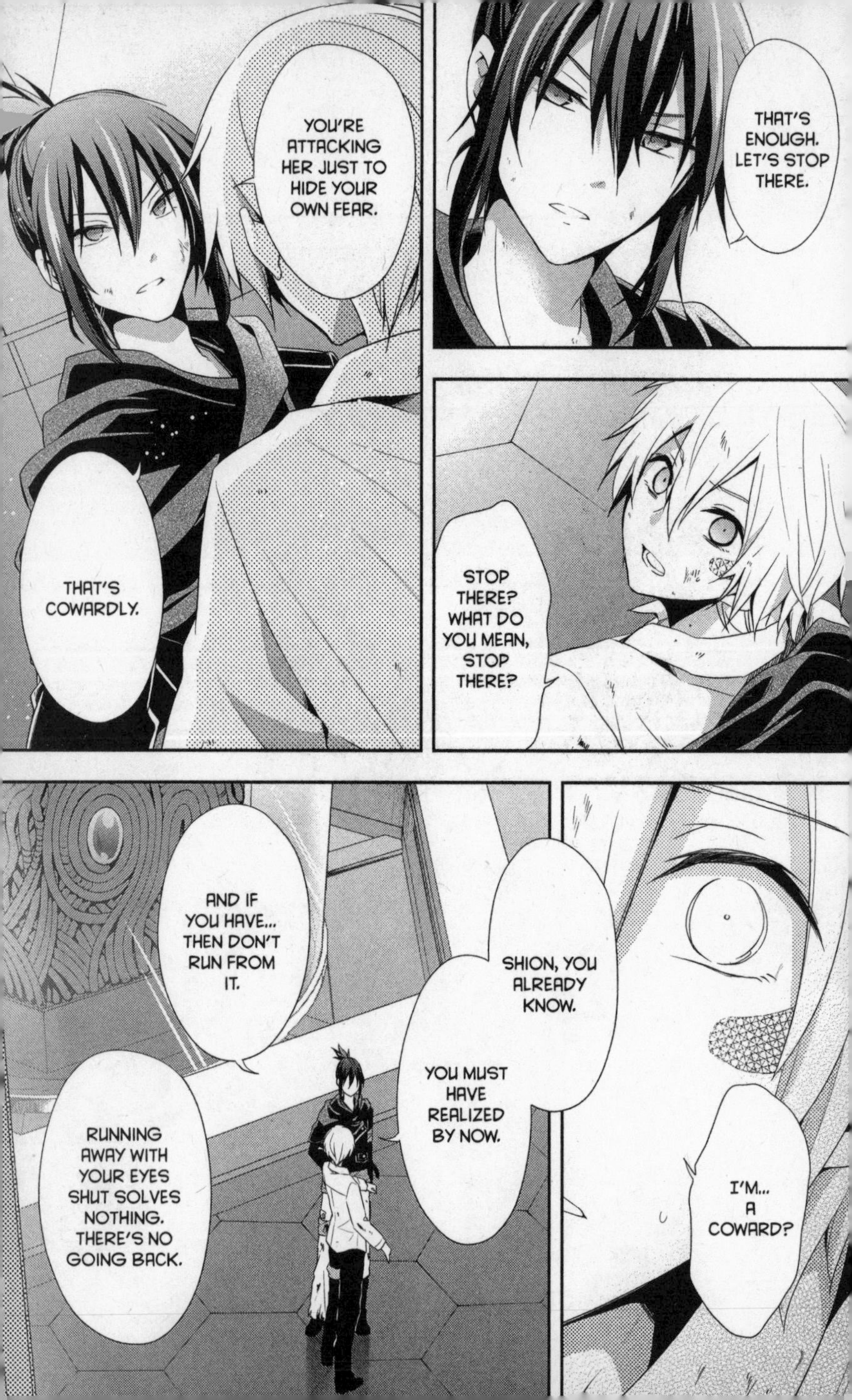
THAT'S ENOUGH. LET'S STOP THERE.
STOP THERE? WHAT DO YOU MEAN, STOP THERE?
YOU'RE ATTACKING HER JUST TO HIDE YOUR OWN FEAR.
THAT'S COWARDLY.
I'M... A COWARD?
SHION, YOU ALREADY KNOW.
YOU MUST HAVE REALIZED BY NOW.
AND IF YOU HAVE... THEN DON'T RUN FROM IT.
RUNNING AWAY WITH YOUR EYES SHUT SOLVES NOTHING. THERE'S NO GOING BACK.

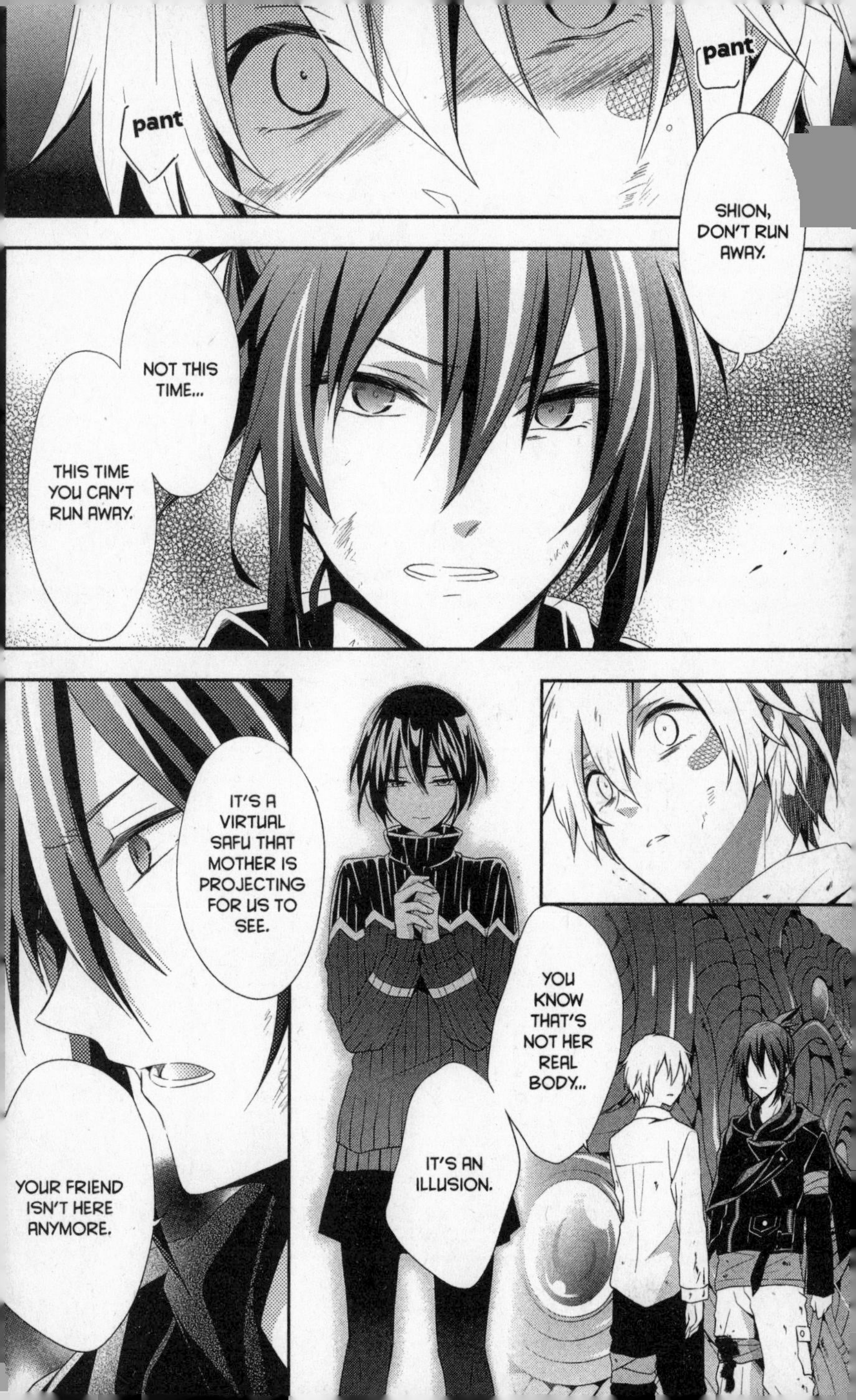
pant
pant
SHION, DON'T RUN AWAY.
NOT THIS TIME...
THIS TIME YOU CAN'T RUN AWAY.
YOU KNOW THAT'S NOT HER REAL BODY...
IT'S AN ILLUSION.
IT'S A VIRTUAL SAFU THAT MOTHER IS PROJECTING FOR US TO SEE.
YOUR FRIEND ISN'T HERE ANYMORE.

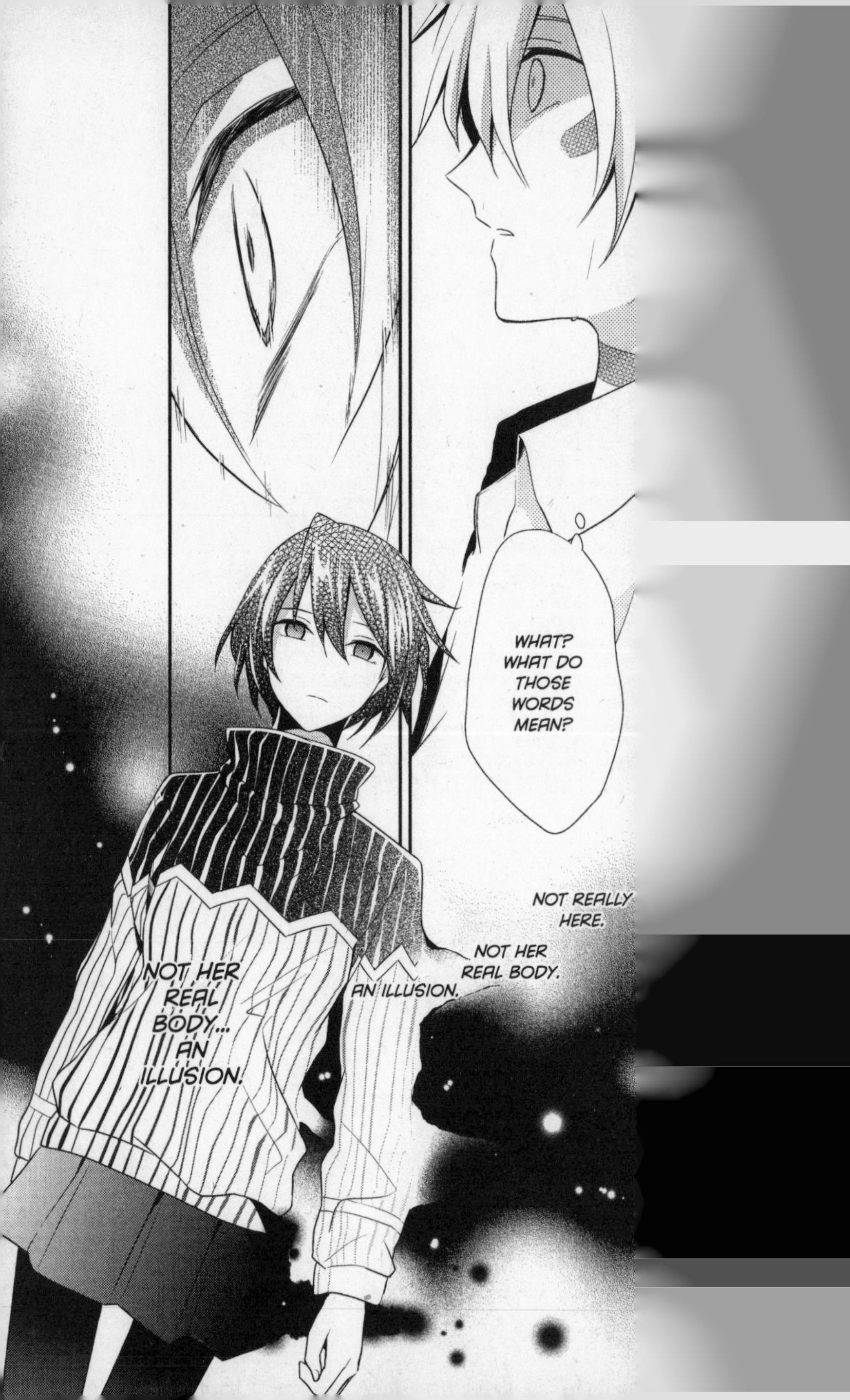
WHAT? WHAT DO THOSE WORDS MEAN?
NOT REALLY HERE.
NOT HER REAL BODY.
AN ILLUSION.
NOT HER REAL BODY... AN ILLUSION.

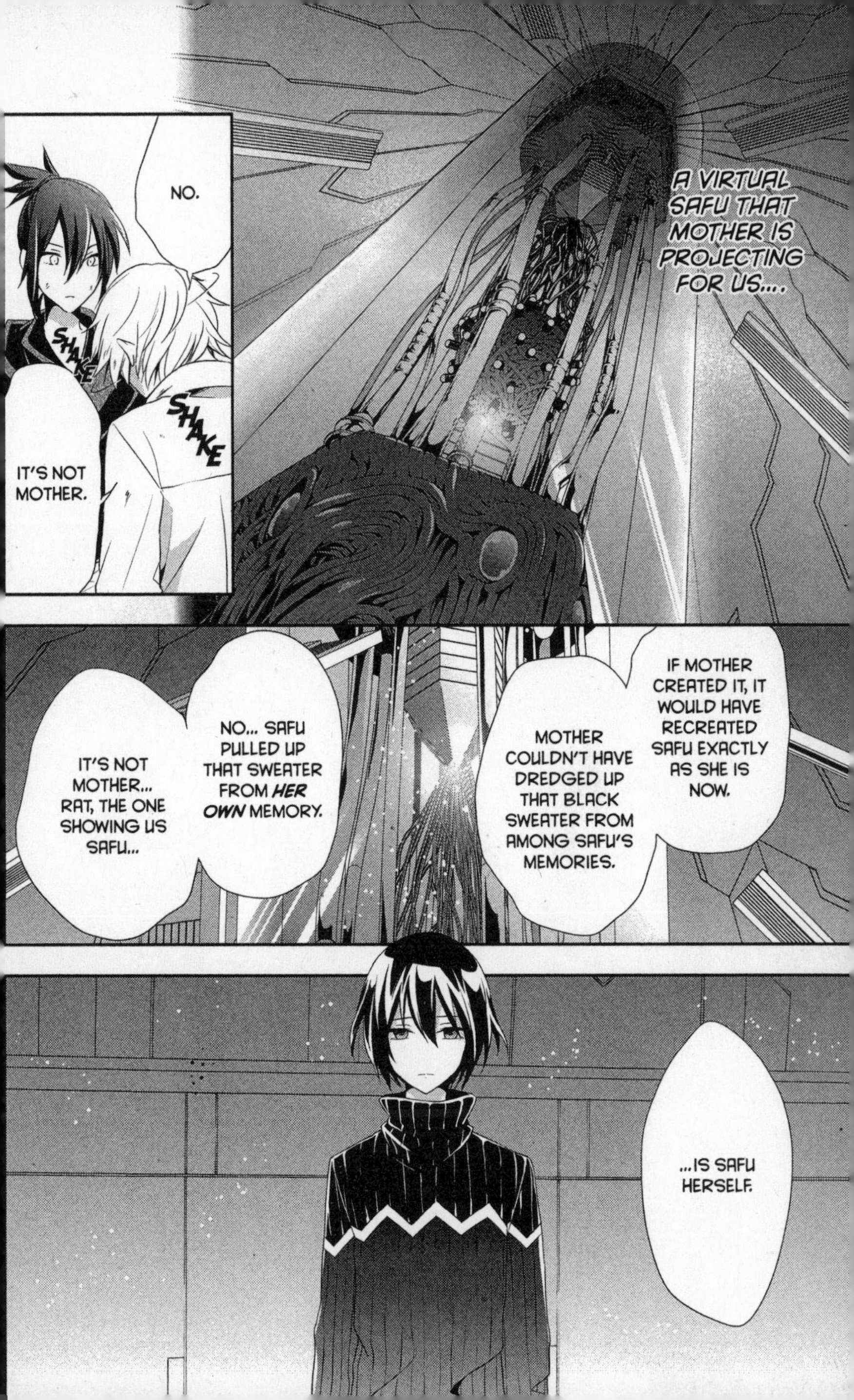
A VIRTUAL SAFU THAT MOTHER IS PROJECTING FOR US....
NO.
SHAKE
SHAKE
IT'S NOT MOTHER.
IF MOTHER CREATED IT, IT WOULD HAVE RECREATED SAFU EXACTLY AS SHE IS NOW.
MOTHER COULDN'T HAVE DREDGED UP THAT BLACK SWEATER FROM AMONG SAFU'S MEMORIES.
NO... SAFU PULLED UP THAT SWEATER FROM *HER OWN* MEMORY.
IT'S NOT MOTHER... RAT, THE ONE SHOWING US SAFU...
...IS SAFU HERSELF.

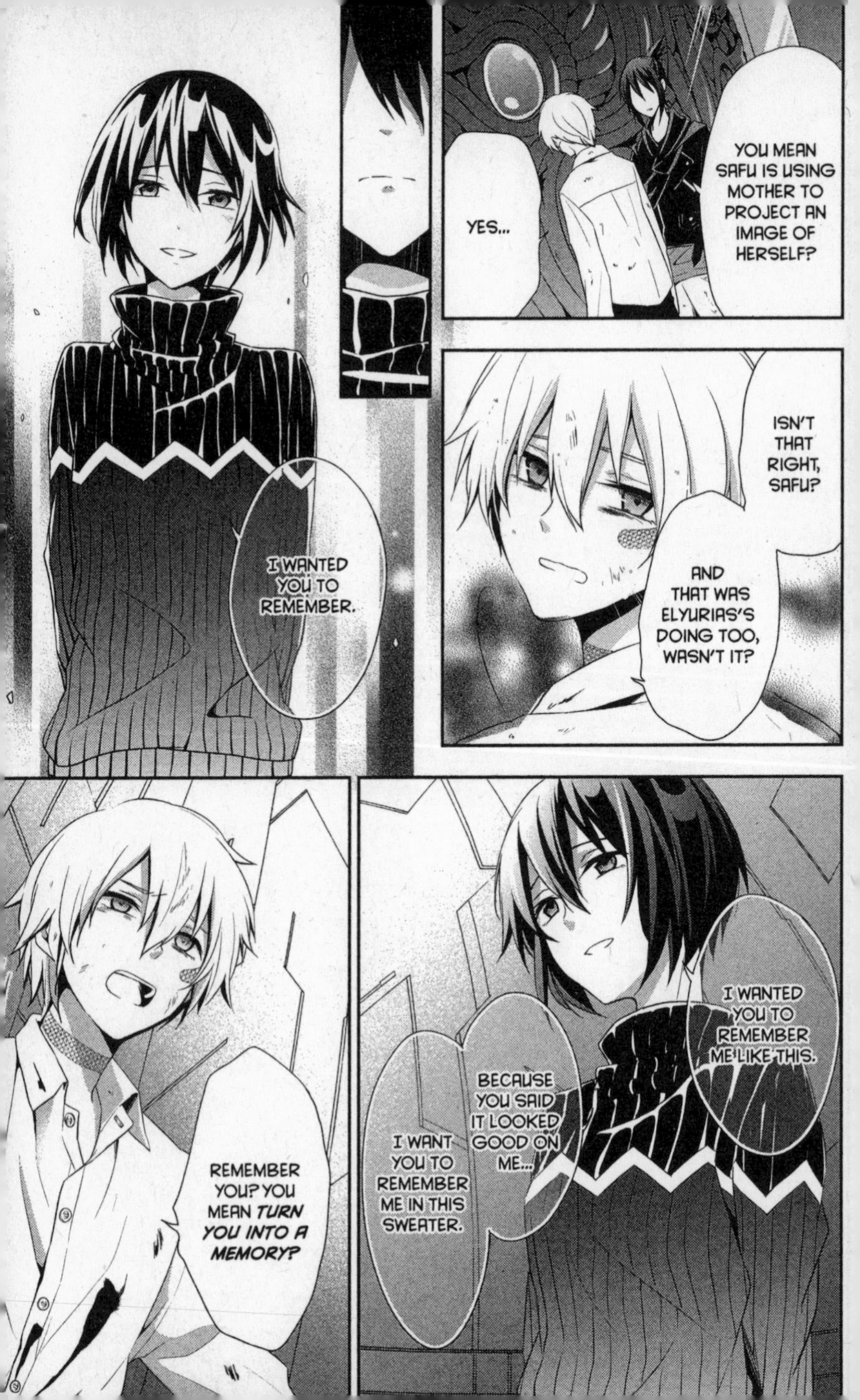
YOU MEAN SAFU IS USING MOTHER TO PROJECT AN IMAGE OF HERSELF?
YES...
ISN'T THAT RIGHT, SAFU?
AND THAT WAS ELYURIAS'S DOING TOO, WASN'T IT?
I WANTED YOU TO REMEMBER.
I WANTED YOU TO REMEMBER ME LIKE THIS.
BECAUSE YOU SAID IT LOOKED GOOD ON ME...
I WANT YOU TO REMEMBER ME IN THIS SWEATER.
REMEMBER YOU? YOU MEAN *TURN YOU INTO A MEMORY?*

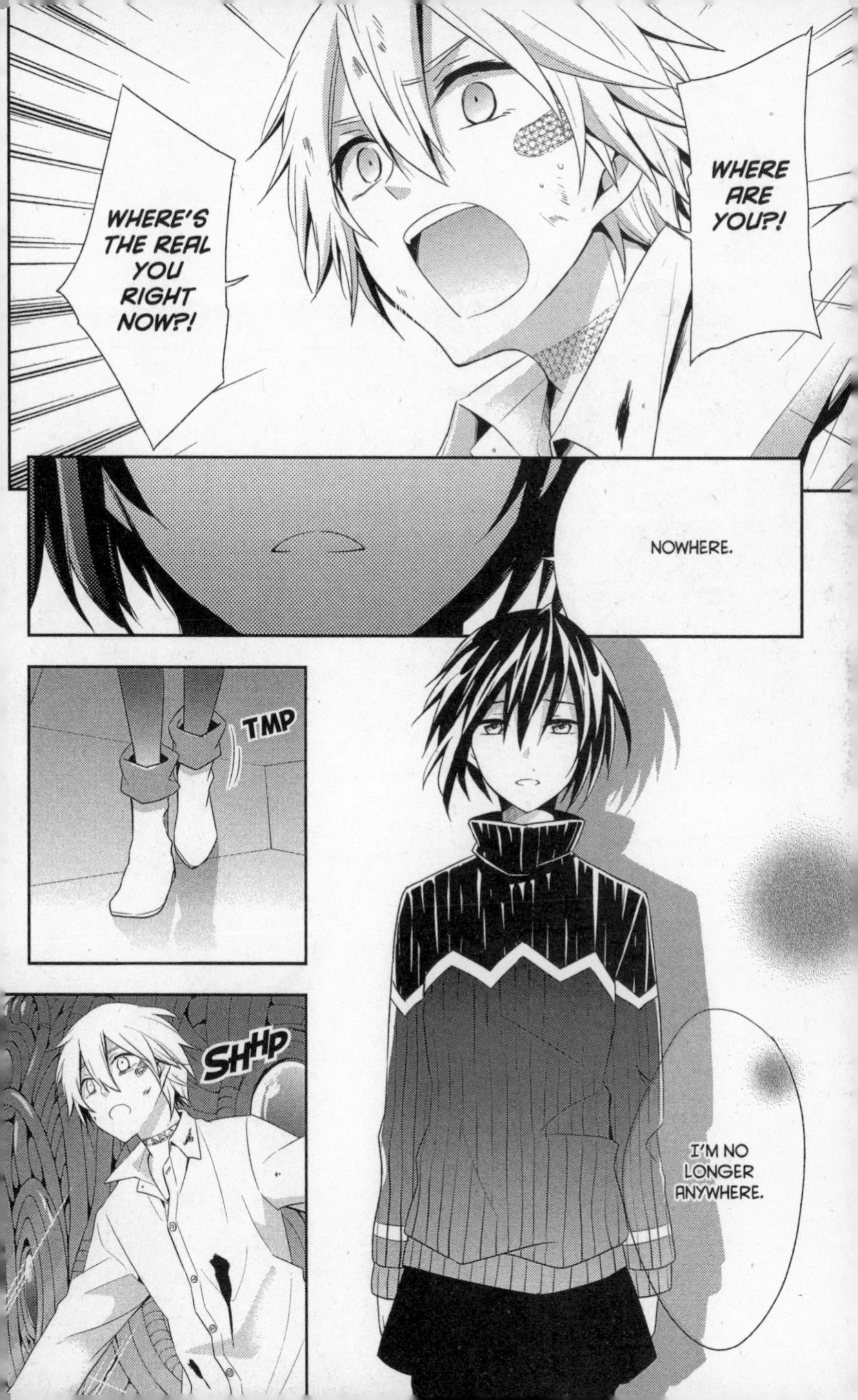
WHERE ARE YOU?!
WHERE'S THE REAL YOU RIGHT NOW?!
NOWHERE.
I'M NO LONGER ANYWHERE.
TMP
SHHp

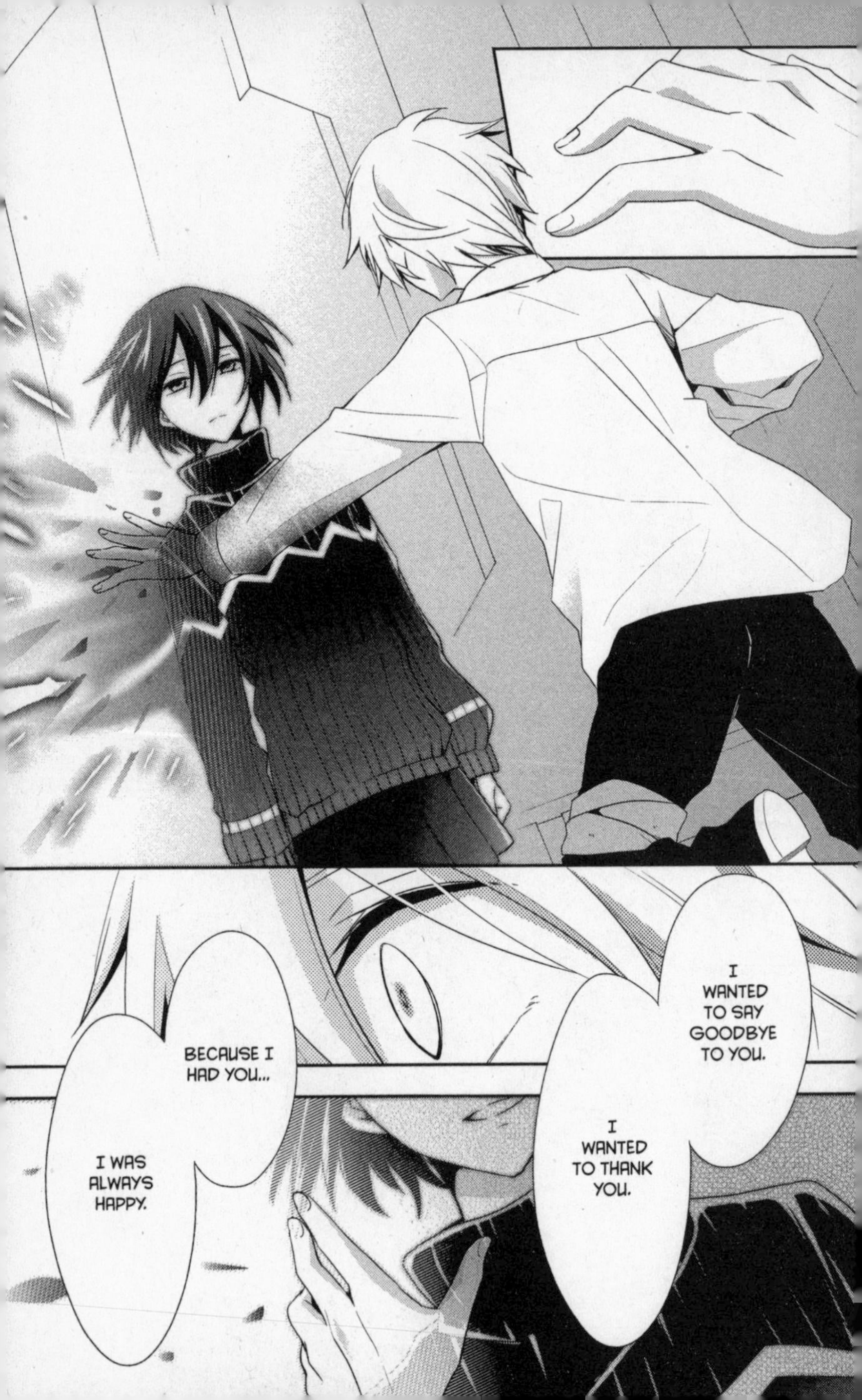
I WANTED TO SAY GOODBYE TO YOU.
I WANTED TO THANK YOU.
BECAUSE I HAD YOU...
I WAS ALWAYS HAPPY.

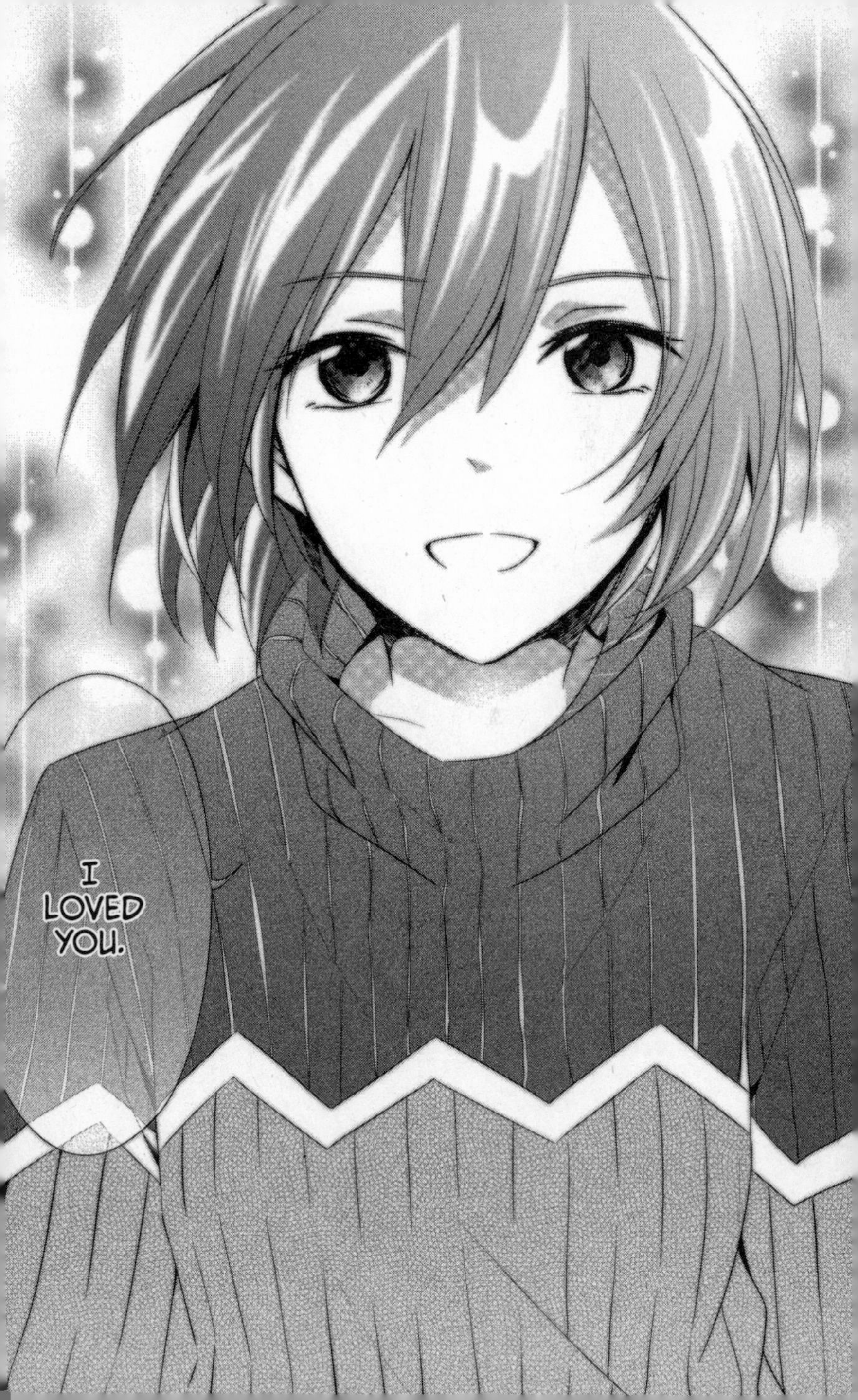
I LOVED YOU.

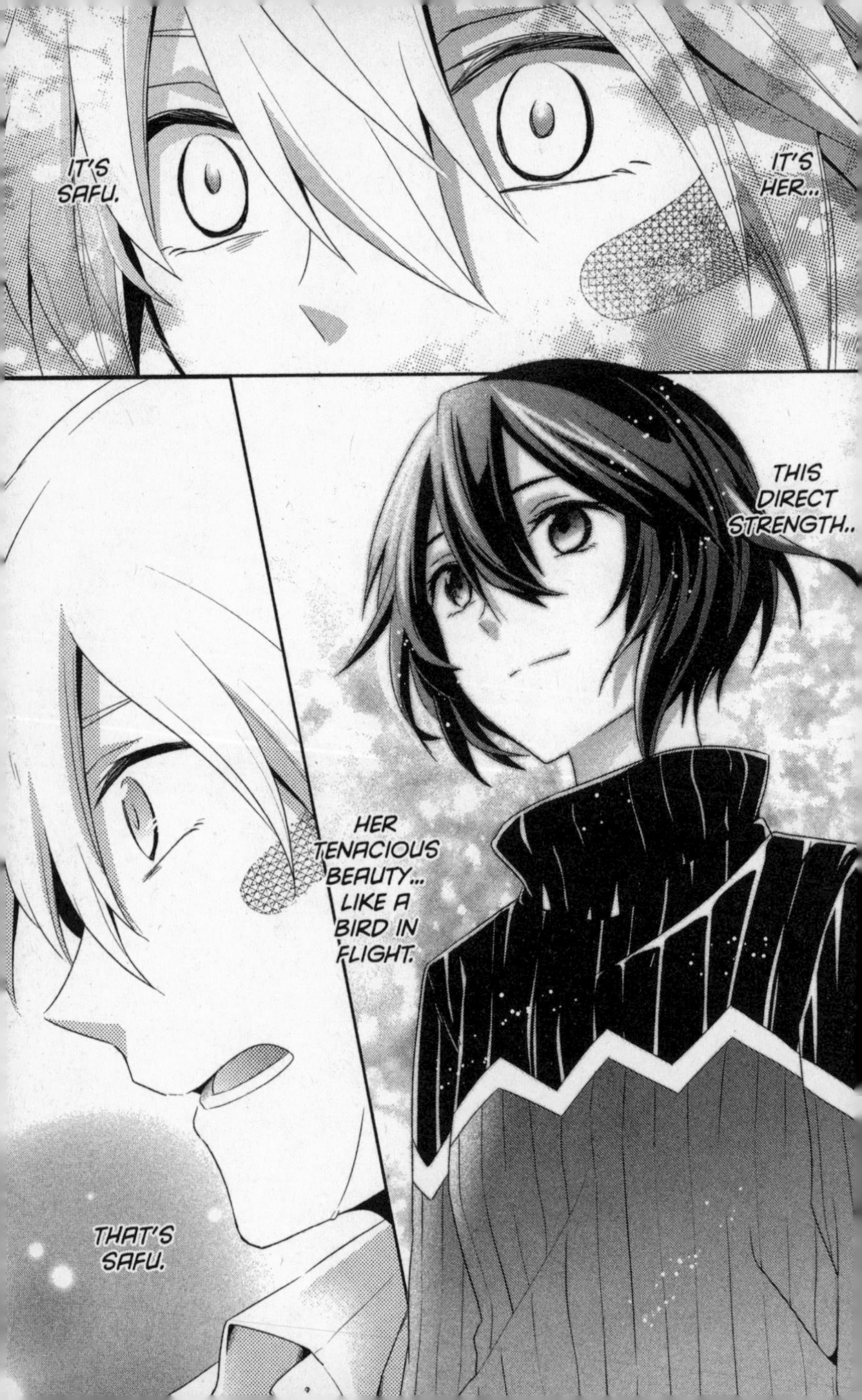
IT'S HER...
IT'S SAFU.
THIS DIRECT STRENGTH..
HER TENACIOUS BEAUTY... LIKE A BIRD IN FLIGHT.
THAT'S SAFU.

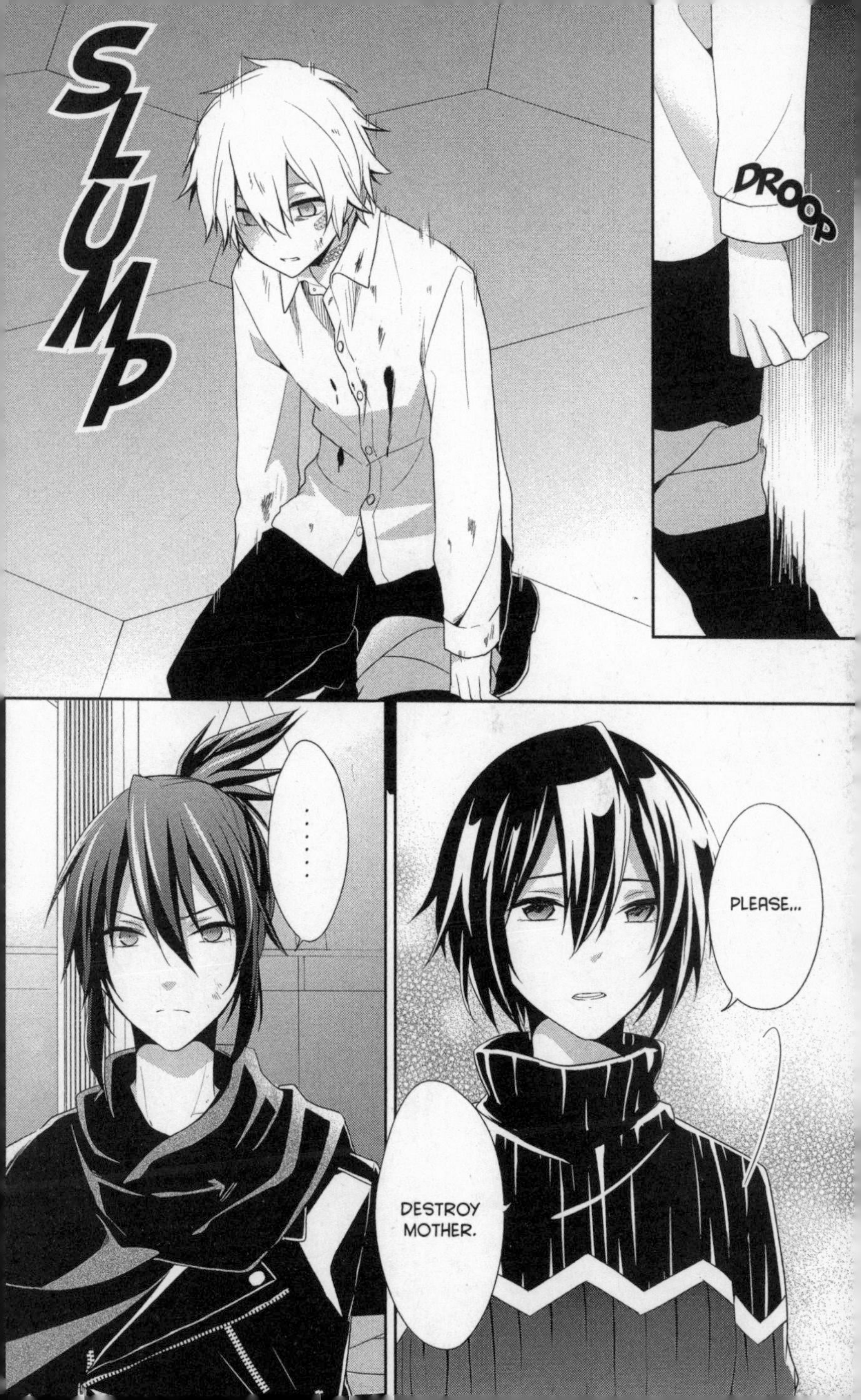
DROOP
SLUMP
PLEASE...
DESTROY MOTHER.
......

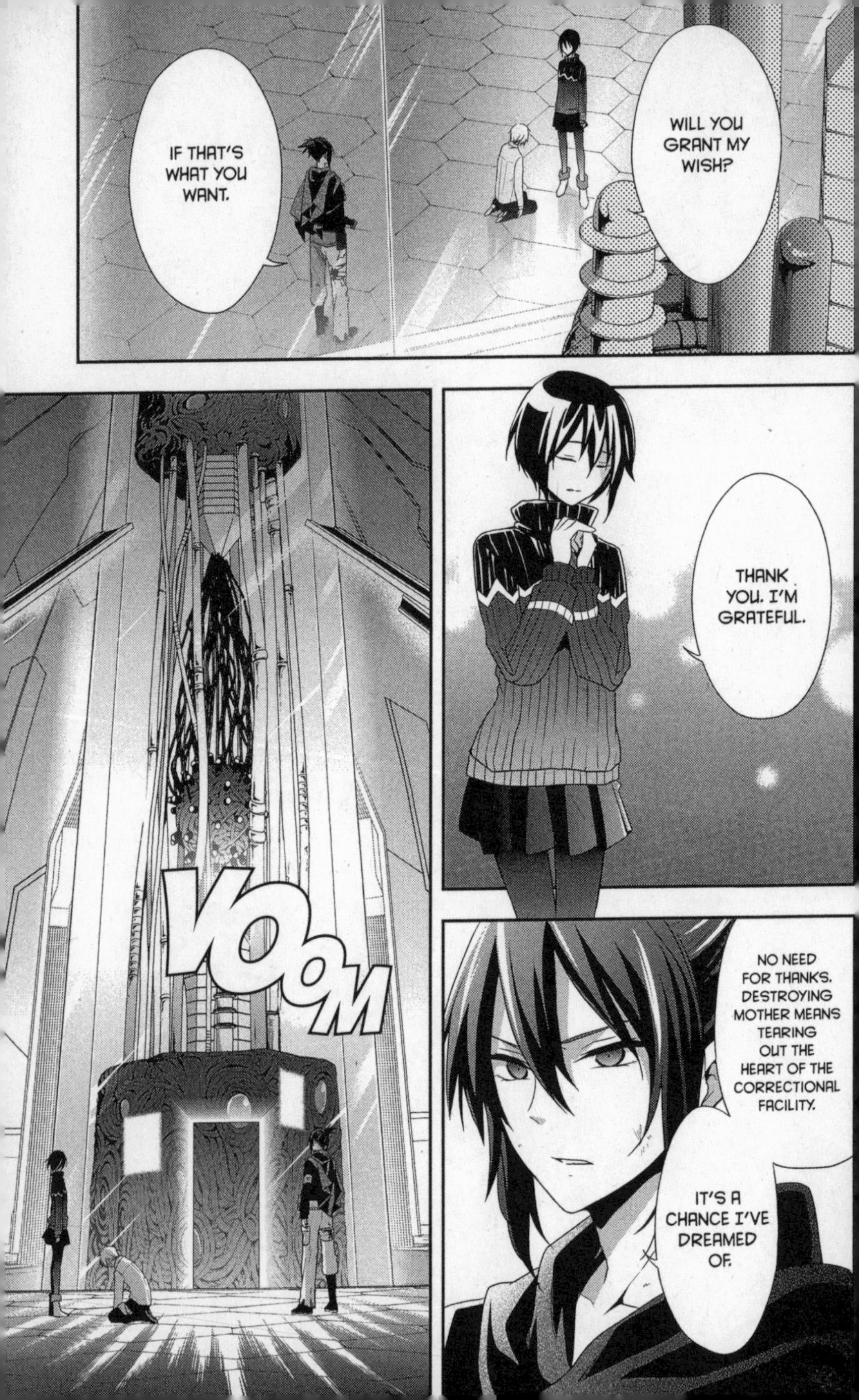
WILL YOU GRANT MY WISH?
IF THAT'S WHAT YOU WANT.
THANK YOU. I'M GRATEFUL.
NO NEED FOR THANKS. DESTROYING MOTHER MEANS TEARING OUT THE HEART OF THE CORRECTIONAL FACILITY.
IT'S A CHANCE I'VE DREAMED OF.
VOOM

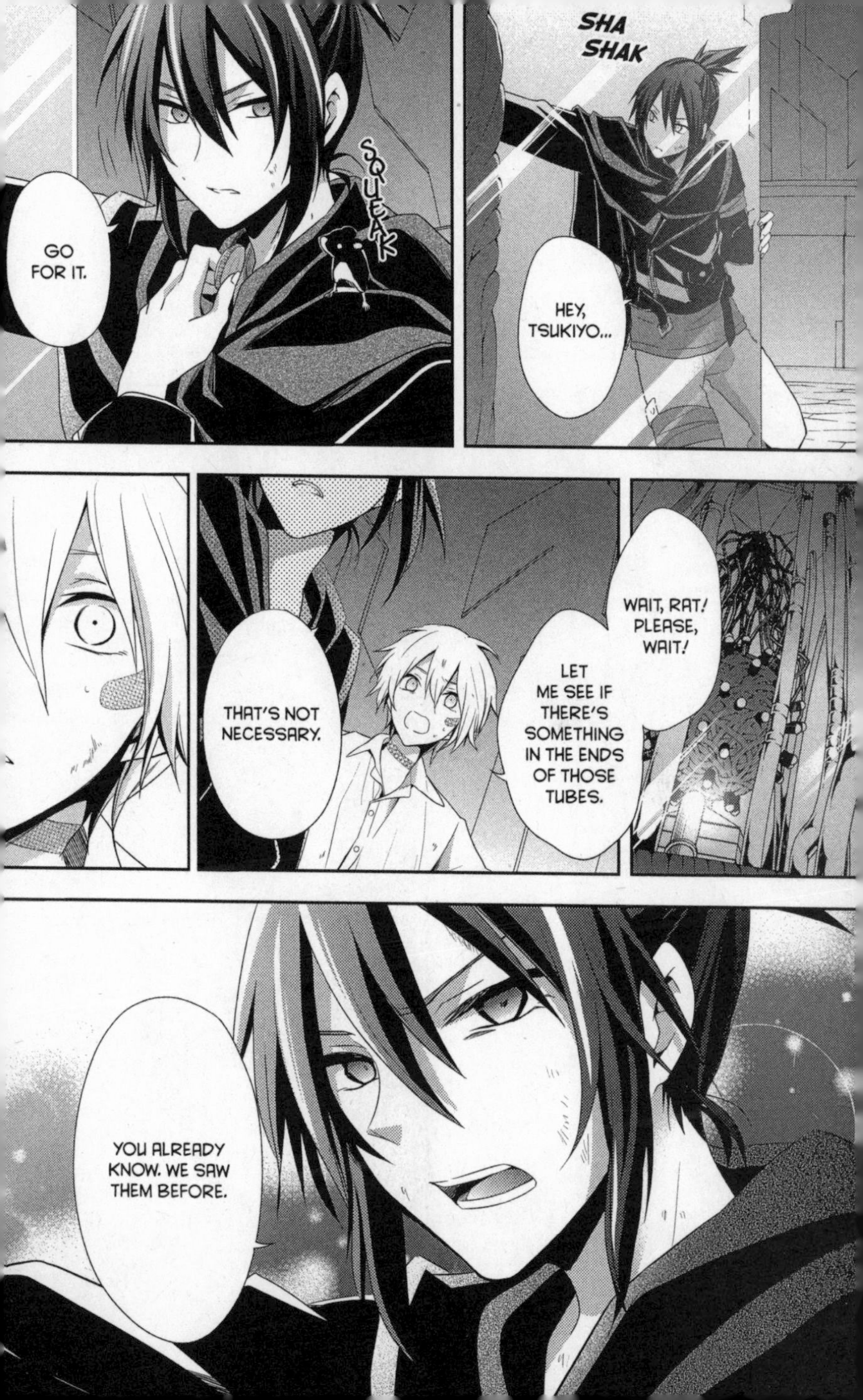
SHA SHAK
HEY, TSUKIYO...
SQUEAK
GO FOR IT.
WAIT, RAT! PLEASE, WAIT!
LET ME SEE IF THERE'S SOMETHING IN THE ENDS OF THOSE TUBES.
THAT'S NOT NECESSARY.
YOU ALREADY KNOW. WE SAW THEM BEFORE.

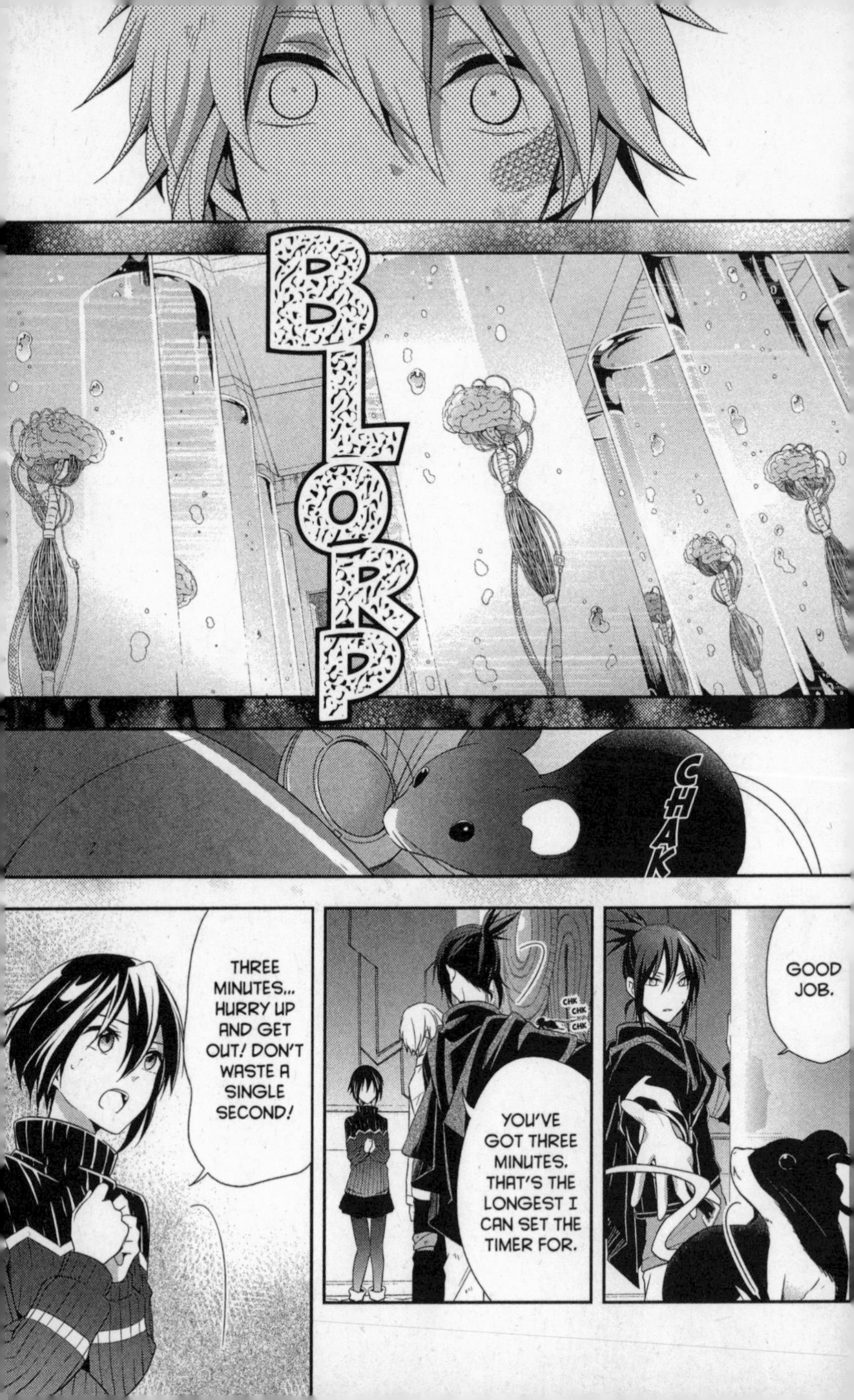
BLORP
CHAK
GOOD JOB.
CHK CHK CHK
YOU'VE GOT THREE MINUTES. THAT'S THE LONGEST I CAN SET THE TIMER FOR.
THREE MINUTES... HURRY UP AND GET OUT! DON'T WASTE A SINGLE SECOND!

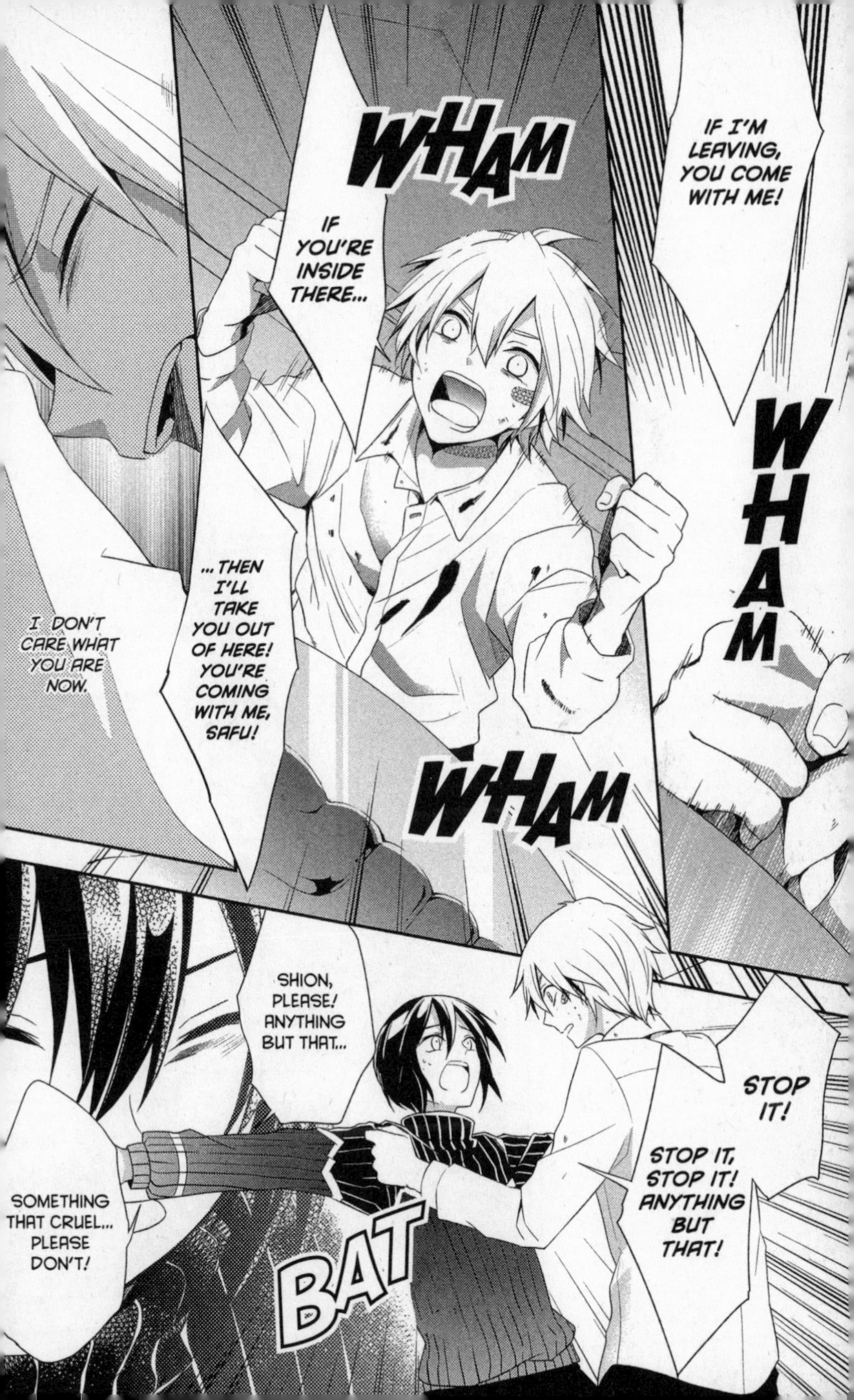
IF I'M LEAVING, YOU COME WITH ME!
WHAM
WHAM
IF YOU'RE INSIDE THERE...
...THEN I'LL TAKE YOU OUT OF HERE! YOU'RE COMING WITH ME, SAFU!
WHAM
I DON'T CARE WHAT YOU ARE NOW.
STOP IT!
STOP IT, STOP IT! ANYTHING BUT THAT!
SHION, PLEASE! ANYTHING BUT THAT...
BAT
SOMETHING THAT CRUEL... PLEASE DON'T!

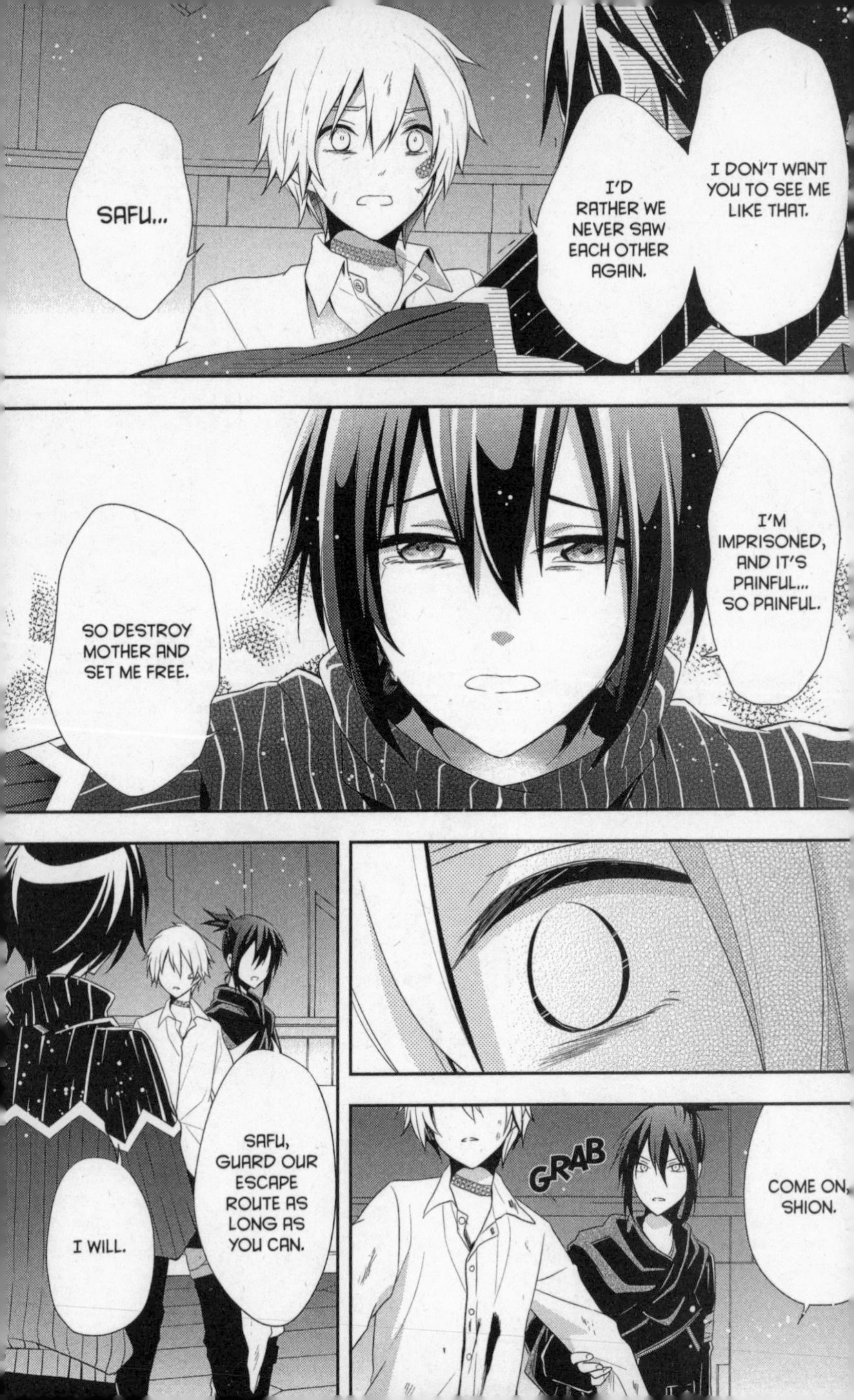
I DON'T WANT YOU TO SEE ME LIKE THAT.
I'D RATHER WE NEVER SAW EACH OTHER AGAIN.
SAFU...
I'M IMPRISONED, AND IT'S PAINFUL... SO PAINFUL.
SO DESTROY MOTHER AND SET ME FREE.
COME ON, SHION.
GRAB
SAFU, GUARD OUR ESCAPE ROUTE AS LONG AS YOU CAN.
I WILL.

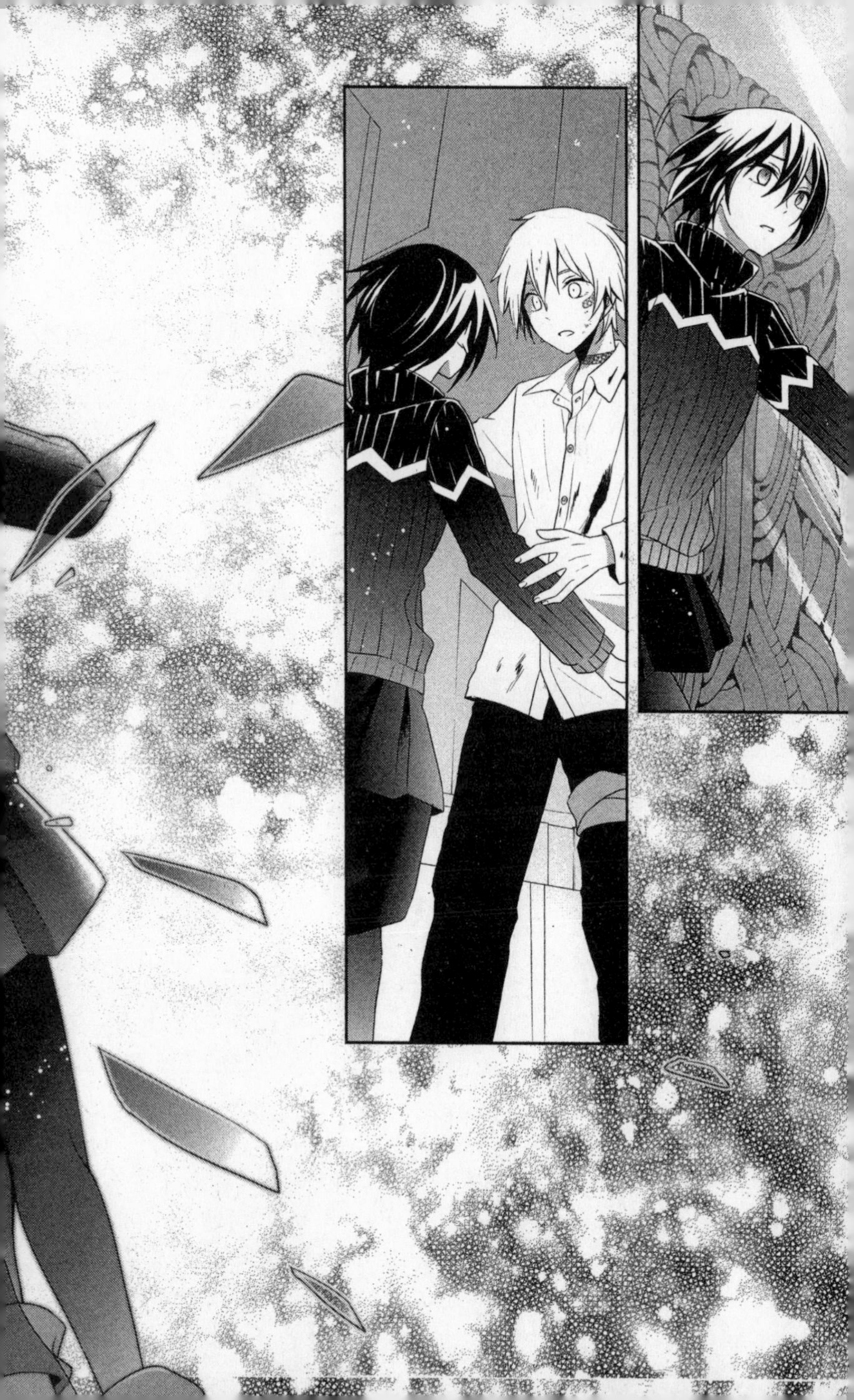

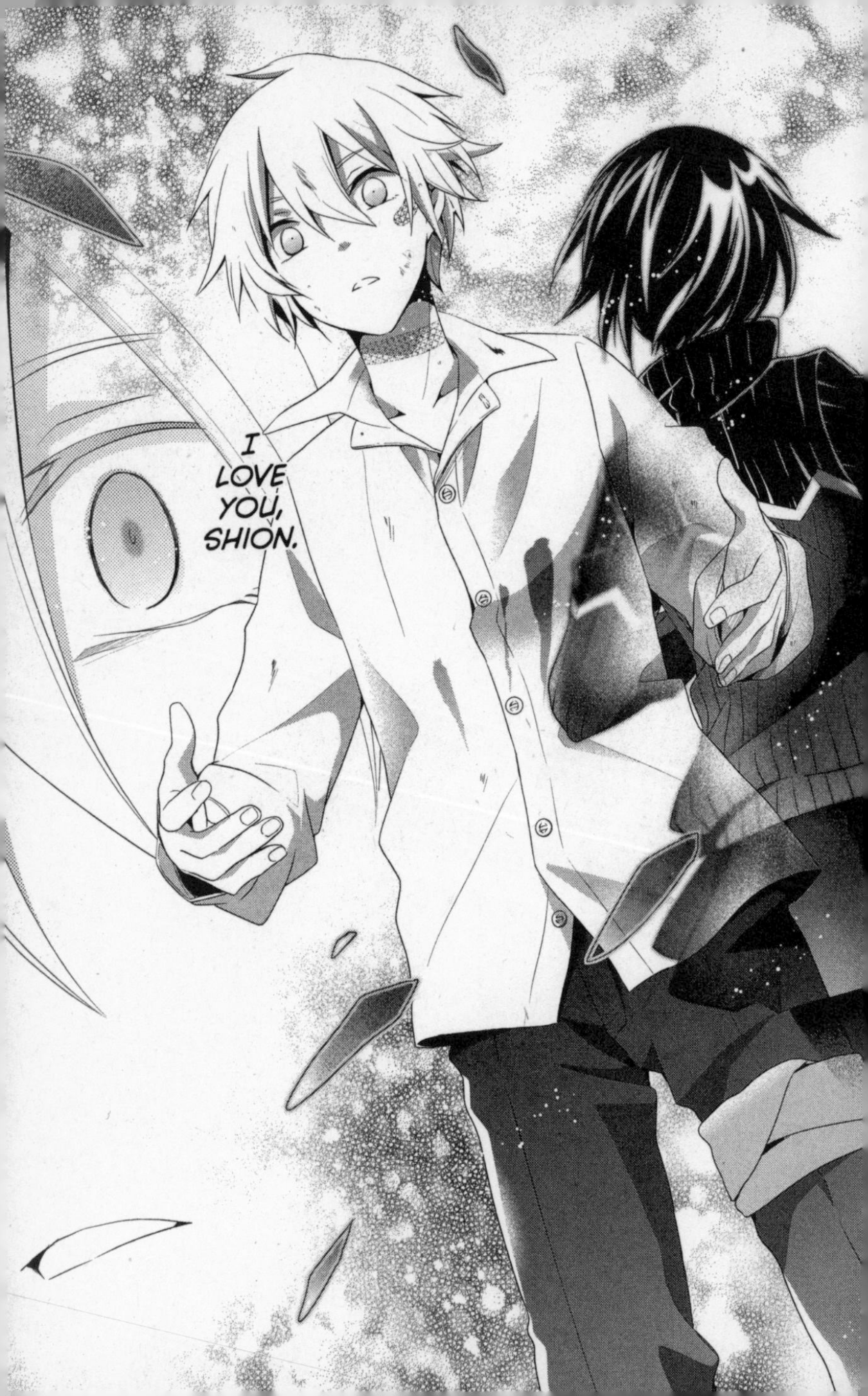
I LOVE YOU, SHION.

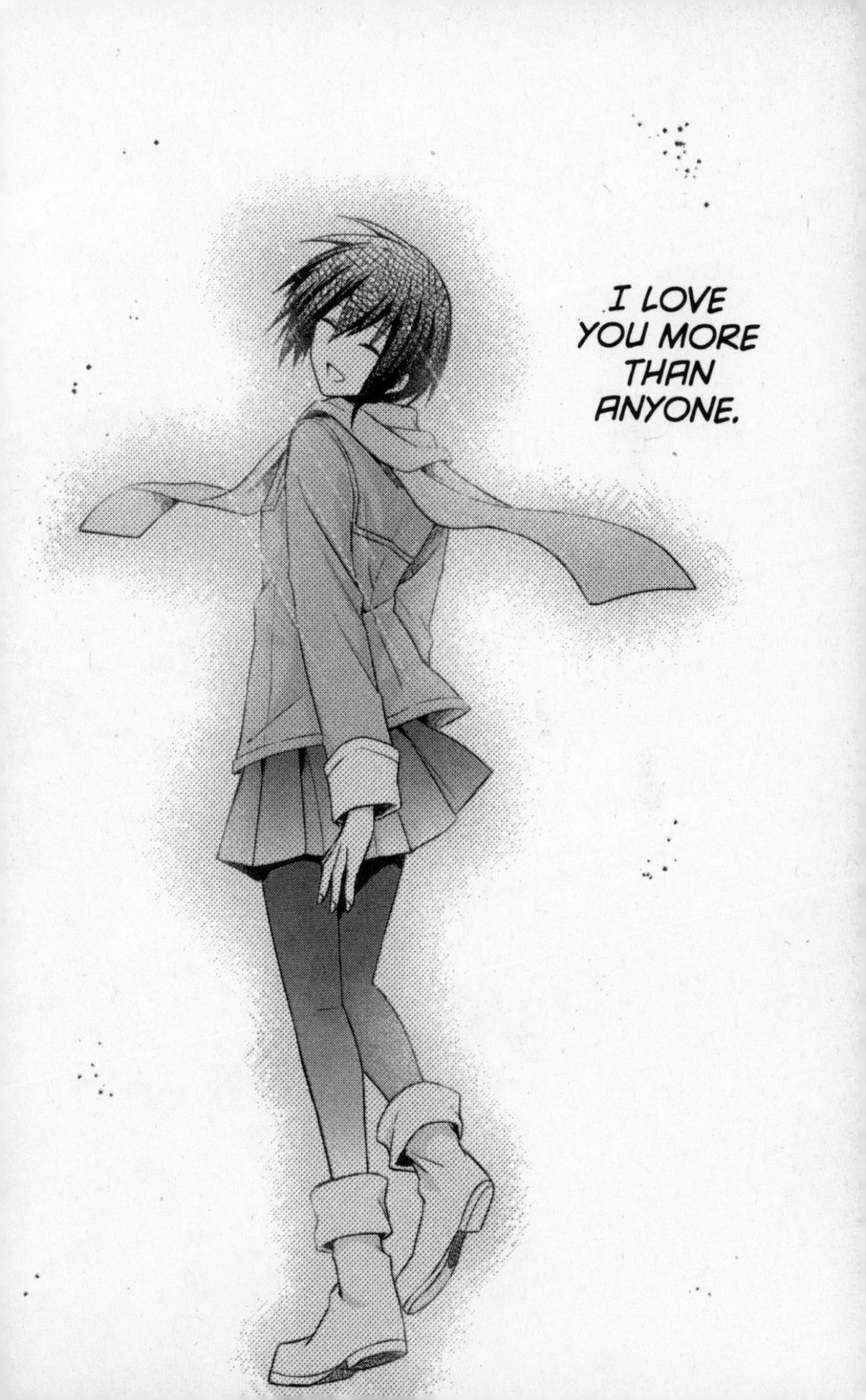
I LOVE YOU MORE THAN ANYONE.

Chapter 29: Get Out of Here!

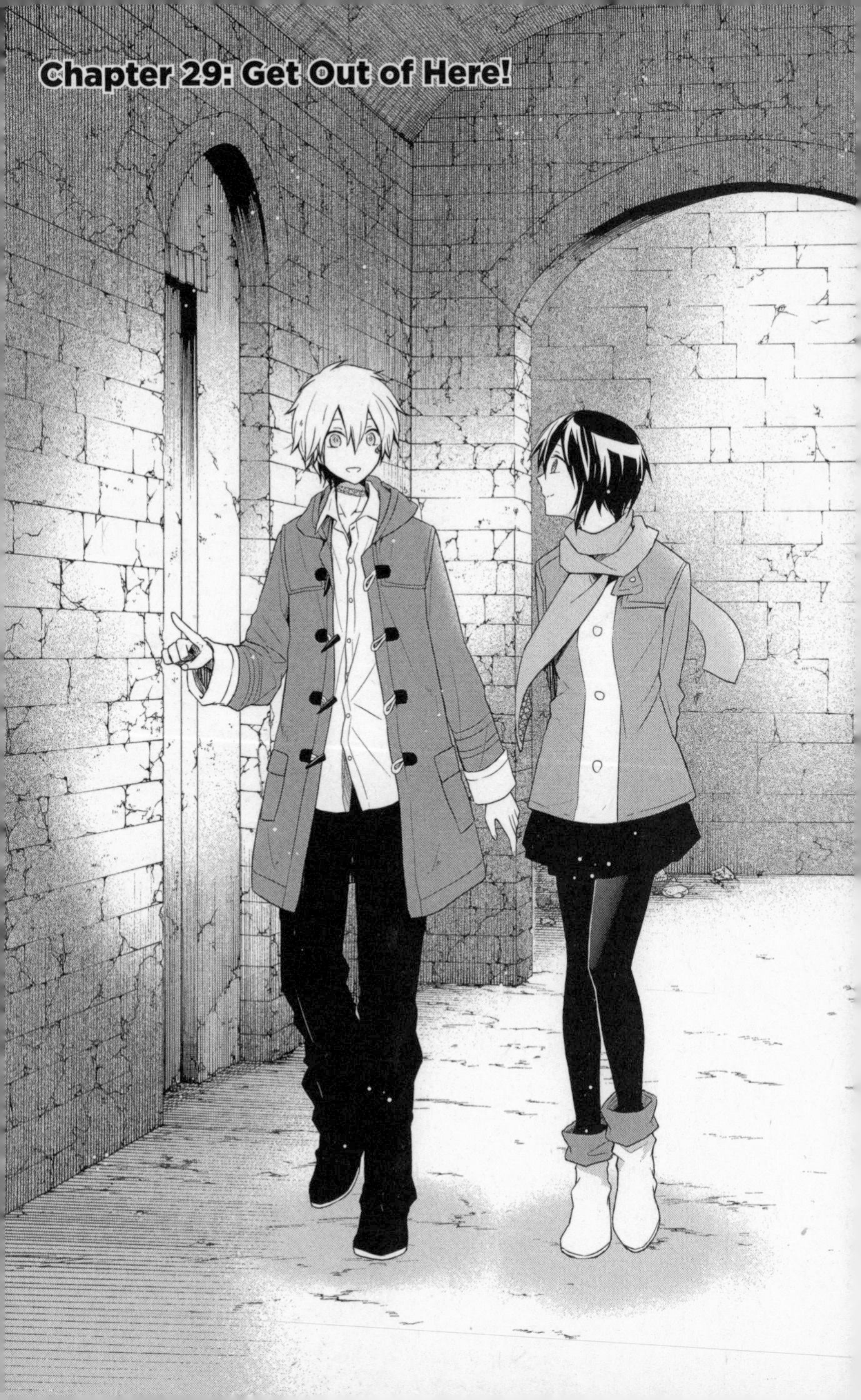

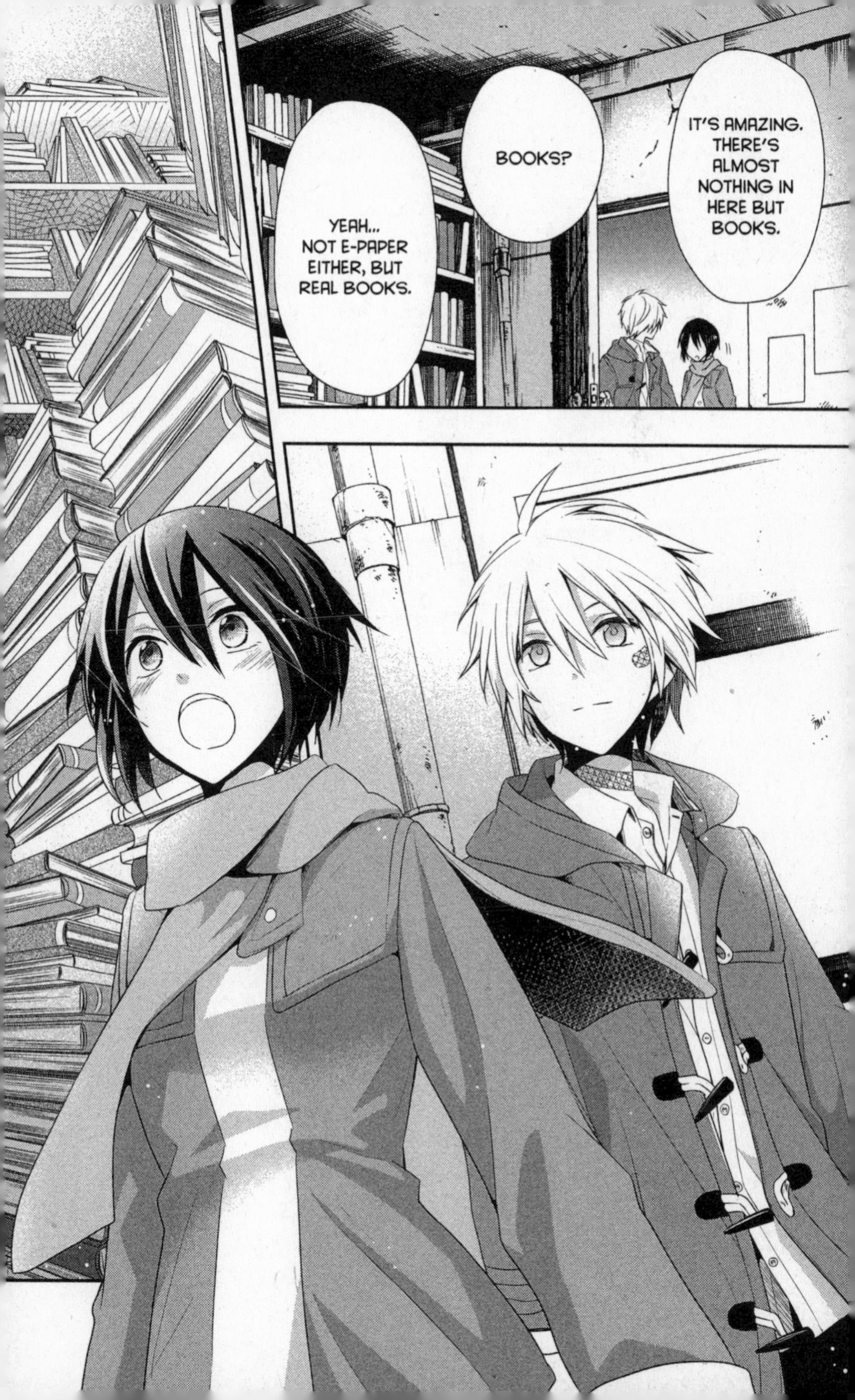
IT'S AMAZING. THERE'S ALMOST NOTHING IN HERE BUT BOOKS.
BOOKS?
YEAH... NOT E-PAPER EITHER, BUT REAL BOOKS.

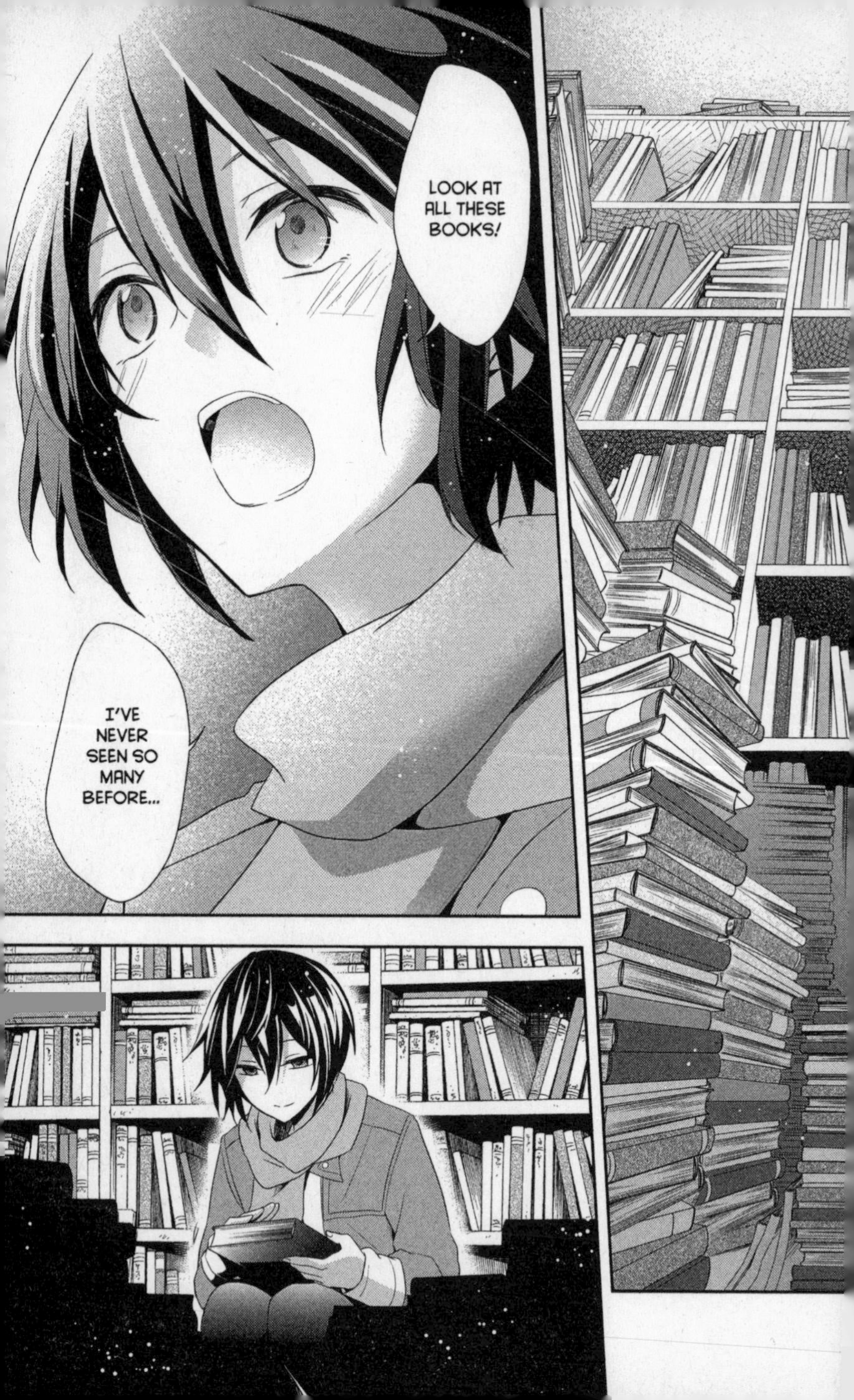
LOOK AT ALL THESE BOOKS!
I'VE NEVER SEEN SO MANY BEFORE...

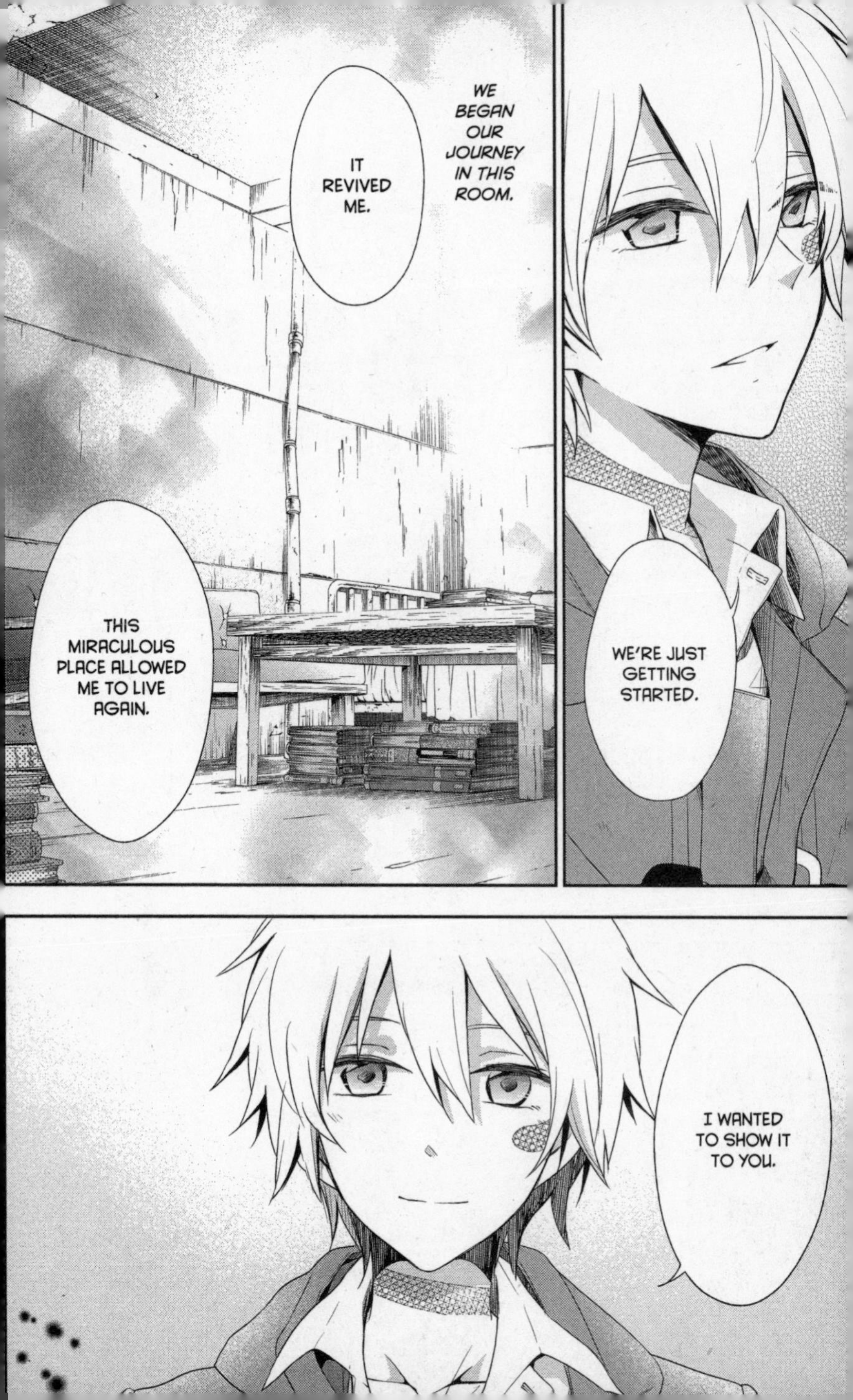
WE'RE JUST GETTING STARTED.
WE BEGAN OUR JOURNEY IN THIS ROOM.
IT REVIVED ME.
THIS MIRACULOUS PLACE ALLOWED ME TO LIVE AGAIN.
I WANTED TO SHOW IT TO YOU.

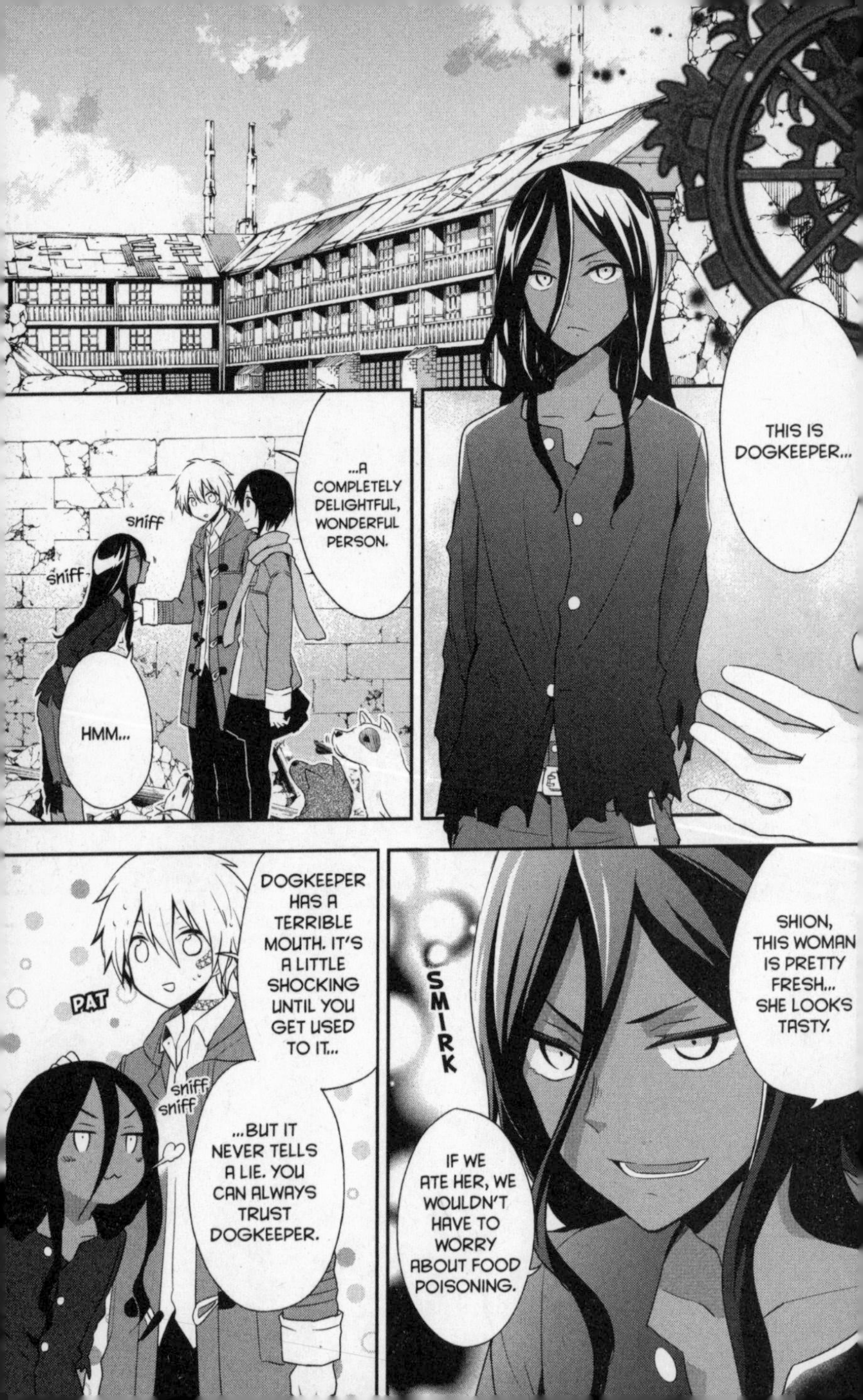
THIS IS DOGKEEPER...
...A COMPLETELY DELIGHTFUL, WONDERFUL PERSON.
sniff
sniff
HMM...
SHION, THIS WOMAN IS PRETTY FRESH... SHE LOOKS TASTY.
SMIRK
IF WE ATE HER, WE WOULDN'T HAVE TO WORRY ABOUT FOOD POISONING.
DOGKEEPER HAS A TERRIBLE MOUTH. IT'S A LITTLE SHOCKING UNTIL YOU GET USED TO IT...
PAT
sniff sniff
...BUT IT NEVER TELLS A LIE. YOU CAN ALWAYS TRUST DOGKEEPER.

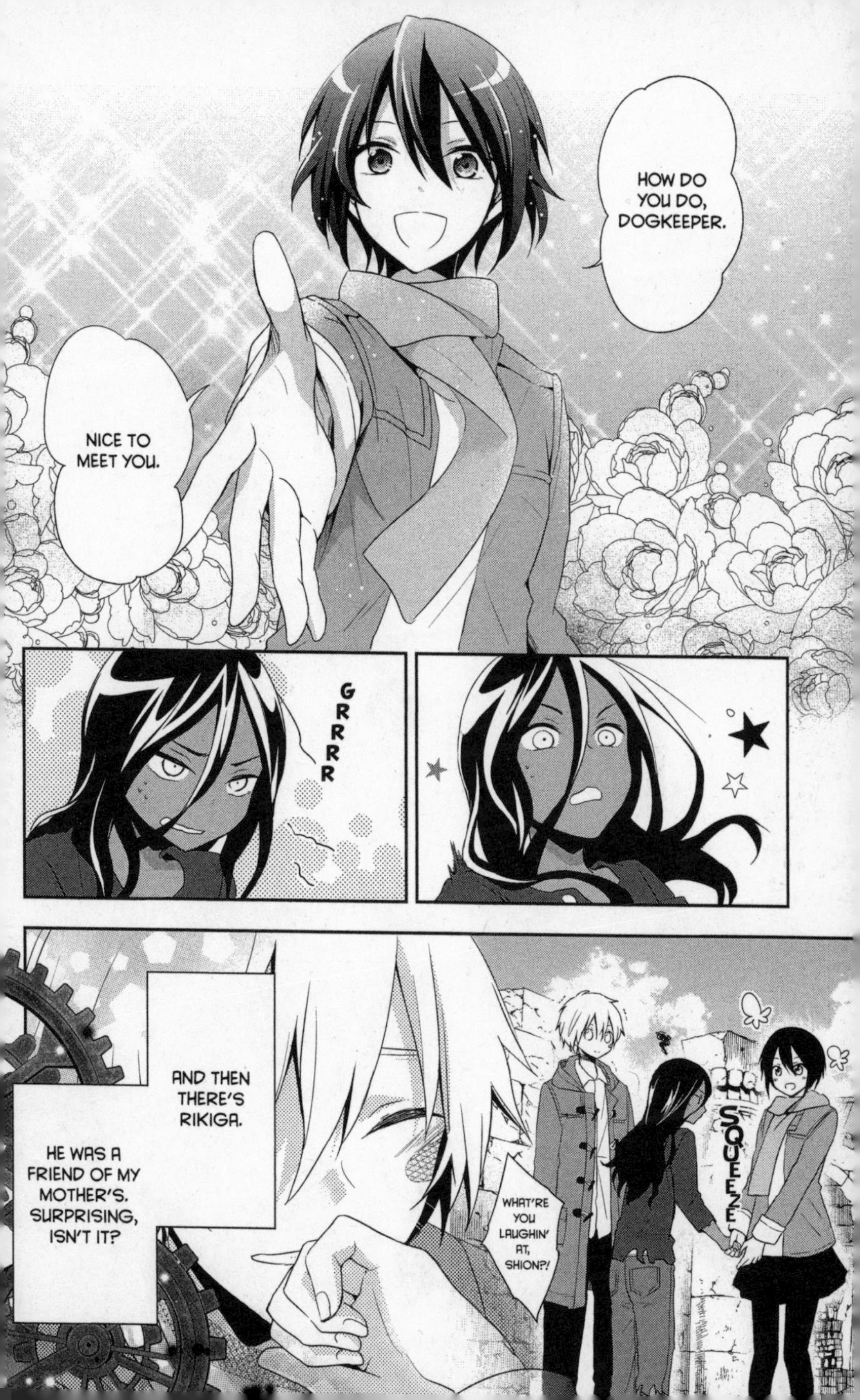
HOW DO YOU DO, DOGKEEPER.
NICE TO MEET YOU.
GRRRR
SQUEEZE
WHAT'RE YOU LAUGHIN' AT, SHION?!
AND THEN THERE'S RIKIGA.
HE WAS A FRIEND OF MY MOTHER'S. SURPRISING, ISN'T IT?

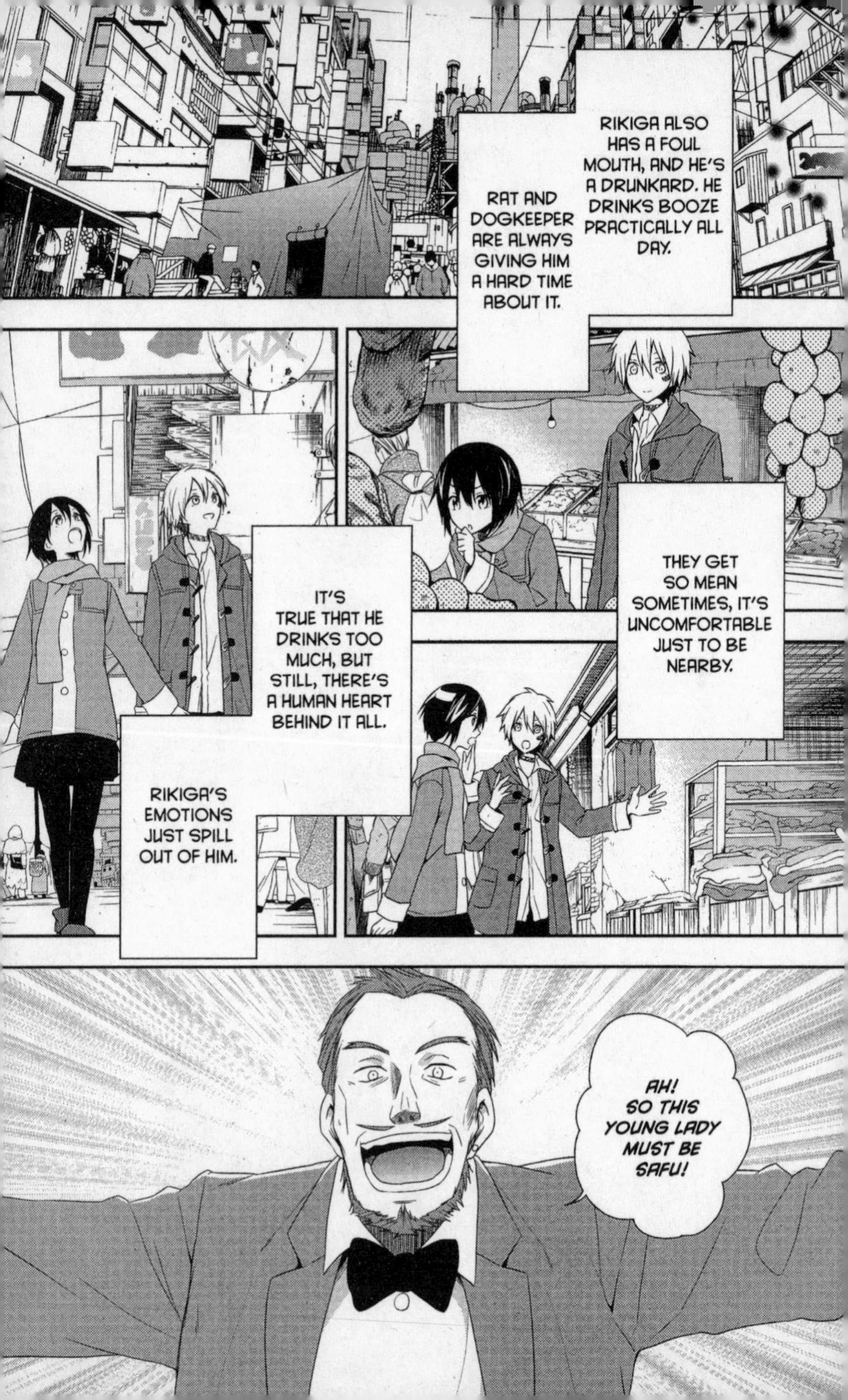
RIKIGA ALSO HAS A FOUL MOUTH, AND HE'S A DRUNKARD. HE DRINKS BOOZE PRACTICALLY ALL DAY.
RAT AND DOGKEEPER ARE ALWAYS GIVING HIM A HARD TIME ABOUT IT.
THEY GET SO MEAN SOMETIMES, IT'S UNCOMFORTABLE JUST TO BE NEARBY.
IT'S TRUE THAT HE DRINKS TOO MUCH, BUT STILL, THERE'S A HUMAN HEART BEHIND IT ALL.
RIKIGA'S EMOTIONS JUST SPILL OUT OF HIM.
AH! SO THIS YOUNG LADY MUST BE SAFU!

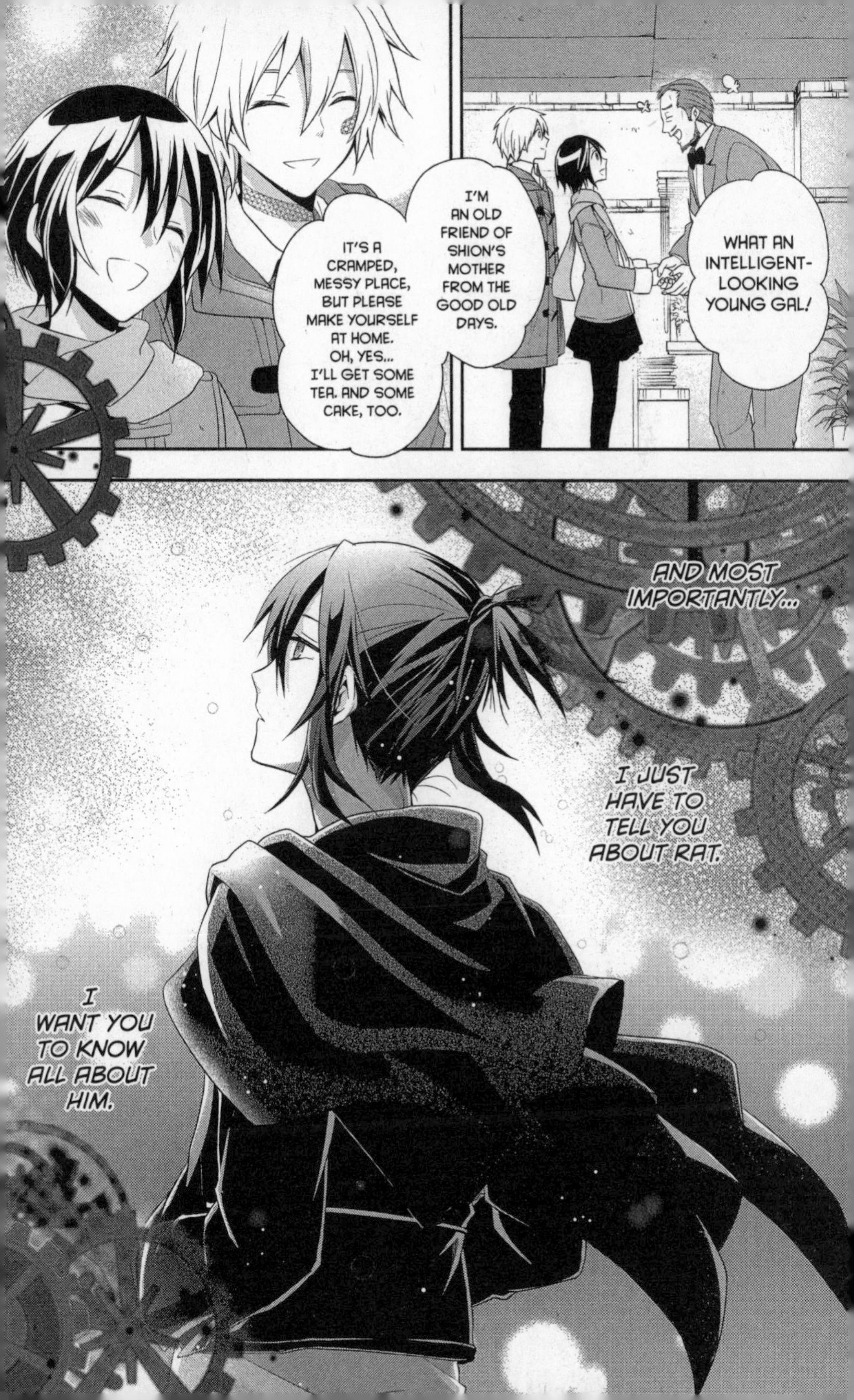
WHAT AN INTELLIGENT-LOOKING YOUNG GAL!
I'M AN OLD FRIEND OF SHION'S MOTHER FROM THE GOOD OLD DAYS.
IT'S A CRAMPED, MESSY PLACE, BUT PLEASE MAKE YOURSELF AT HOME. OH, YES... I'LL GET SOME TEA. AND SOME CAKE, TOO.
AND MOST IMPORTANTLY...
I JUST HAVE TO TELL YOU ABOUT RAT.
I WANT YOU TO KNOW ALL ABOUT HIM.

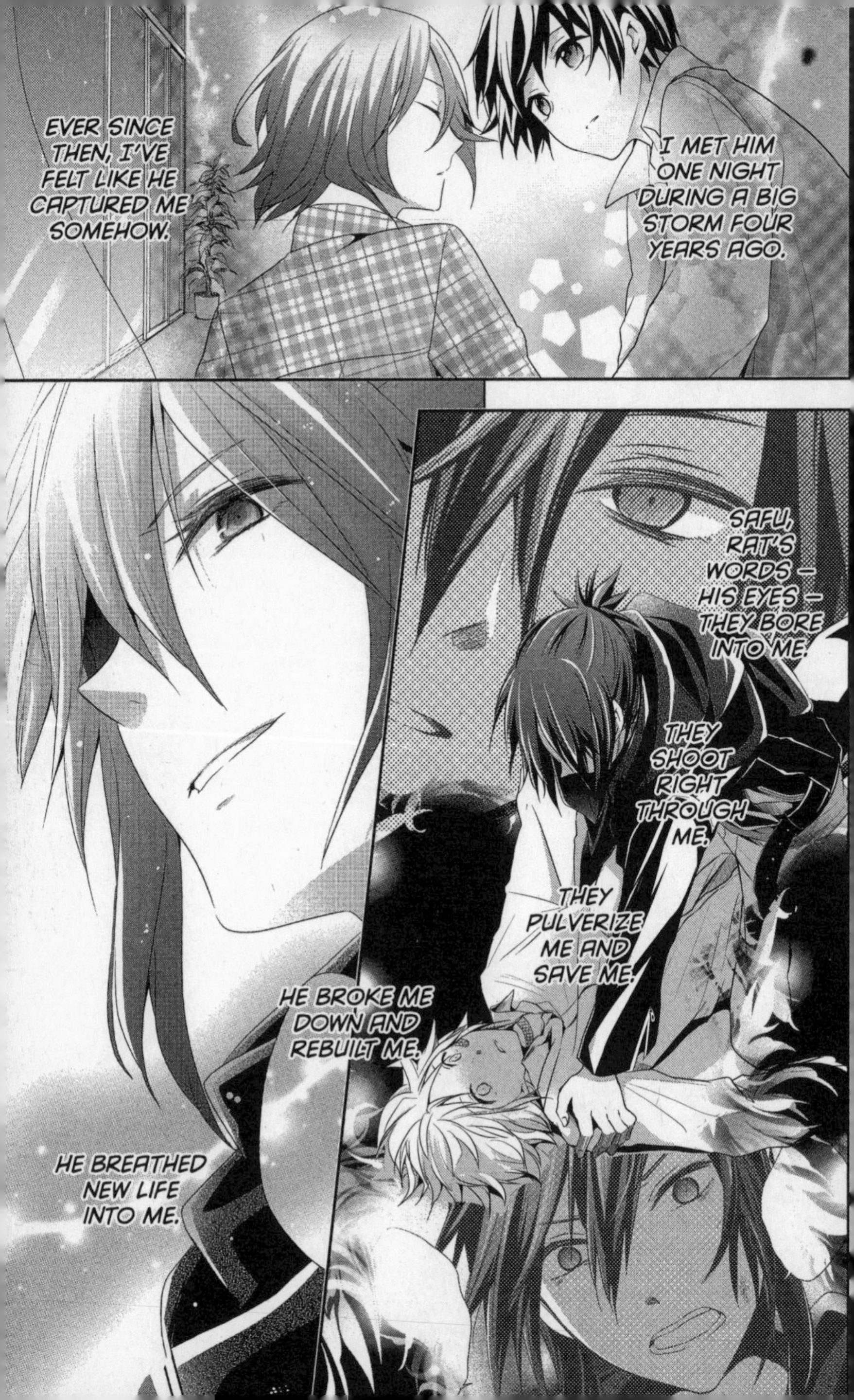
I MET HIM ONE NIGHT DURING A BIG STORM FOUR YEARS AGO.
EVER SINCE THEN, I'VE FELT LIKE HE CAPTURED ME SOMEHOW.
SAFU, RAT'S WORDS – HIS EYES – THEY BORE INTO ME.
THEY SHOOT RIGHT THROUGH ME.
THEY PULVERIZE ME AND SAVE ME.
HE BROKE ME DOWN AND REBUILT ME.
HE BREATHED NEW LIFE INTO ME.

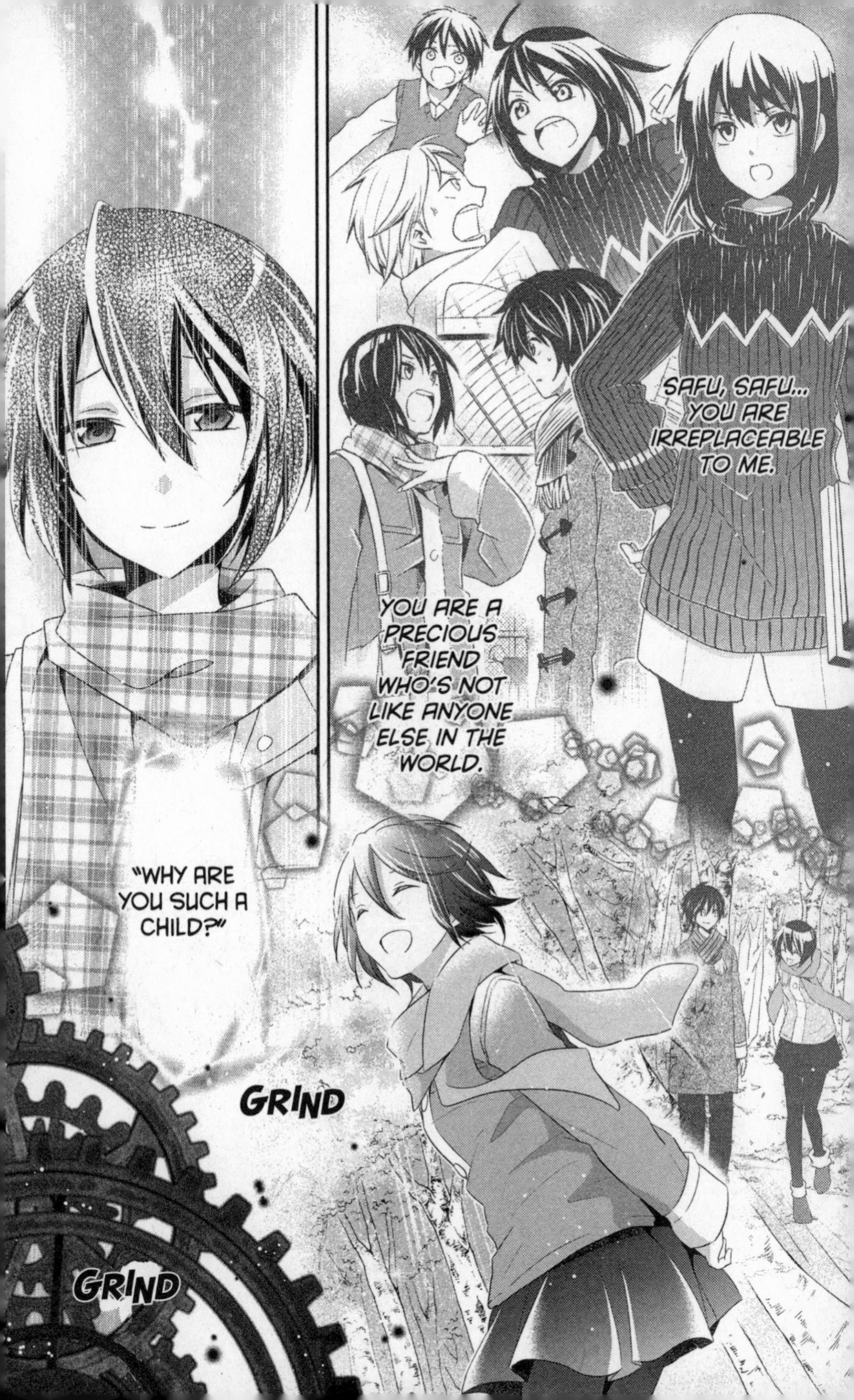
SAFU, SAFU... YOU ARE IRREPLACEABLE TO ME.
YOU ARE A PRECIOUS FRIEND WHO'S NOT LIKE ANYONE ELSE IN THE WORLD.
"WHY ARE YOU SUCH A CHILD?"
GRIND
GRIND

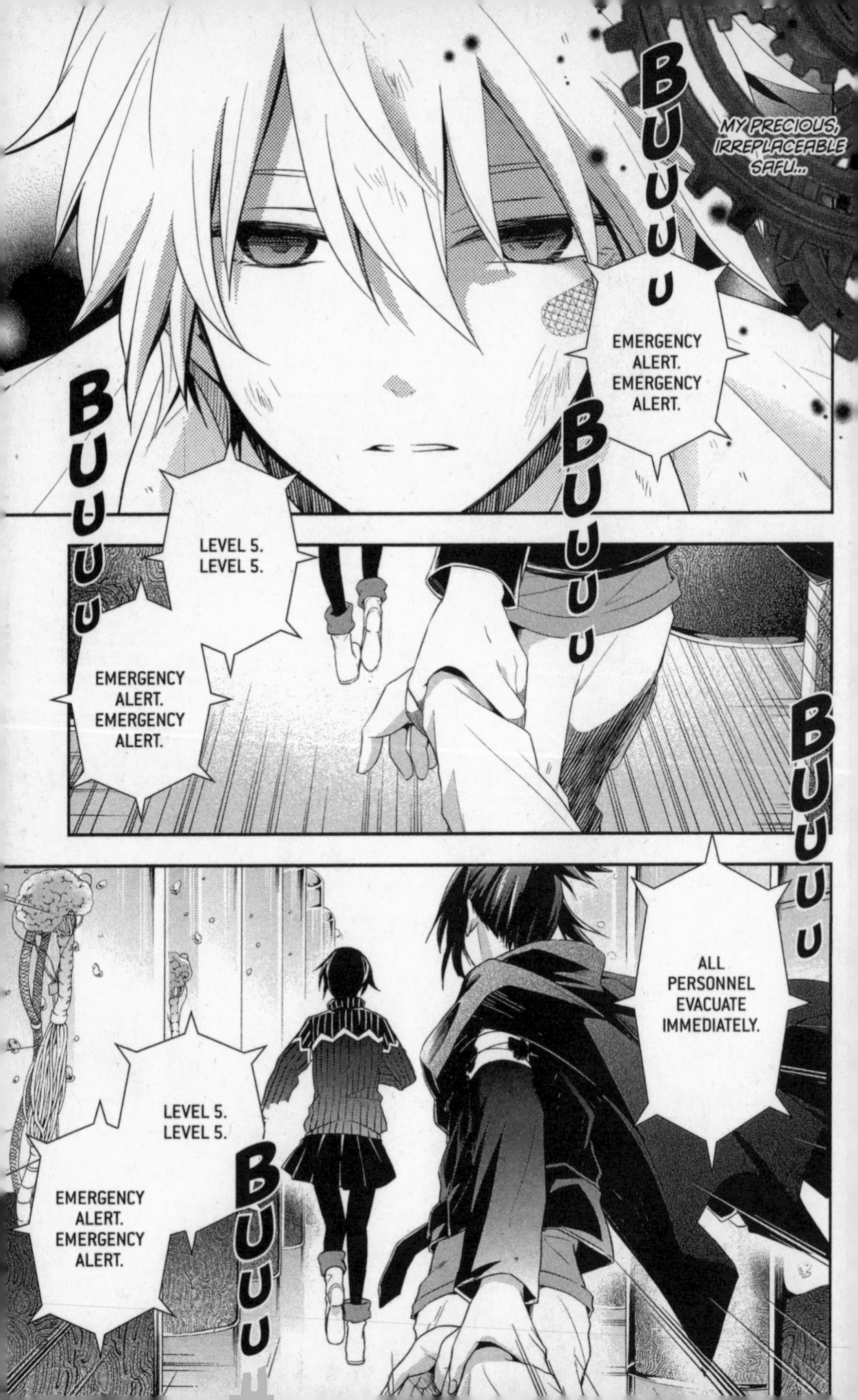
MY PRECIOUS, IRREPLACEABLE SAFU...
BUUUUU
EMERGENCY ALERT. EMERGENCY ALERT.
BUUUUU
LEVEL 5. LEVEL 5.
BUUUUU
EMERGENCY ALERT. EMERGENCY ALERT.
BUUUUU
ALL PERSONNEL EVACUATE IMMEDIATELY.
LEVEL 5. LEVEL 5.
BUUUU
EMERGENCY ALERT. EMERGENCY ALERT.

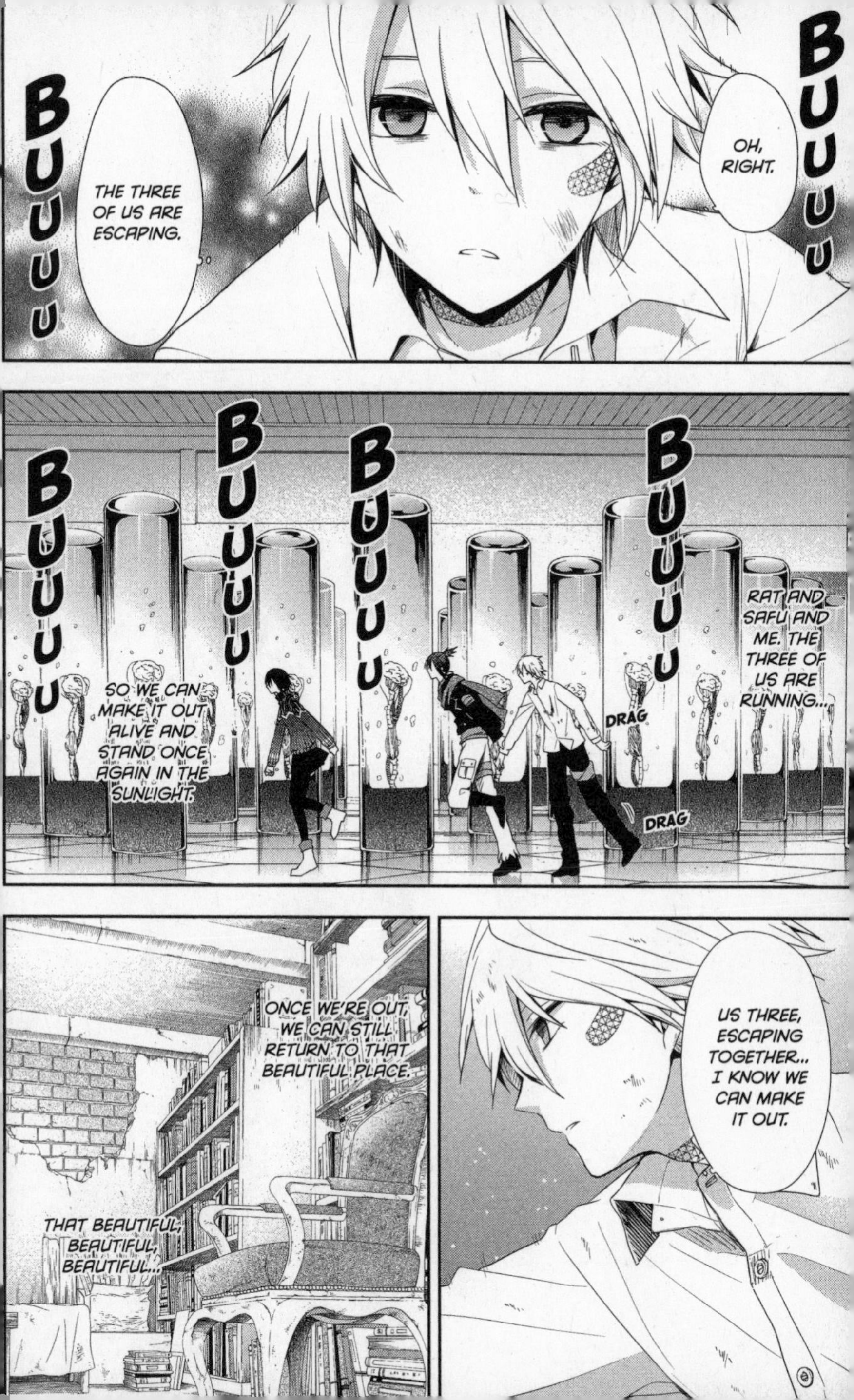
BUUUU
OH, RIGHT.
THE THREE OF US ARE ESCAPING.
BUUUUU
BUUUU
RAT AND SAFU AND ME. THE THREE OF US ARE RUNNING...
DRAG
DRAG
BUUUUU
BUUUUU
BUUUUU
SO WE CAN MAKE IT OUT ALIVE AND STAND ONCE AGAIN IN THE SUNLIGHT.
US THREE, ESCAPING TOGETHER... I KNOW WE CAN MAKE IT OUT.
ONCE WE'RE OUT, WE CAN STILL RETURN TO THAT BEAUTIFUL PLACE.
THAT BEAUTIFUL, BEAUTIFUL, BEAUTIFUL...

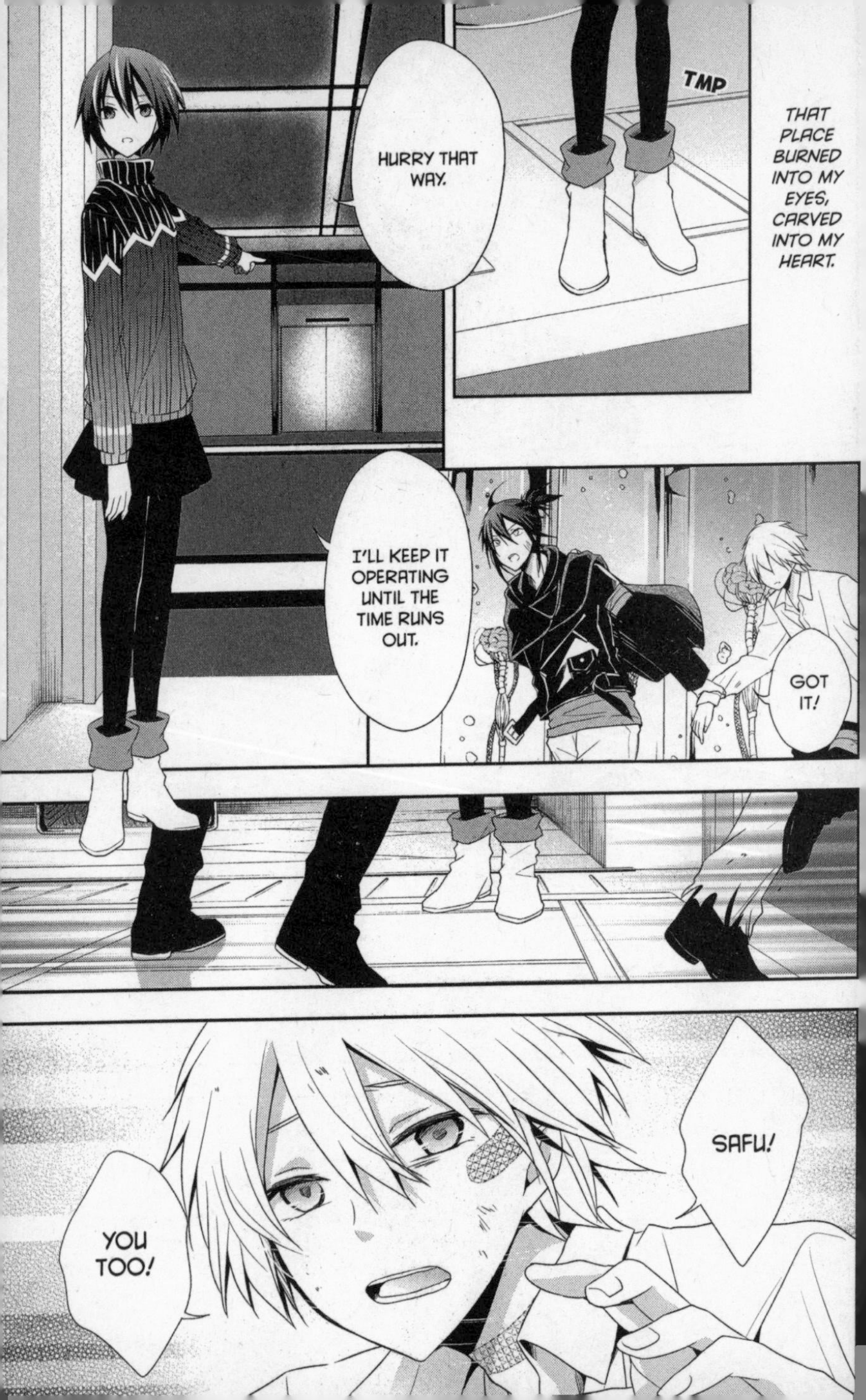
THAT PLACE BURNED INTO MY EYES, CARVED INTO MY HEART.
TMP
HURRY THAT WAY.
I'LL KEEP IT OPERATING UNTIL THE TIME RUNS OUT.
GOT IT!
SAFU!
YOU TOO!

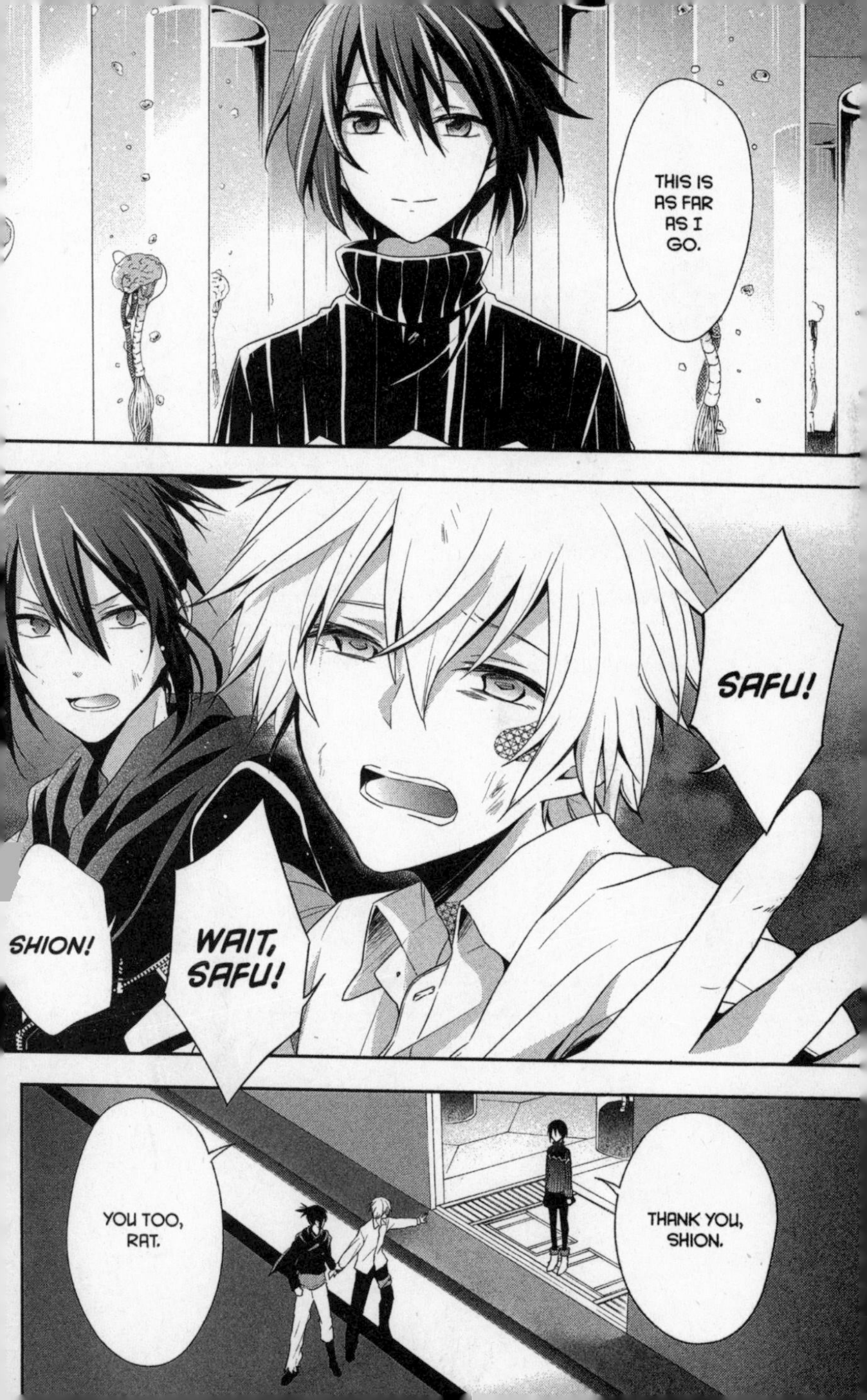
THIS IS AS FAR AS I GO.
SAFU!
WAIT, SAFU!
SHION!
THANK YOU, SHION.
YOU TOO, RAT.

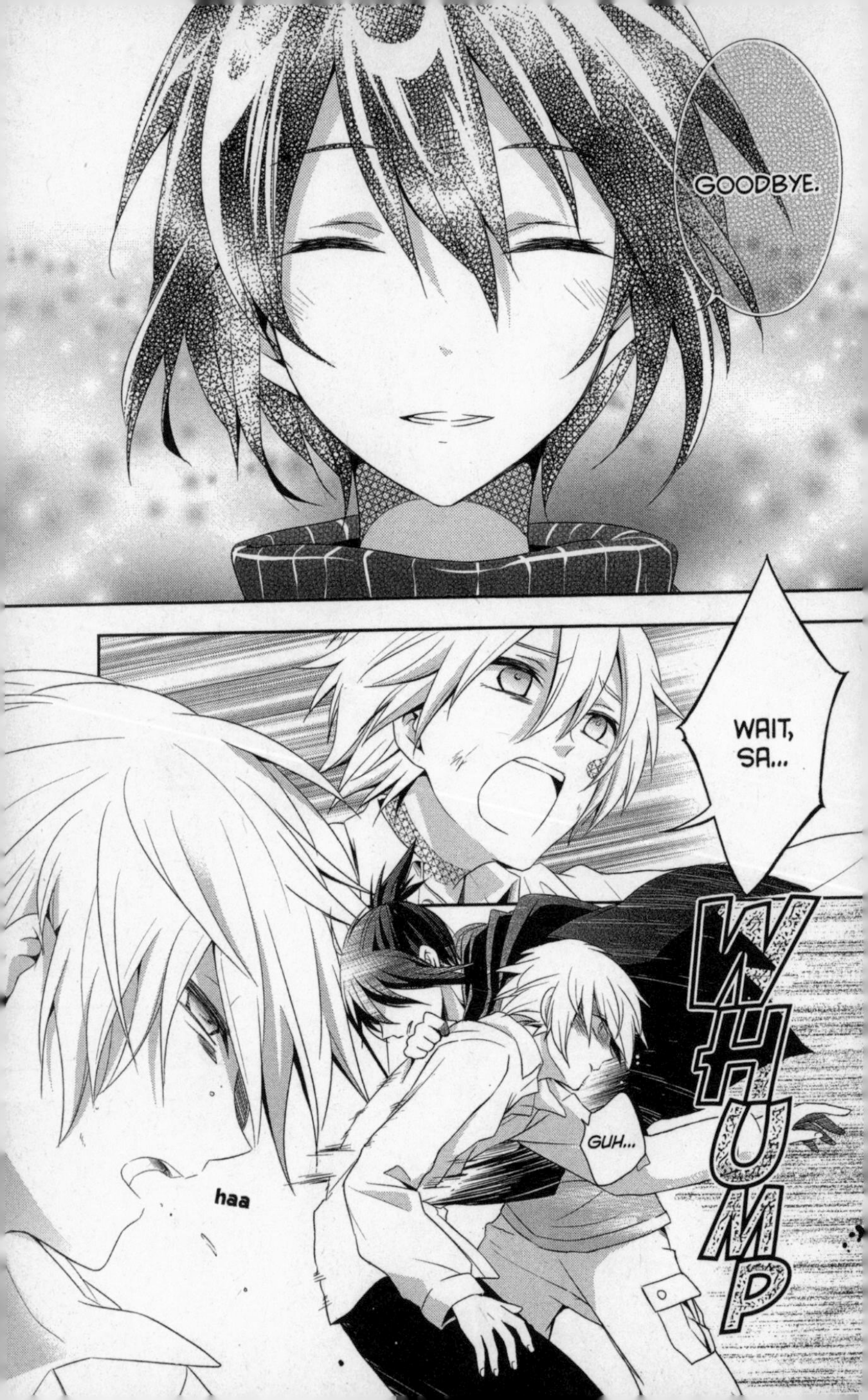
GOODBYE.
WAIT, SA...
WHUMP
GUH...
haa

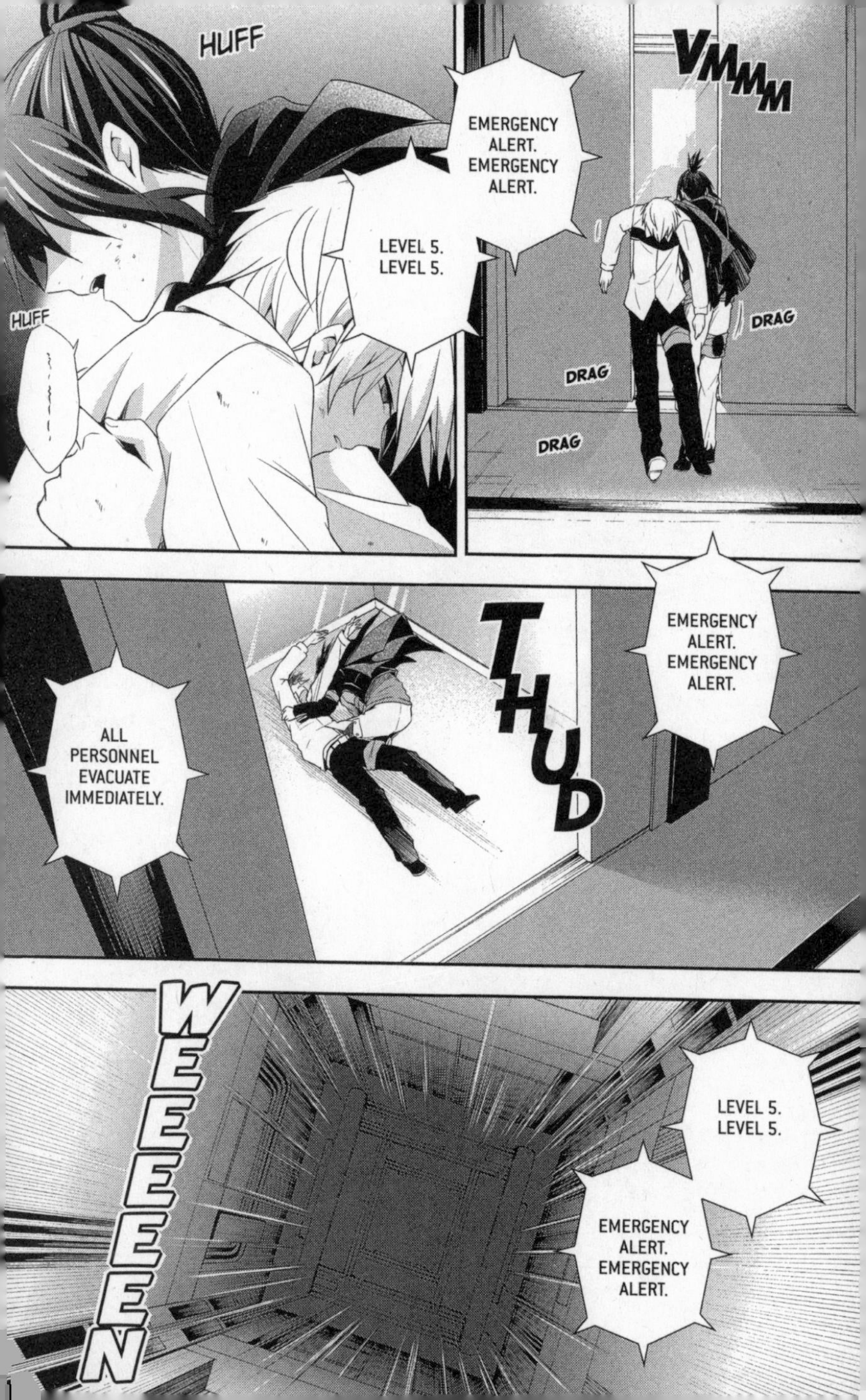
VMMM
EMERGENCY ALERT. EMERGENCY ALERT.
DRAG
DRAG
DRAG
HUFF
LEVEL 5. LEVEL 5.
HUFF
EMERGENCY ALERT. EMERGENCY ALERT.
THUD
ALL PERSONNEL EVACUATE IMMEDIATELY.
LEVEL 5. LEVEL 5.
EMERGENCY ALERT. EMERGENCY ALERT.
WEEEEEEN

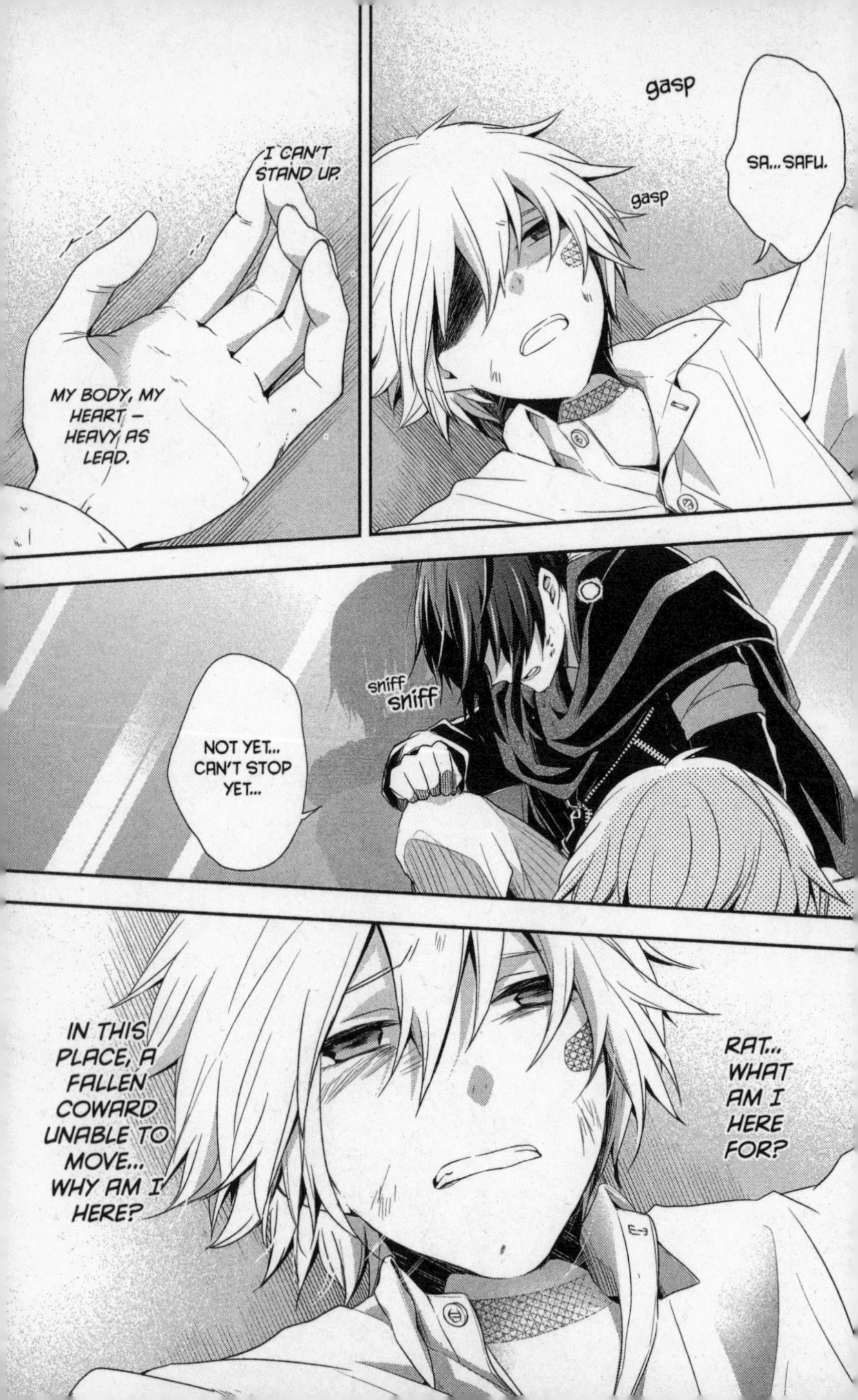
gasp
SA... SAFU.
gasp
I CAN'T STAND UP.
MY BODY, MY HEART — HEAVY AS LEAD.
sniff
sniff
NOT YET... CAN'T STOP YET...
RAT... WHAT AM I HERE FOR?
IN THIS PLACE, A FALLEN COWARD UNABLE TO MOVE... WHY AM I HERE?

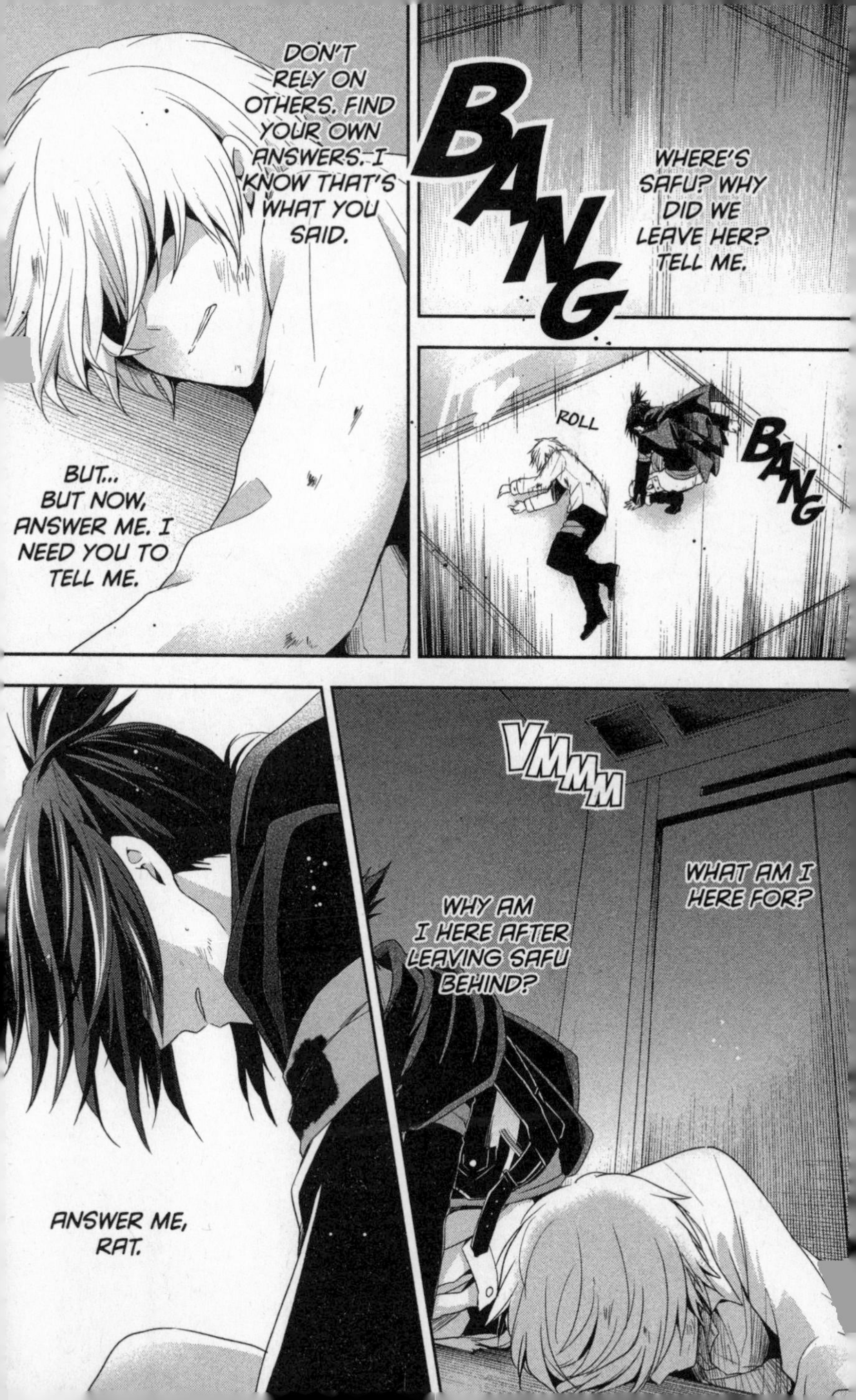
BANG
WHERE'S SAFU? WHY DID WE LEAVE HER? TELL ME.
ROLL
BANG
DON'T RELY ON OTHERS. FIND YOUR OWN ANSWERS. I KNOW THAT'S WHAT YOU SAID.
BUT... BUT NOW, ANSWER ME. I NEED YOU TO TELL ME.
VMMM
WHAT AM I HERE FOR?
WHY AM I HERE AFTER LEAVING SAFU BEHIND?
ANSWER ME, RAT.

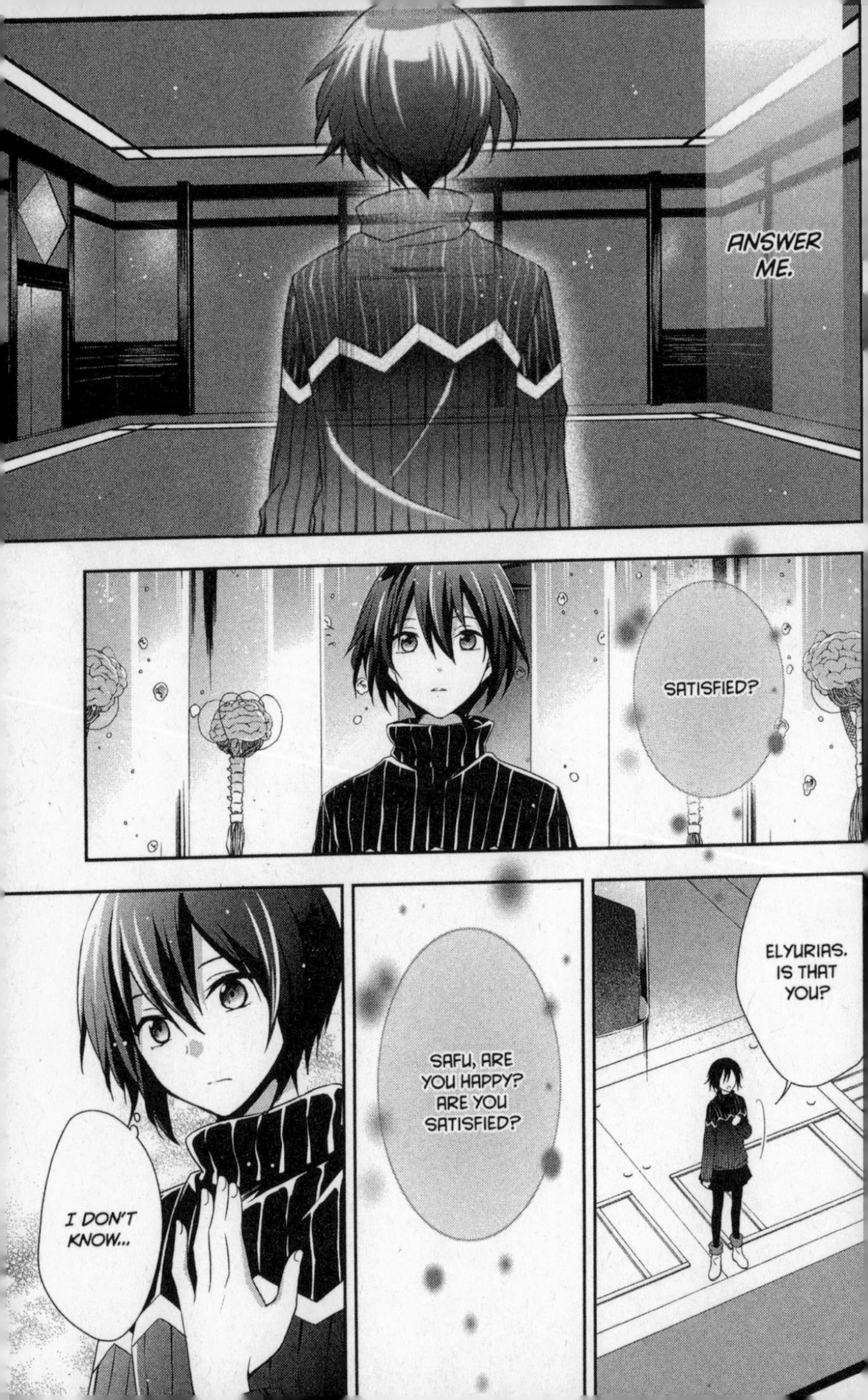
ANSWER ME.
SATISFIED?
ELYURIAS. IS THAT YOU?
SAFU, ARE YOU HAPPY? ARE YOU SATISFIED?
I DON'T KNOW...

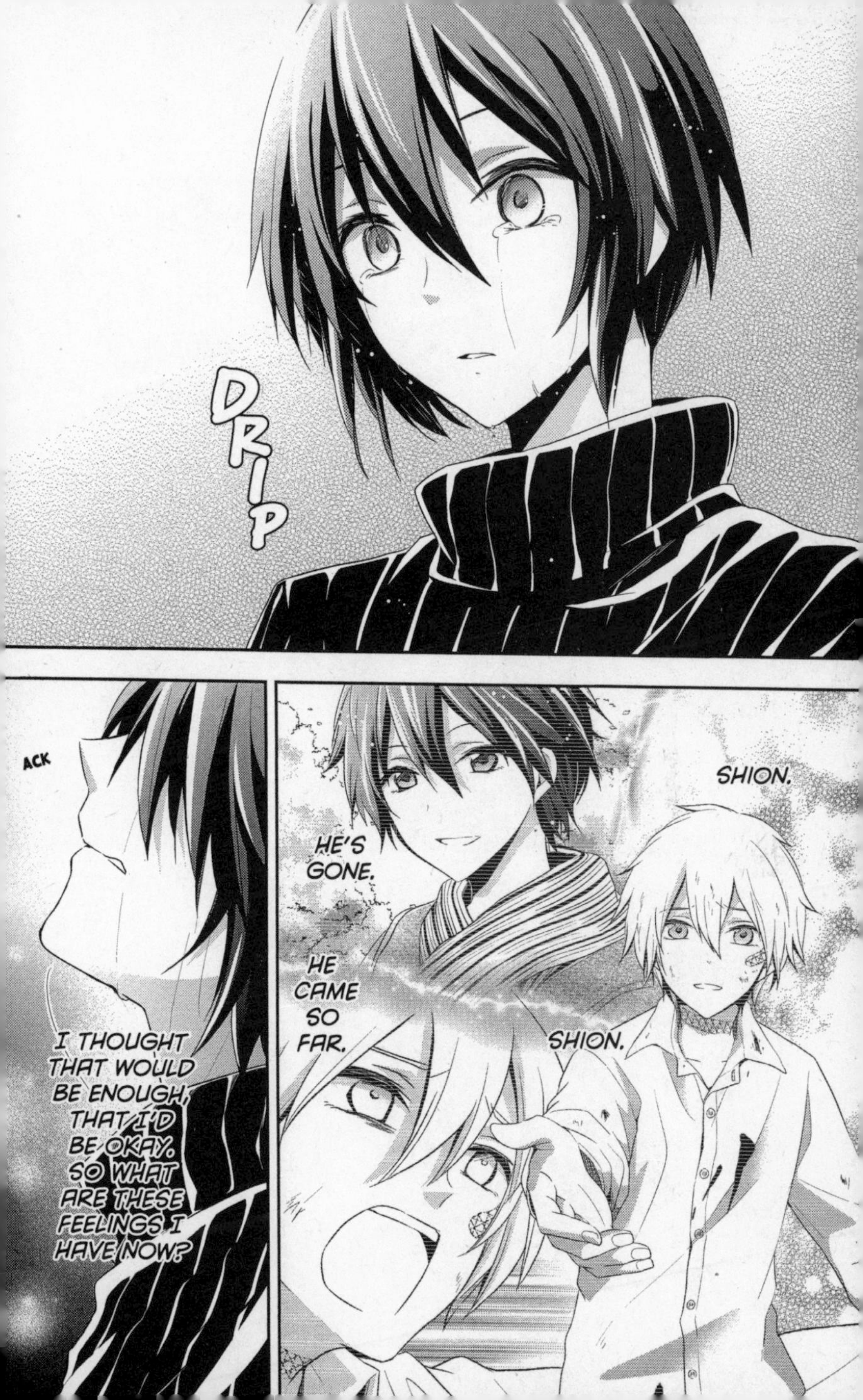
DRIP
SHION.
HE'S GONE.
SHION.
HE CAME SO FAR.
ACK
I THOUGHT THAT WOULD BE ENOUGH, THAT I'D BE OKAY. SO WHAT ARE THESE FEELINGS I HAVE NOW?

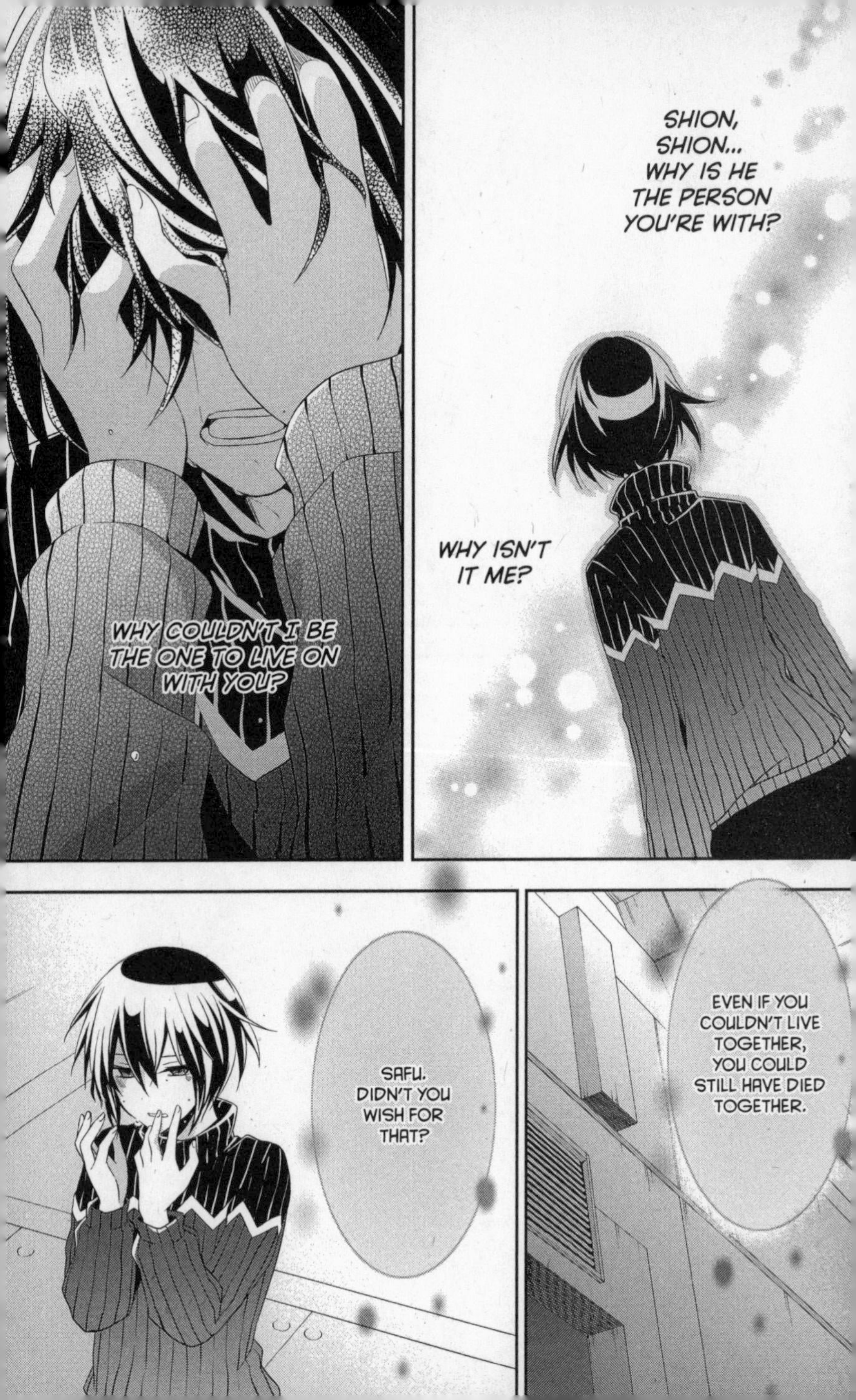
SHION, SHION... WHY IS HE THE PERSON YOU'RE WITH?
WHY ISN'T IT ME?
WHY COULDN'T I BE THE ONE TO LIVE ON WITH YOU?
EVEN IF YOU COULDN'T LIVE TOGETHER, YOU COULD STILL HAVE DIED TOGETHER.
SAFU. DIDN'T YOU WISH FOR THAT?

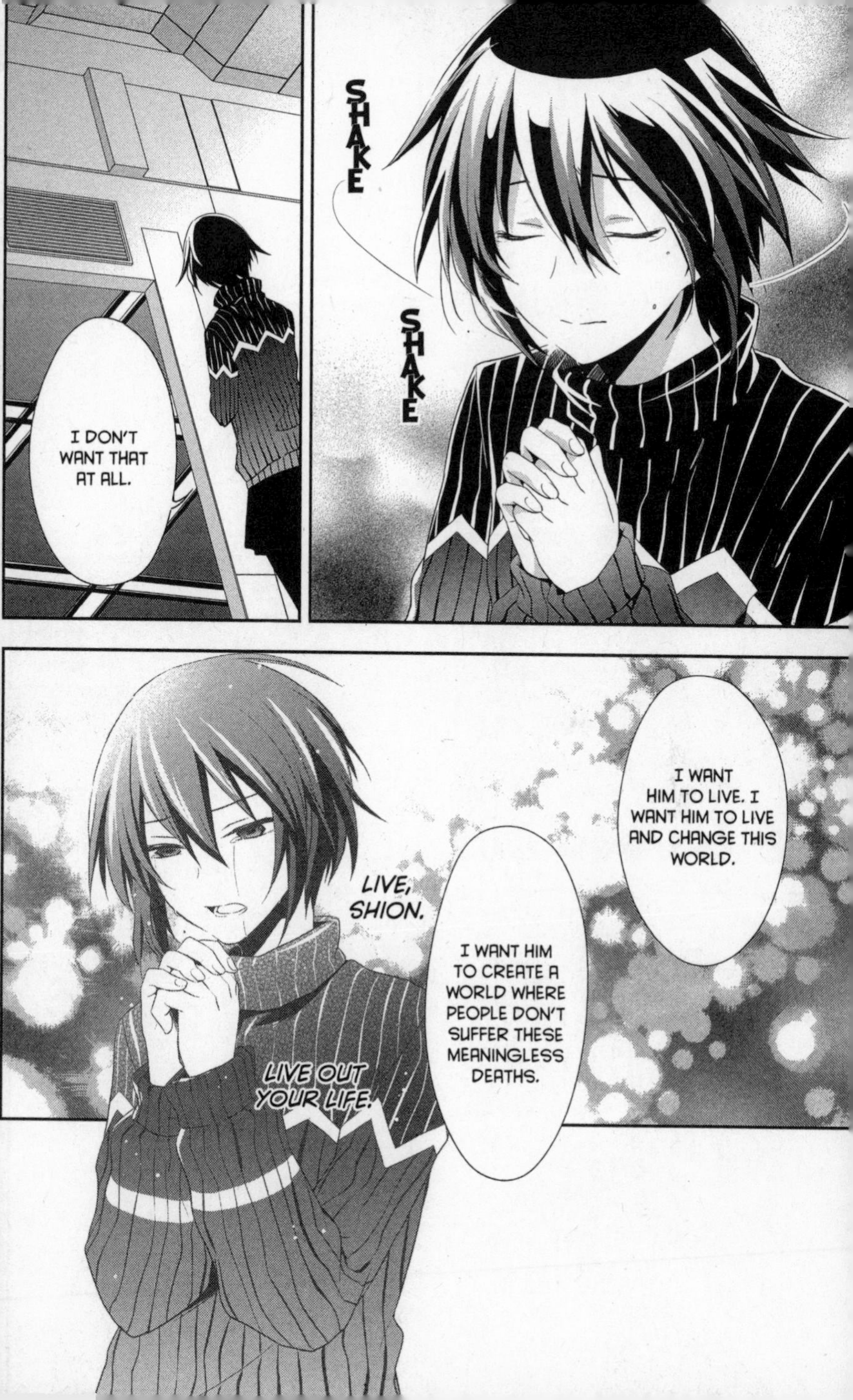
SHAKE
SHAKE
I DON'T WANT THAT AT ALL.
I WANT HIM TO LIVE. I WANT HIM TO LIVE AND CHANGE THIS WORLD.
I WANT HIM TO CREATE A WORLD WHERE PEOPLE DON'T SUFFER THESE MEANINGLESS DEATHS.
LIVE, SHION.
LIVE OUT YOUR LIFE.

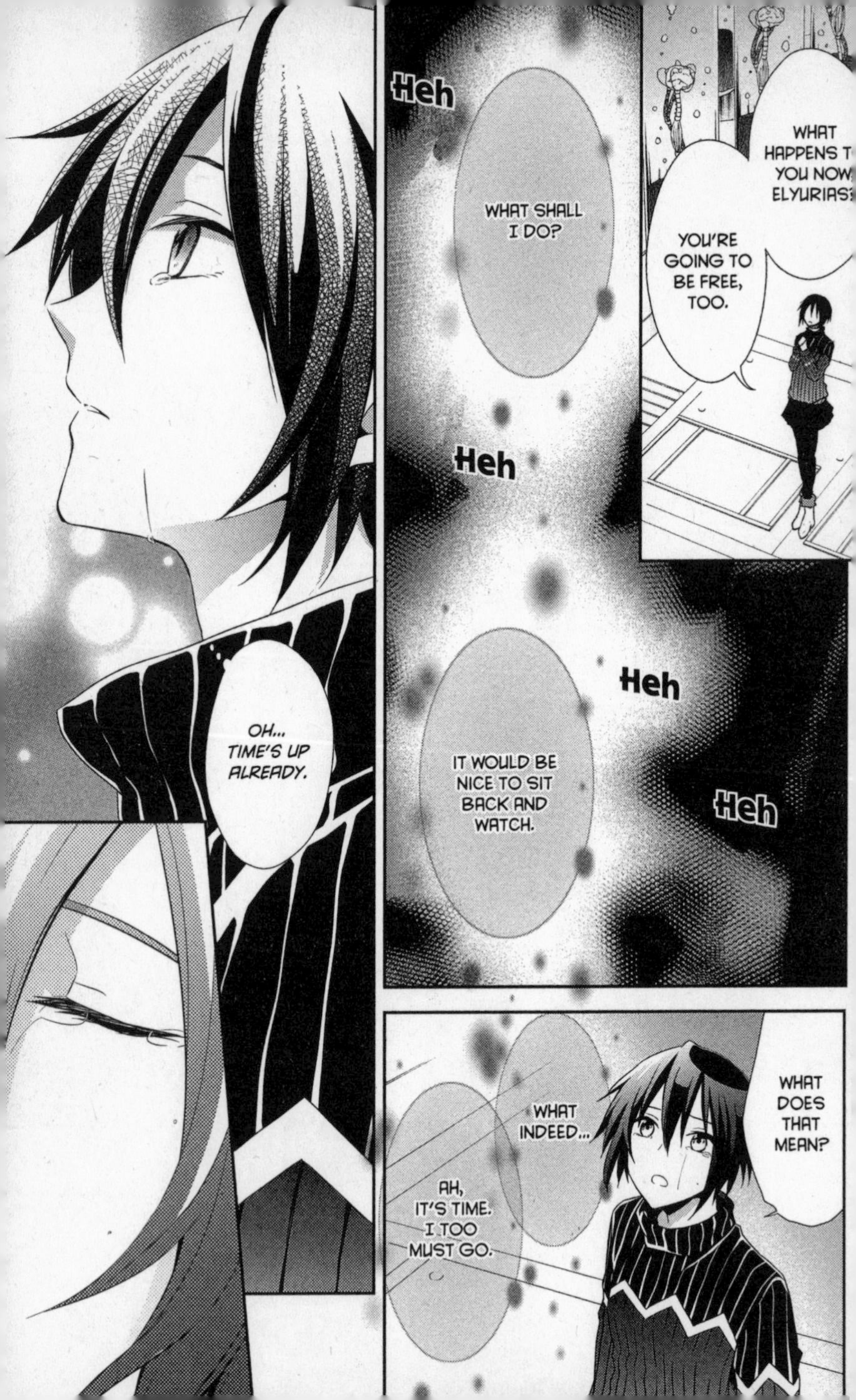
WHAT HAPPENS T YOU NOW, ELYURIAS?
YOU'RE GOING TO BE FREE, TOO.
Heh
WHAT SHALL I DO?
Heh
Heh
IT WOULD BE NICE TO SIT BACK AND WATCH.
Heh
OH... TIME'S UP ALREADY.
WHAT DOES THAT MEAN?
WHAT INDEED...
AH, IT'S TIME. I TOO MUST GO.

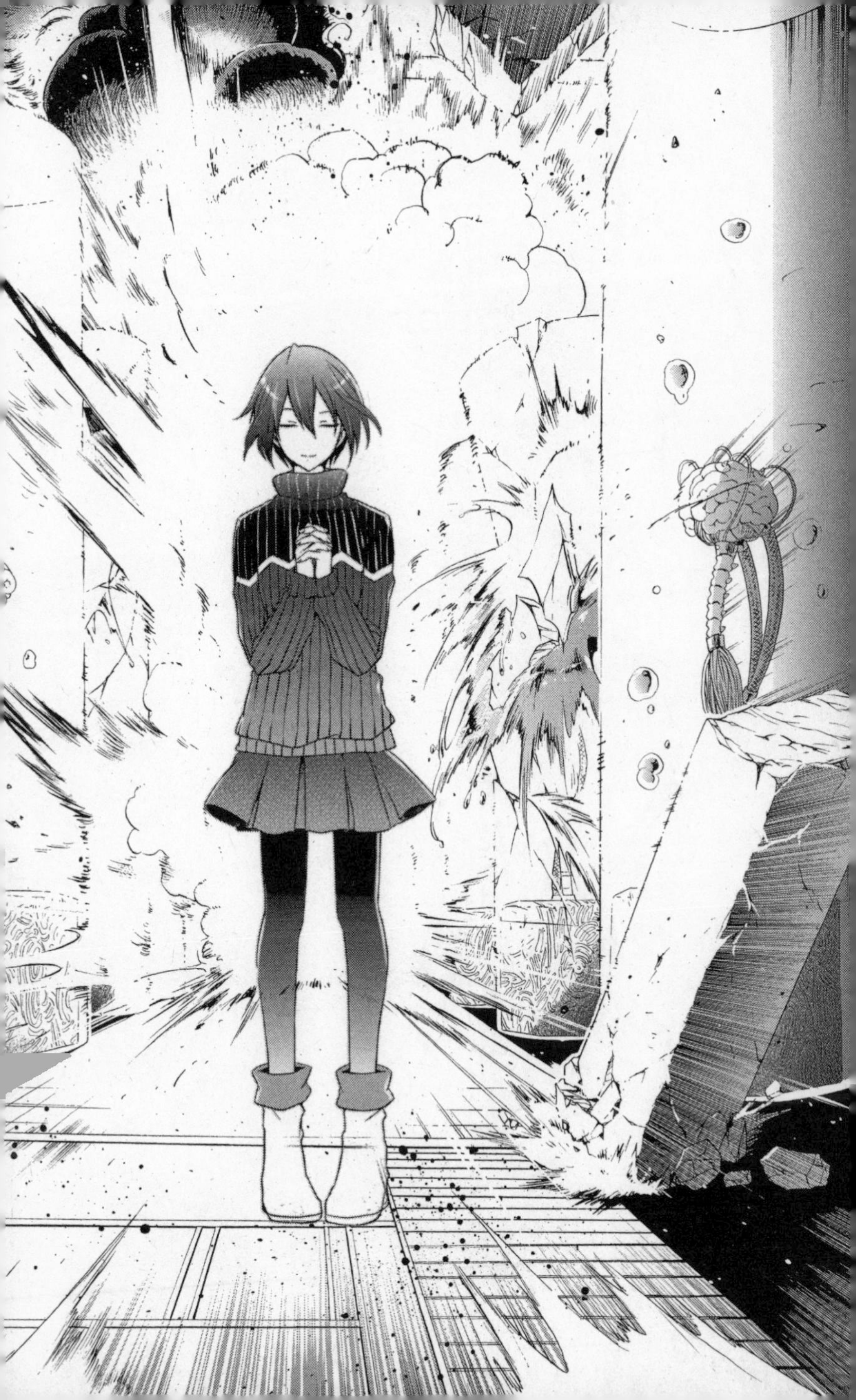

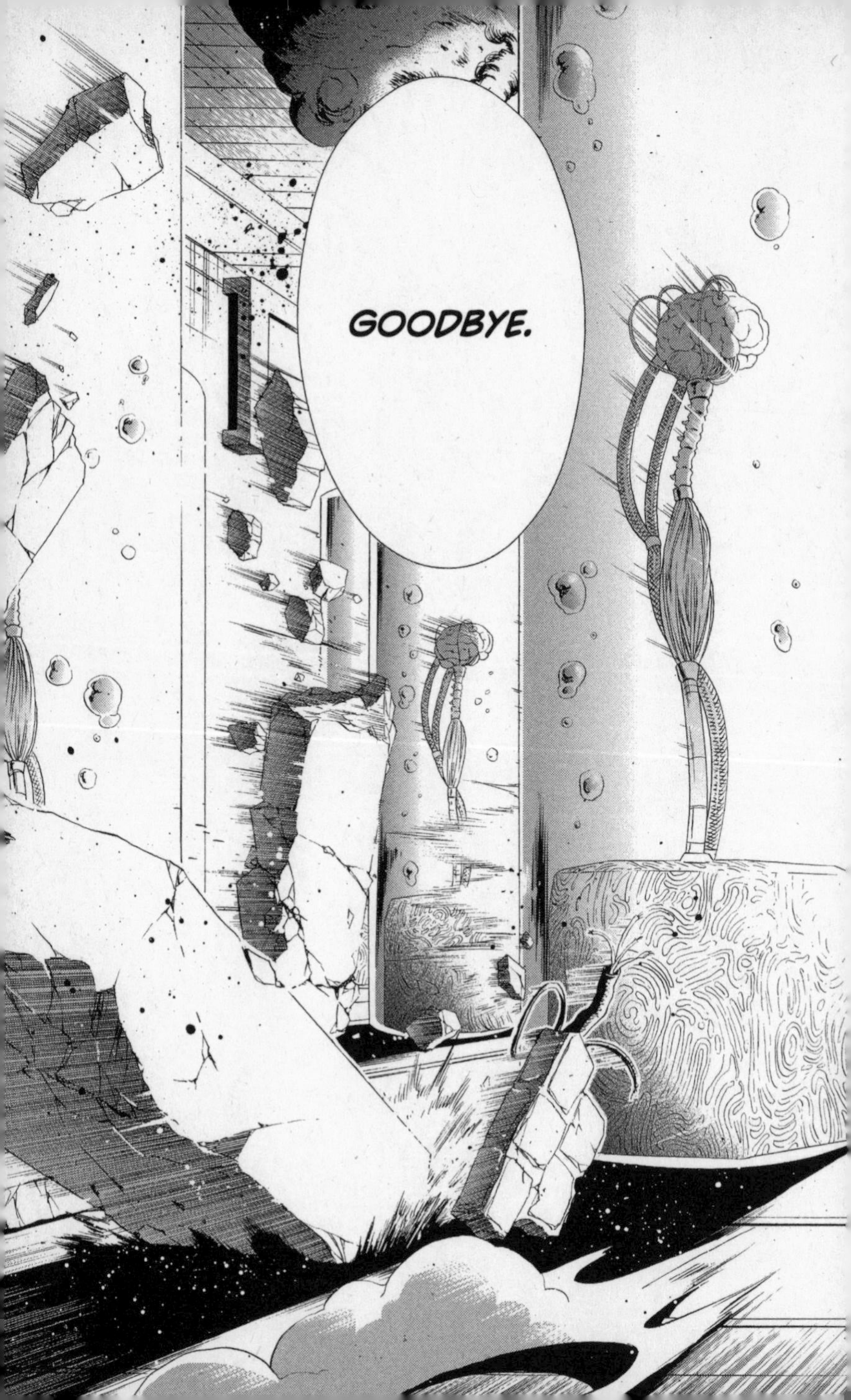
GOODBYE.

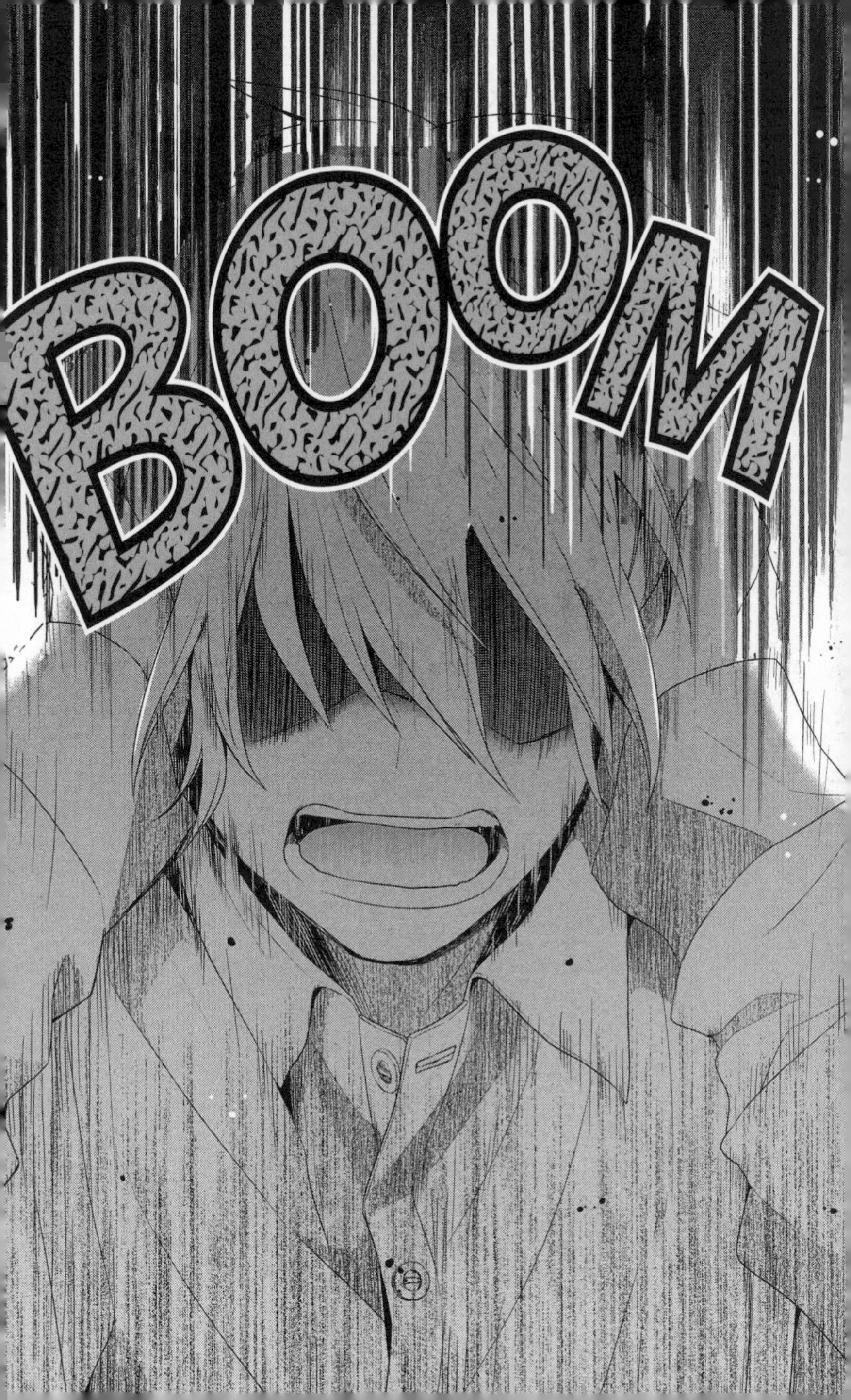
BOOM

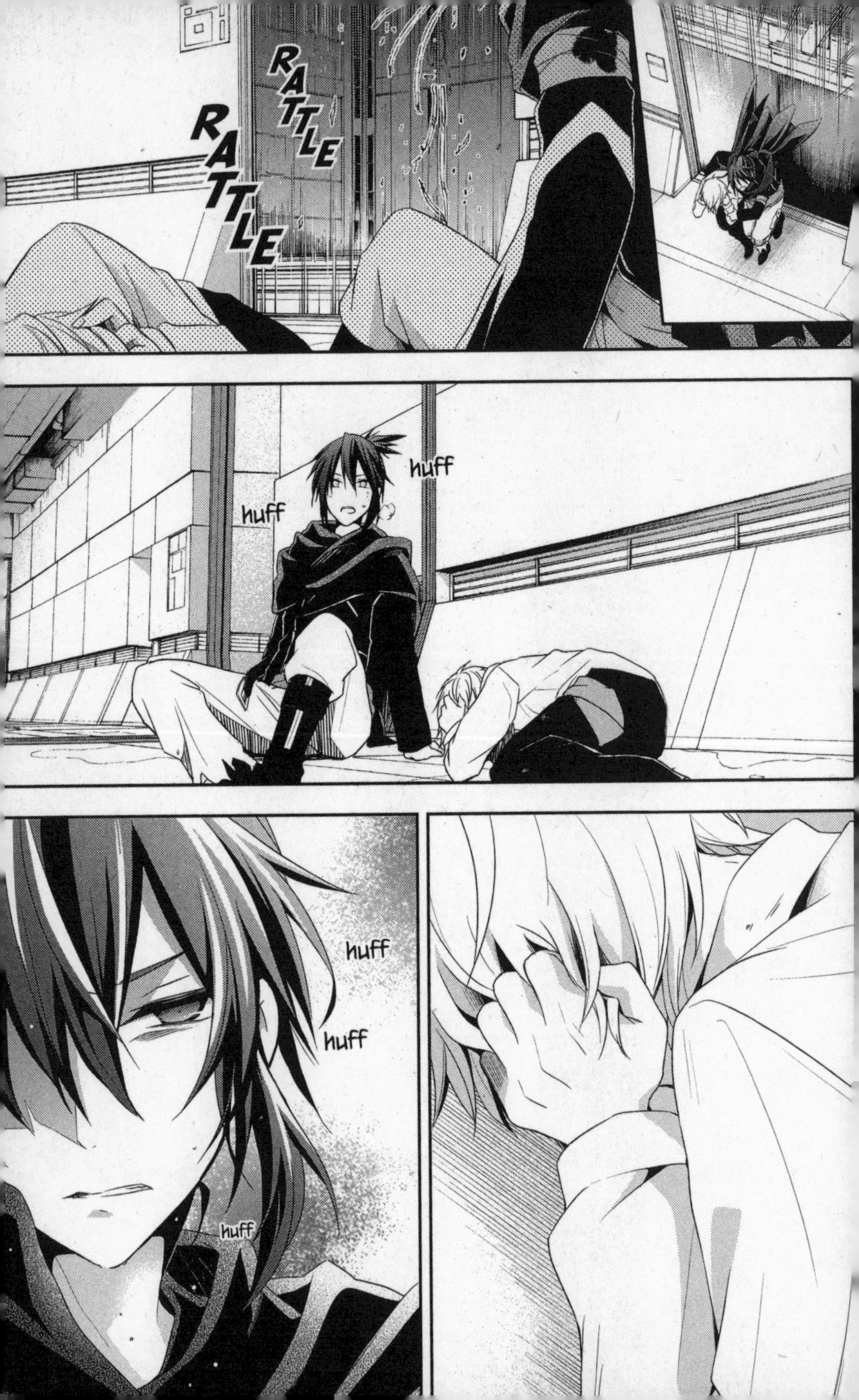
RATTLE
RATTLE
huff
huff
huff
huff
huff

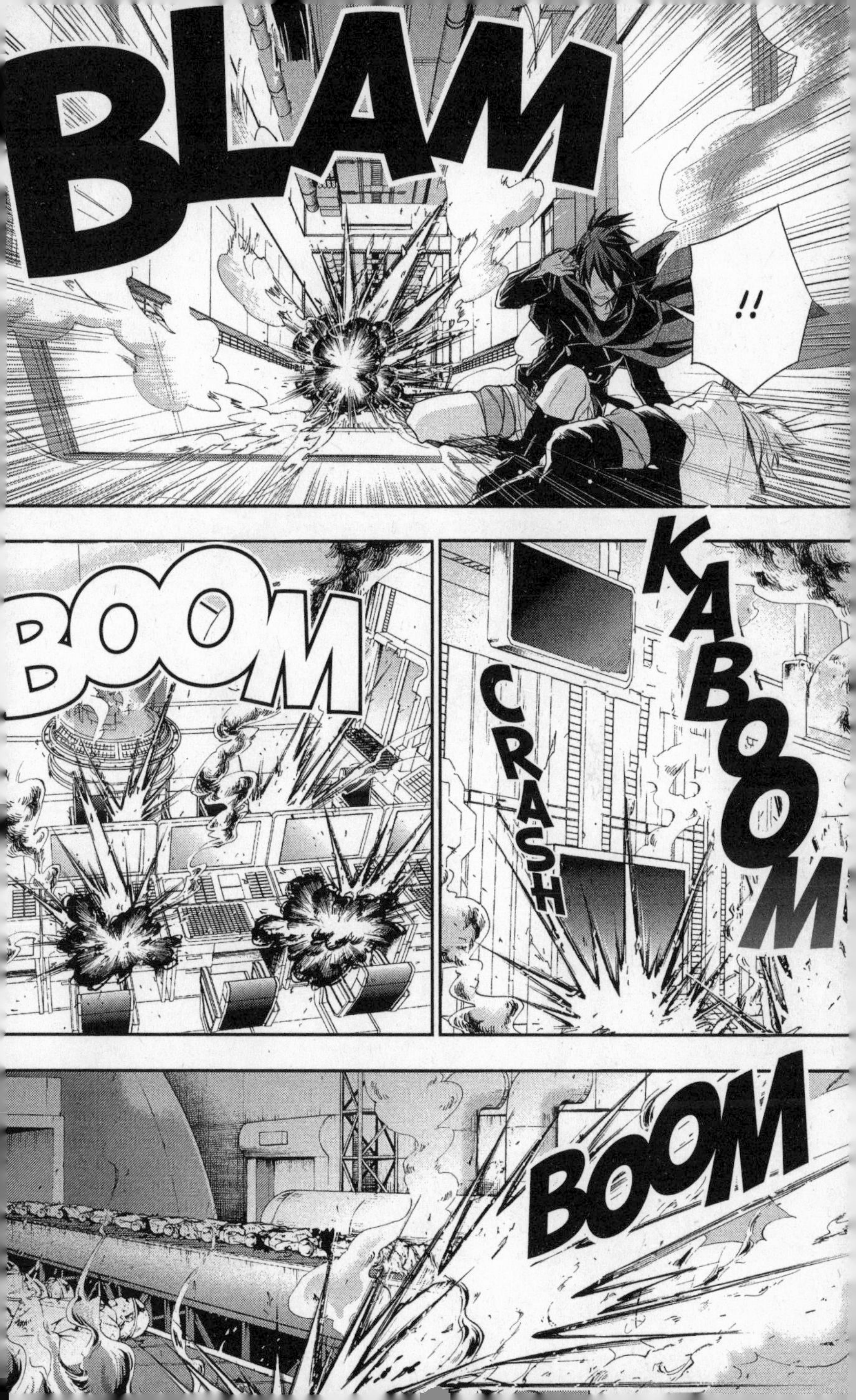
BLAM
!!
KABOOM
CRASH
BOOM
BOOM

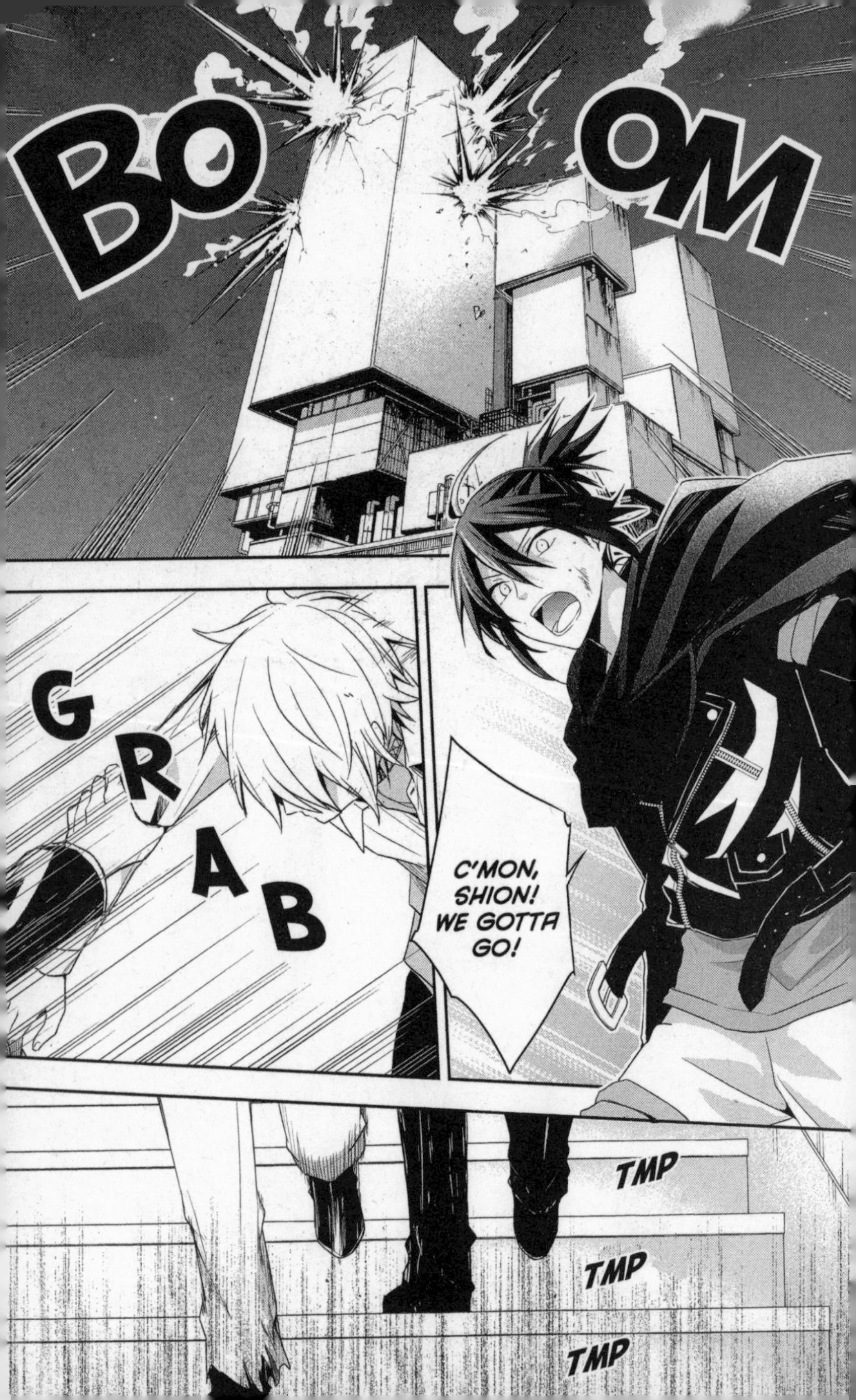
BOOM
C'MON, SHION! WE GOTTA GO!
GRAB
TMP
TMP
TMP

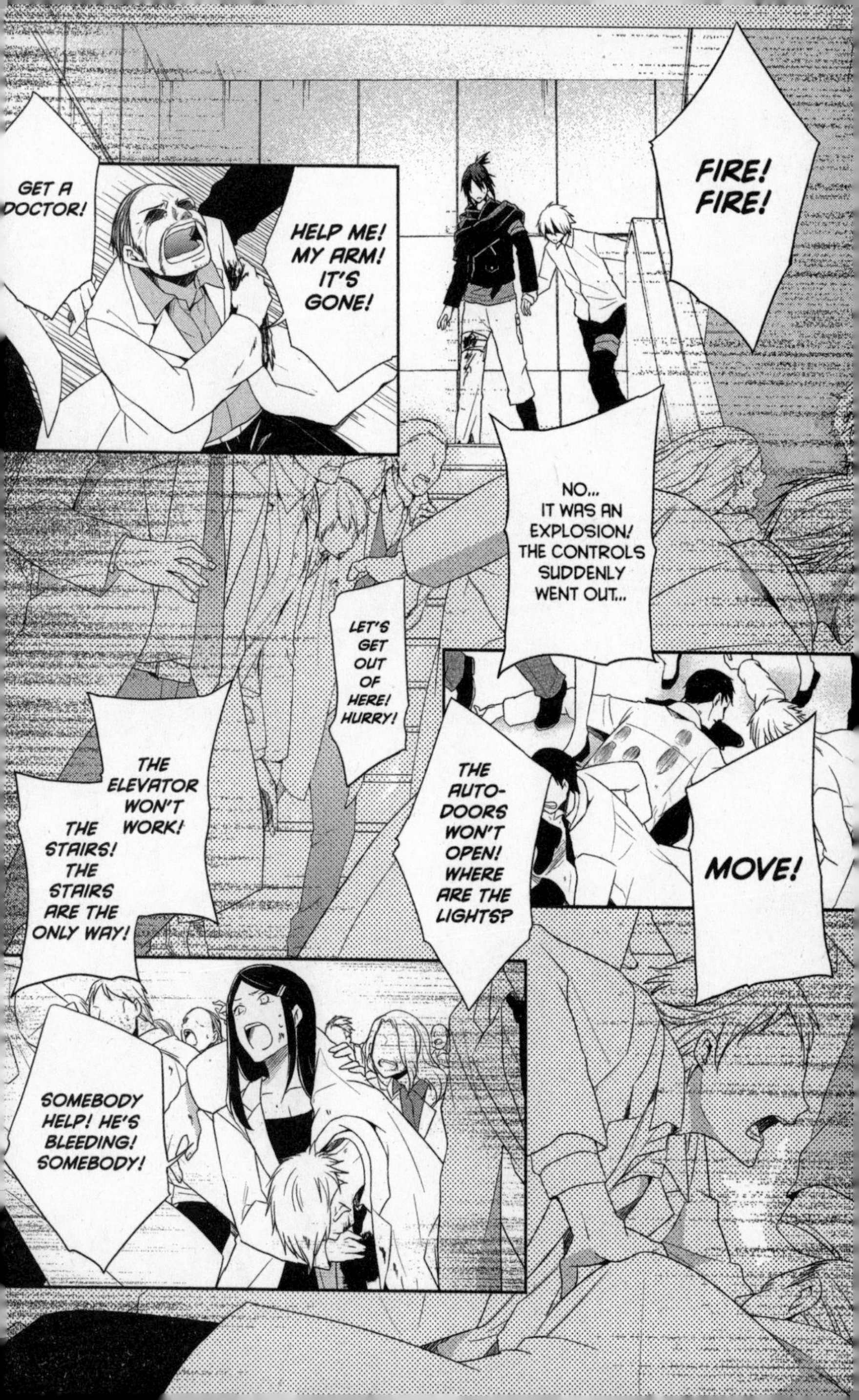
FIRE! FIRE!
HELP ME! MY ARM! IT'S GONE!
GET A DOCTOR!
NO... IT WAS AN EXPLOSION! THE CONTROLS SUDDENLY WENT OUT...
LET'S GET OUT OF HERE! HURRY!
MOVE!
THE AUTO-DOORS WON'T OPEN! WHERE ARE THE LIGHTS?
THE ELEVATOR WON'T WORK!
THE STAIRS! THE STAIRS ARE THE ONLY WAY!
SOMEBODY HELP! HE'S BLEEDING! SOMEBODY!

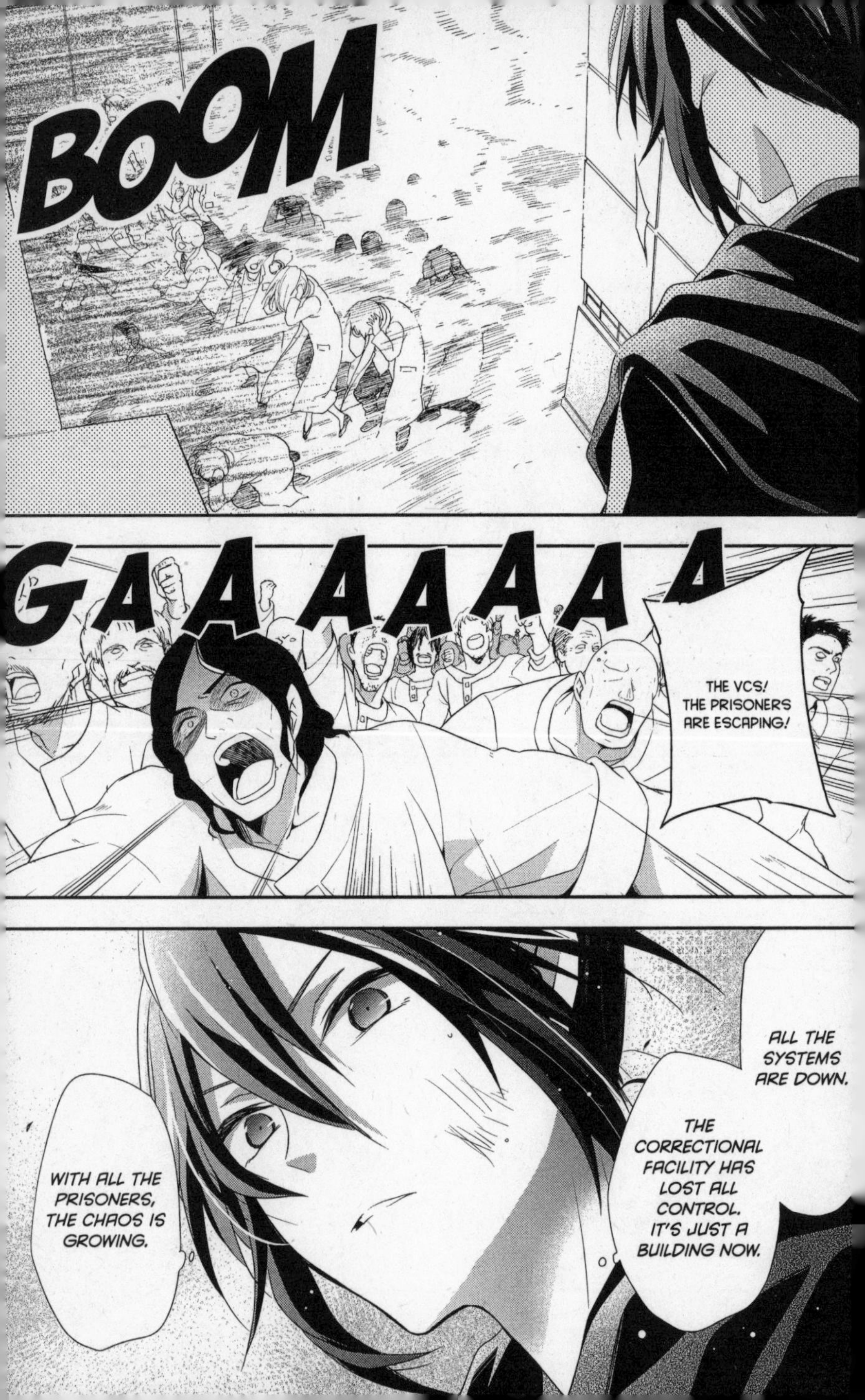
BOOM
GAAAAAA
THE VCS! THE PRISONERS ARE ESCAPING!
ALL THE SYSTEMS ARE DOWN.
THE CORRECTIONAL FACILITY HAS LOST ALL CONTROL. IT'S JUST A BUILDING NOW.
WITH ALL THE PRISONERS, THE CHAOS IS GROWING.

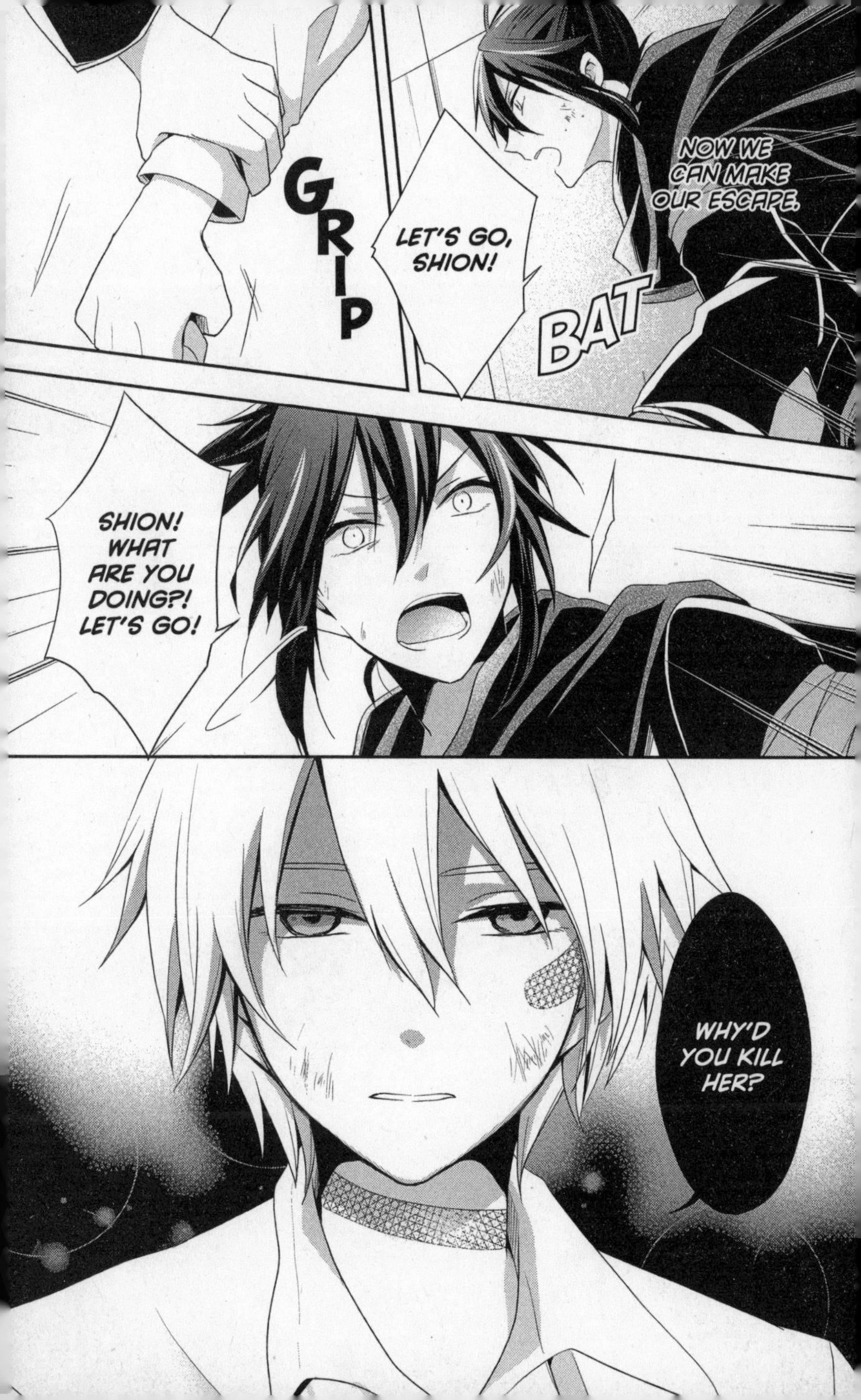
NOW WE CAN MAKE OUR ESCAPE.
BAT
LET'S GO, SHION!
GRIP
SHION! WHAT ARE YOU DOING?! LET'S GO!
WHY'D YOU KILL HER?

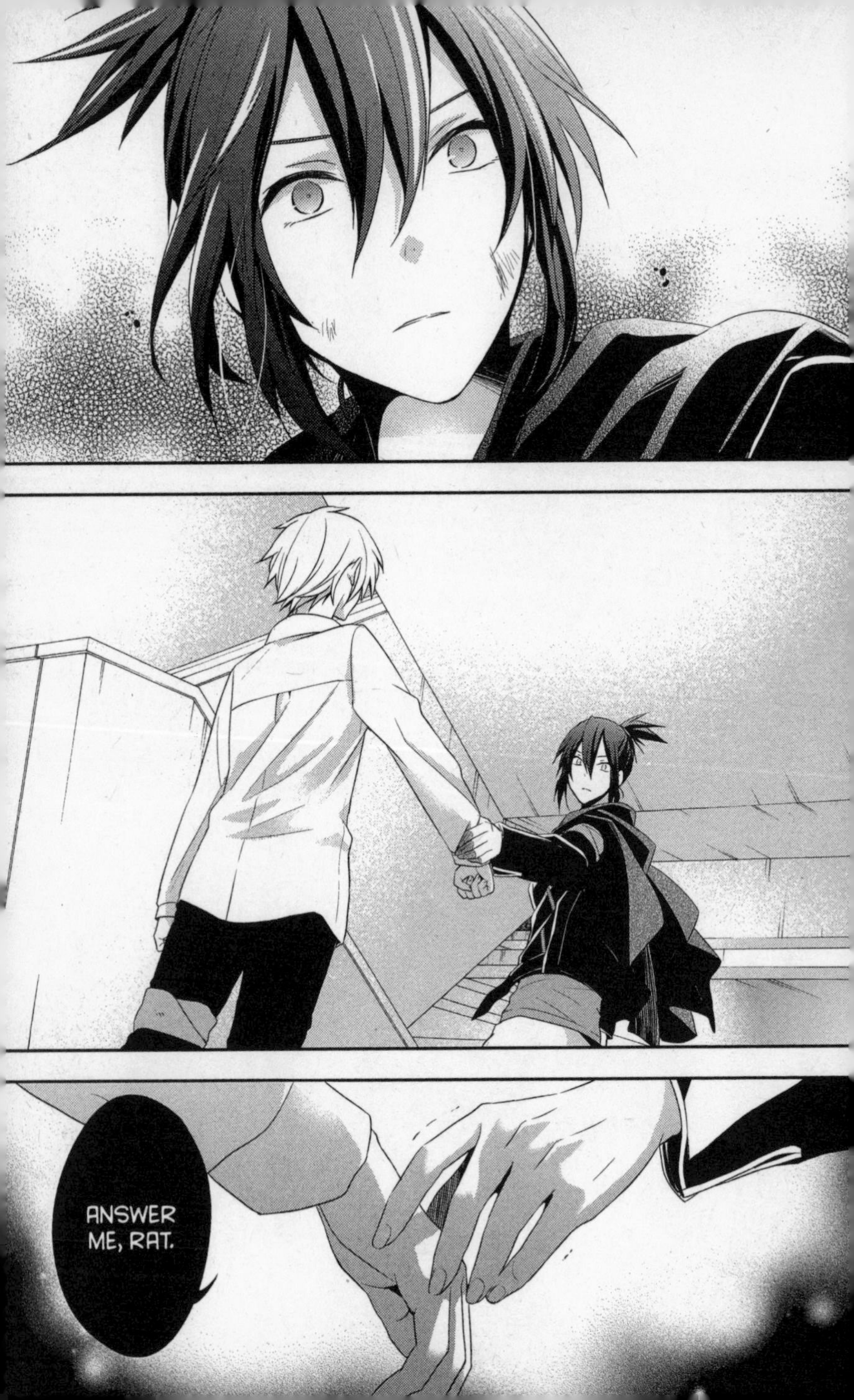
ANSWER ME, RAT.

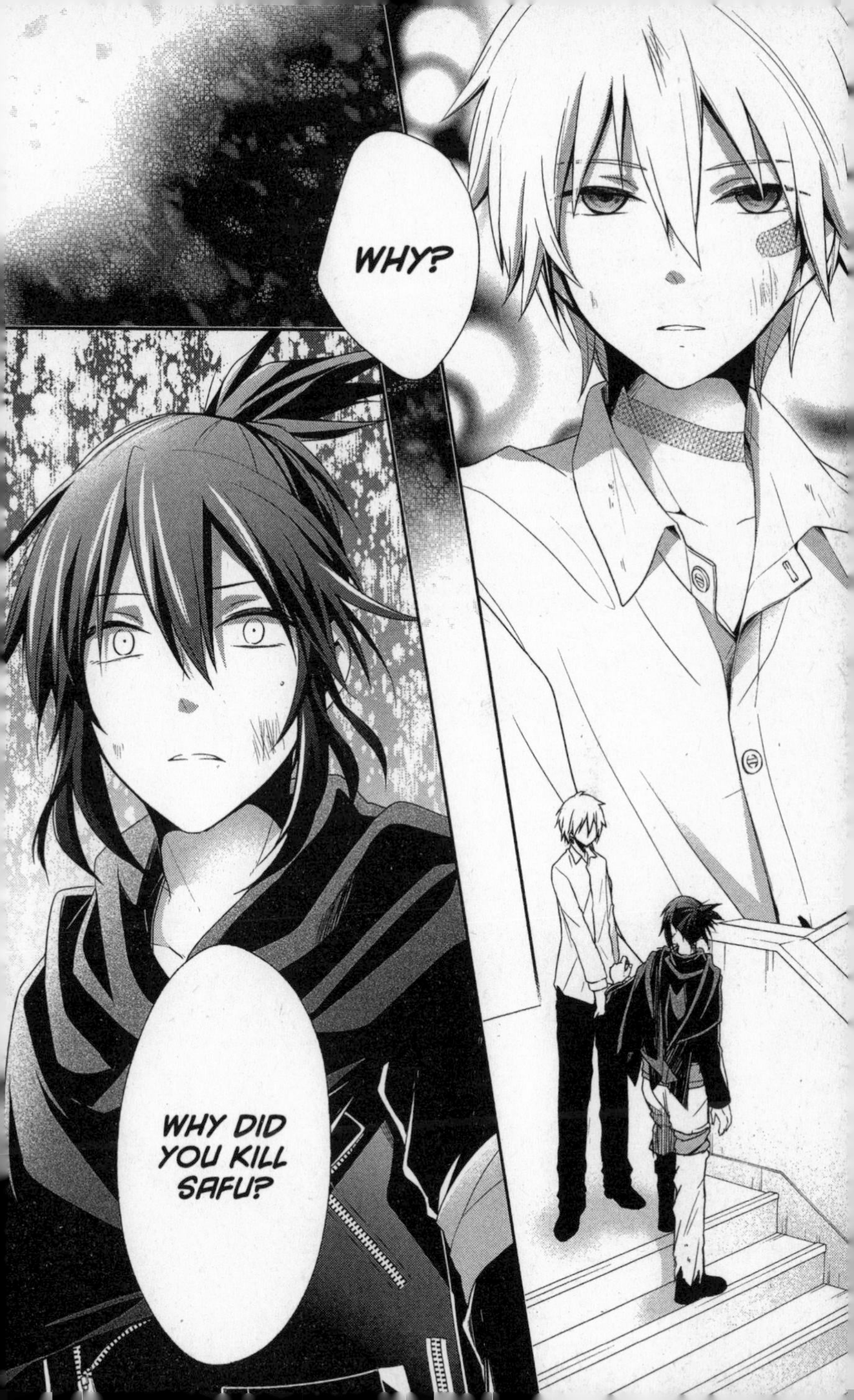
WHY?
WHY DID YOU KILL SAFU?

Chapter 30: Cease This Merciless Battle

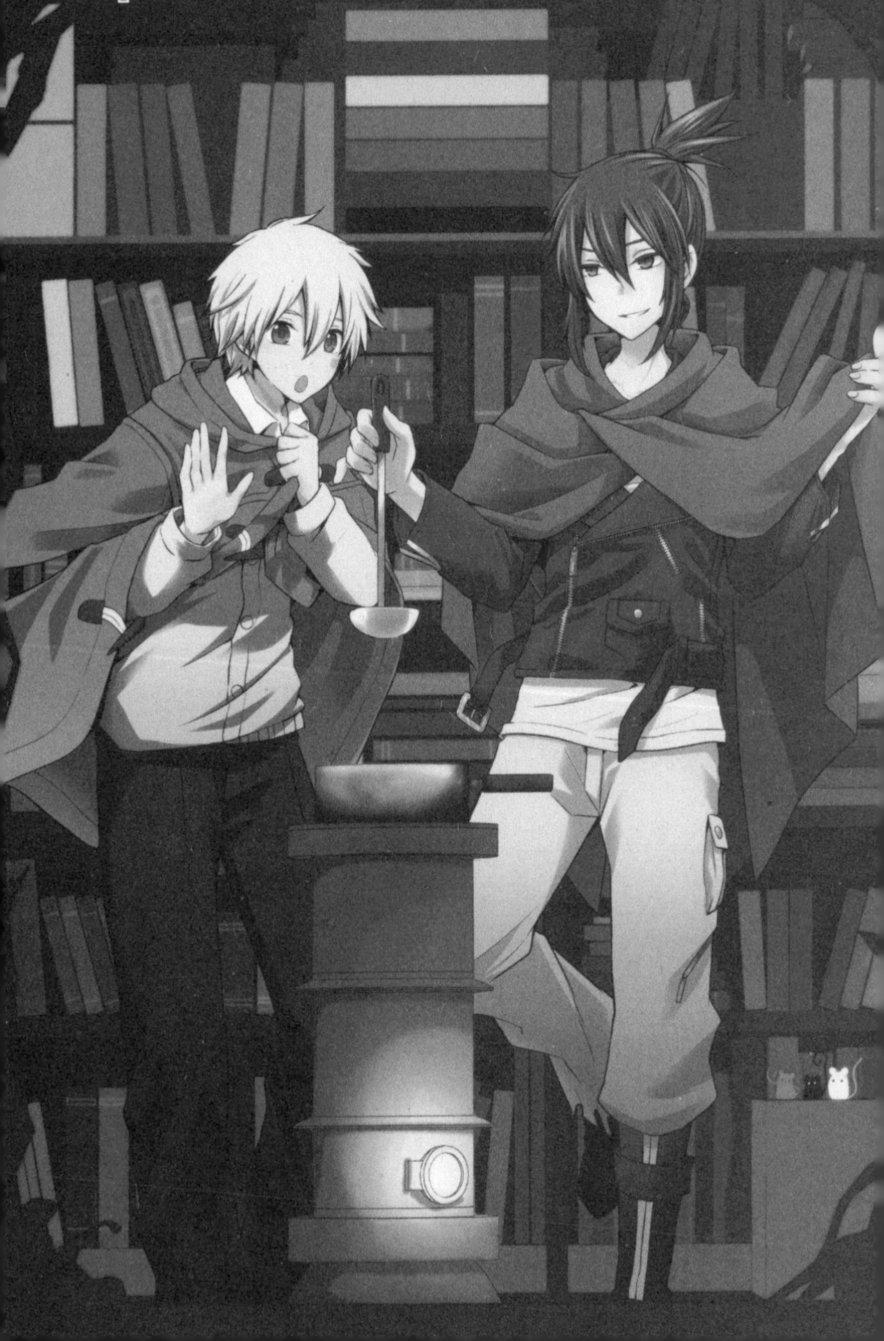

NO.6

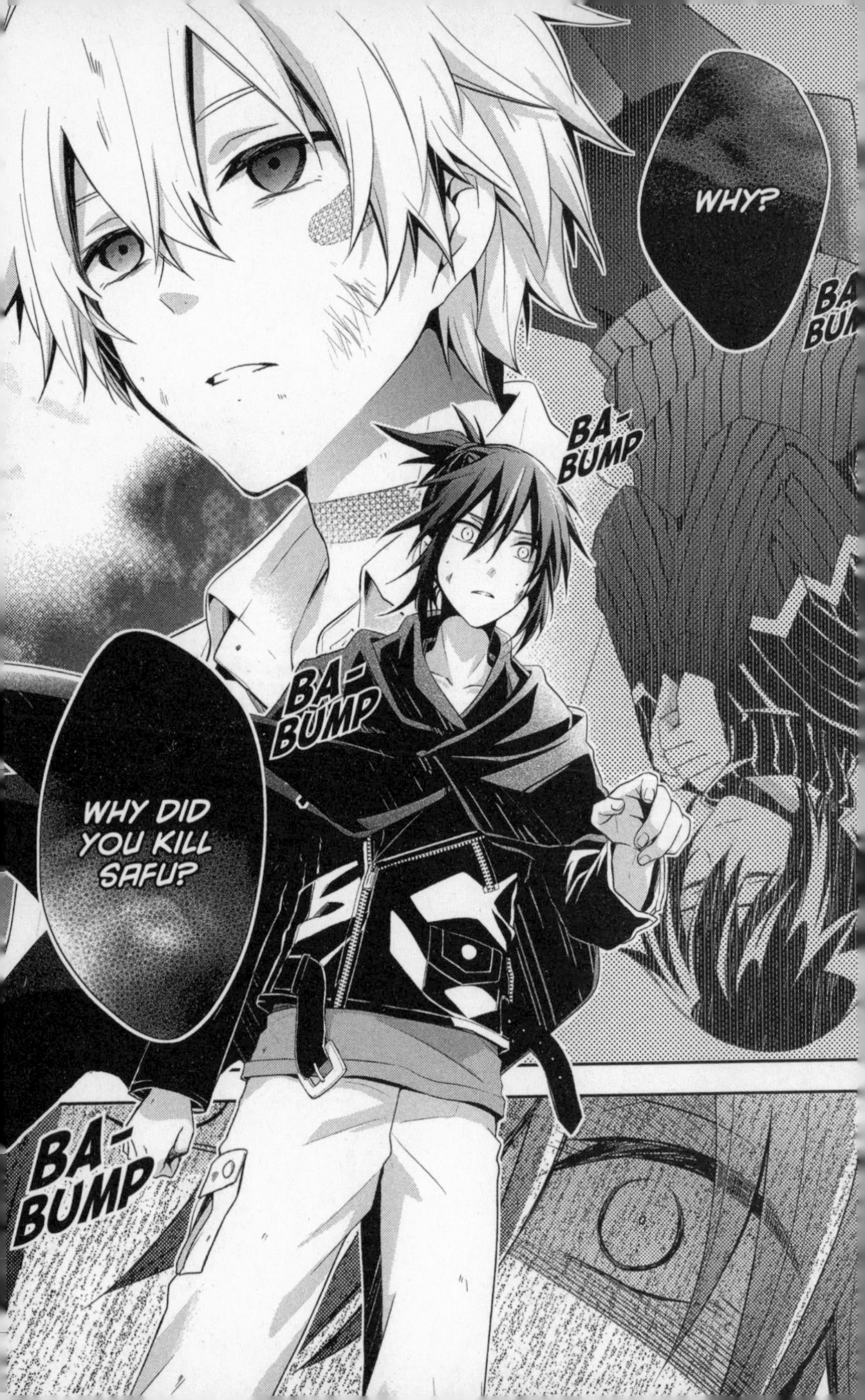
WHY?
BA-
BUM
BA-
BUMP
BA-
BUMP
WHY DID YOU KILL SAFU?
BA-
BUMP

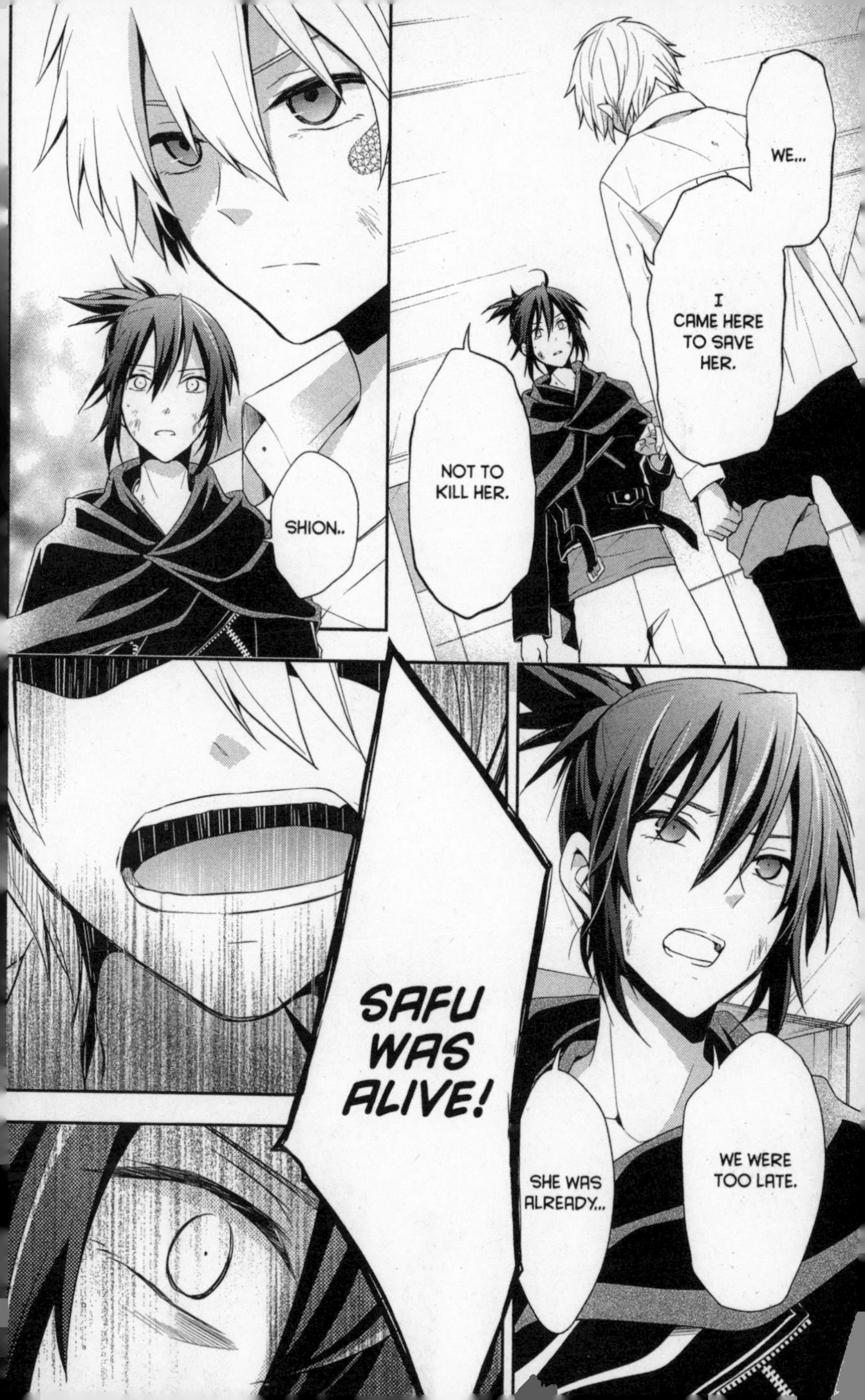
WE...
I CAME HERE TO SAVE HER.
NOT TO KILL HER.
SHION..
WE WERE TOO LATE.
SHE WAS ALREADY...
SAFU WAS ALIVE!

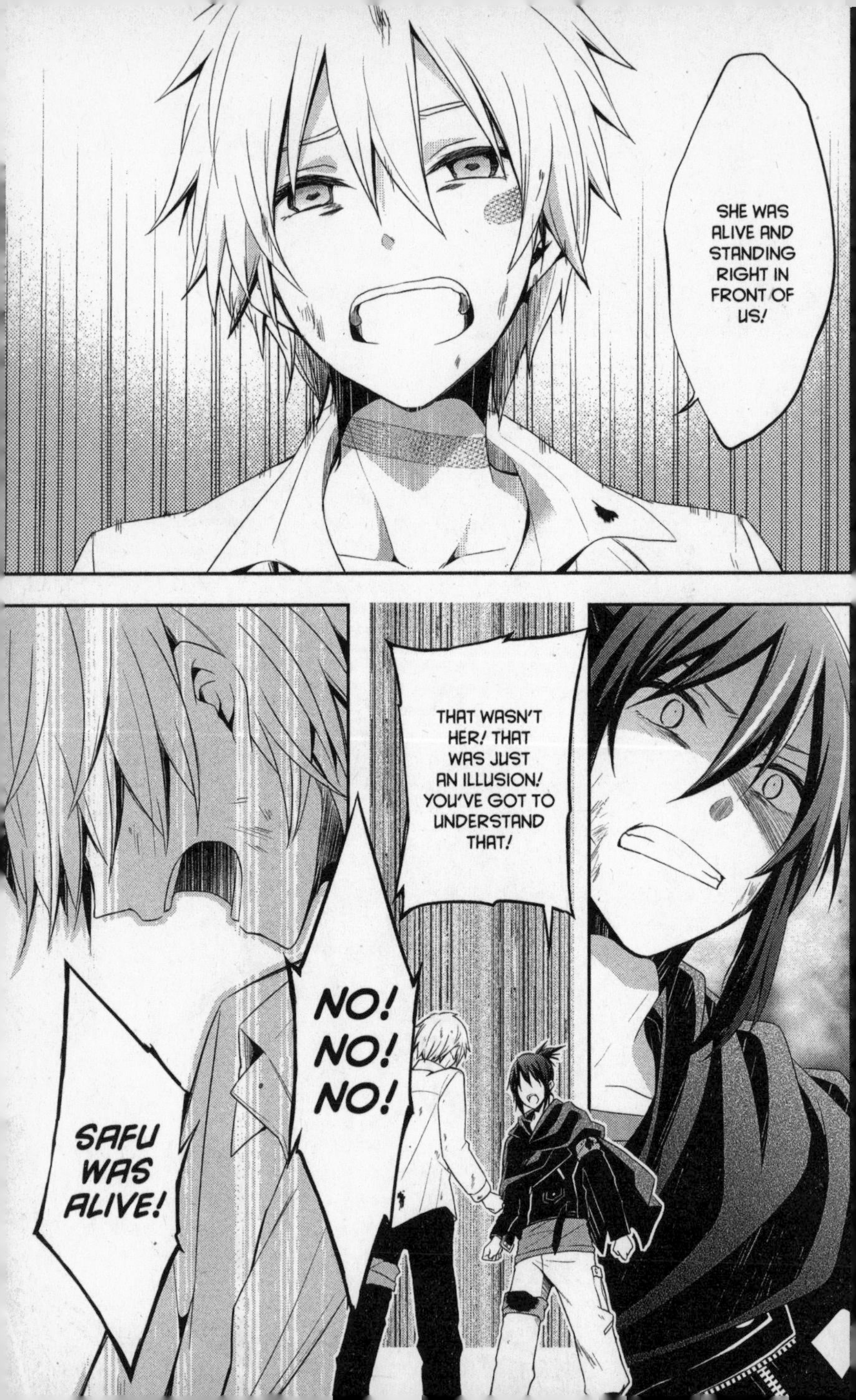
SHE WAS ALIVE AND STANDING RIGHT IN FRONT OF US!
THAT WASN'T HER! THAT WAS JUST AN ILLUSION! YOU'VE GOT TO UNDERSTAND THAT!
NO! NO! NO!
SAFU WAS ALIVE!

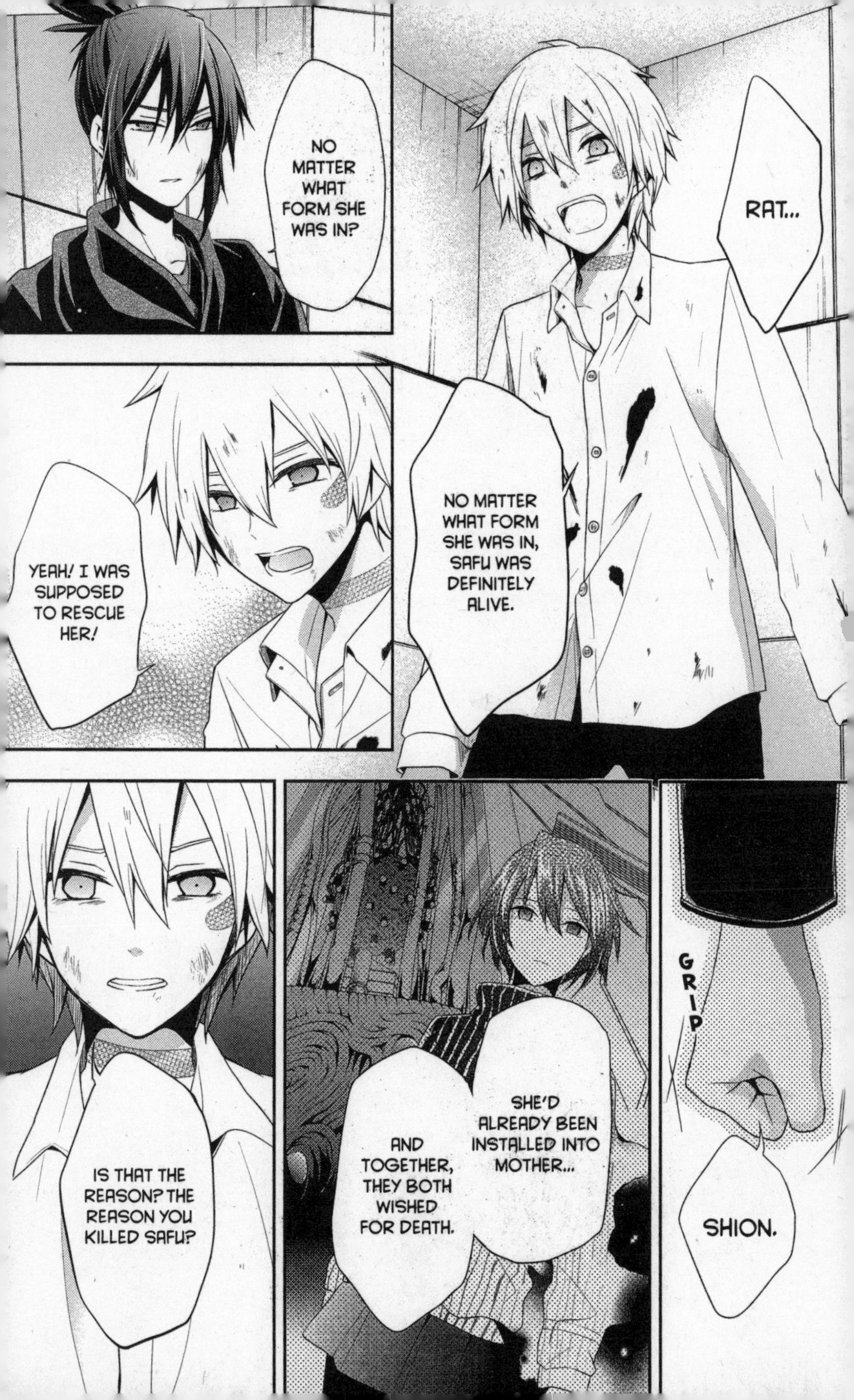
RAT...
NO MATTER WHAT FORM SHE WAS IN, SAFU WAS DEFINITELY ALIVE.
NO MATTER WHAT FORM SHE WAS IN?
YEAH! I WAS SUPPOSED TO RESCUE HER!
GRIP
SHION.
SHE'D ALREADY BEEN INSTALLED INTO MOTHER...
AND TOGETHER, THEY BOTH WISHED FOR DEATH.
IS THAT THE REASON? THE REASON YOU KILLED SAFU?

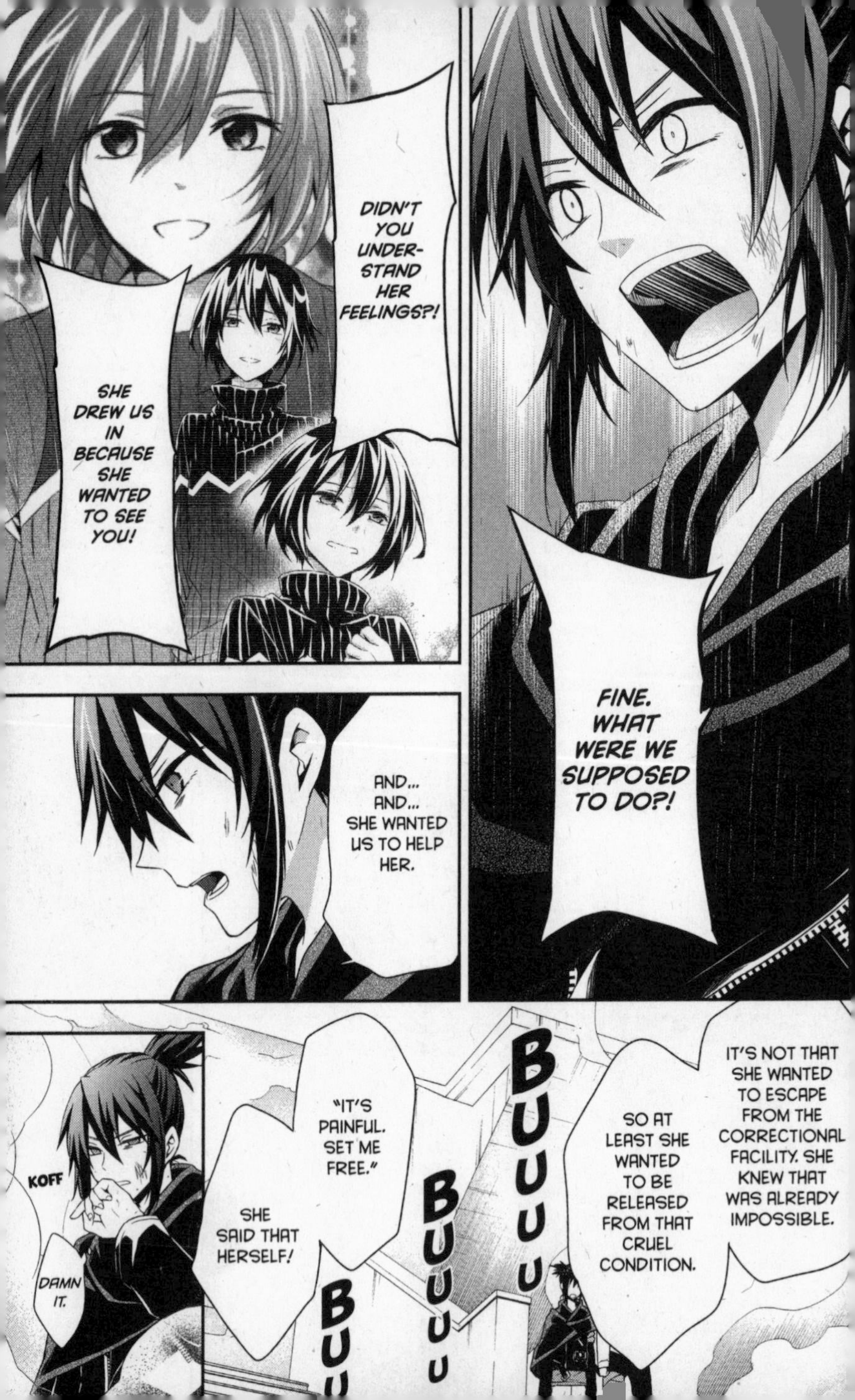
FINE. WHAT WERE WE SUPPOSED TO DO?!
DIDN'T YOU UNDER-STAND HER FEELINGS?!
SHE DREW US IN BECAUSE SHE WANTED TO SEE YOU!
AND... AND... SHE WANTED US TO HELP HER.
IT'S NOT THAT SHE WANTED TO ESCAPE FROM THE CORRECTIONAL FACILITY. SHE KNEW THAT WAS ALREADY IMPOSSIBLE.
SO AT LEAST SHE WANTED TO BE RELEASED FROM THAT CRUEL CONDITION.
BUUUU
BUUUU
BUUU
"IT'S PAINFUL. SET ME FREE."
SHE SAID THAT HERSELF!
KOFF
DAMN IT.

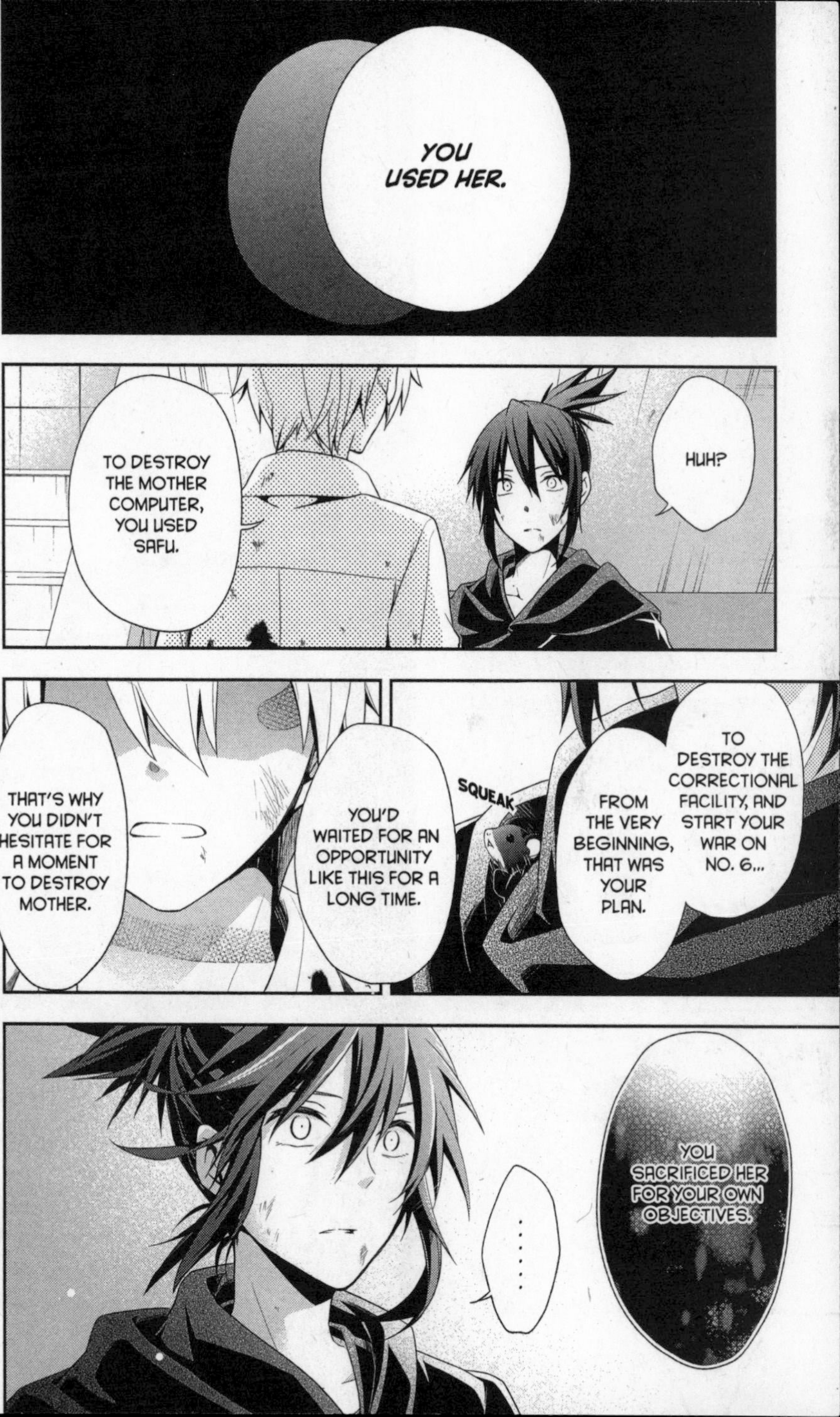
YOU USED HER.
HUH?
TO DESTROY THE MOTHER COMPUTER, YOU USED SAFU.
TO DESTROY THE CORRECTIONAL FACILITY, AND START YOUR WAR ON NO. 6...
FROM THE VERY BEGINNING, THAT WAS YOUR PLAN.
SQUEAK
YOU'D WAITED FOR AN OPPORTUNITY LIKE THIS FOR A LONG TIME.
THAT'S WHY YOU DIDN'T HESITATE FOR A MOMENT TO DESTROY MOTHER.
YOU SACRIFICED HER FOR YOUR OWN OBJECTIVES.
......

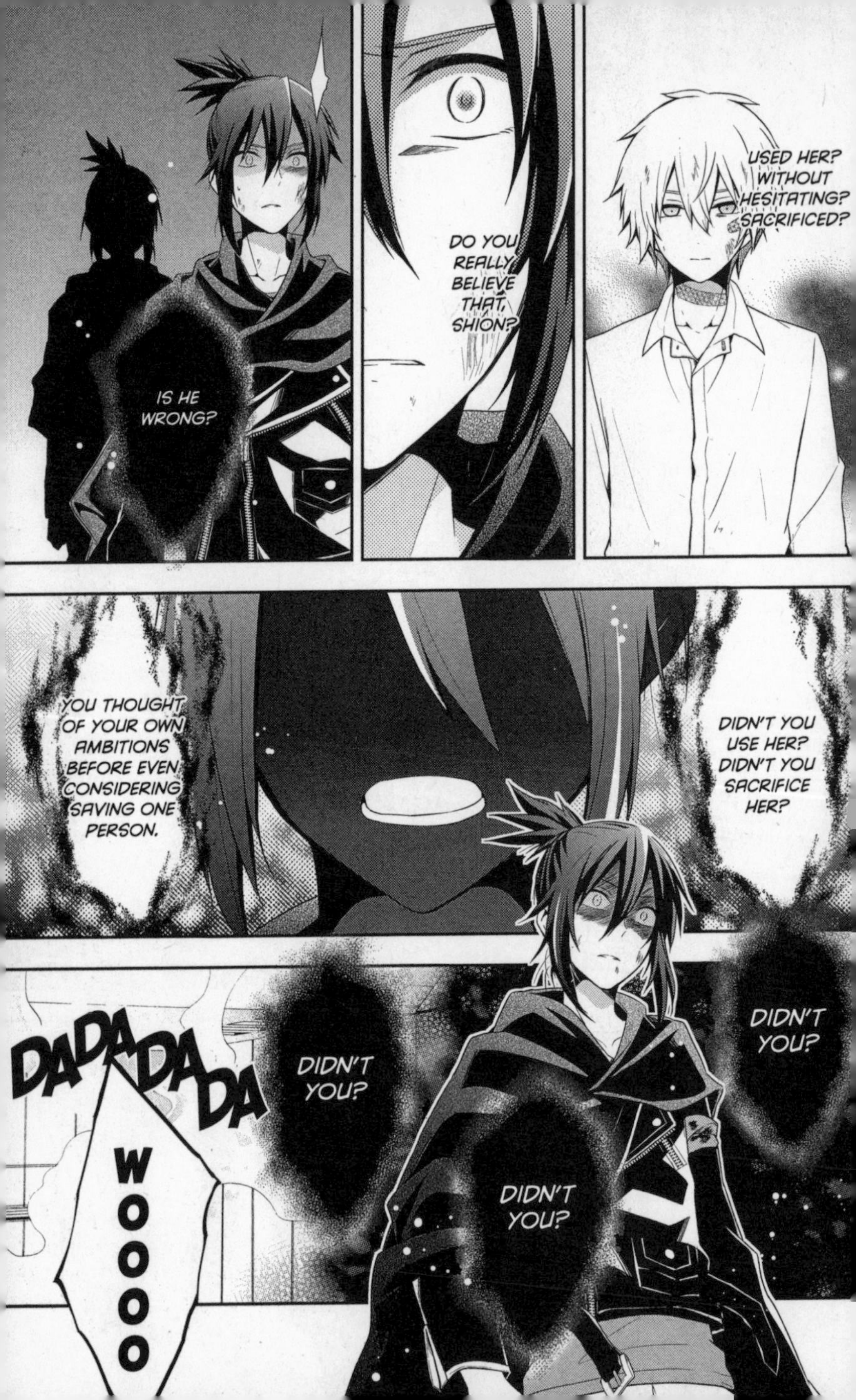
USED HER? WITHOUT HESITATING? SACRIFICED?
DO YOU REALLY BELIEVE THAT, SHION?
IS HE WRONG?
DIDN'T YOU USE HER? DIDN'T YOU SACRIFICE HER?
YOU THOUGHT OF YOUR OWN AMBITIONS BEFORE EVEN CONSIDERING SAVING ONE PERSON.
DIDN'T YOU?
DIDN'T YOU?
DIDN'T YOU?
DADADADADA
WOOOO

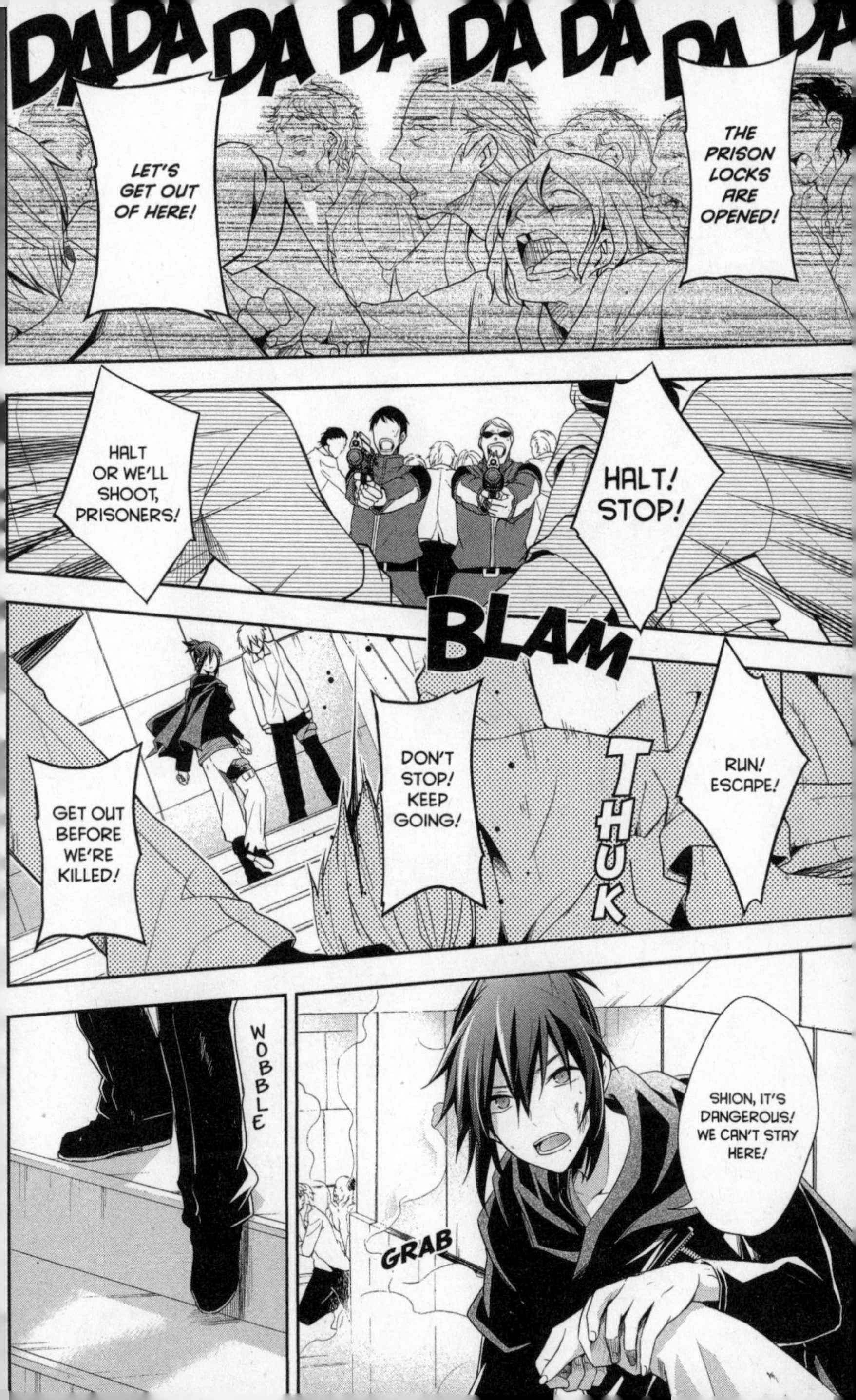
DA DA DA DA DA DA DA DA
THE PRISON LOCKS ARE OPENED!
LET'S GET OUT OF HERE!
HALT! STOP!
HALT OR WE'LL SHOOT, PRISONERS!
BLAM
RUN! ESCAPE!
THUK
DON'T STOP! KEEP GOING!
GET OUT BEFORE WE'RE KILLED!
SHION, IT'S DANGEROUS! WE CAN'T STAY HERE!
GRAB
WOBBLE

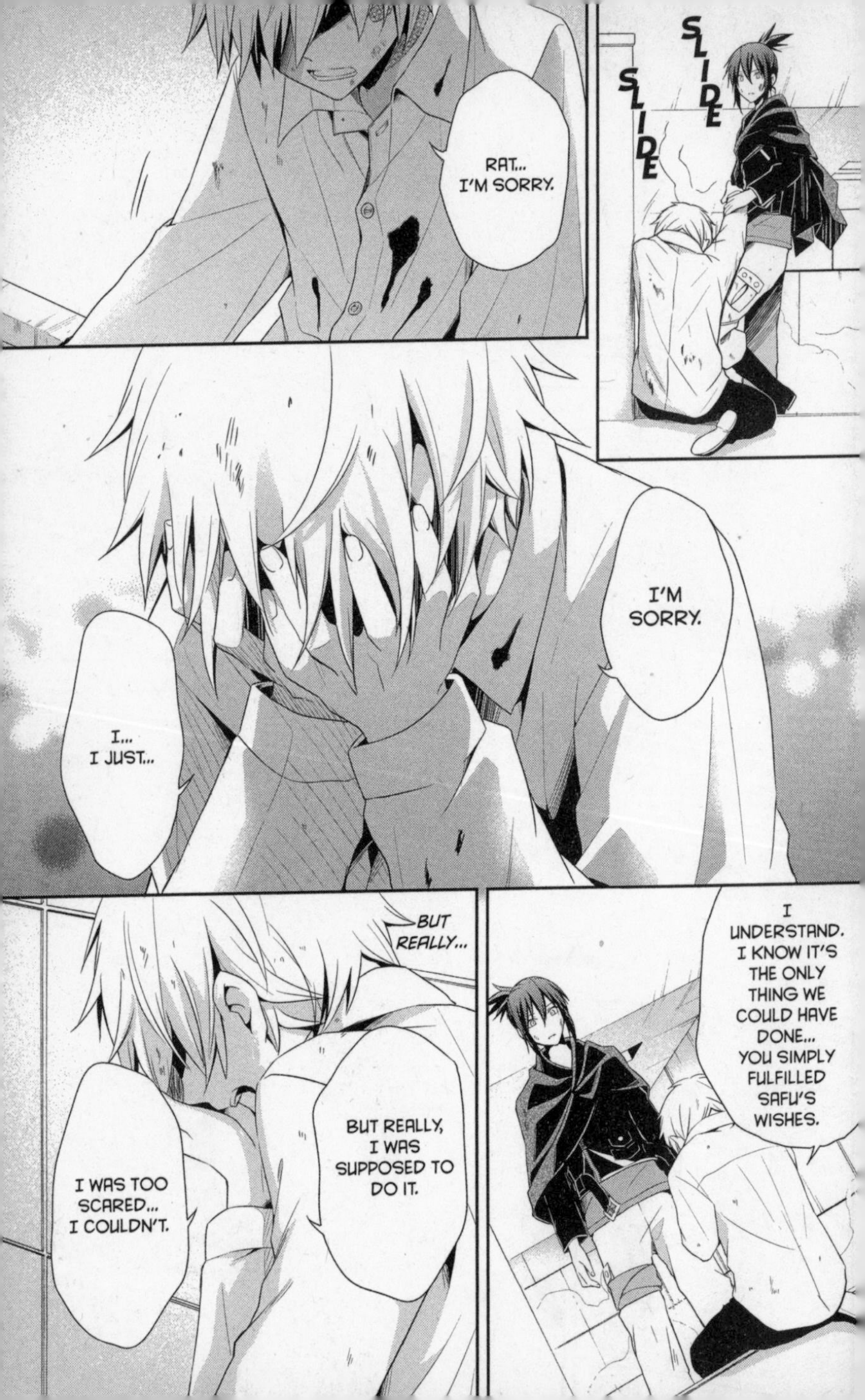
SLIDE
SLIDE
RAT... I'M SORRY.
I'M SORRY.
I... I JUST...
I UNDERSTAND. I KNOW IT'S THE ONLY THING WE COULD HAVE DONE... YOU SIMPLY FULFILLED SAFU'S WISHES.
BUT REALLY...
BUT REALLY, I WAS SUPPOSED TO DO IT.
I WAS TOO SCARED... I COULDN'T.

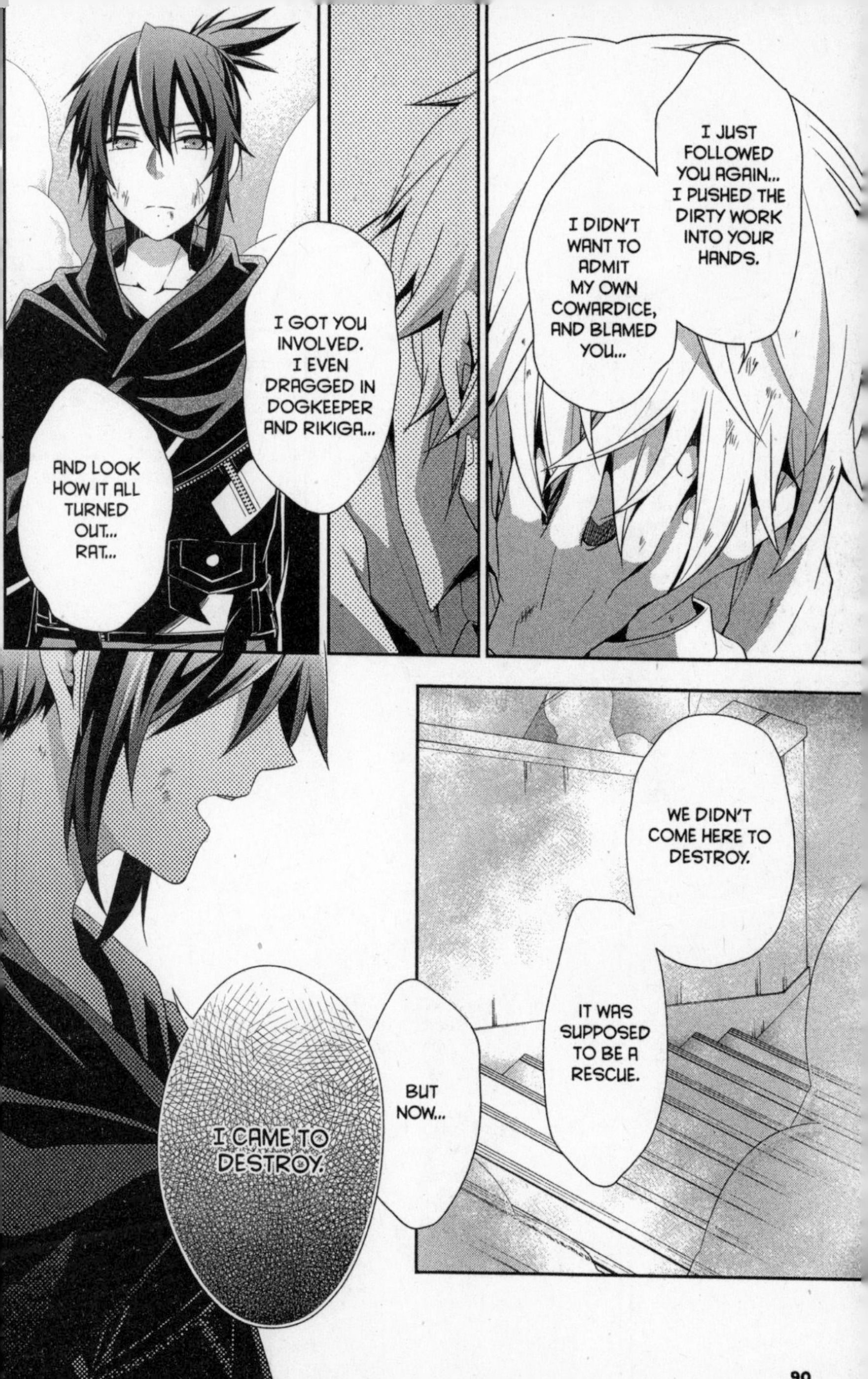
I JUST FOLLOWED YOU AGAIN... I PUSHED THE DIRTY WORK INTO YOUR HANDS.
I DIDN'T WANT TO ADMIT MY OWN COWARDICE, AND BLAMED YOU...
I GOT YOU INVOLVED. I EVEN DRAGGED IN DOGKEEPER AND RIKIGA...
AND LOOK HOW IT ALL TURNED OUT... RAT...
WE DIDN'T COME HERE TO DESTROY.
IT WAS SUPPOSED TO BE A RESCUE.
BUT NOW...
I CAME TO DESTROY.

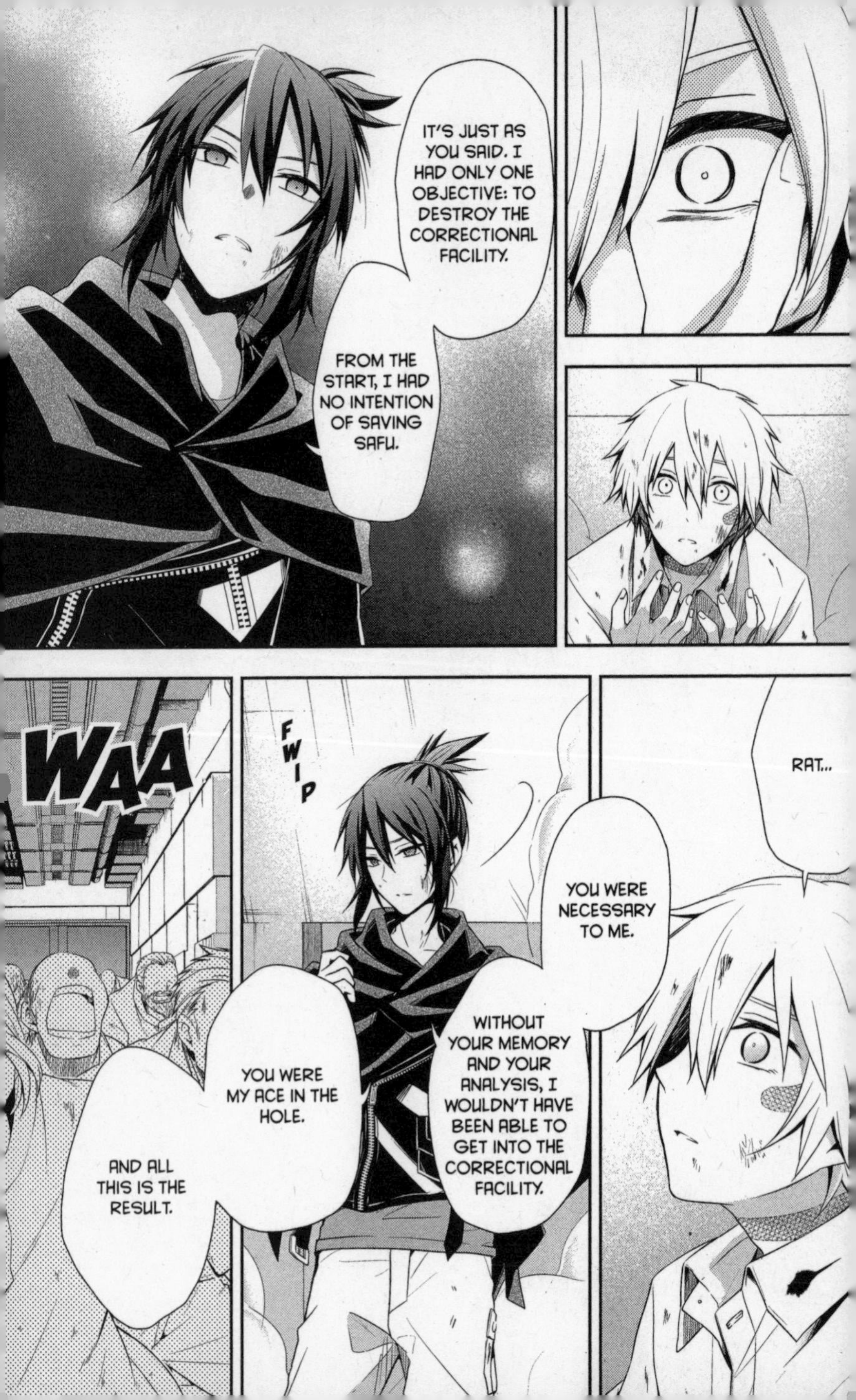
IT'S JUST AS YOU SAID. I HAD ONLY ONE OBJECTIVE: TO DESTROY THE CORRECTIONAL FACILITY.
FROM THE START, I HAD NO INTENTION OF SAVING SAFU.
RAT...
FWIP
YOU WERE NECESSARY TO ME.
WITHOUT YOUR MEMORY AND YOUR ANALYSIS, I WOULDN'T HAVE BEEN ABLE TO GET INTO THE CORRECTIONAL FACILITY.
YOU WERE MY ACE IN THE HOLE.
WAA
AND ALL THIS IS THE RESULT.

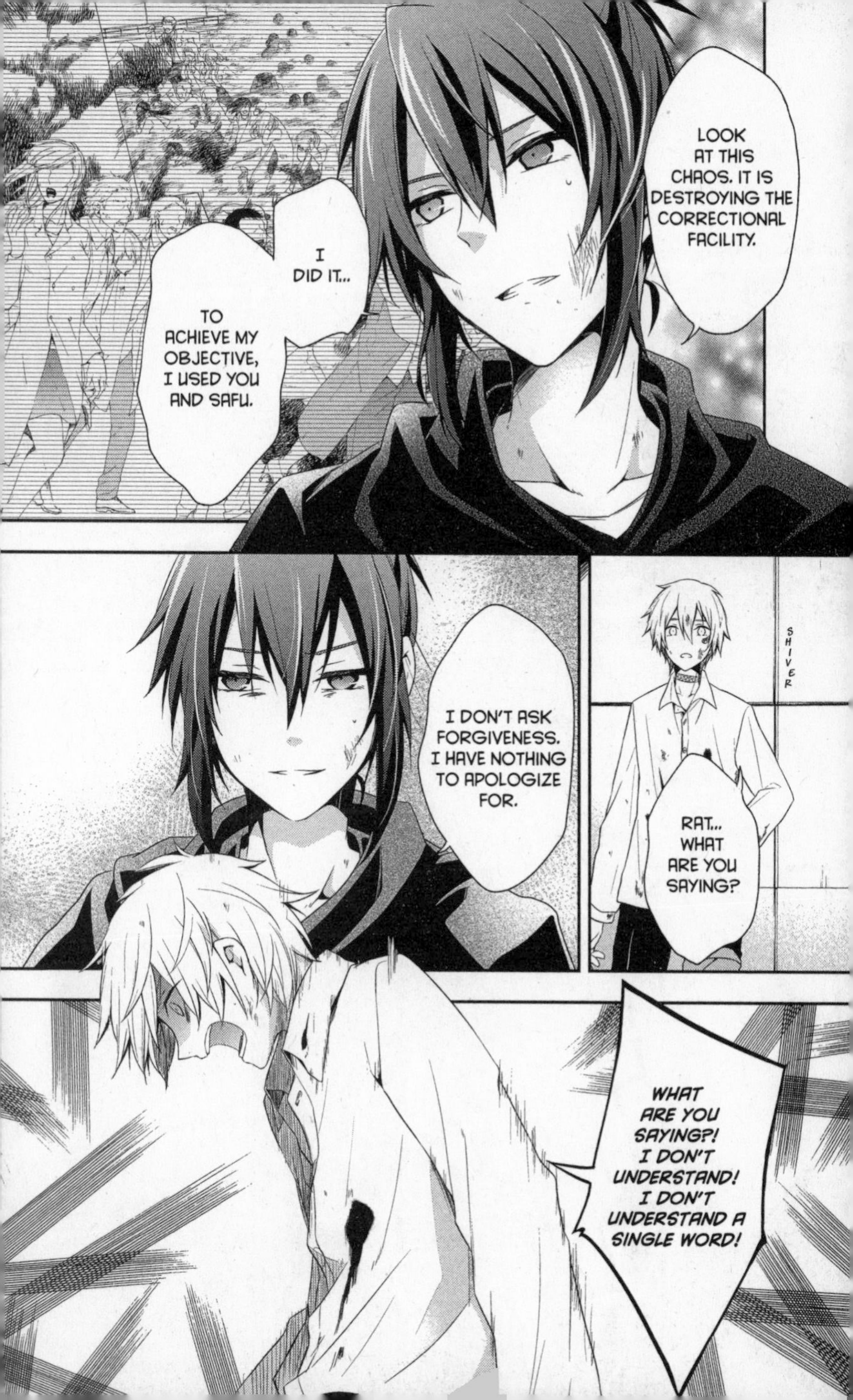
LOOK AT THIS CHAOS. IT IS DESTROYING THE CORRECTIONAL FACILITY.
I DID IT...
TO ACHIEVE MY OBJECTIVE, I USED YOU AND SAFU.
SHIVER
RAT... WHAT ARE YOU SAYING?
I DON'T ASK FORGIVENESS. I HAVE NOTHING TO APOLOGIZE FOR.
WHAT ARE YOU SAYING?! I DON'T UNDERSTAND! I DON'T UNDERSTAND A SINGLE WORD!

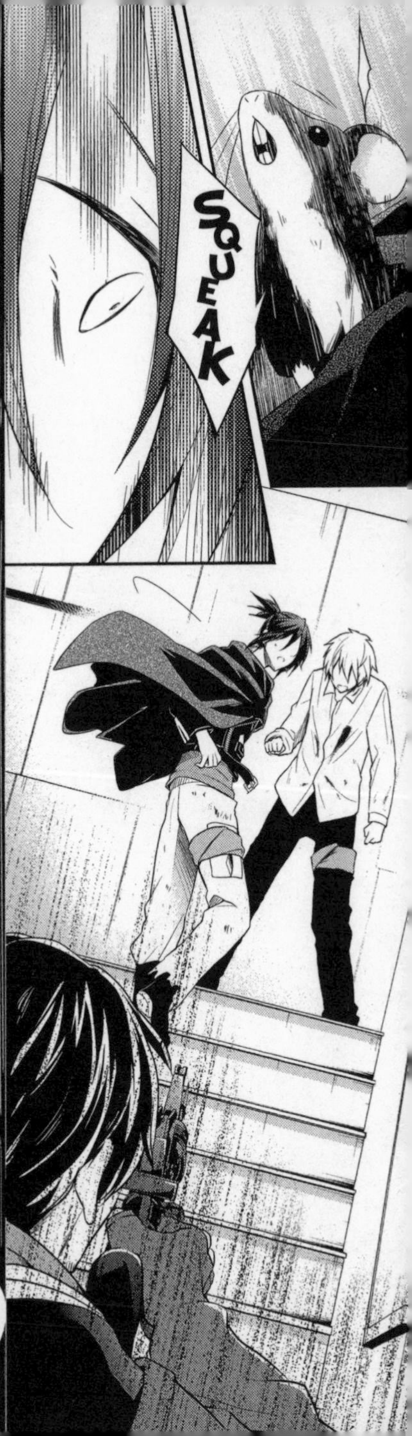
SQUEAK

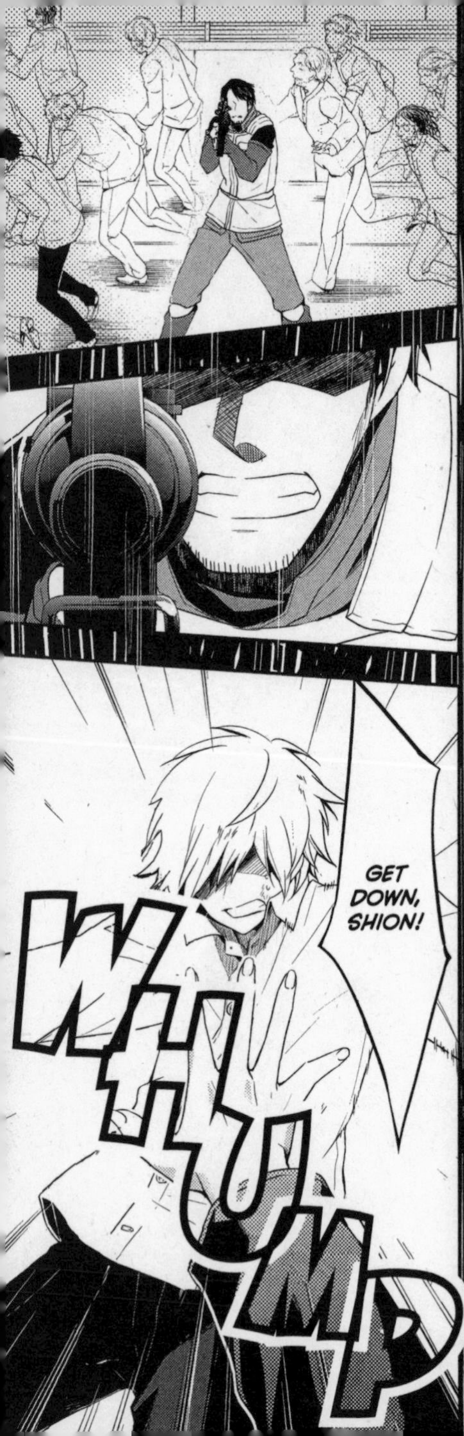
GET DOWN, SHION!
WHUMP

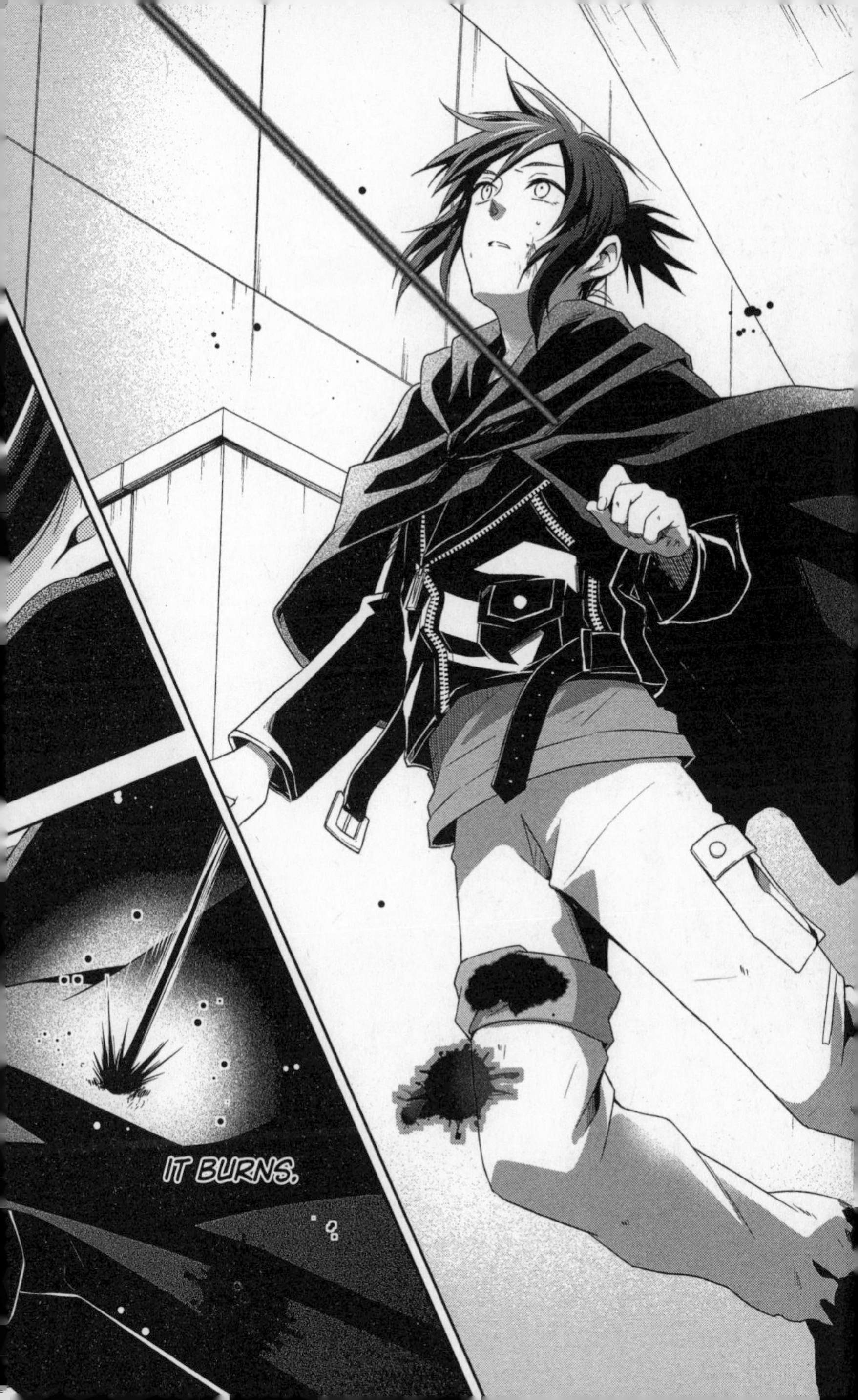
IT BURNS.

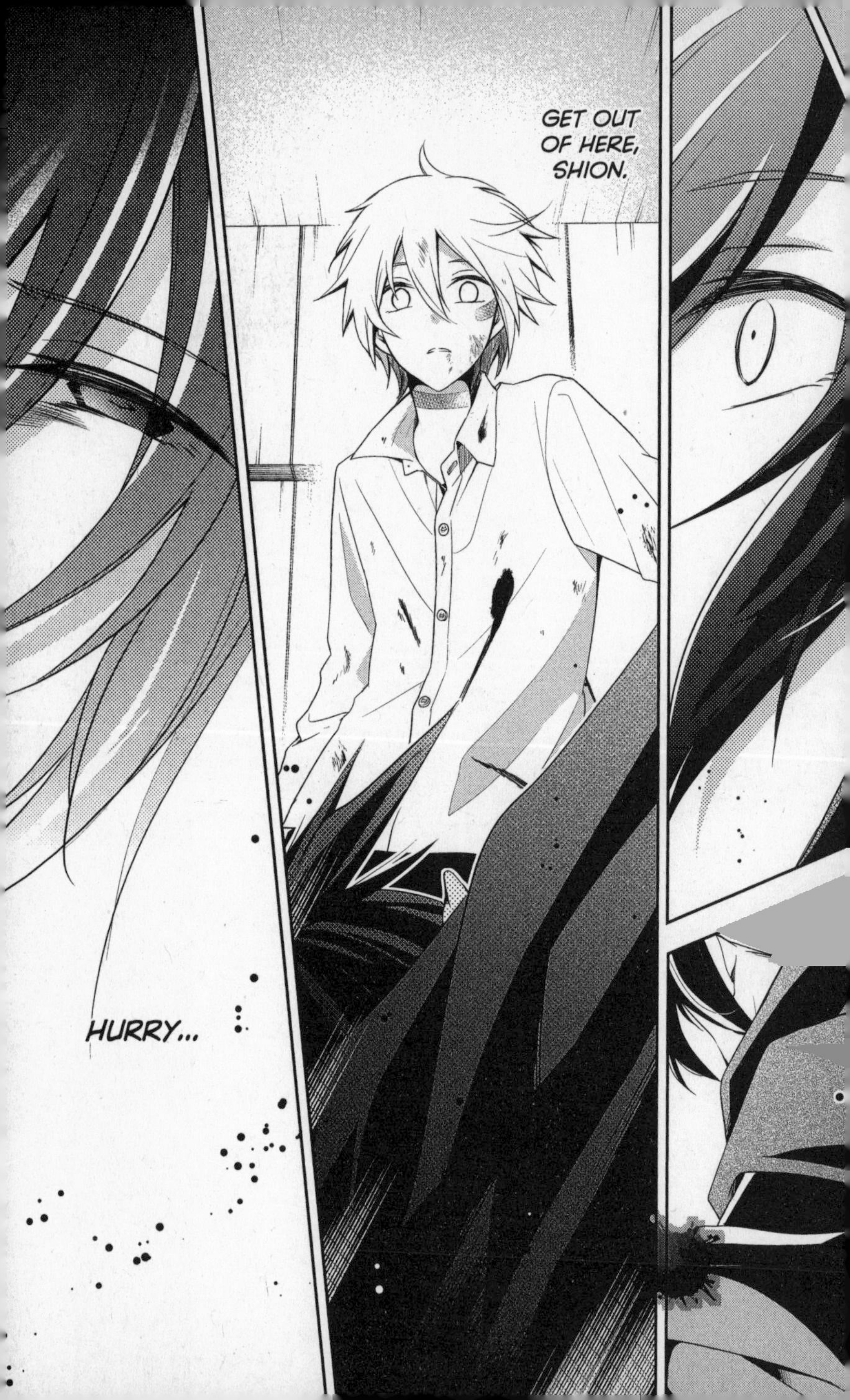
GET OUT OF HERE, SHION.
HURRY...

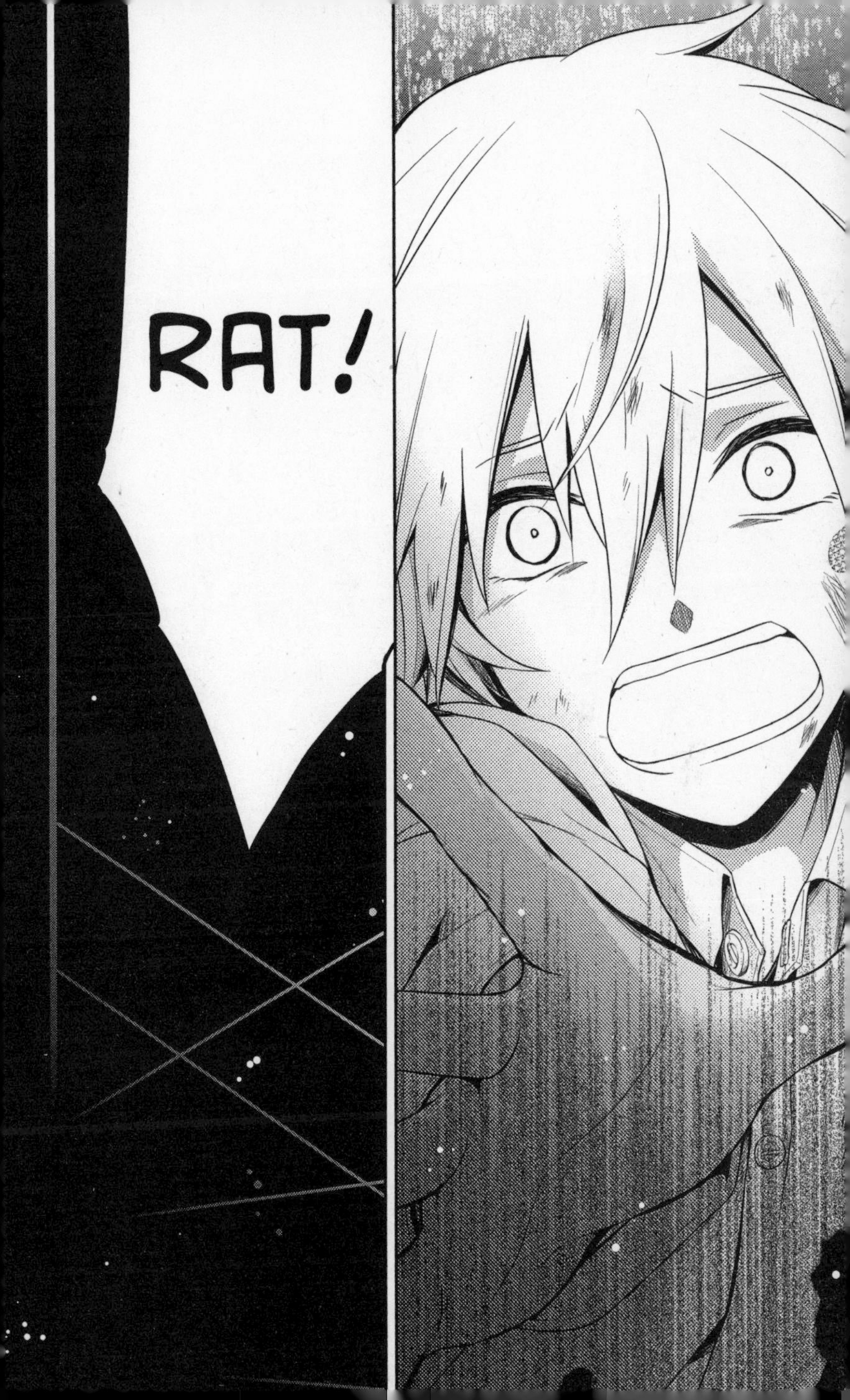
RAT!

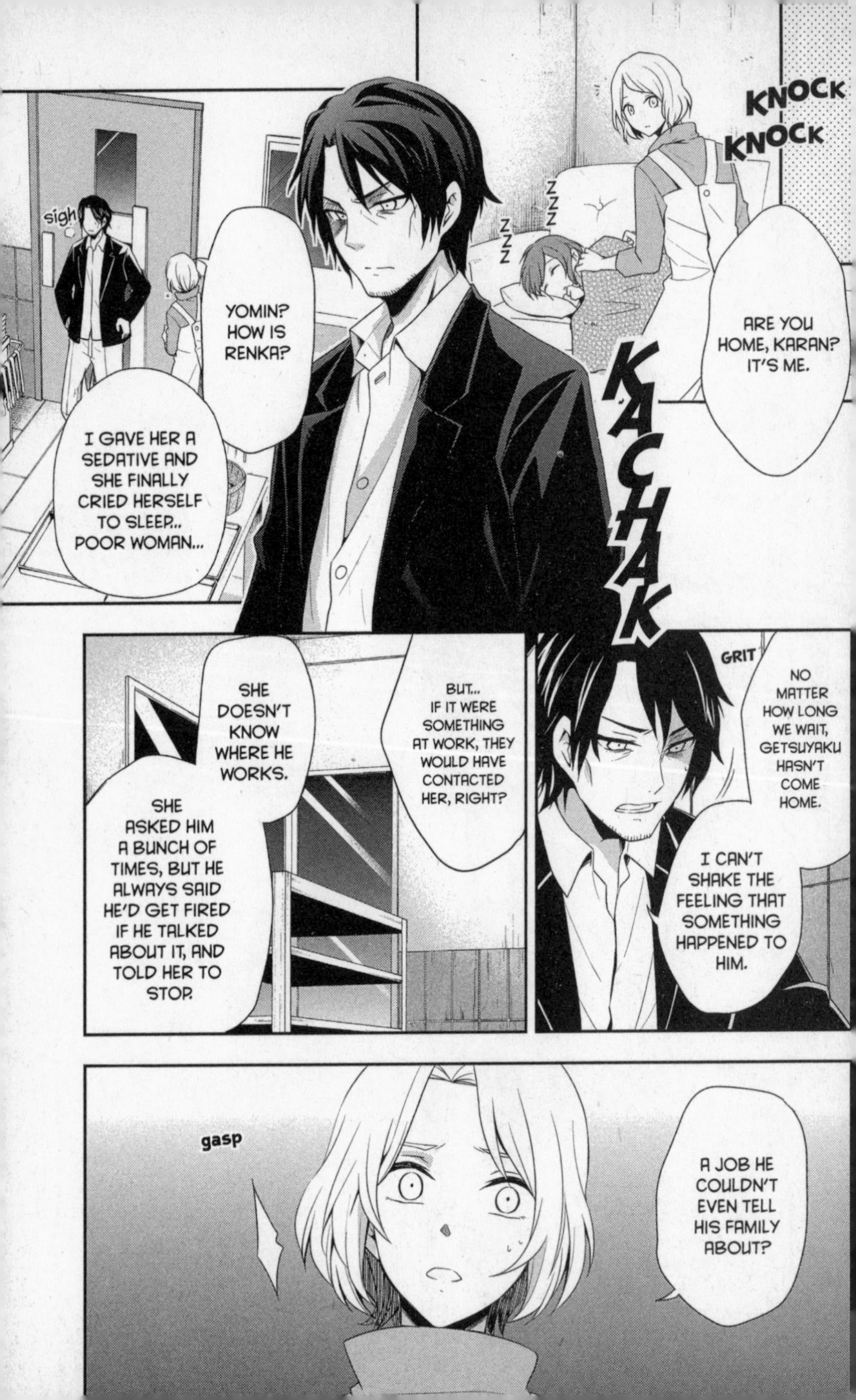
KNOCK KNOCK
ZZZ
ZZZ
ARE YOU HOME, KARAN? IT'S ME.
KACHAK
YOMIN? HOW IS RENKA?
sigh
I GAVE HER A SEDATIVE AND SHE FINALLY CRIED HERSELF TO SLEEP... POOR WOMAN...
GRIT
NO MATTER HOW LONG WE WAIT, GETSUYAKU HASN'T COME HOME.
I CAN'T SHAKE THE FEELING THAT SOMETHING HAPPENED TO HIM.
BUT... IF IT WERE SOMETHING AT WORK, THEY WOULD HAVE CONTACTED HER, RIGHT?
SHE DOESN'T KNOW WHERE HE WORKS.
SHE ASKED HIM A BUNCH OF TIMES, BUT HE ALWAYS SAID HE'D GET FIRED IF HE TALKED ABOUT IT, AND TOLD HER TO STOP.
A JOB HE COULDN'T EVEN TELL HIS FAMILY ABOUT?
gasp

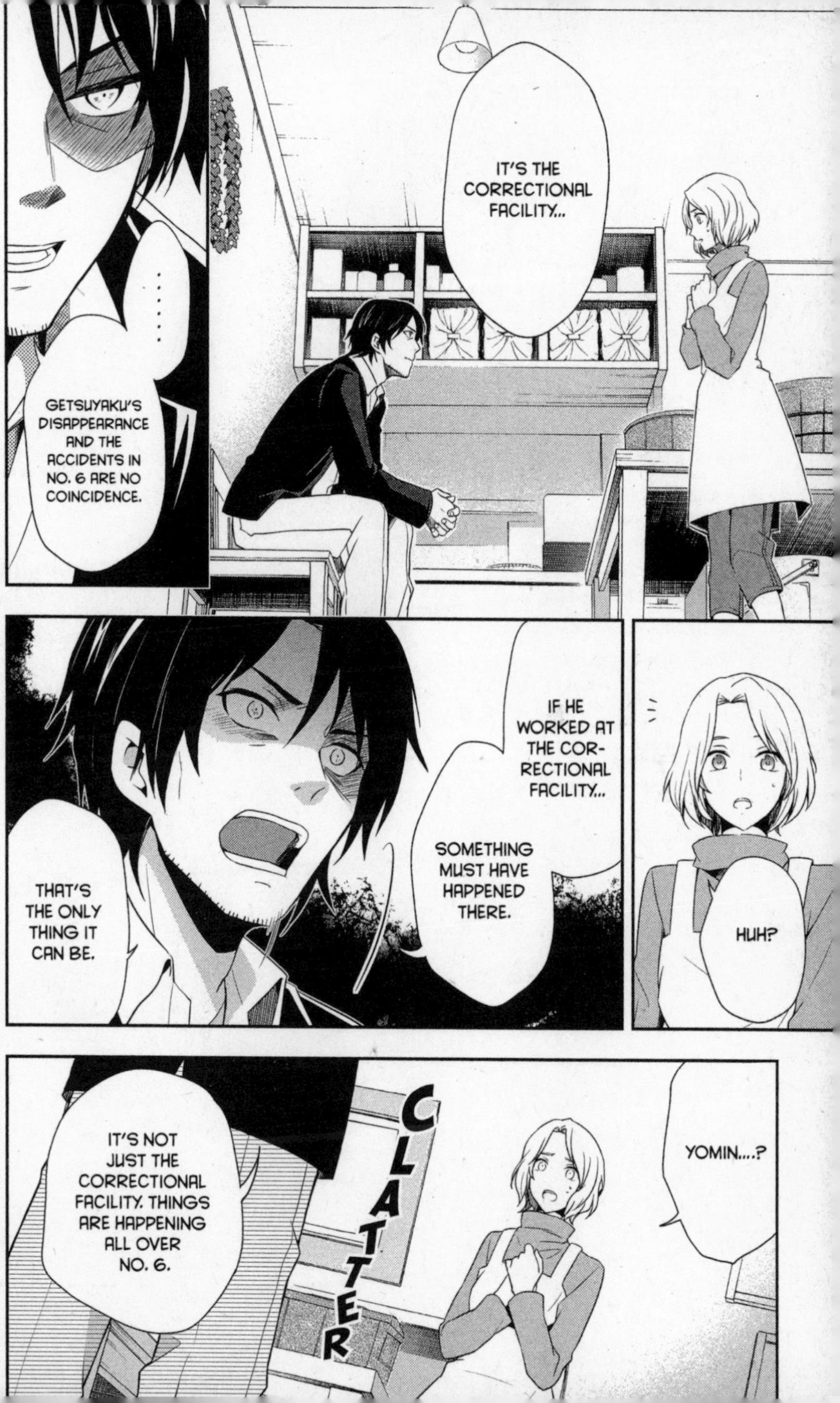
IT'S THE CORRECTIONAL FACILITY...
......
GETSUYAKU'S DISAPPEARANCE AND THE ACCIDENTS IN NO. 6 ARE NO COINCIDENCE.
HUH?
IF HE WORKED AT THE COR-RECTIONAL FACILITY...
SOMETHING MUST HAVE HAPPENED THERE.
THAT'S THE ONLY THING IT CAN BE.
YOMIN....?
CLATTER
IT'S NOT JUST THE CORRECTIONAL FACILITY. THINGS ARE HAPPENING ALL OVER NO. 6.

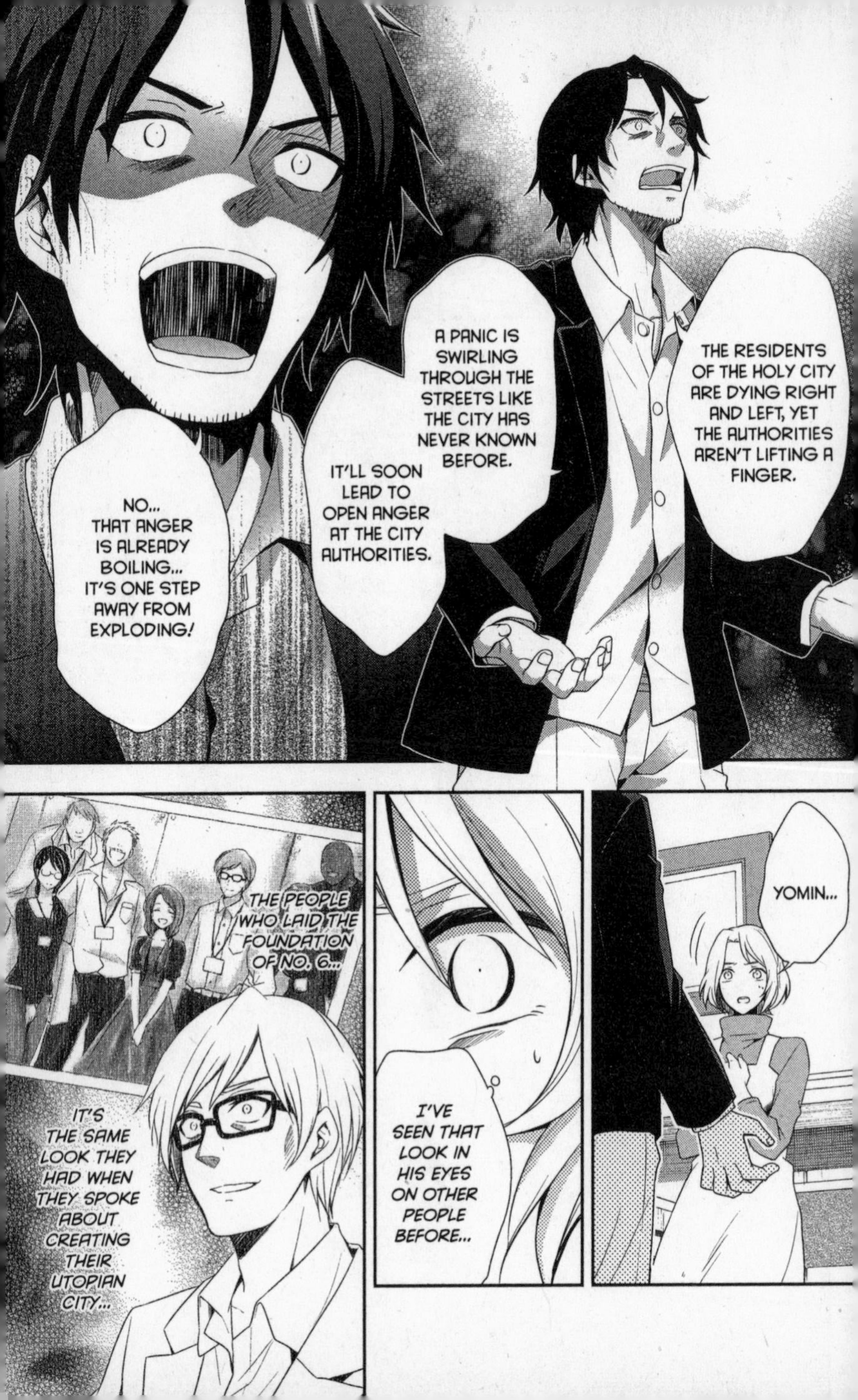
THE RESIDENTS OF THE HOLY CITY ARE DYING RIGHT AND LEFT, YET THE AUTHORITIES AREN'T LIFTING A FINGER.
A PANIC IS SWIRLING THROUGH THE STREETS LIKE THE CITY HAS NEVER KNOWN BEFORE.
IT'LL SOON LEAD TO OPEN ANGER AT THE CITY AUTHORITIES.
NO... THAT ANGER IS ALREADY BOILING... IT'S ONE STEP AWAY FROM EXPLODING!
YOMIN...
I'VE SEEN THAT LOOK IN HIS EYES ON OTHER PEOPLE BEFORE...
THE PEOPLE WHO LAID THE FOUNDATION OF NO. 6...
IT'S THE SAME LOOK THEY HAD WHEN THEY SPOKE ABOUT CREATING THEIR UTOPIAN CITY...

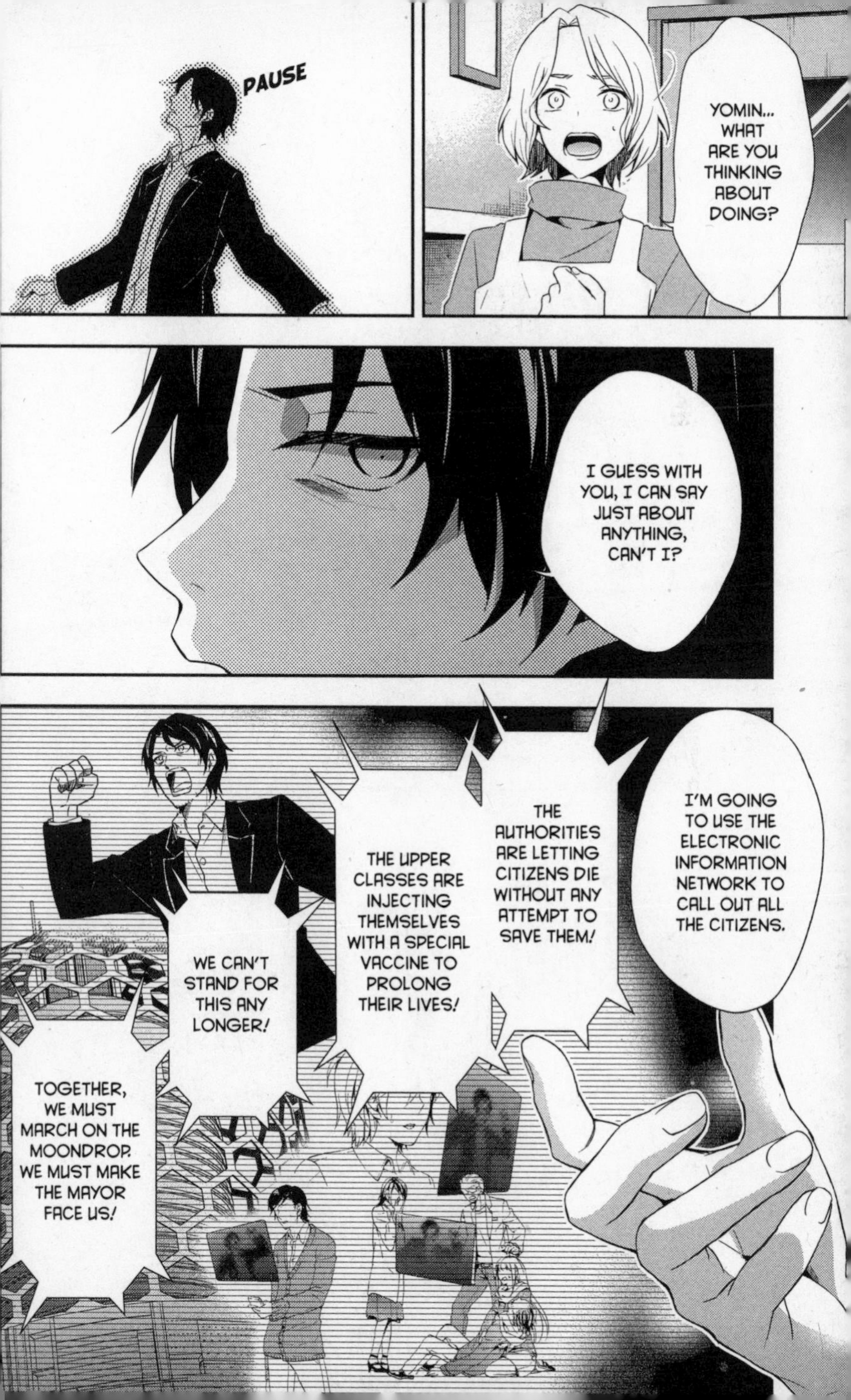
YOMIN... WHAT ARE YOU THINKING ABOUT DOING?
PAUSE
I GUESS WITH YOU, I CAN SAY JUST ABOUT ANYTHING, CAN'T I?
I'M GOING TO USE THE ELECTRONIC INFORMATION NETWORK TO CALL OUT ALL THE CITIZENS.
THE AUTHORITIES ARE LETTING CITIZENS DIE WITHOUT ANY ATTEMPT TO SAVE THEM!
THE UPPER CLASSES ARE INJECTING THEMSELVES WITH A SPECIAL VACCINE TO PROLONG THEIR LIVES!
WE CAN'T STAND FOR THIS ANY LONGER!
TOGETHER, WE MUST MARCH ON THE MOONDROP. WE MUST MAKE THE MAYOR FACE US!

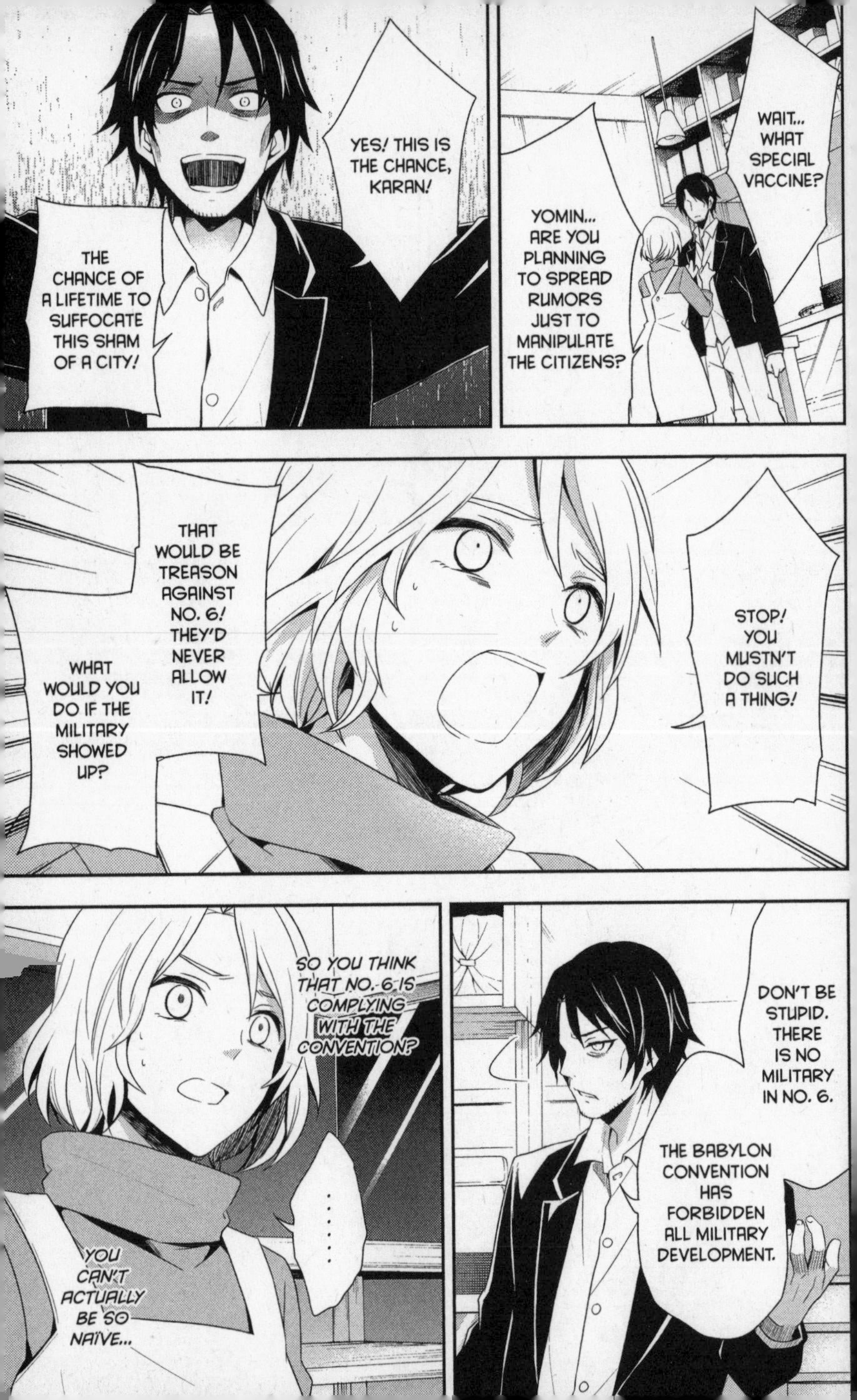
WAIT... WHAT SPECIAL VACCINE?
YOMIN... ARE YOU PLANNING TO SPREAD RUMORS JUST TO MANIPULATE THE CITIZENS?
YES! THIS IS THE CHANCE, KARAN!
THE CHANCE OF A LIFETIME TO SUFFOCATE THIS SHAM OF A CITY!
STOP! YOU MUSTN'T DO SUCH A THING!
THAT WOULD BE TREASON AGAINST NO. 6! THEY'D NEVER ALLOW IT!
WHAT WOULD YOU DO IF THE MILITARY SHOWED UP?
DON'T BE STUPID. THERE IS NO MILITARY IN NO. 6.
THE BABYLON CONVENTION HAS FORBIDDEN ALL MILITARY DEVELOPMENT.
SO YOU THINK THAT NO. 6 IS COMPLYING WITH THE CONVENTION?
......
YOU CAN'T ACTUALLY BE SO NAÏVE...

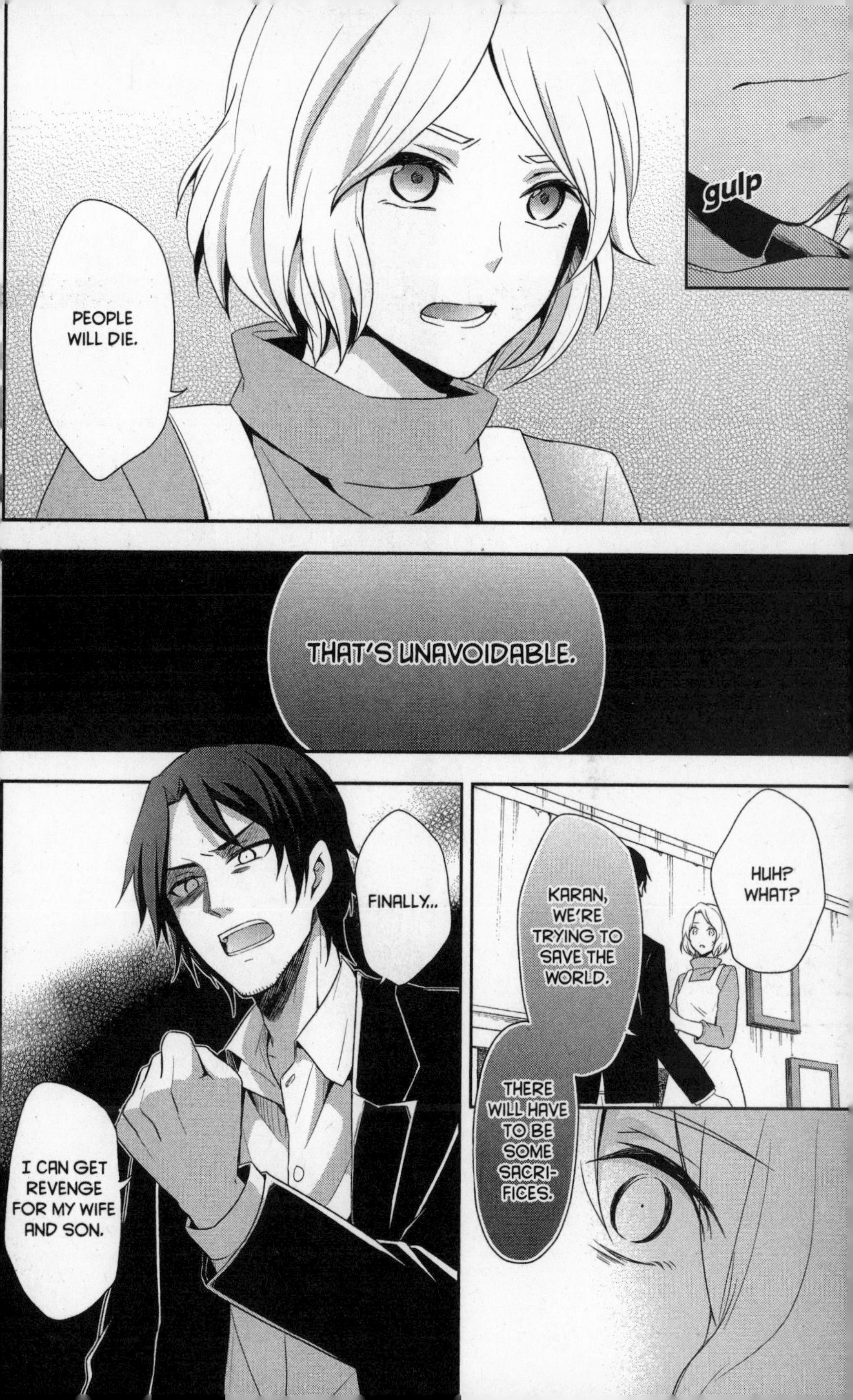
gulp
PEOPLE WILL DIE.
THAT'S UNAVOIDABLE.
HUH? WHAT?
KARAN, WE'RE TRYING TO SAVE THE WORLD.
THERE WILL HAVE TO BE SOME SACRI-FICES.
FINALLY...
I CAN GET REVENGE FOR MY WIFE AND SON.

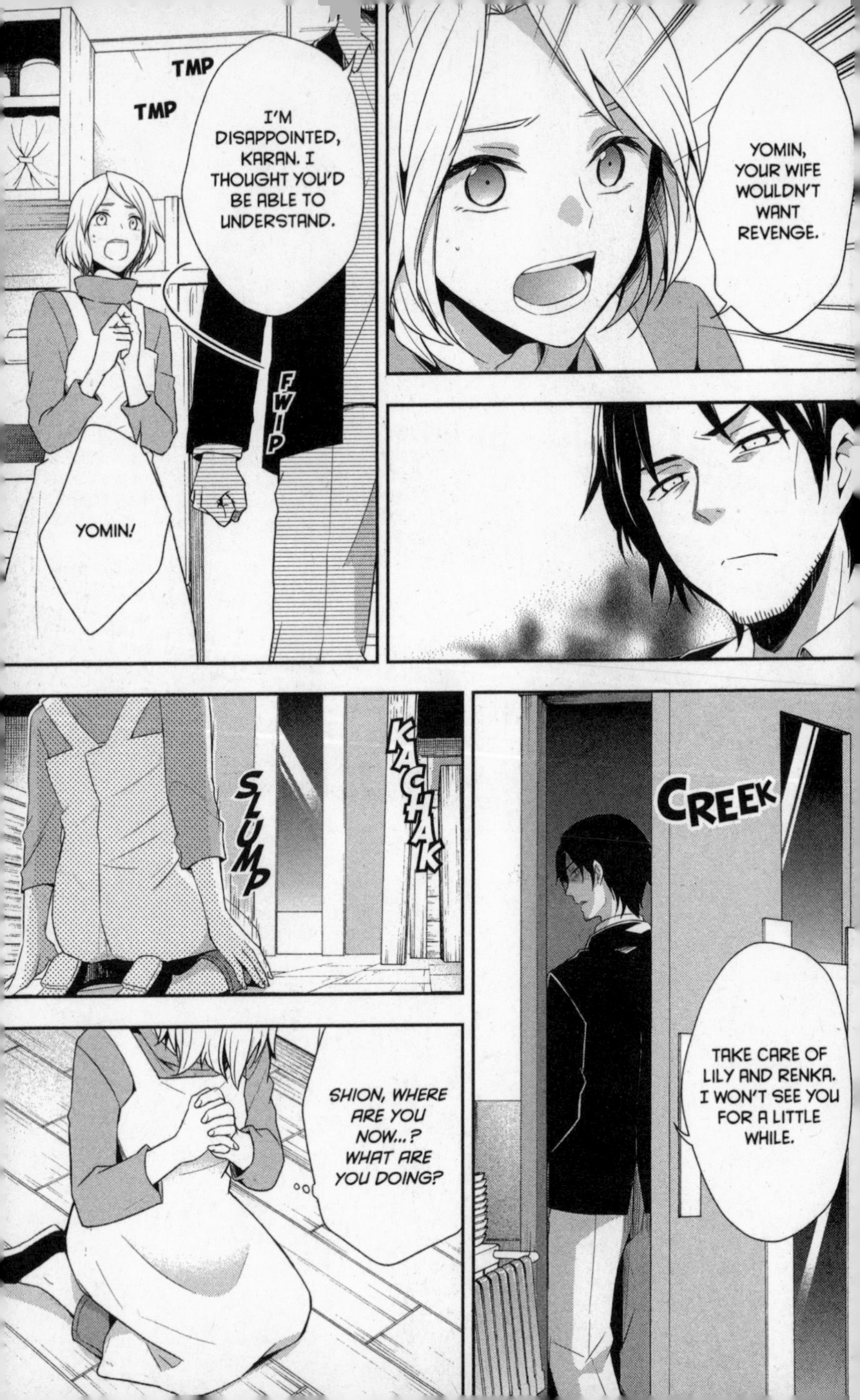
YOMIN, YOUR WIFE WOULDN'T WANT REVENGE.
TMP
TMP
I'M DISAPPOINTED, KARAN. I THOUGHT YOU'D BE ABLE TO UNDERSTAND.
FWIP
YOMIN!
CREEK
TAKE CARE OF LILY AND RENKA. I WON'T SEE YOU FOR A LITTLE WHILE.
KACHAK
SLUMP
SHION, WHERE ARE YOU NOW...? WHAT ARE YOU DOING?

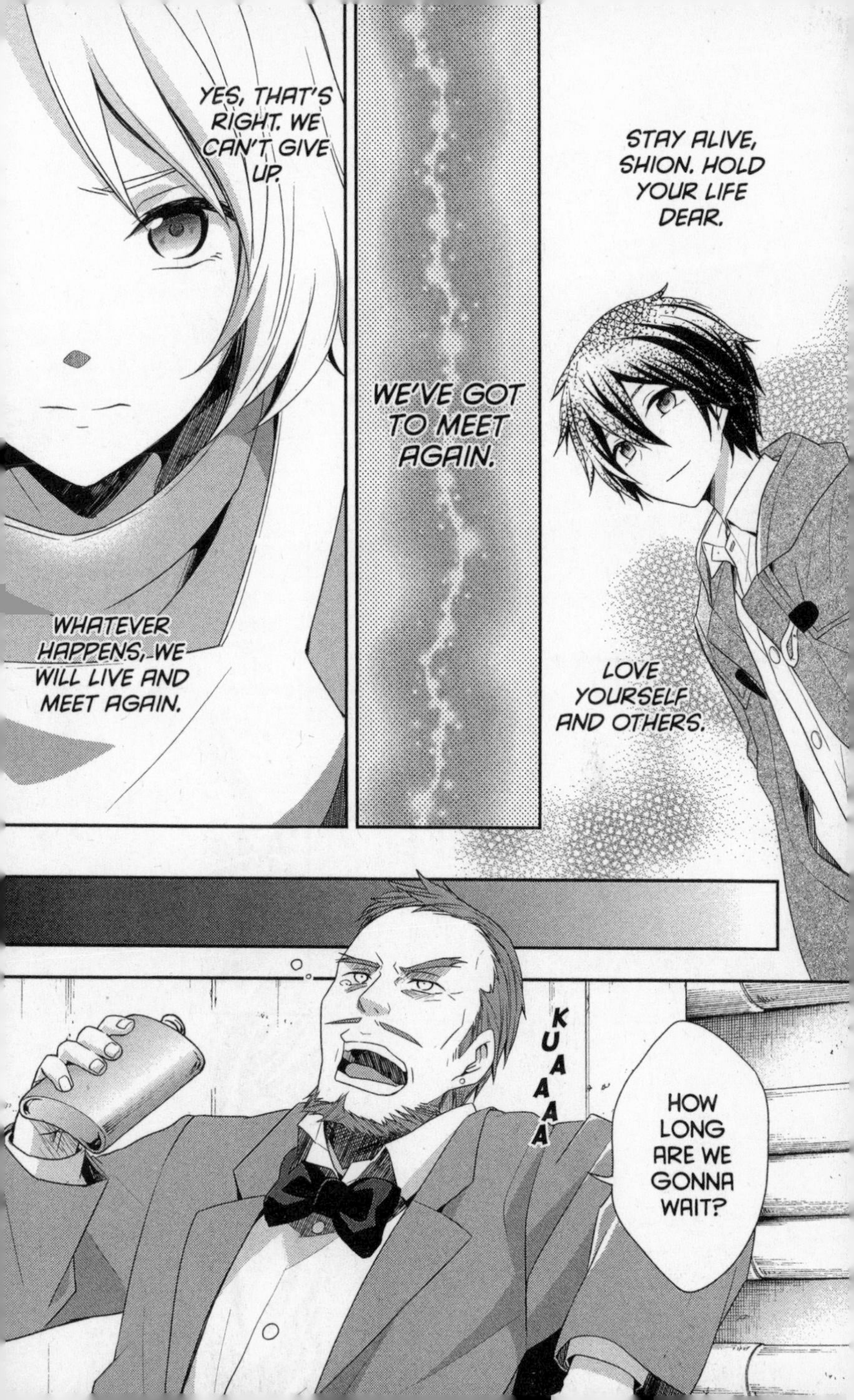
STAY ALIVE, SHION. HOLD YOUR LIFE DEAR.
LOVE YOURSELF AND OTHERS.
WE'VE GOT TO MEET AGAIN.
YES, THAT'S RIGHT. WE CAN'T GIVE UP.
WHATEVER HAPPENS, WE WILL LIVE AND MEET AGAIN.
KUAAAA
HOW LONG ARE WE GONNA WAIT?

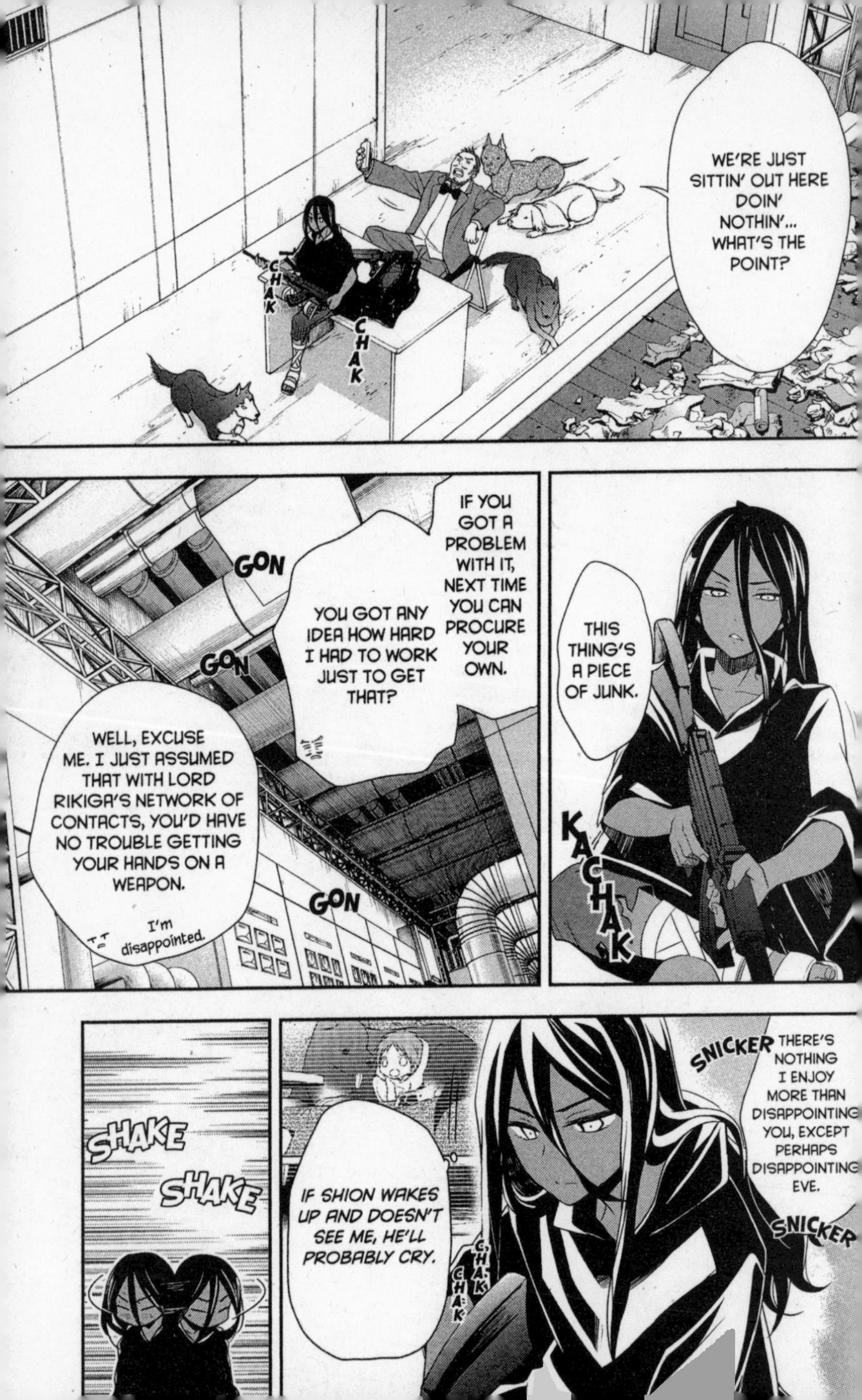
WE'RE JUST SITTIN' OUT HERE DOIN' NOTHIN'... WHAT'S THE POINT?
CHAK
CHAK
THIS THING'S A PIECE OF JUNK.
KACHAK
IF YOU GOT A PROBLEM WITH IT, NEXT TIME YOU CAN PROCURE YOUR OWN.
YOU GOT ANY IDEA HOW HARD I HAD TO WORK JUST TO GET THAT?
GON
GON
WELL, EXCUSE ME. I JUST ASSUMED THAT WITH LORD RIKIGA'S NETWORK OF CONTACTS, YOU'D HAVE NO TROUBLE GETTING YOUR HANDS ON A WEAPON.
GON
I'm disappointed.
SNICKER
THERE'S NOTHING I ENJOY MORE THAN DISAPPOINTING YOU, EXCEPT PERHAPS DISAPPOINTING EVE.
SNICKER
CHAK
CHAK
IF SHION WAKES UP AND DOESN'T SEE ME, HE'LL PROBABLY CRY.
SHAKE
SHAKE

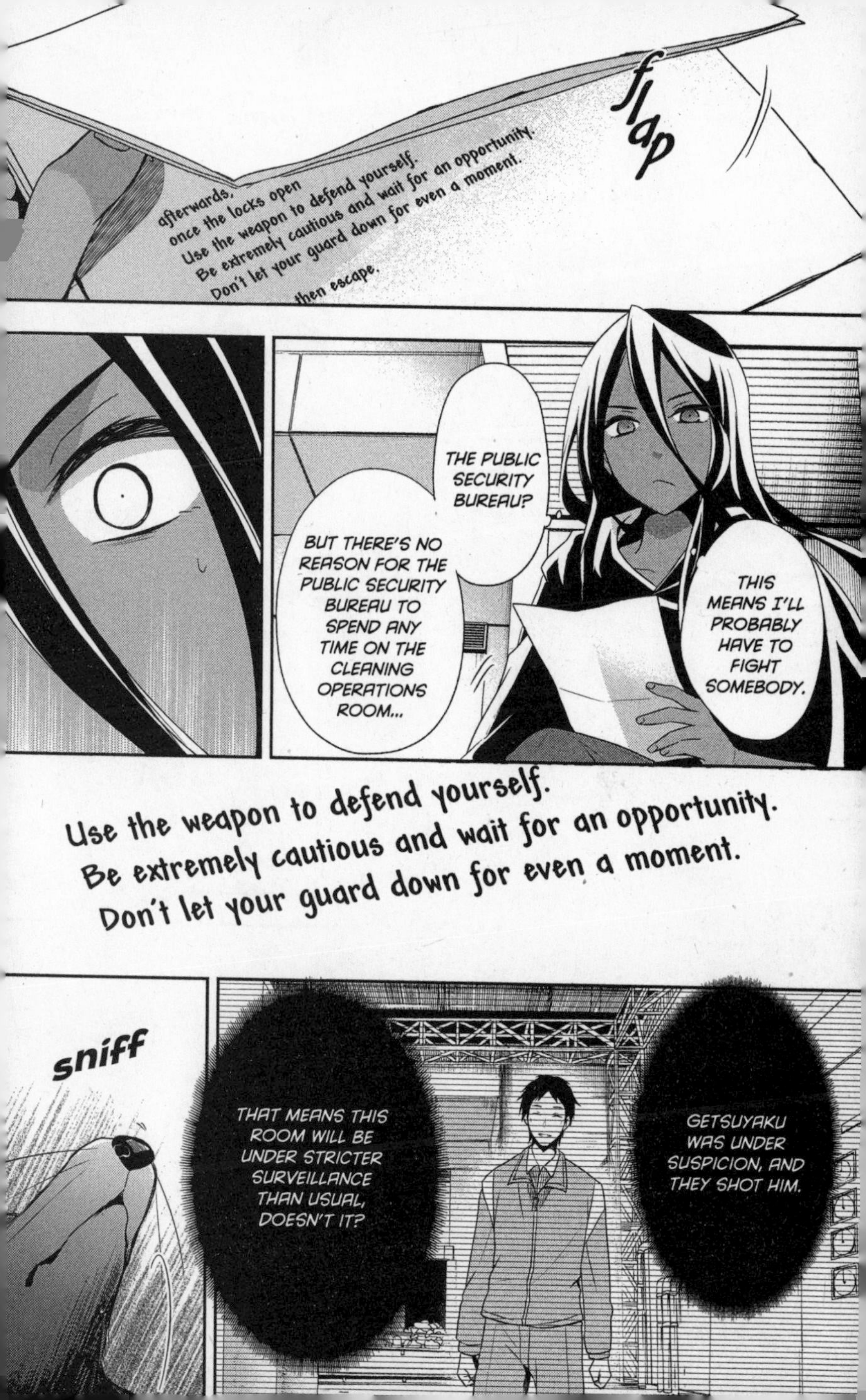
flap
afterwards,
once the locks open
Use the weapon to defend yourself.
Be extremely cautious and wait for an opportunity.
Don't let your guard down for even a moment.
then escape.
THIS MEANS I'LL PROBABLY HAVE TO FIGHT SOMEBODY.
THE PUBLIC SECURITY BUREAU?
BUT THERE'S NO REASON FOR THE PUBLIC SECURITY BUREAU TO SPEND ANY TIME ON THE CLEANING OPERATIONS ROOM...
Use the weapon to defend yourself.
Be extremely cautious and wait for an opportunity.
Don't let your guard down for even a moment.
GETSUYAKU WAS UNDER SUSPICION, AND THEY SHOT HIM.
THAT MEANS THIS ROOM WILL BE UNDER STRICTER SURVEILLANCE THAN USUAL, DOESN'T IT?
sniff

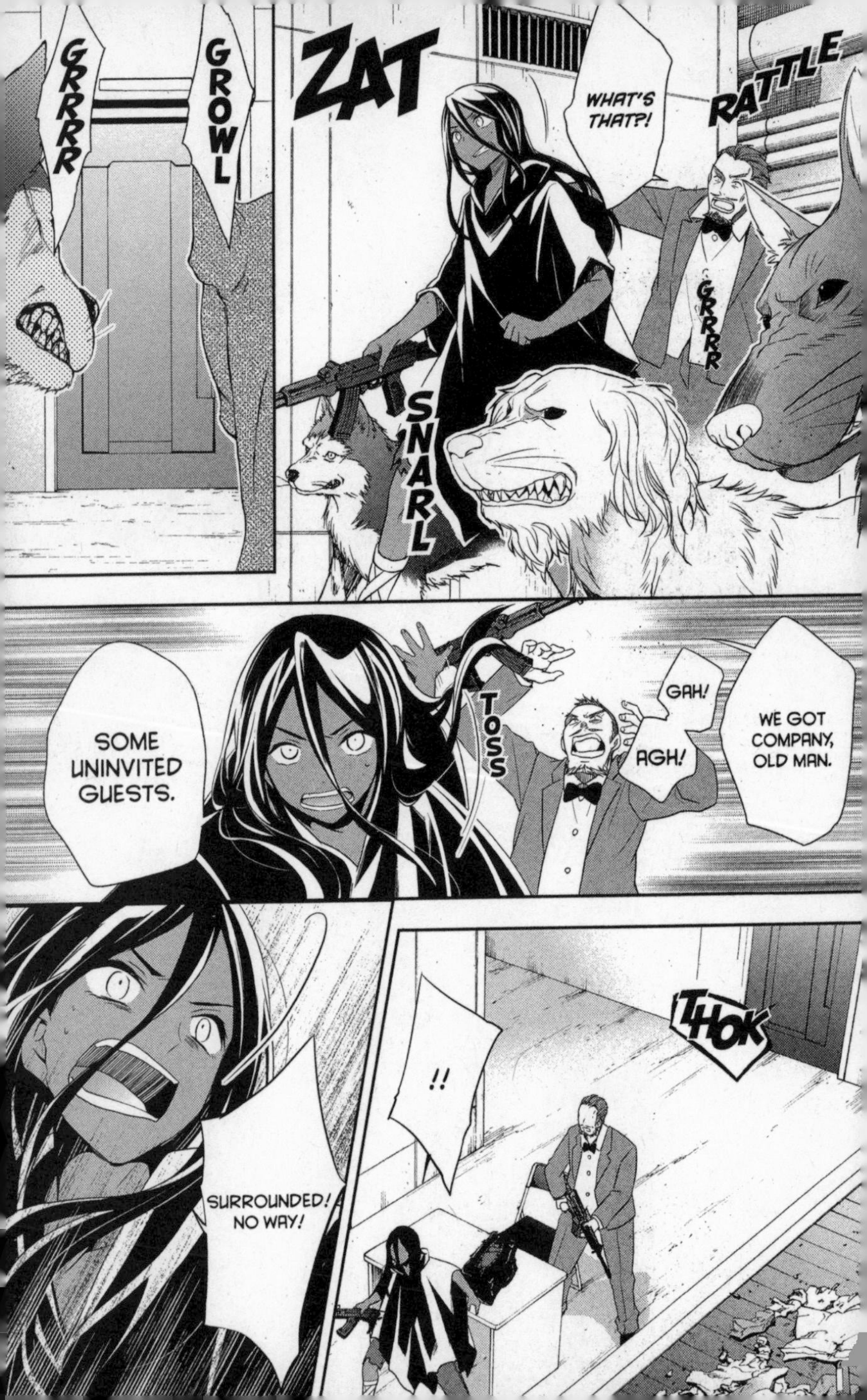
RATTLE
WHAT'S THAT?!
ZAT
GRRRR
SNARL
GROWL
GRRRR
WE GOT COMPANY, OLD MAN.
GAH!
AGH!
TOSS
SOME UNINVITED GUESTS.
THOK
!!
SURROUNDED! NO WAY!

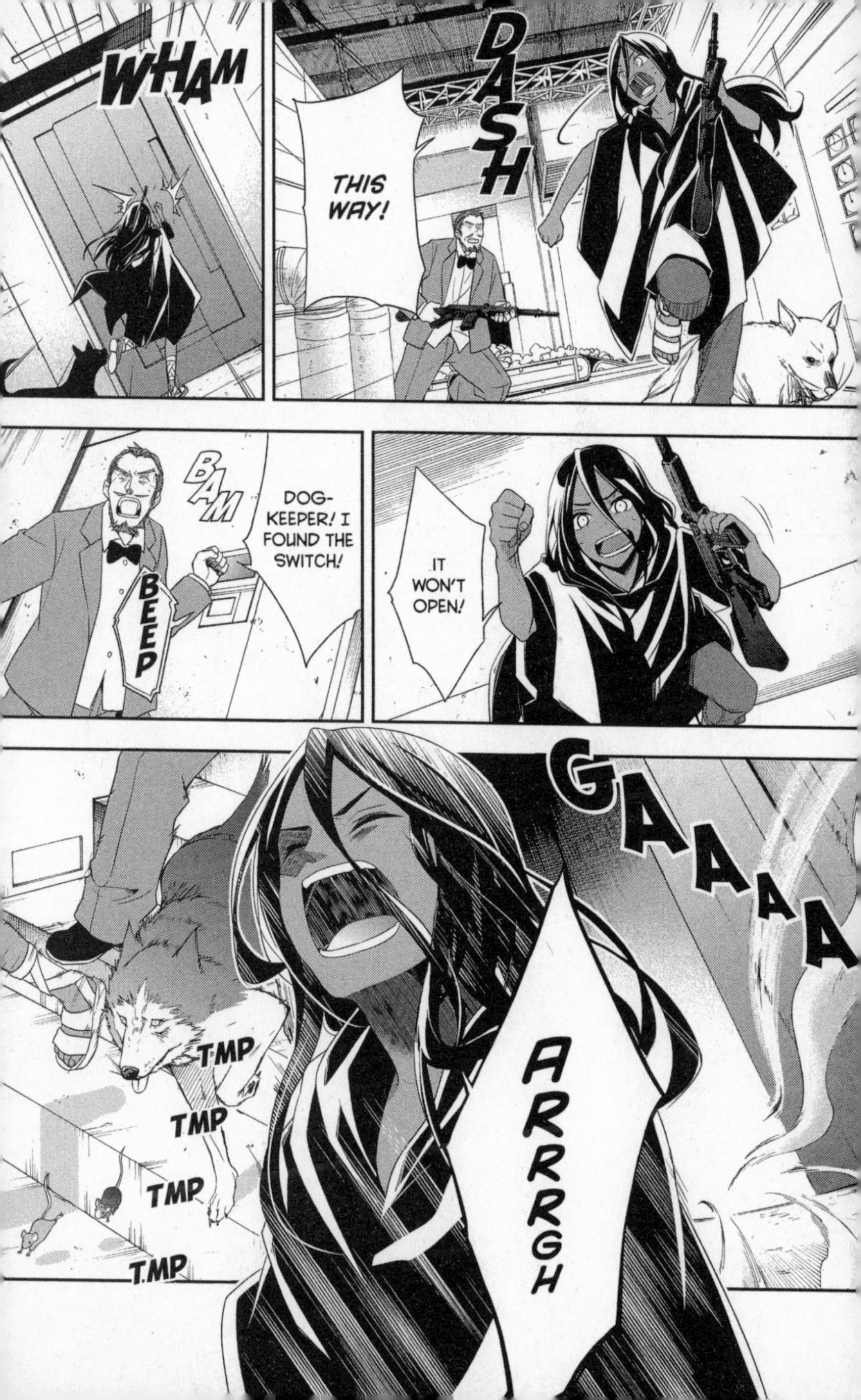
DASH
THIS WAY!
WHAM
IT WON'T OPEN!
BAM
DOG-KEEPER! I FOUND THE SWITCH!
BEEP
GAAAAA
ARRRGH
TMP
TMP
TMP
TMP

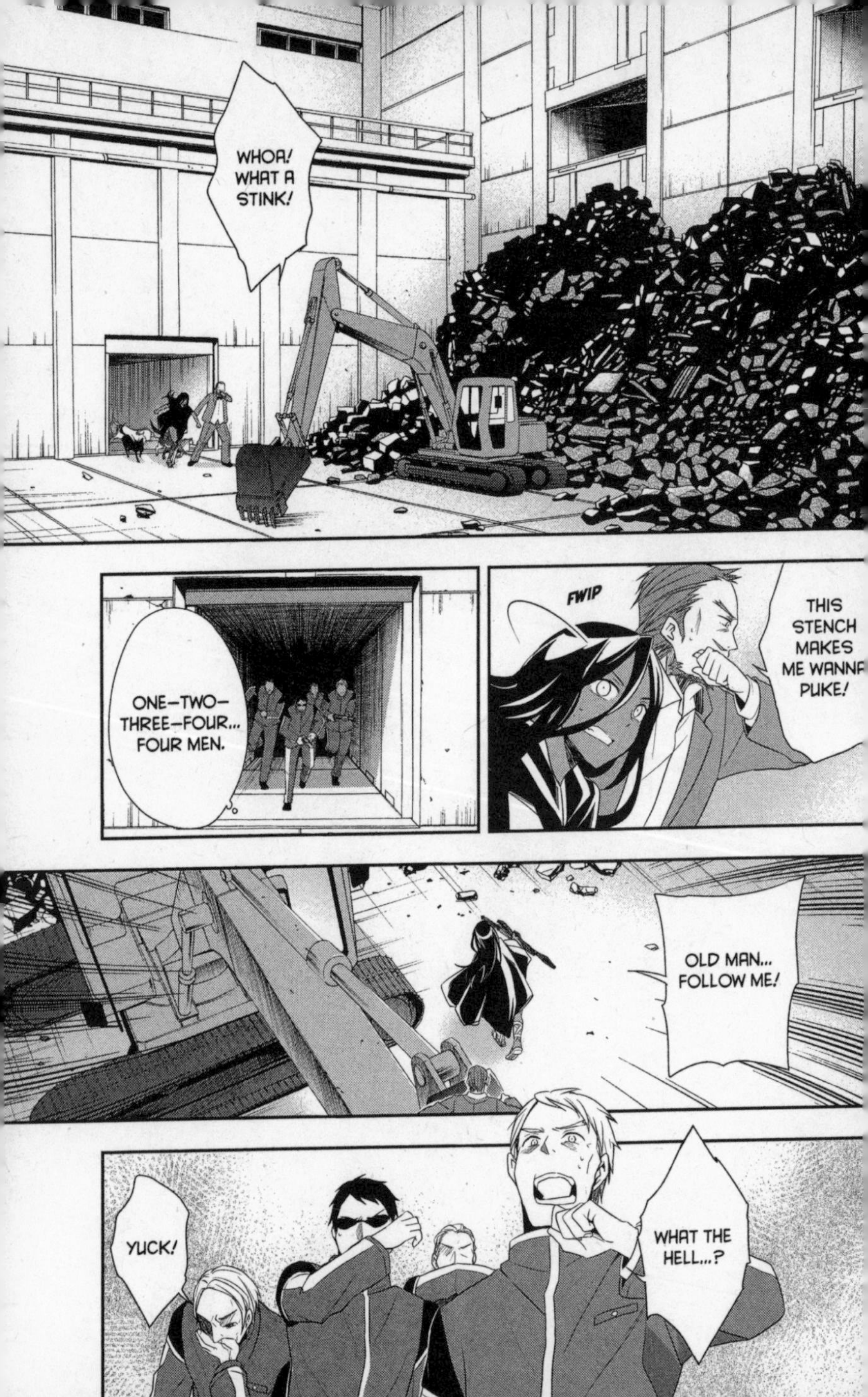
WHOA! WHAT A STINK!
FWIP
THIS STENCH MAKES ME WANNA PUKE!
ONE-TWO-THREE-FOUR... FOUR MEN.
OLD MAN... FOLLOW ME!
WHAT THE HELL...?
YUCK!

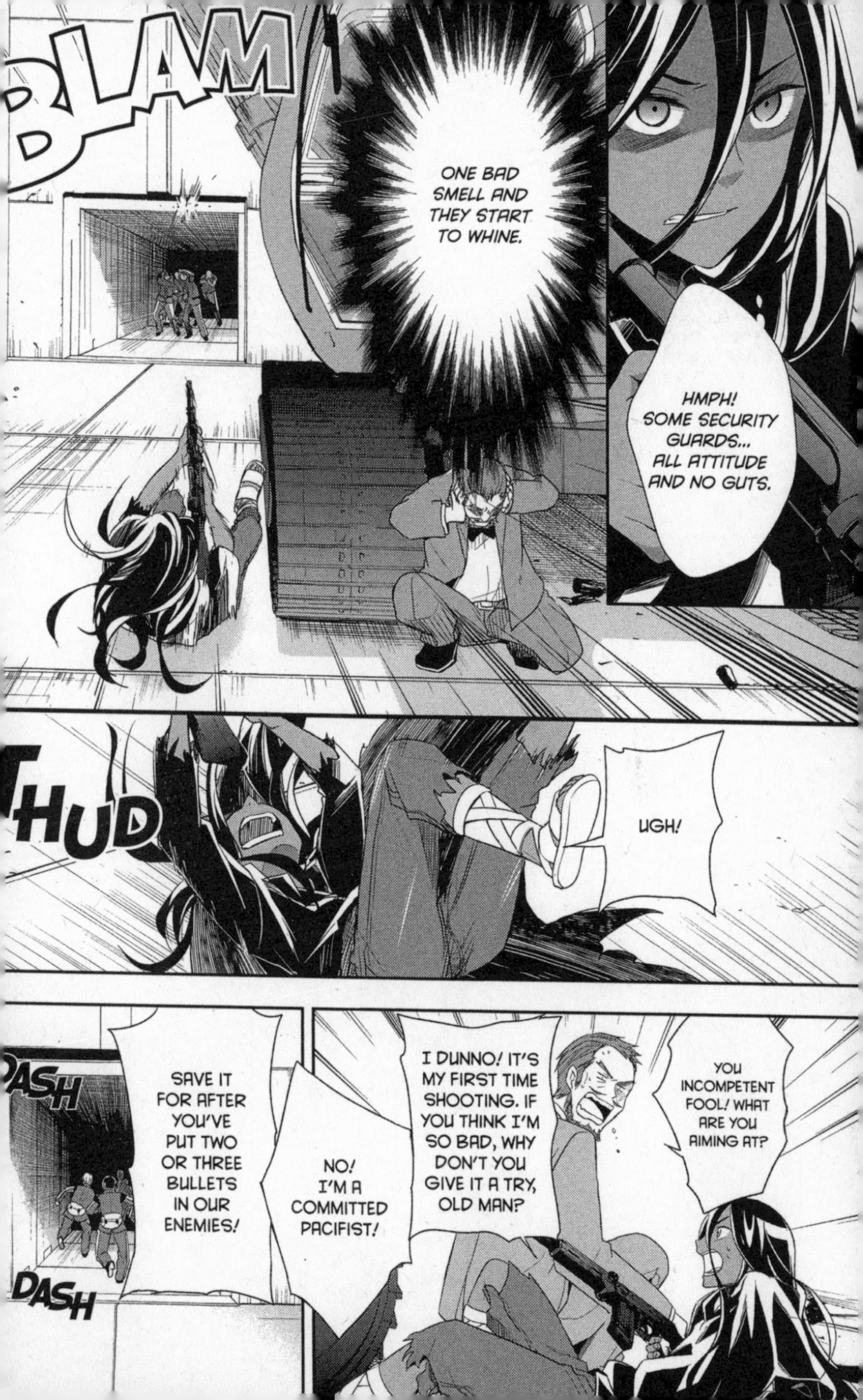
HMPH! SOME SECURITY GUARDS... ALL ATTITUDE AND NO GUTS.
BLAM
ONE BAD SMELL AND THEY START TO WHINE.
UGH!
THUD
YOU INCOMPETENT FOOL! WHAT ARE YOU AIMING AT?
I DUNNO! IT'S MY FIRST TIME SHOOTING. IF YOU THINK I'M SO BAD, WHY DON'T YOU GIVE IT A TRY, OLD MAN?
NO! I'M A COMMITTED PACIFIST!
SAVE IT FOR AFTER YOU'VE PUT TWO OR THREE BULLETS IN OUR ENEMIES!
DASH
DASH

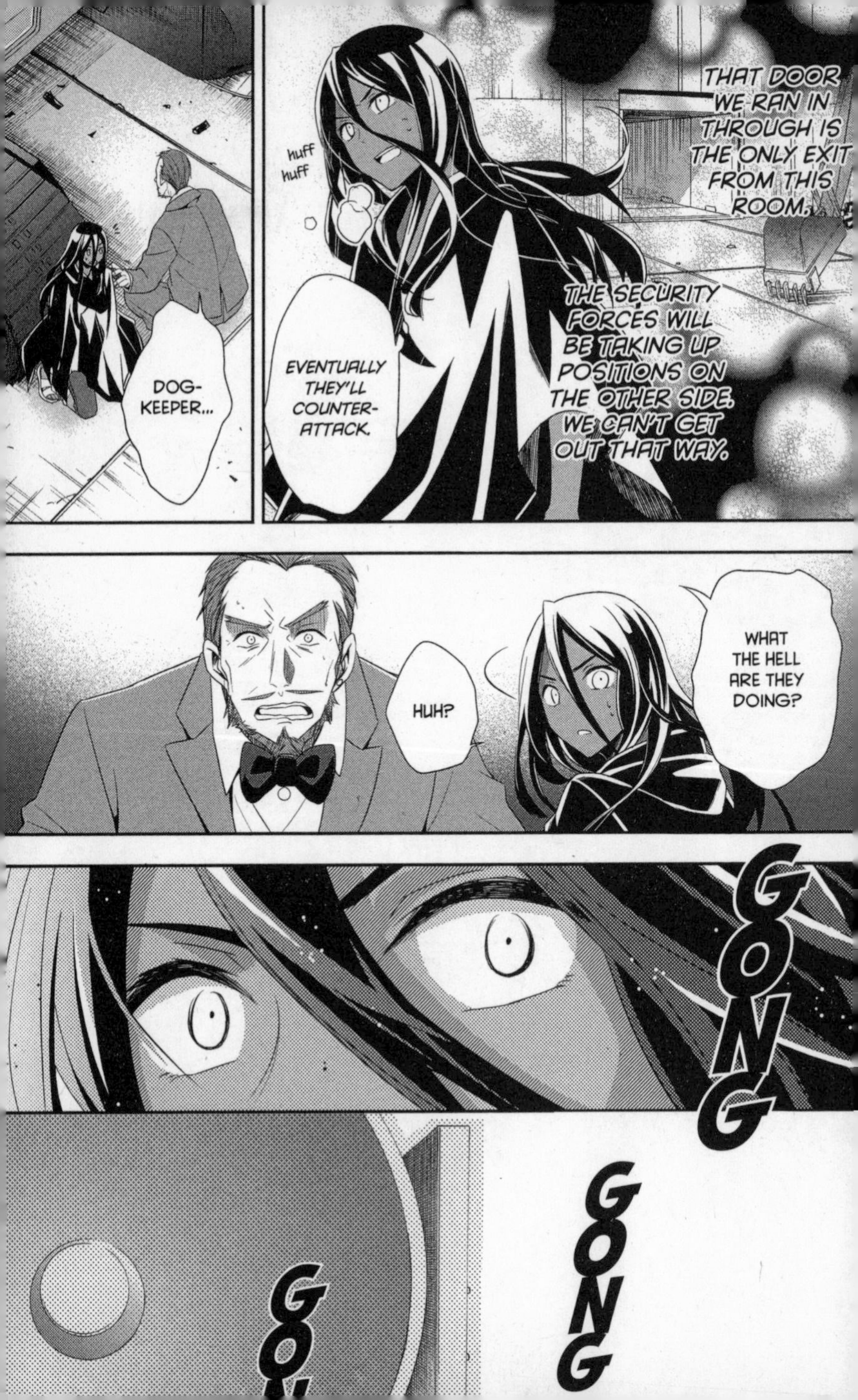
THAT DOOR WE RAN IN THROUGH IS THE ONLY EXIT FROM THIS ROOM.
THE SECURITY FORCES WILL BE TAKING UP POSITIONS ON THE OTHER SIDE. WE CAN'T GET OUT THAT WAY.
huff huff
EVENTUALLY THEY'LL COUNTER-ATTACK.
DOG-KEEPER...
WHAT THE HELL ARE THEY DOING?
HUH?
GONG
GONG

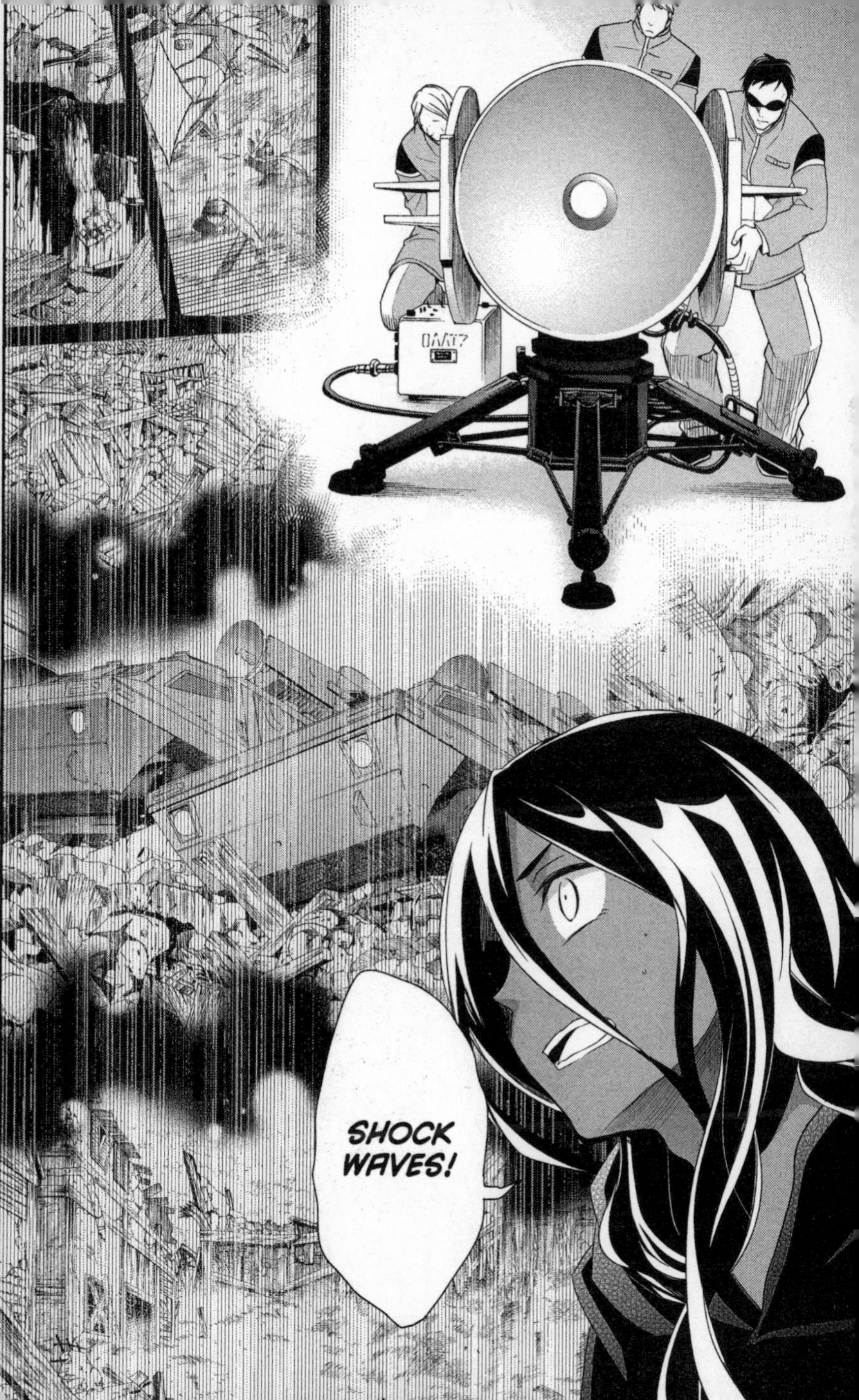
OAAT7
SHOCK WAVES!

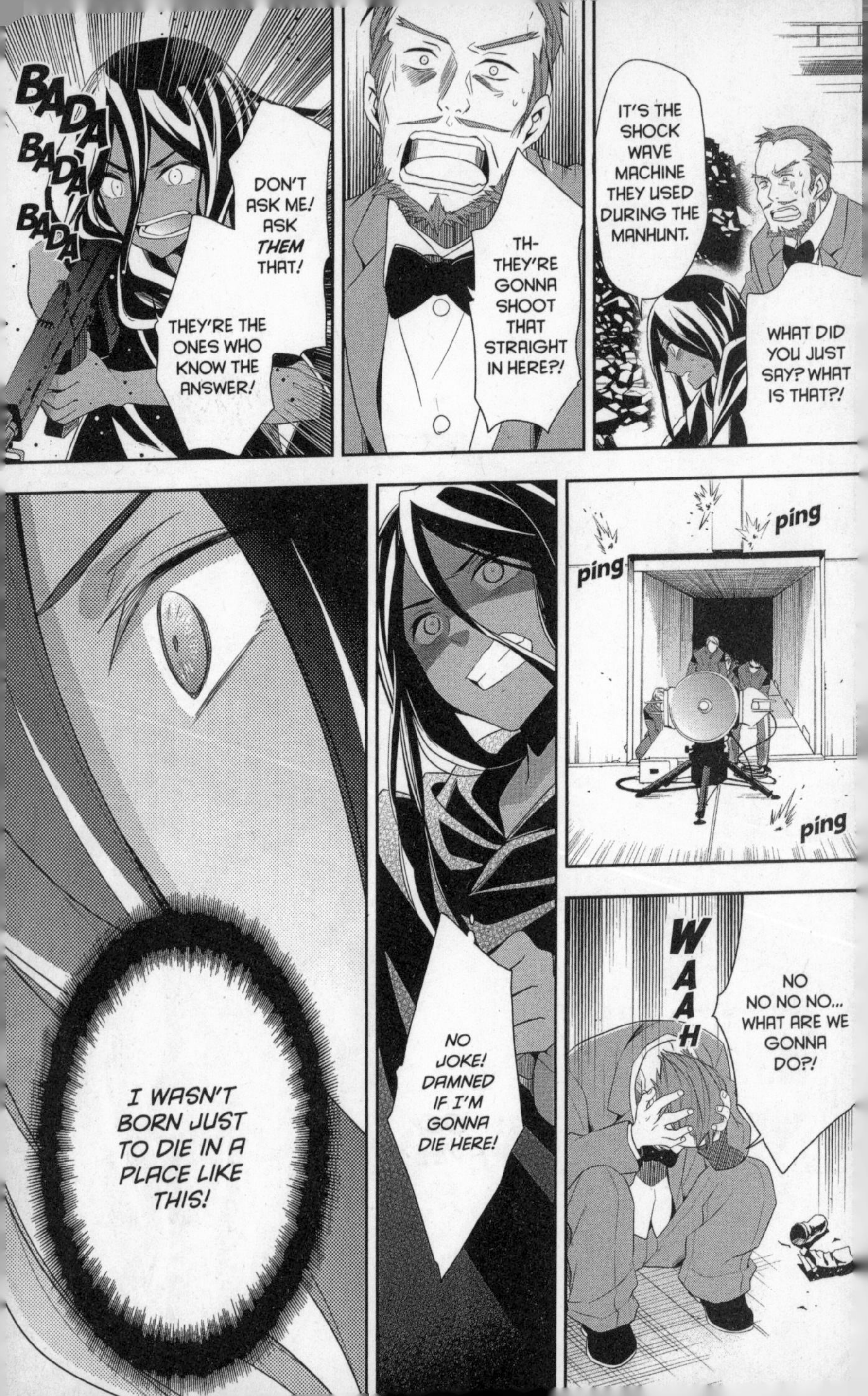
IT'S THE SHOCK WAVE MACHINE THEY USED DURING THE MANHUNT.
WHAT DID YOU JUST SAY? WHAT IS THAT?!
TH- THEY'RE GONNA SHOOT THAT STRAIGHT IN HERE?!
BADA BADA BADA
DON'T ASK ME! ASK *THEM* THAT!
THEY'RE THE ONES WHO KNOW THE ANSWER!
ping
ping
ping
NO NO NO NO... WHAT ARE WE GONNA DO?!
WAAAH
NO JOKE! DAMNED IF I'M GONNA DIE HERE!
I WASN'T BORN JUST TO DIE IN A PLACE LIKE THIS!

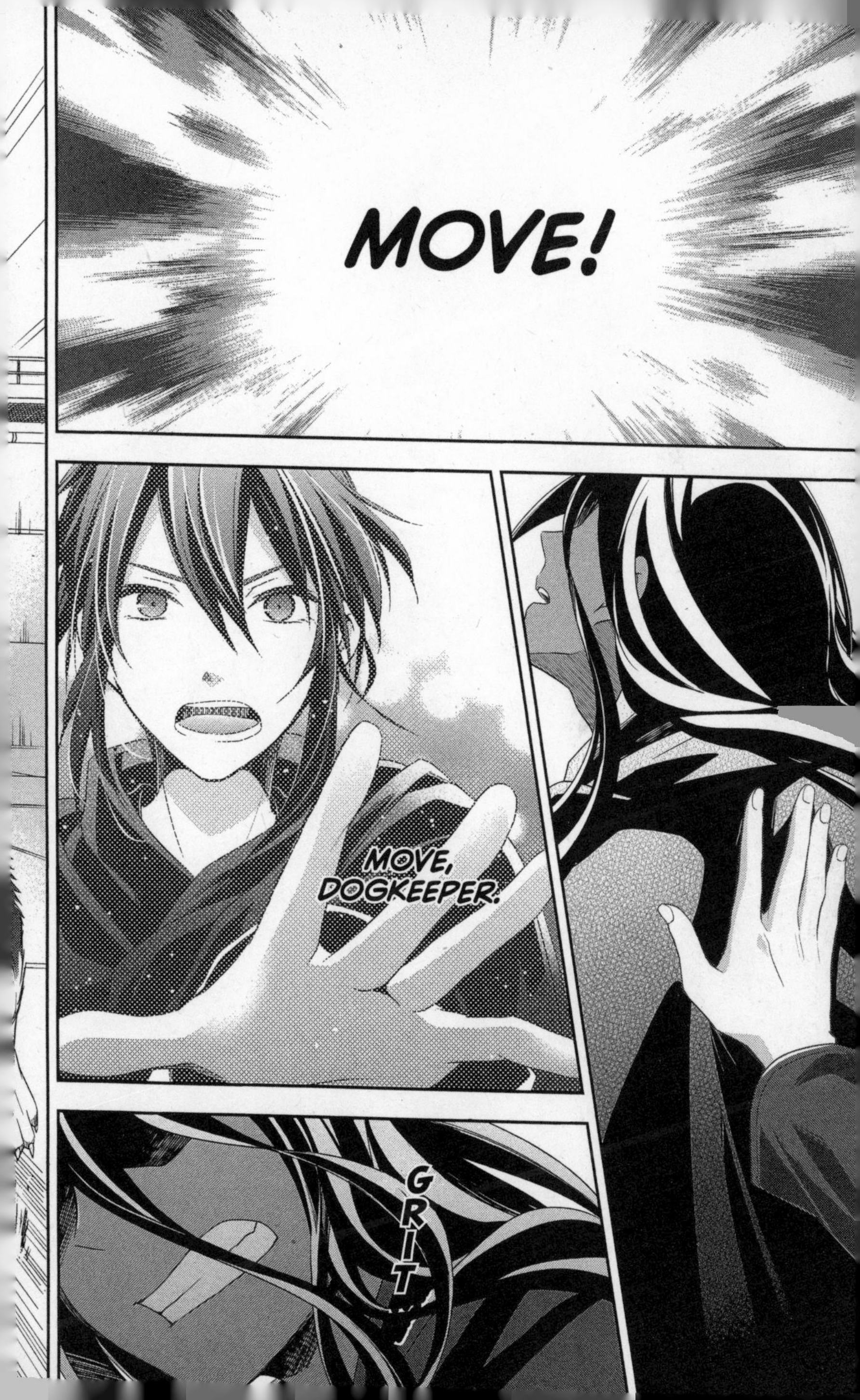
MOVE!
MOVE, DOGKEEPER.
GRIT

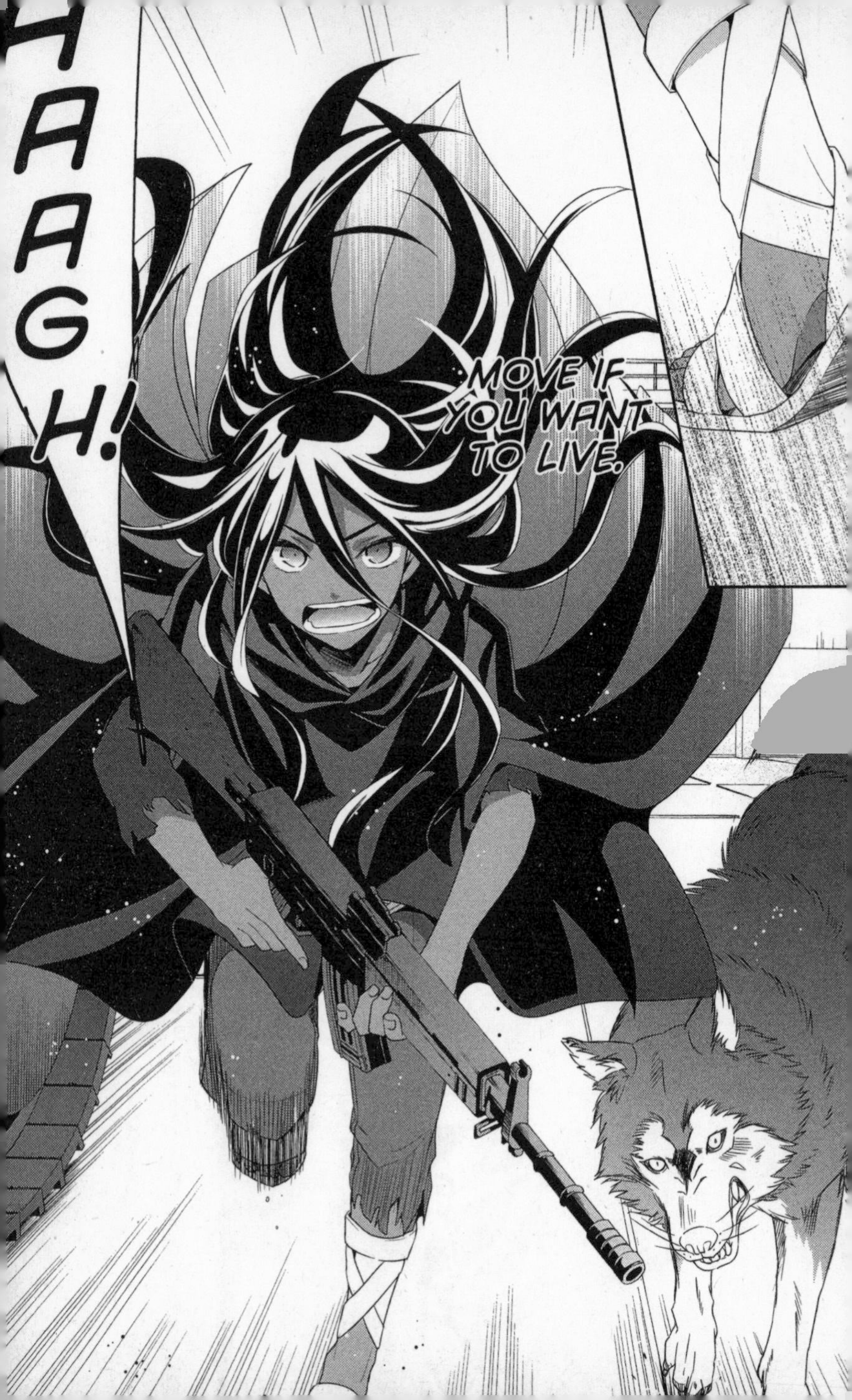
MOVE IF YOU WANT TO LIVE.
HAAAGH!

NO.6

Chapter 31: Amidst the Evening Winc

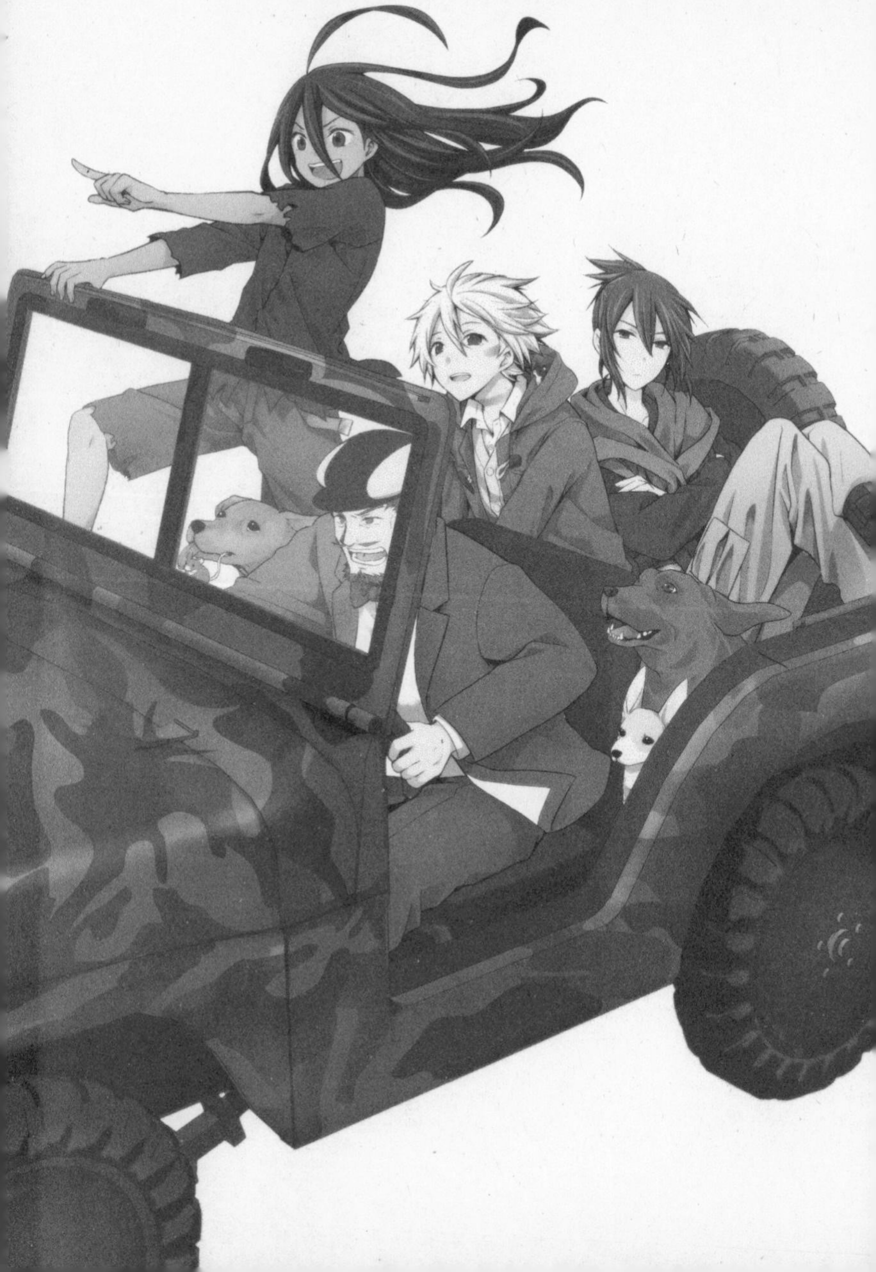

NO.6

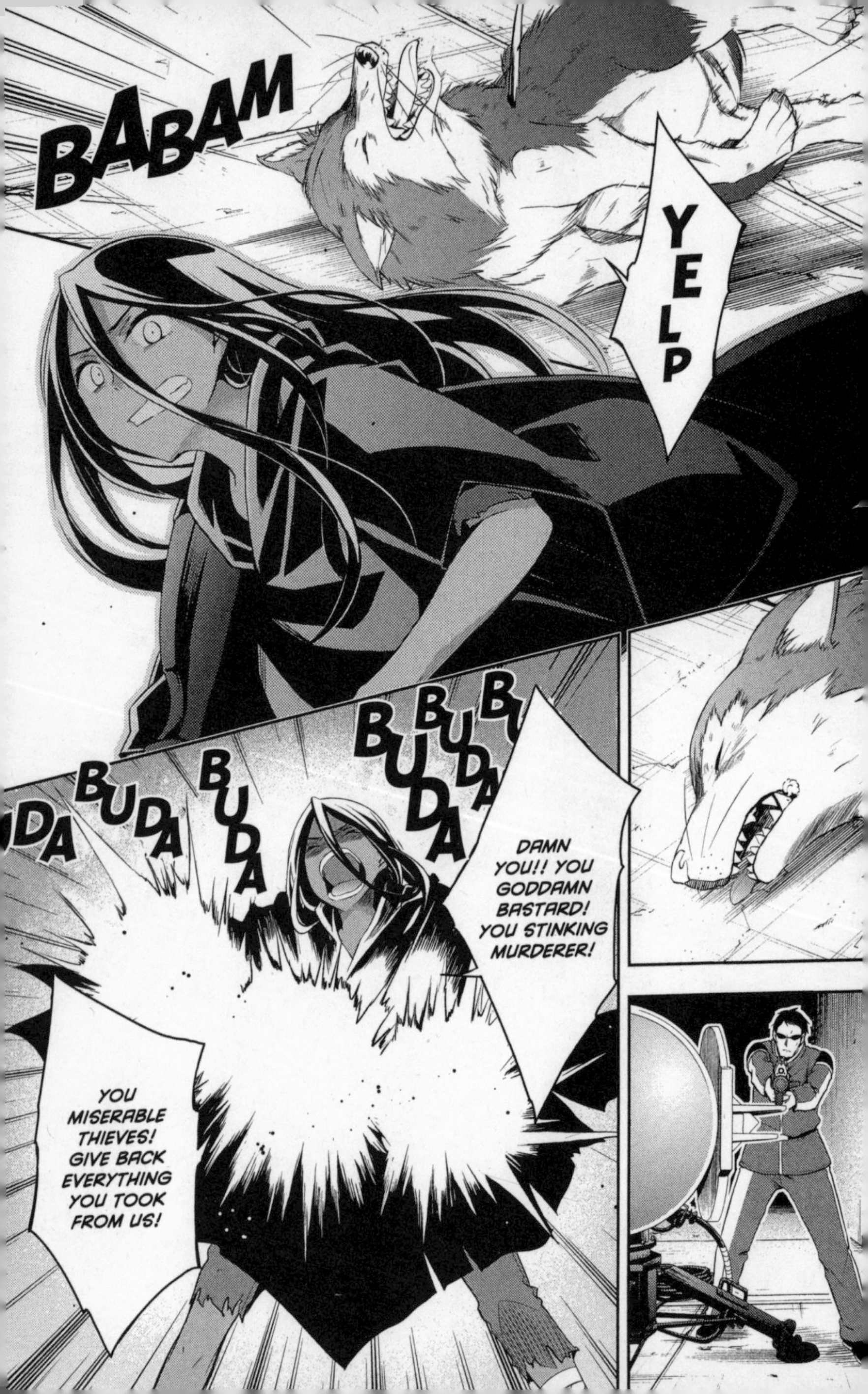
BABAM
YELP
BUDA BUDA B
DAMN YOU!! YOU GODDAMN BASTARD! YOU STINKING MURDERER!
BUDA
BUDA
DA
YOU MISERABLE THIEVES! GIVE BACK EVERYTHING YOU TOOK FROM US!

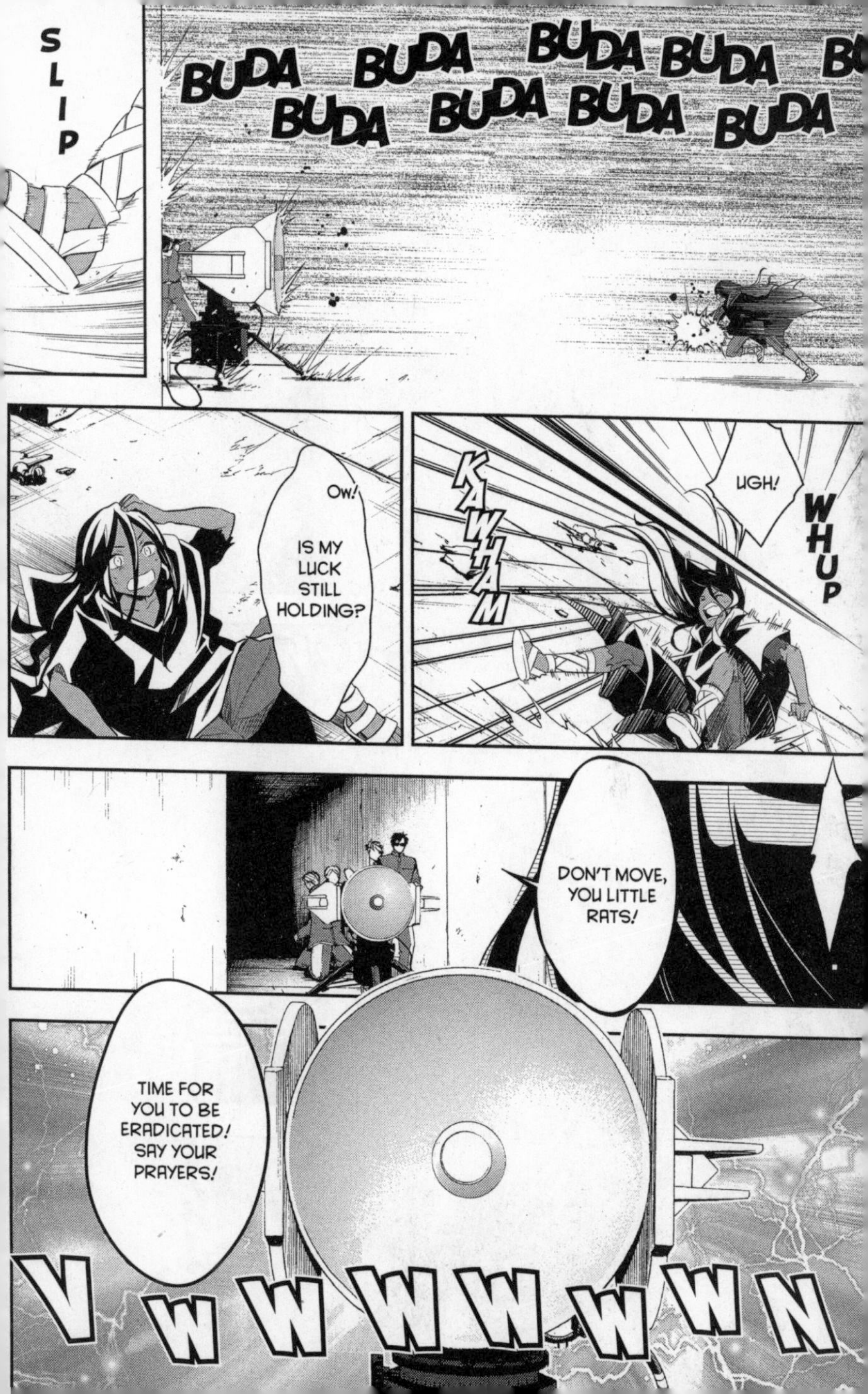
BUDA BUDA BUDA BUDA BU
BUDA BUDA BUDA BUDA
SLIP
KAWHAM
UGH!
WHUP
OW!
IS MY LUCK STILL HOLDING?
DON'T MOVE, YOU LITTLE RATS!
TIME FOR YOU TO BE ERADICATED! SAY YOUR PRAYERS!
VWWWWWWN

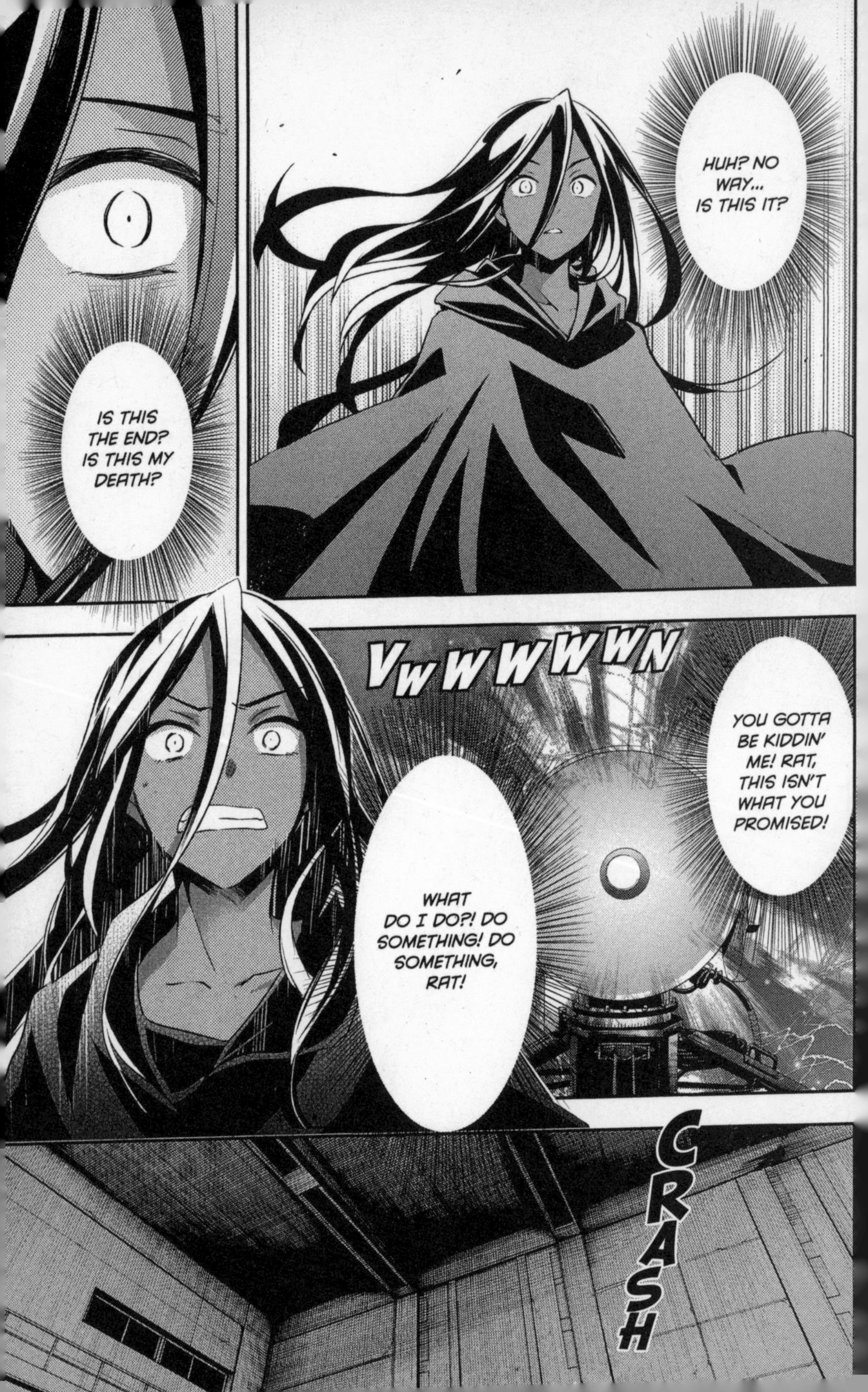
HUH? NO WAY... IS THIS IT?
IS THIS THE END? IS THIS MY DEATH?
VWWWWWN
YOU GOTTA BE KIDDIN' ME! RAT, THIS ISN'T WHAT YOU PROMISED!
WHAT DO I DO?! DO SOMETHING! DO SOMETHING, RAT!
CRASH

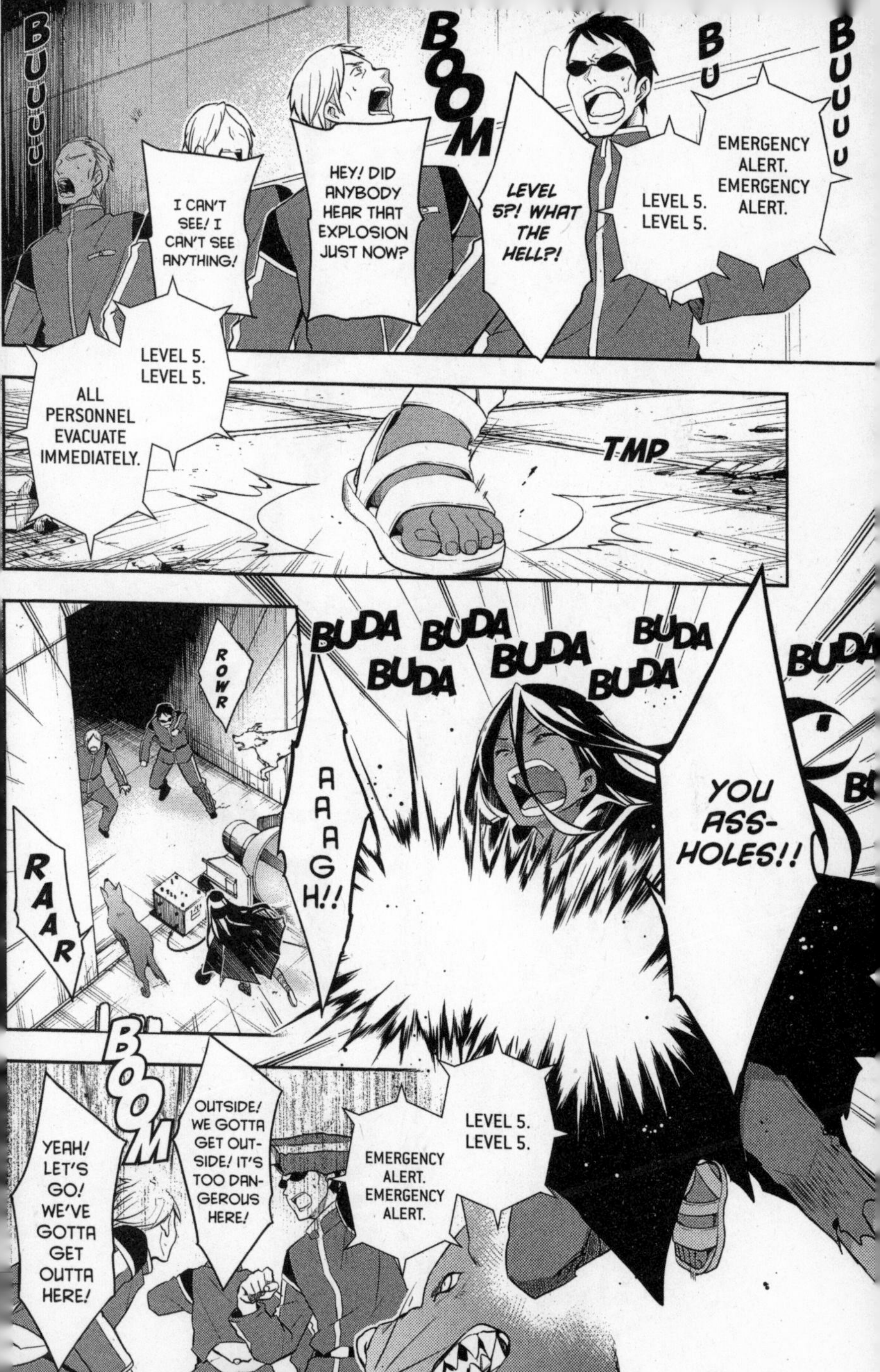
BUUUU
BU
EMERGENCY ALERT. EMERGENCY ALERT.
LEVEL 5. LEVEL 5.
LEVEL 5?! WHAT THE HELL?!
BOOM
HEY! DID ANYBODY HEAR THAT EXPLOSION JUST NOW?
I CAN'T SEE! I CAN'T SEE ANYTHING!
BUUUUU
LEVEL 5. LEVEL 5.
ALL PERSONNEL EVACUATE IMMEDIATELY.
TMP
BUDA BUDA BUDA BUDA BUDA BUDA BUDA BUDA
YOU ASS-HOLES!!
AAAAGH!!
ROWR
RAAR
LEVEL 5. LEVEL 5.
EMERGENCY ALERT. EMERGENCY ALERT.
OUTSIDE! WE GOTTA GET OUT-SIDE! IT'S TOO DAN-GEROUS HERE!
BOOM
YEAH! LET'S GO! WE'VE GOTTA GET OUTTA HERE!

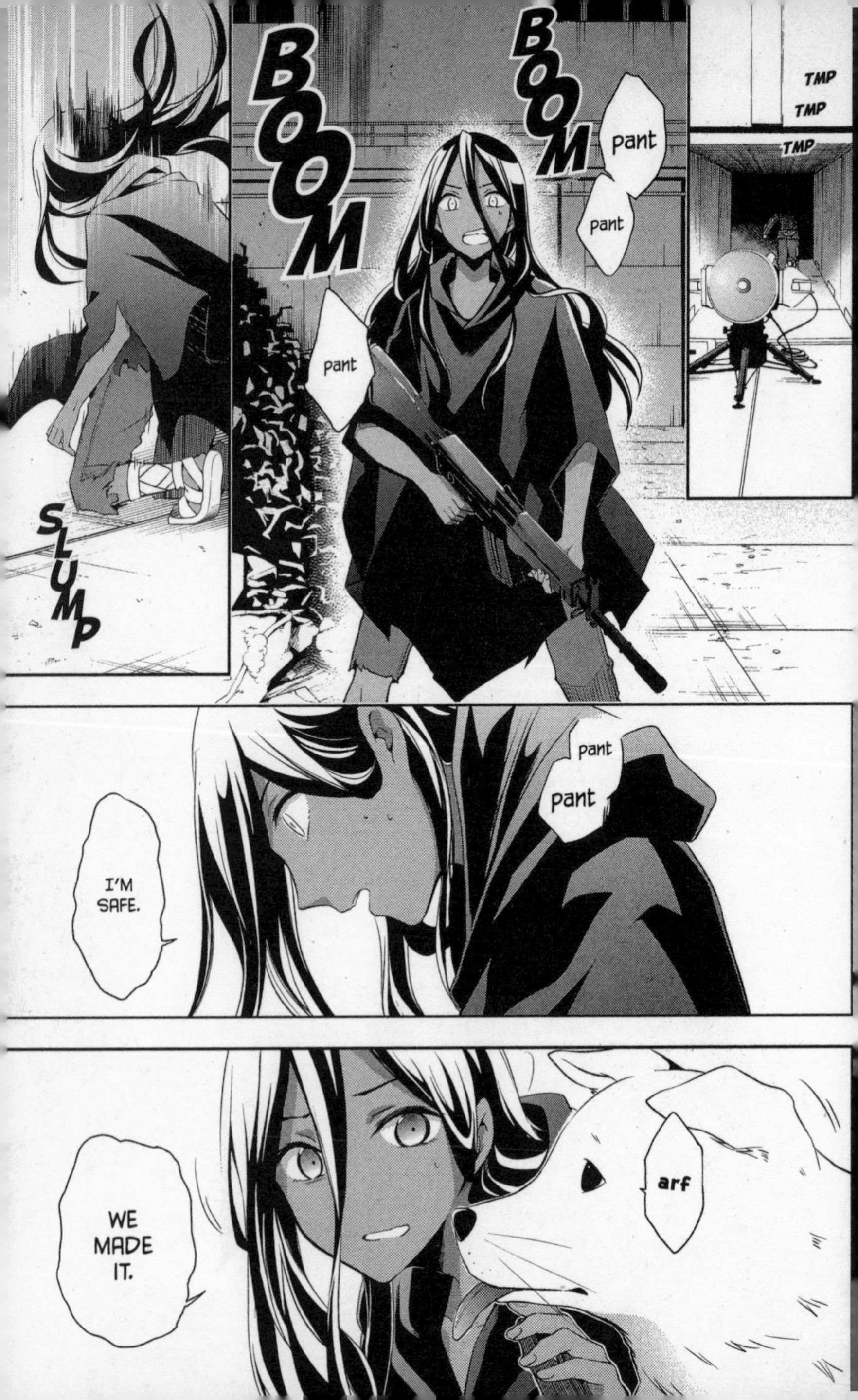
TMP
TMP
TMP
BOOM
pant
pant
BOOM
pant
SLUMP
pant
pant
I'M SAFE.
arf
WE MADE IT.

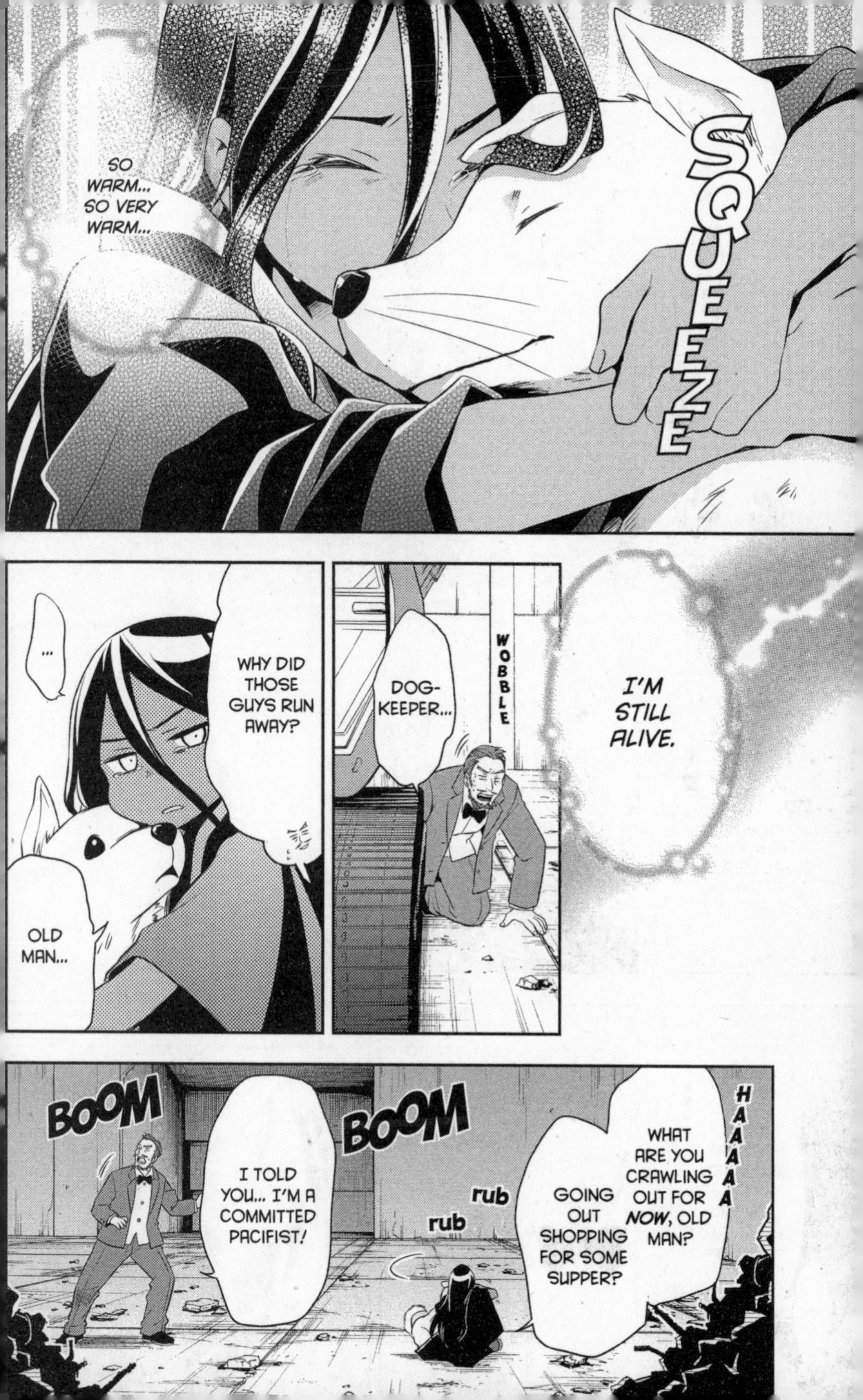
SQUEEZE
SO WARM... SO VERY WARM...
I'M STILL ALIVE.
WOBBLE
DOG-KEEPER...
WHY DID THOSE GUYS RUN AWAY?
...
OLD MAN...
HAAAAA
WHAT ARE YOU CRAWLING OUT FOR *NOW*, OLD MAN?
GOING OUT SHOPPING FOR SOME SUPPER?
rub
rub
BOOM
I TOLD YOU... I'M A COMMITTED PACIFIST!
BOOM

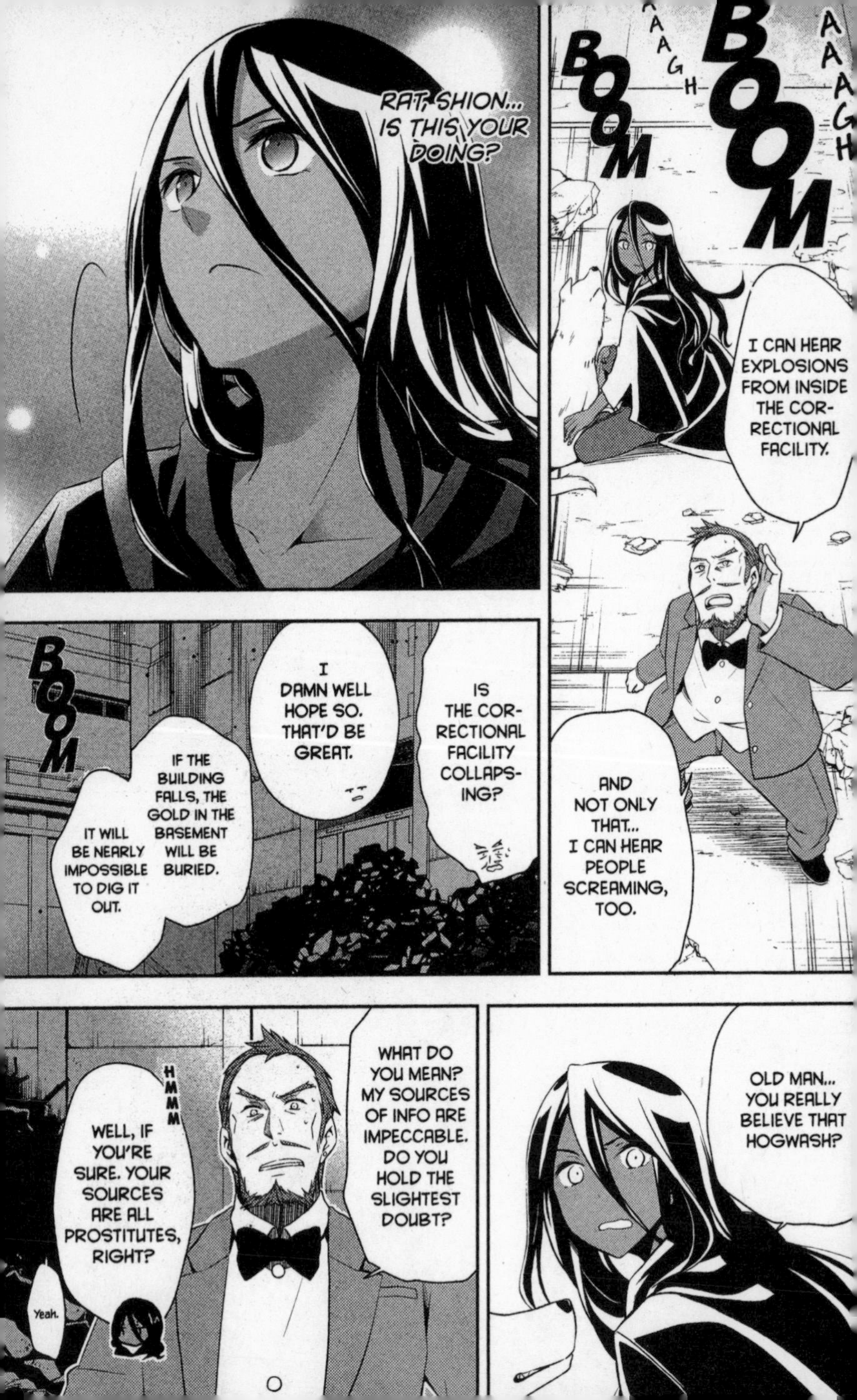
AAAGH
BOOM
BOOM
AAAAGH
I CAN HEAR EXPLOSIONS FROM INSIDE THE CORRECTIONAL FACILITY.
AND NOT ONLY THAT... I CAN HEAR PEOPLE SCREAMING, TOO.
RAT, SHION... IS THIS YOUR DOING?
BOOM
IS THE CORRECTIONAL FACILITY COLLAPSING?
I DAMN WELL HOPE SO. THAT'D BE GREAT.
IF THE BUILDING FALLS, THE GOLD IN THE BASEMENT WILL BE BURIED.
IT WILL BE NEARLY IMPOSSIBLE TO DIG IT OUT.
OLD MAN... YOU REALLY BELIEVE THAT HOGWASH?
WHAT DO YOU MEAN? MY SOURCES OF INFO ARE IMPECCABLE. DO YOU HOLD THE SLIGHTEST DOUBT?
HMMM
WELL, IF YOU'RE SURE. YOUR SOURCES ARE ALL PROSTITUTES, RIGHT?
Yeah.

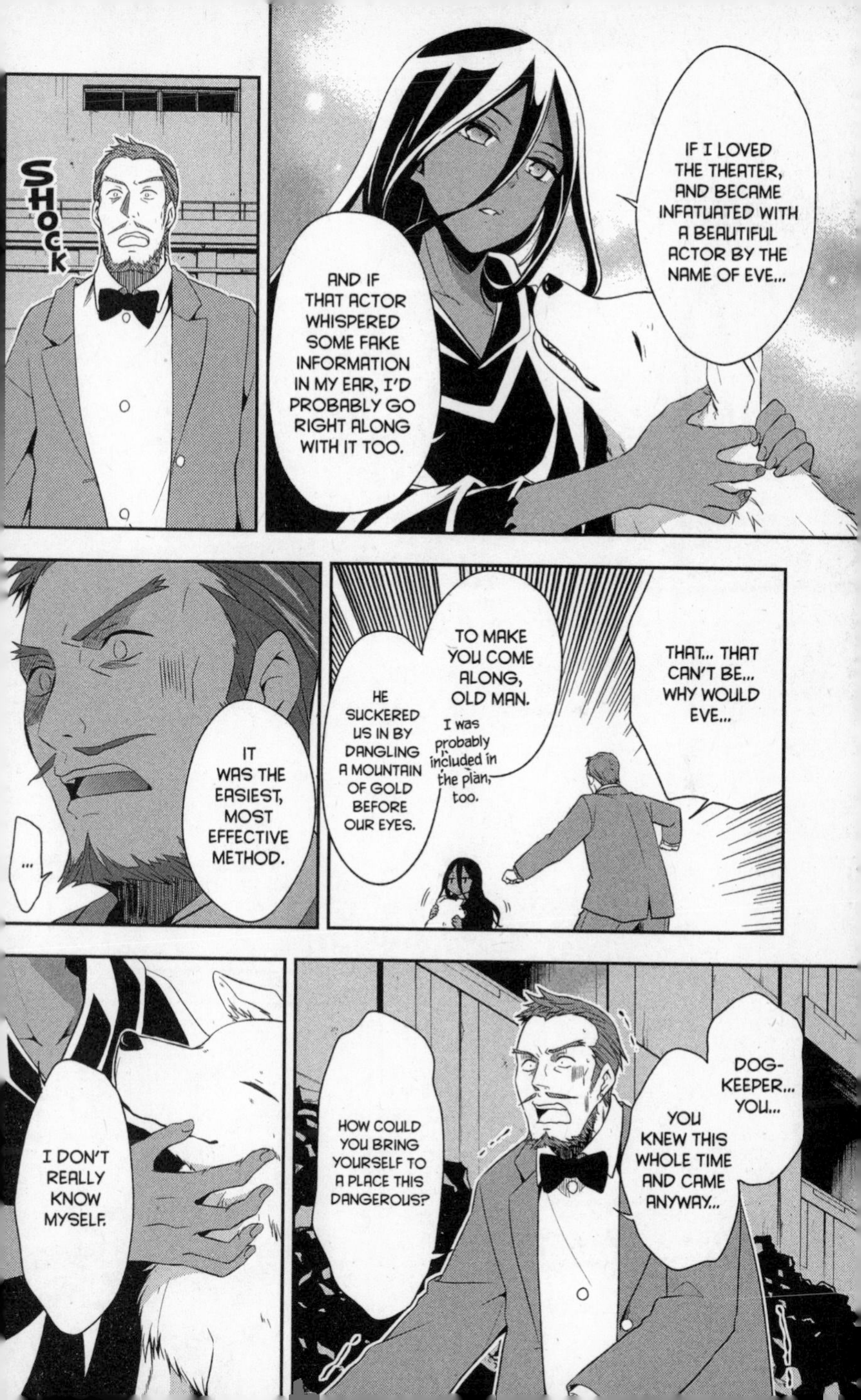
IF I LOVED THE THEATER, AND BECAME INFATUATED WITH A BEAUTIFUL ACTOR BY THE NAME OF EVE...
AND IF THAT ACTOR WHISPERED SOME FAKE INFORMATION IN MY EAR, I'D PROBABLY GO RIGHT ALONG WITH IT TOO.
SHOCK
THAT... THAT CAN'T BE... WHY WOULD EVE...
TO MAKE YOU COME ALONG, OLD MAN.
I was probably included in the plan, too.
HE SUCKERED US IN BY DANGLING A MOUNTAIN OF GOLD BEFORE OUR EYES.
IT WAS THE EASIEST, MOST EFFECTIVE METHOD.
...
DOG-KEEPER... YOU...
YOU KNEW THIS WHOLE TIME AND CAME ANYWAY...
HOW COULD YOU BRING YOURSELF TO A PLACE THIS DANGEROUS?
I DON'T REALLY KNOW MYSELF.

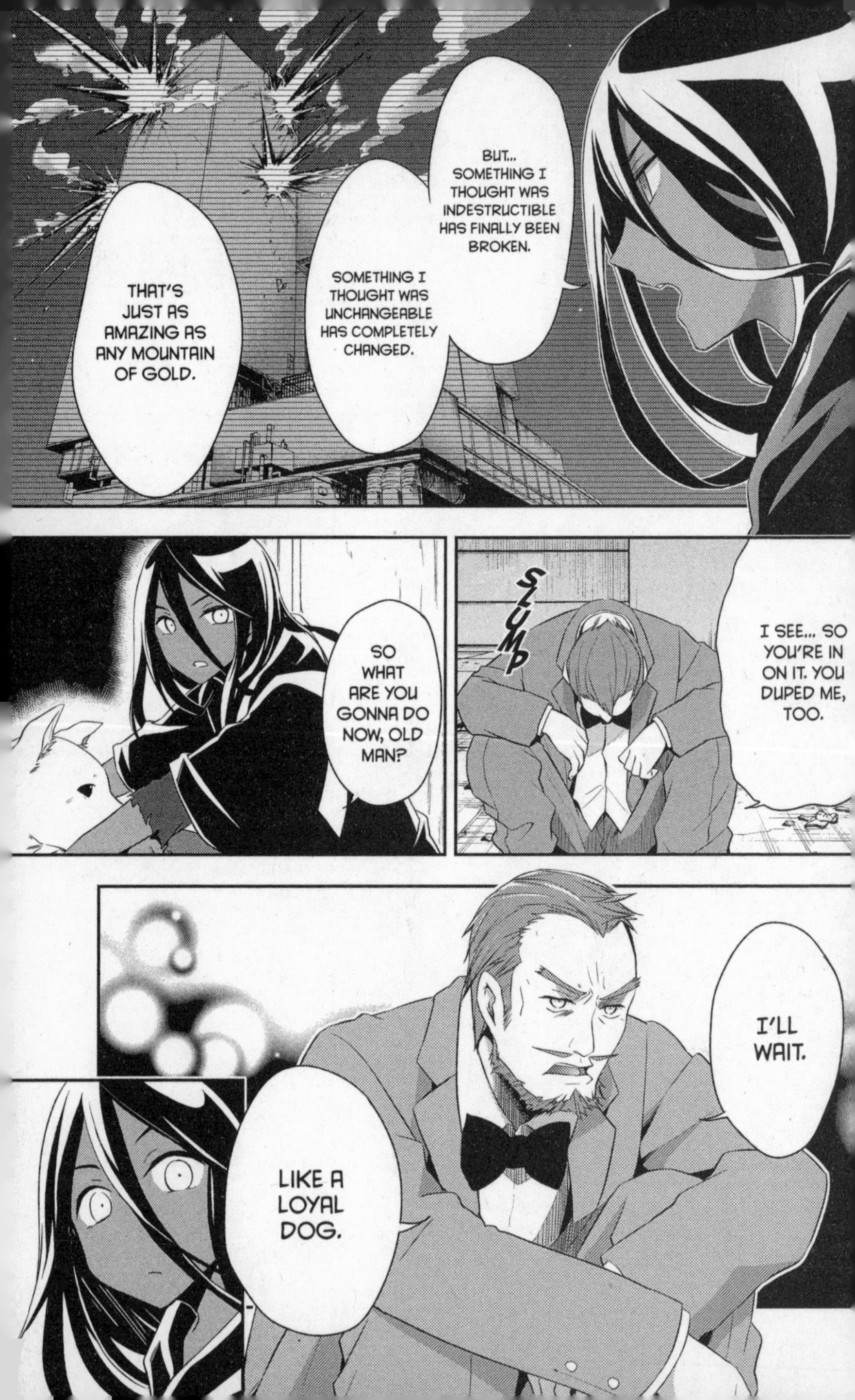
BUT... SOMETHING I THOUGHT WAS INDESTRUCTIBLE HAS FINALLY BEEN BROKEN.
SOMETHING I THOUGHT WAS UNCHANGEABLE HAS COMPLETELY CHANGED.
THAT'S JUST AS AMAZING AS ANY MOUNTAIN OF GOLD.
I SEE... SO YOU'RE IN ON IT. YOU DUPED ME, TOO.
SLUMP
SO WHAT ARE YOU GONNA DO NOW, OLD MAN?
I'LL WAIT.
LIKE A LOYAL DOG.

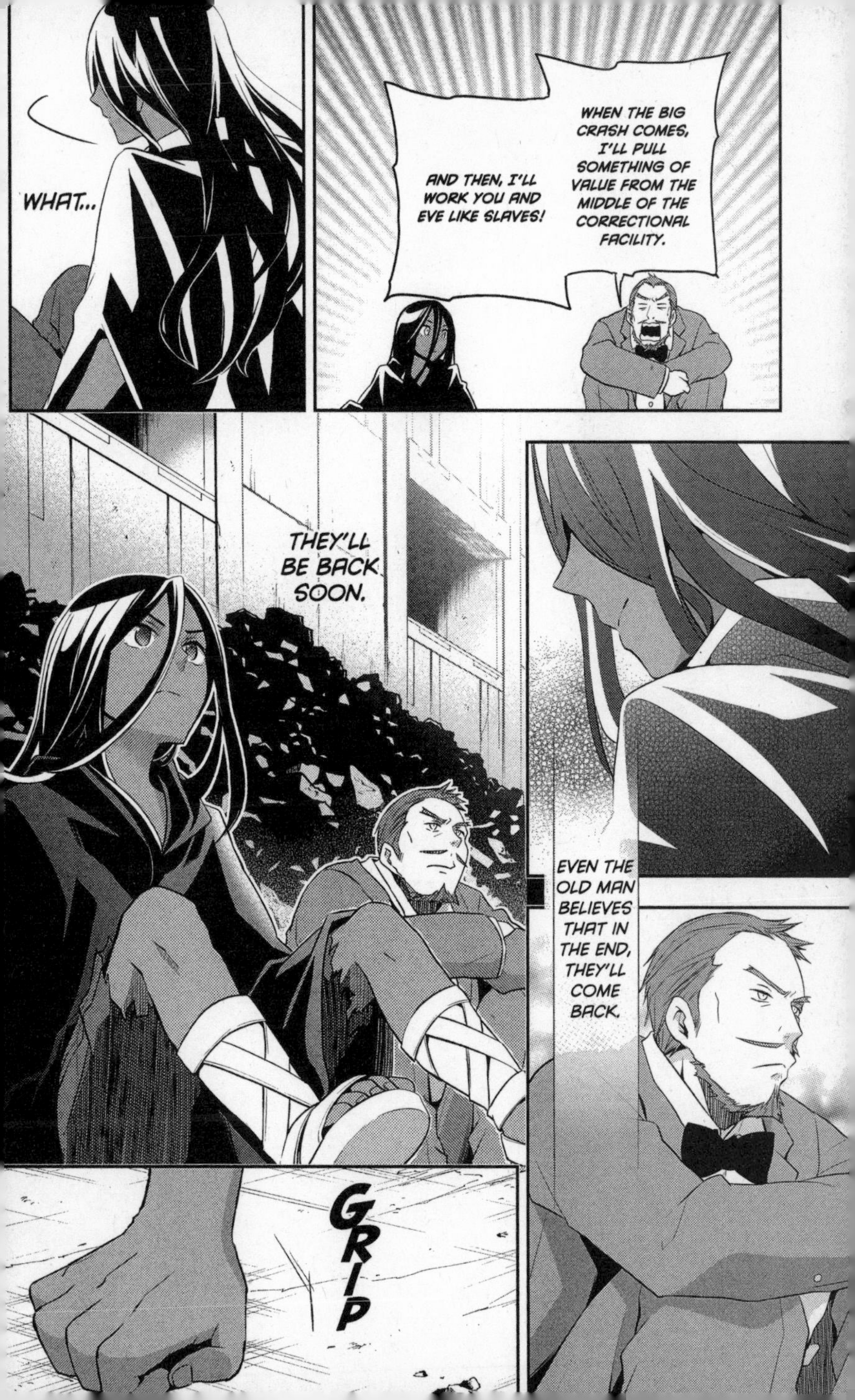
WHEN THE BIG CRASH COMES, I'LL PULL SOMETHING OF VALUE FROM THE MIDDLE OF THE CORRECTIONAL FACILITY.
AND THEN, I'LL WORK YOU AND EVE LIKE SLAVES!
WHAT...
EVEN THE OLD MAN BELIEVES THAT IN THE END, THEY'LL COME BACK.
THEY'LL BE BACK SOON.
GRIP

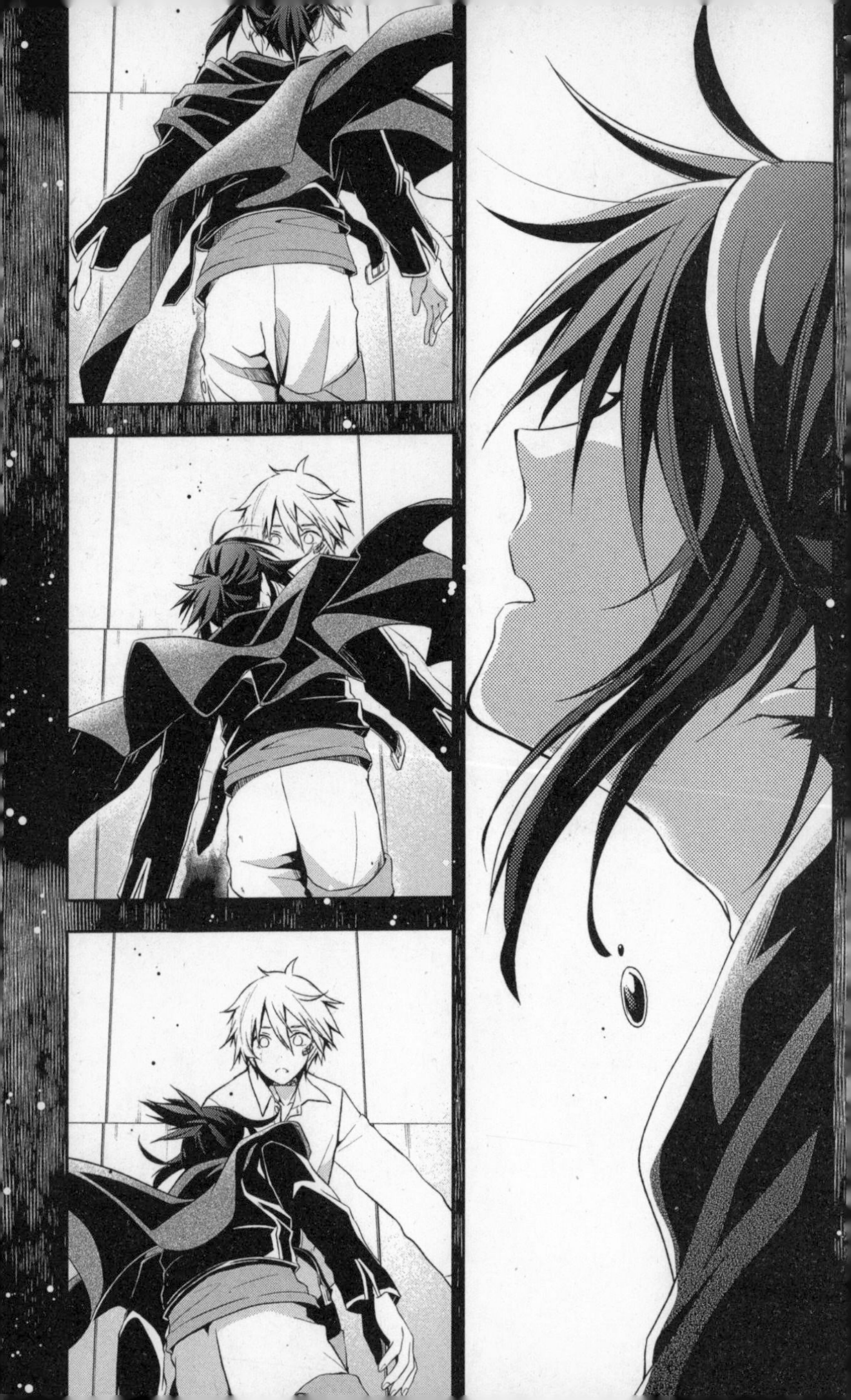

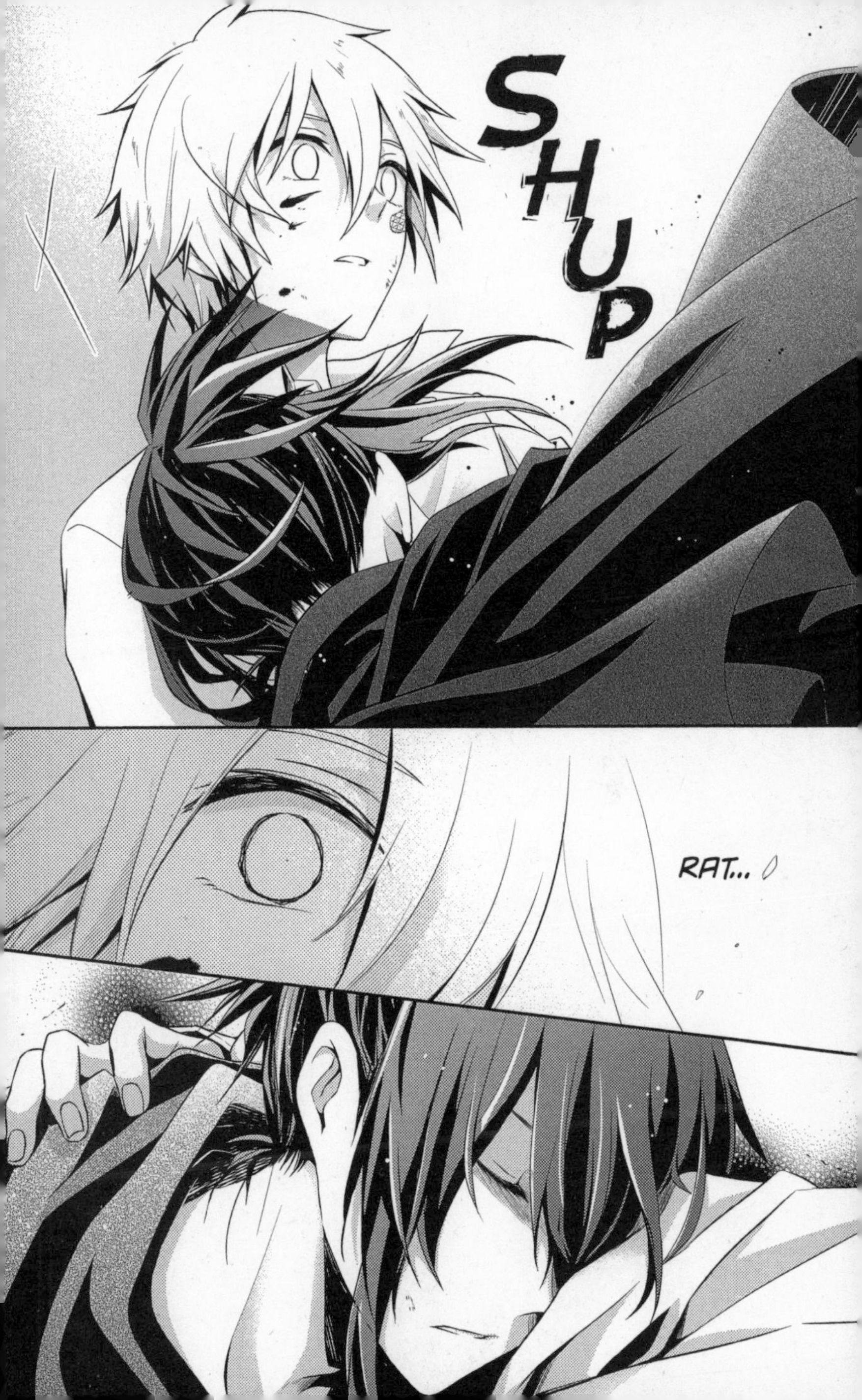
SHUP
RAT...

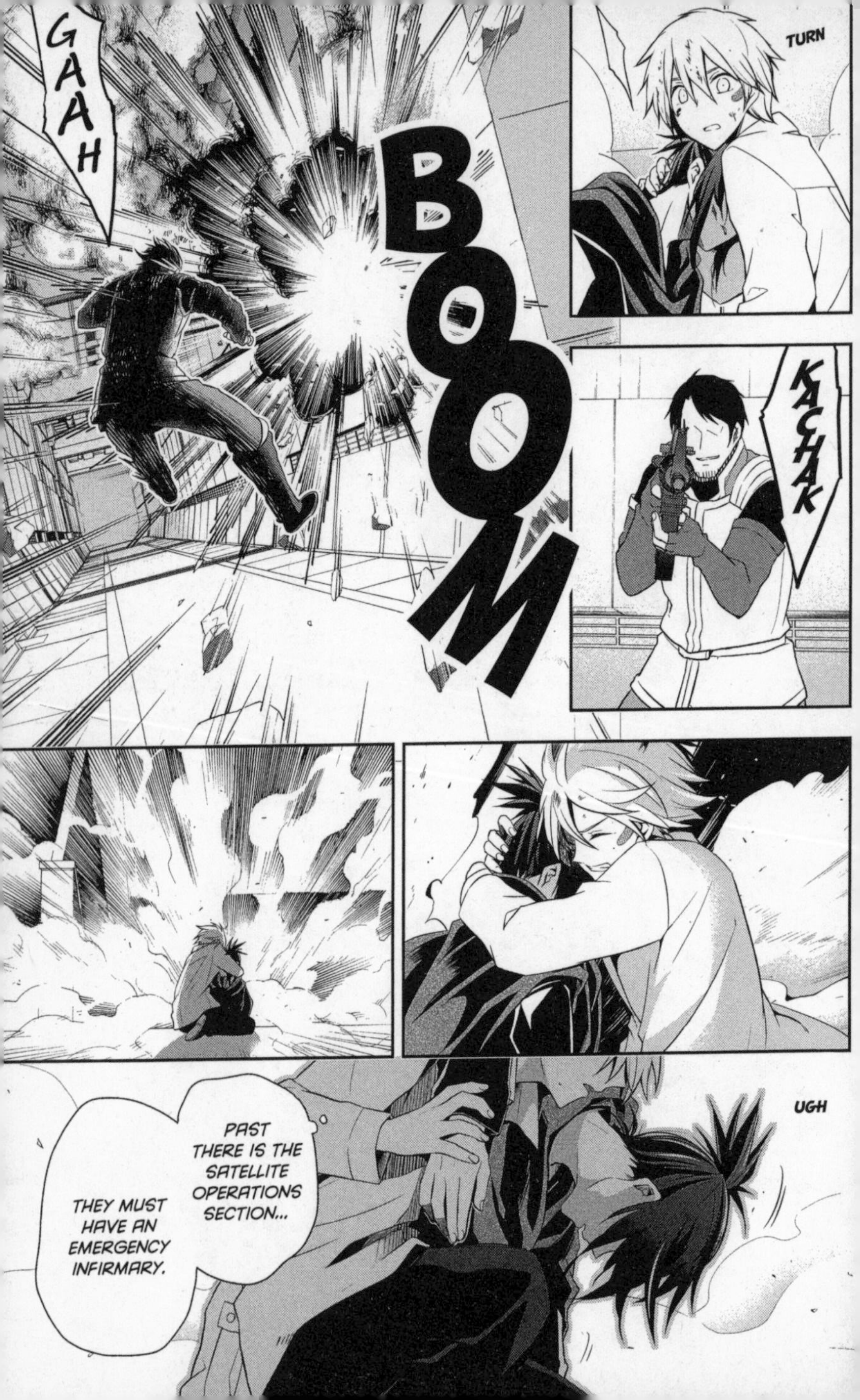
TURN
KACHAK
BOOM
GAAH
UGH
PAST THERE IS THE SATELLITE OPERATIONS SECTION...
THEY MUST HAVE AN EMERGENCY INFIRMARY.

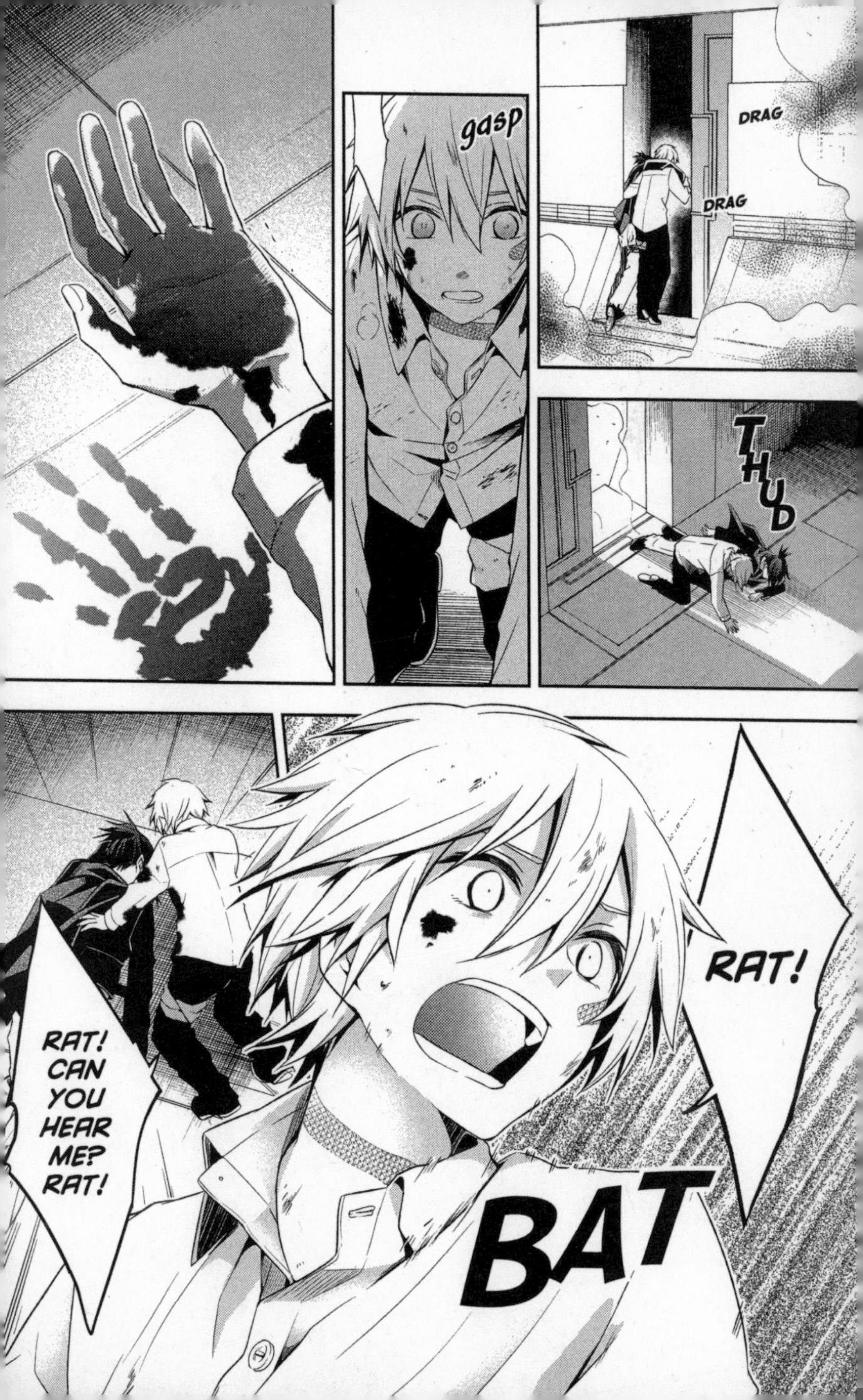
DRAG
DRAG
THUD
gasp
RAT!
RAT! CAN YOU HEAR ME? RAT!
BAT

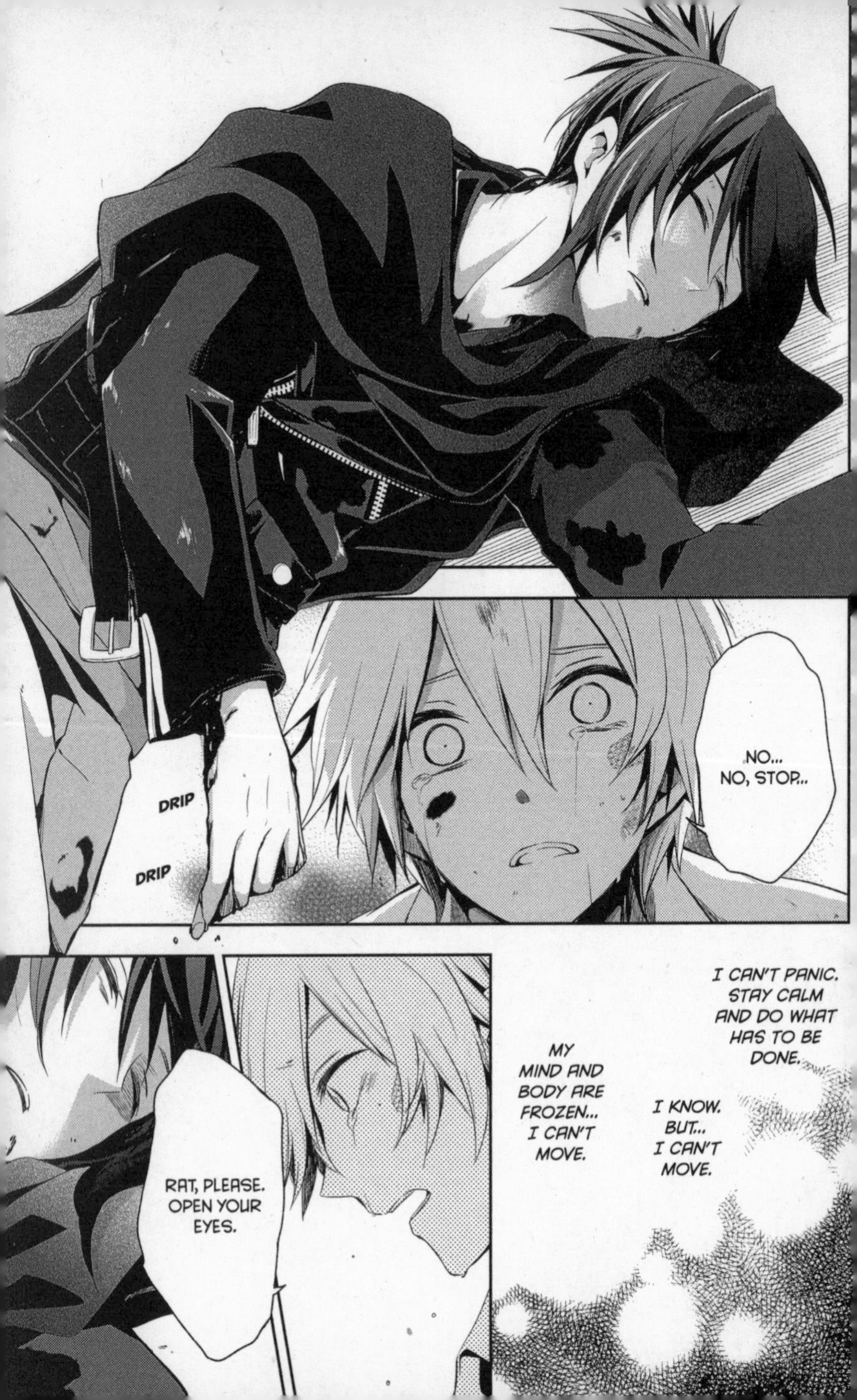
NO... NO, STOP...
DRIP
DRIP
I CAN'T PANIC. STAY CALM AND DO WHAT HAS TO BE DONE.
I KNOW. BUT... I CAN'T MOVE.
MY MIND AND BODY ARE FROZEN... I CAN'T MOVE.
RAT, PLEASE. OPEN YOUR EYES.

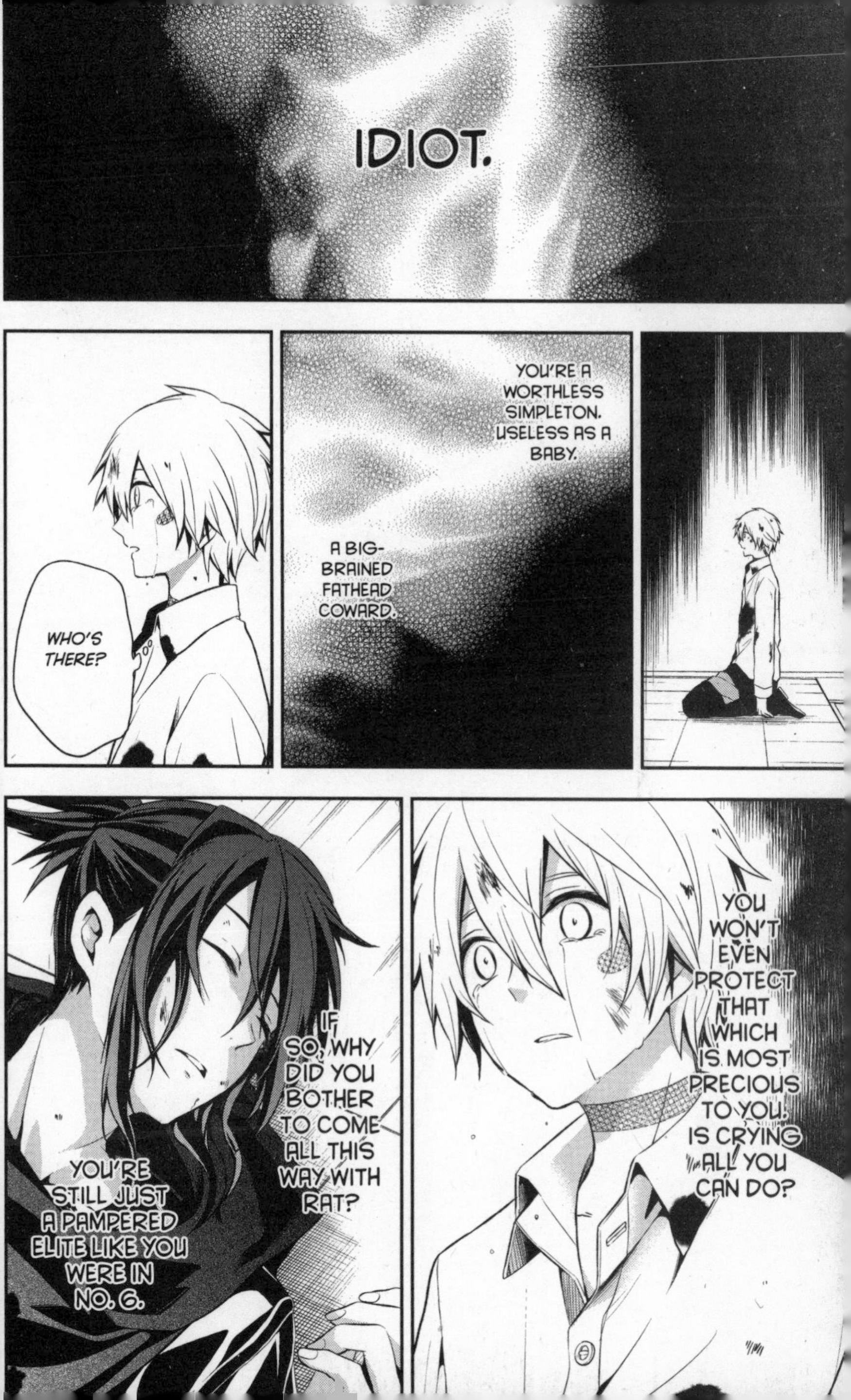
IDIOT.
YOU'RE A WORTHLESS SIMPLETON. USELESS AS A BABY.
A BIG-BRAINED FATHEAD COWARD.
WHO'S THERE?
YOU WON'T EVEN PROTECT THAT WHICH IS MOST PRECIOUS TO YOU. IS CRYING ALL YOU CAN DO?
IF SO, WHY DID YOU BOTHER TO COME ALL THIS WAY WITH RAT?
YOU'RE STILL JUST A PAMPERED ELITE LIKE YOU WERE IN NO. 6.

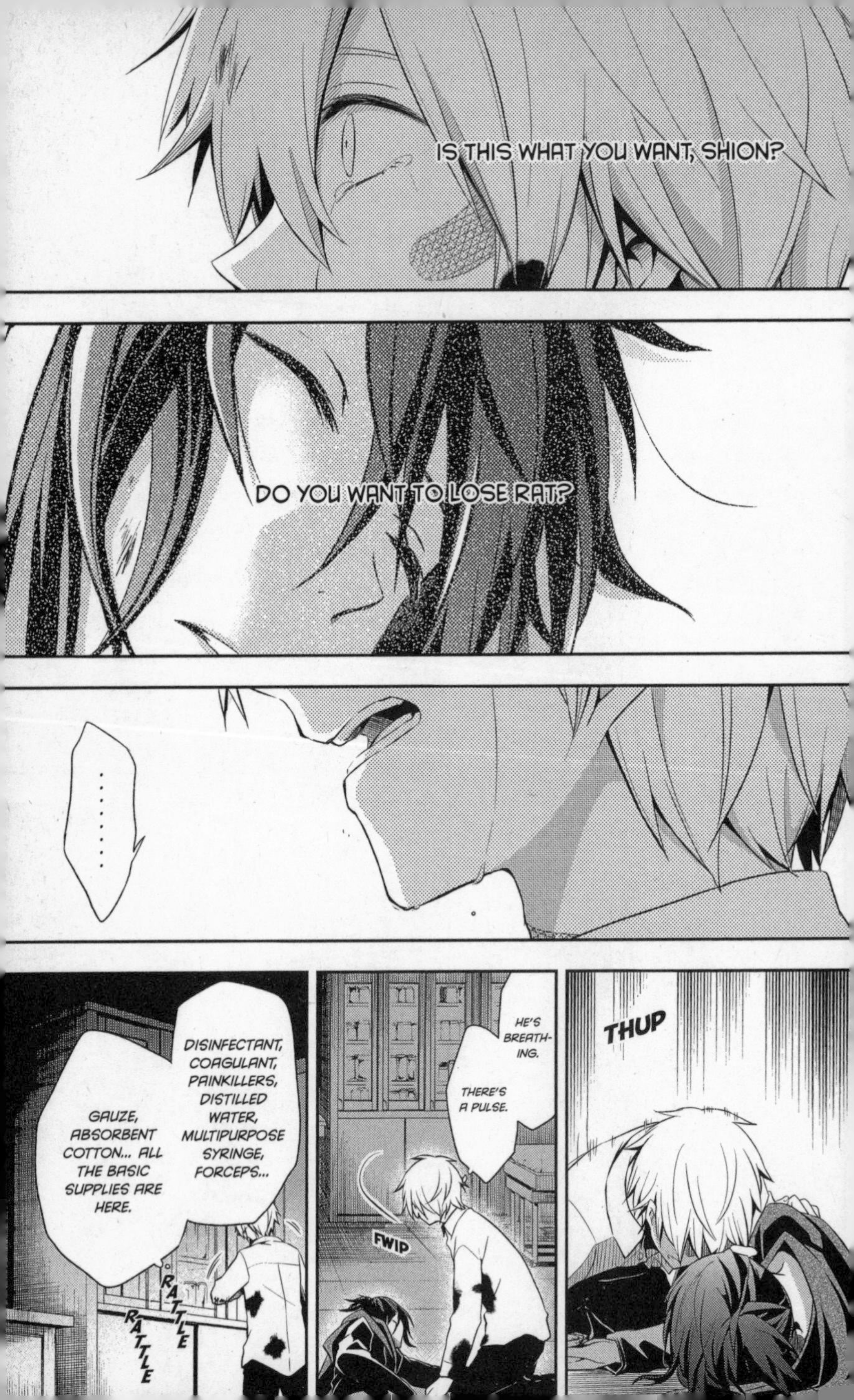
IS THIS WHAT YOU WANT, SHION?
DO YOU WANT TO LOSE RAT?
......
THUP
HE'S BREATHING.
THERE'S A PULSE.
FWIP
DISINFECTANT, COAGULANT, PAINKILLERS, DISTILLED WATER, MULTIPURPOSE SYRINGE, FORCEPS...
GAUZE, ABSORBENT COTTON... ALL THE BASIC SUPPLIES ARE HERE.
RATTLE
RATTLE

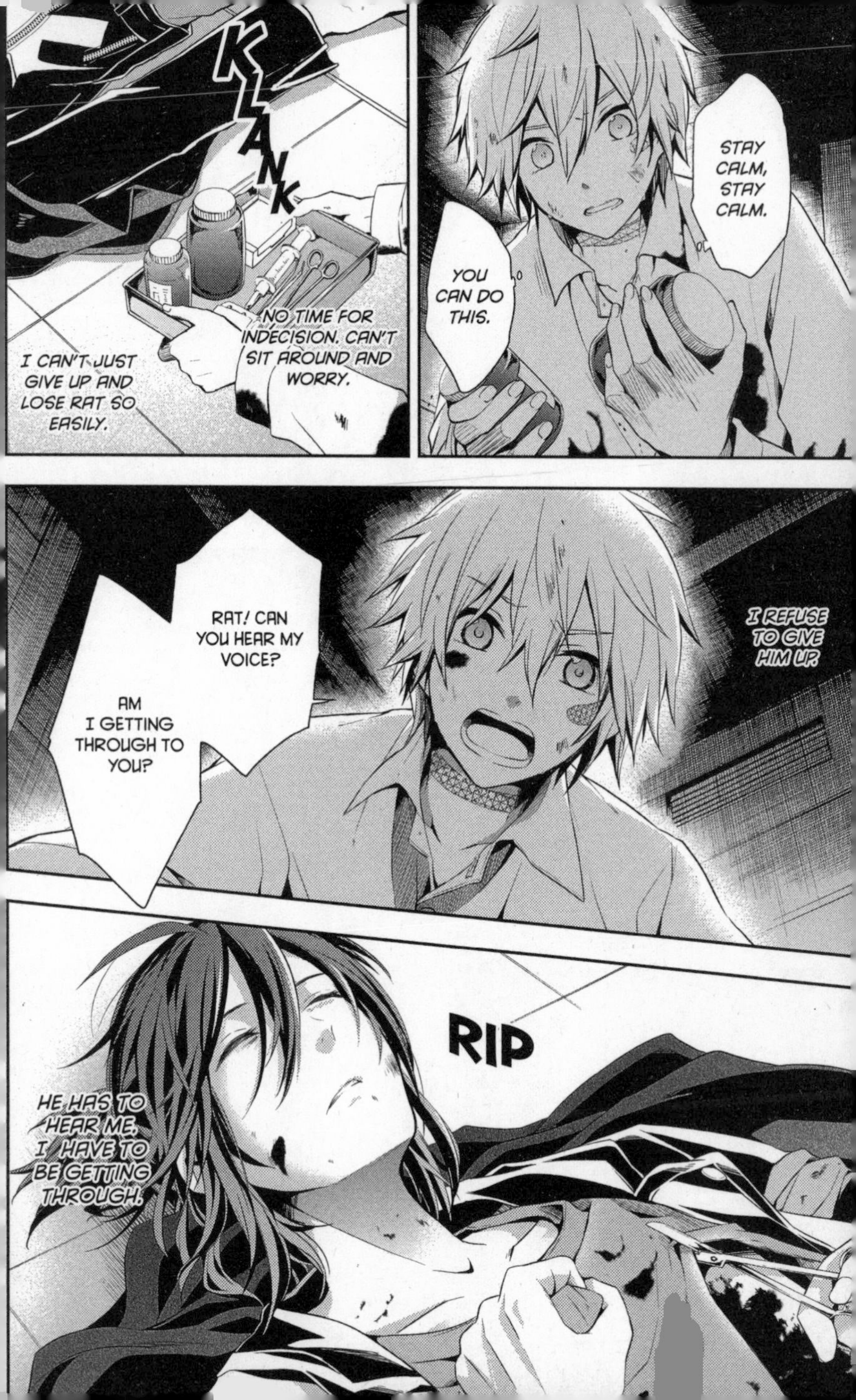
STAY CALM, STAY CALM.
YOU CAN DO THIS.
KLANK
NO TIME FOR INDECISION. CAN'T SIT AROUND AND WORRY.
I CAN'T JUST GIVE UP AND LOSE RAT SO EASILY.
I REFUSE TO GIVE HIM UP.
RAT! CAN YOU HEAR MY VOICE?
AM I GETTING THROUGH TO YOU?
RIP
HE HAS TO HEAR ME. I HAVE TO BE GETTING THROUGH.

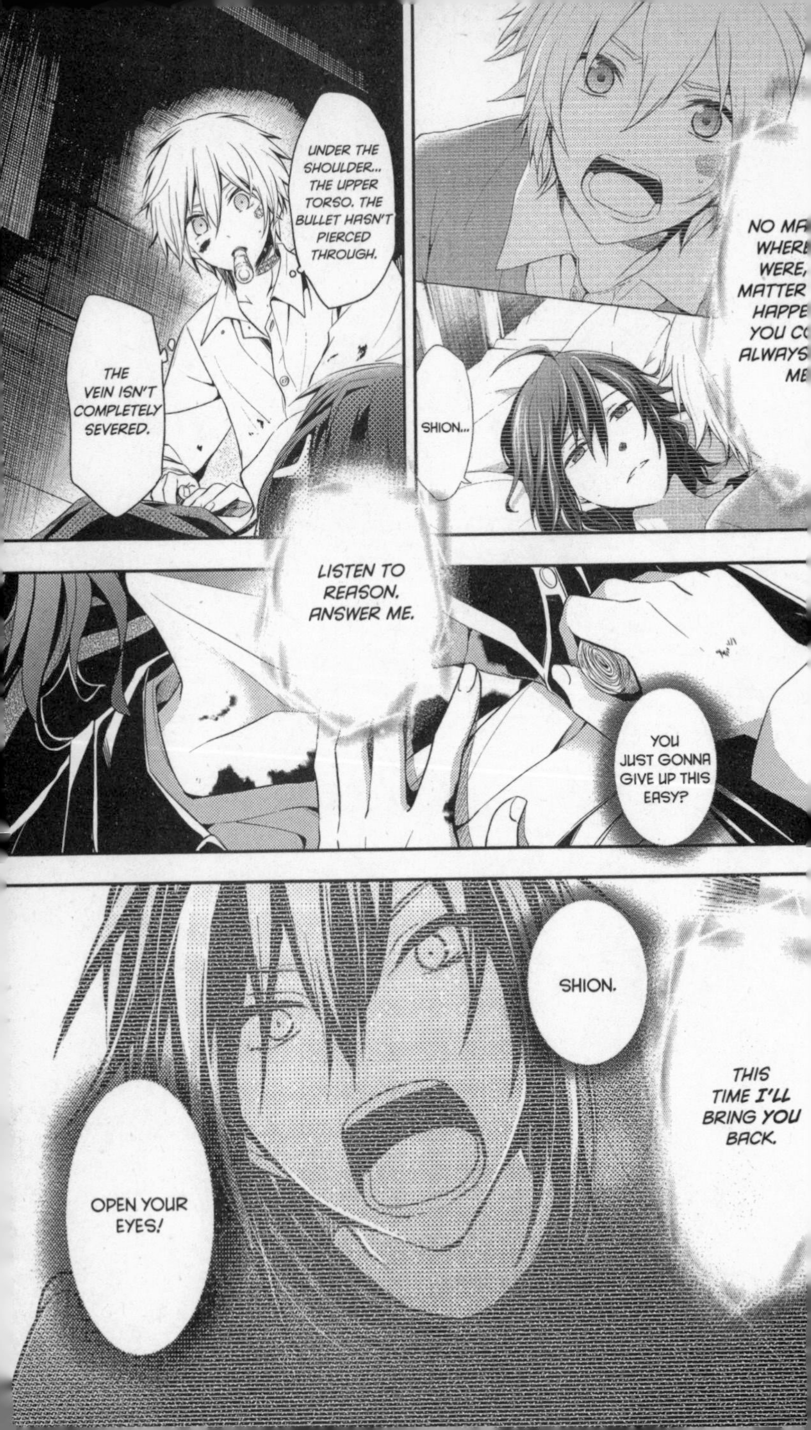
NO MA WHERE WERE, MATTER HAPPE YOU C ALWAYS ME
SHION...
UNDER THE SHOULDER... THE UPPER TORSO. THE BULLET HASN'T PIERCED THROUGH.
THE VEIN ISN'T COMPLETELY SEVERED.
YOU JUST GONNA GIVE UP THIS EASY?
LISTEN TO REASON. ANSWER ME.
THIS TIME I'LL BRING YOU BACK.
SHION.
OPEN YOUR EYES!

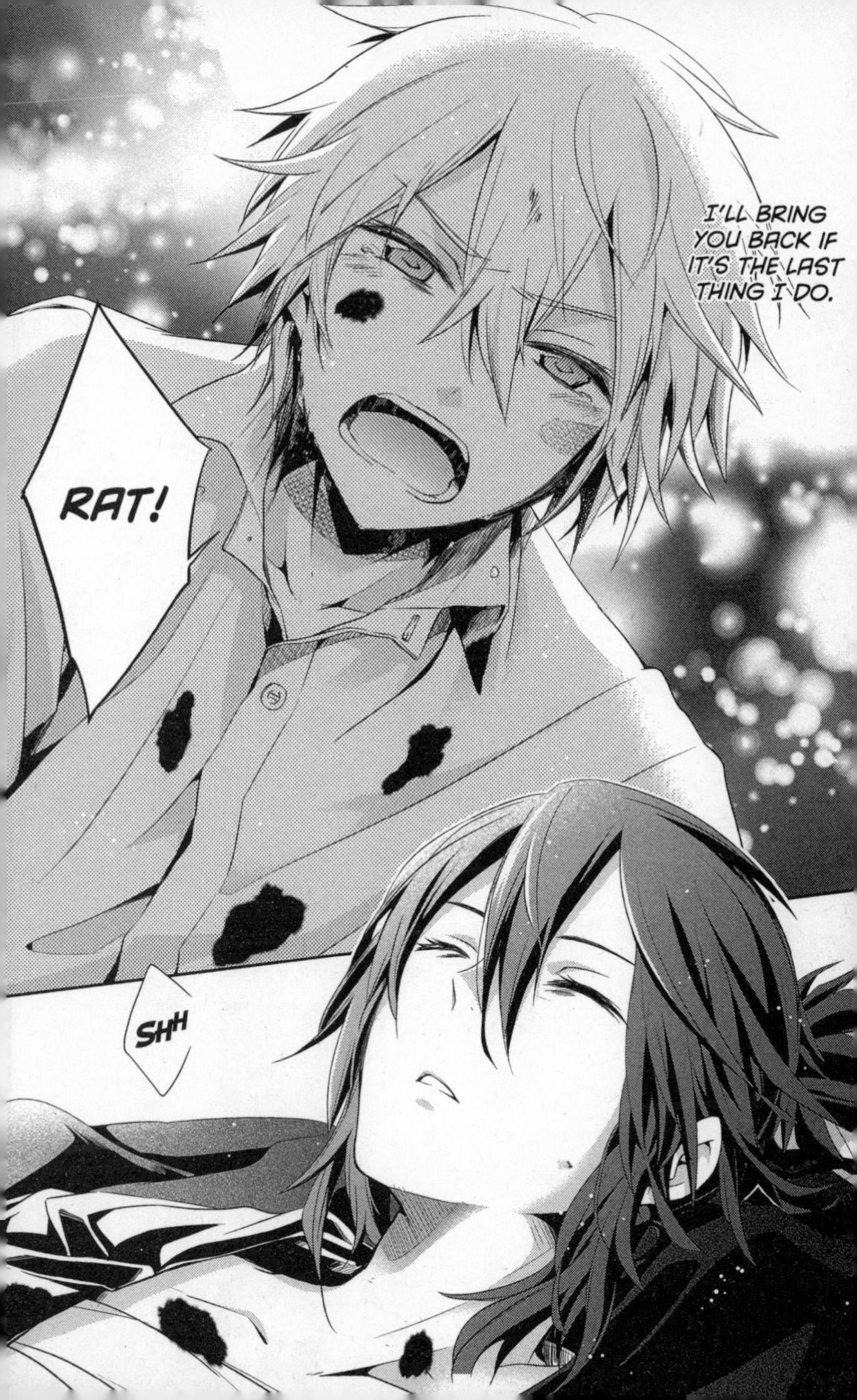
I'LL BRING YOU BACK IF IT'S THE LAST THING I DO.
RAT!
SHH

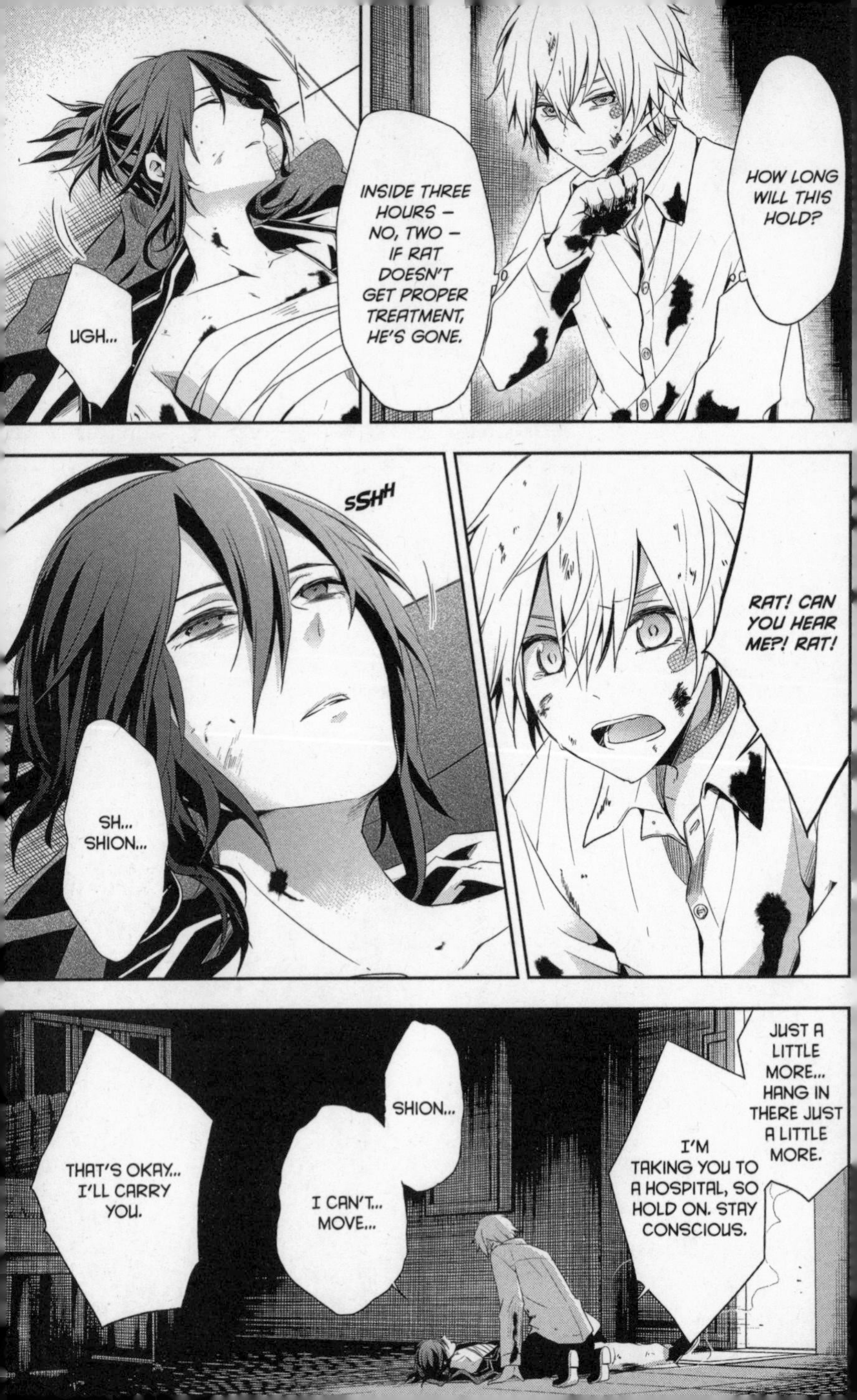
HOW LONG WILL THIS HOLD?
INSIDE THREE HOURS – NO, TWO – IF RAT DOESN'T GET PROPER TREATMENT, HE'S GONE.
UGH...
RAT! CAN YOU HEAR ME?! RAT!
SSHH
SH... SHION...
JUST A LITTLE MORE... HANG IN THERE JUST A LITTLE MORE.
I'M TAKING YOU TO A HOSPITAL, SO HOLD ON. STAY CONSCIOUS.
SHION...
I CAN'T... MOVE...
THAT'S OKAY... I'LL CARRY YOU.

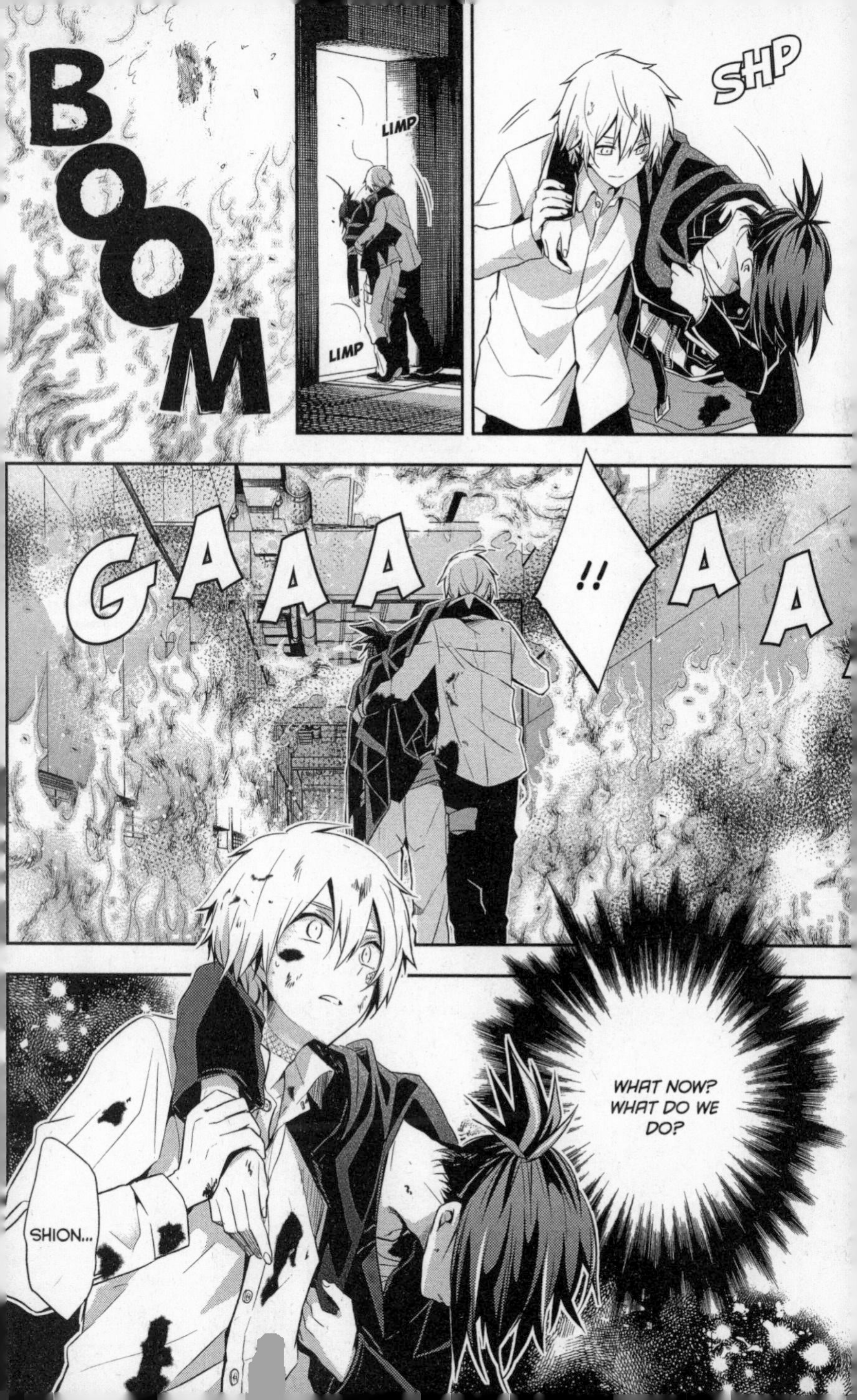
SHP
LIMP
LIMP
BOOM
GAAAAA
!!
WHAT NOW? WHAT DO WE DO?
SHION...

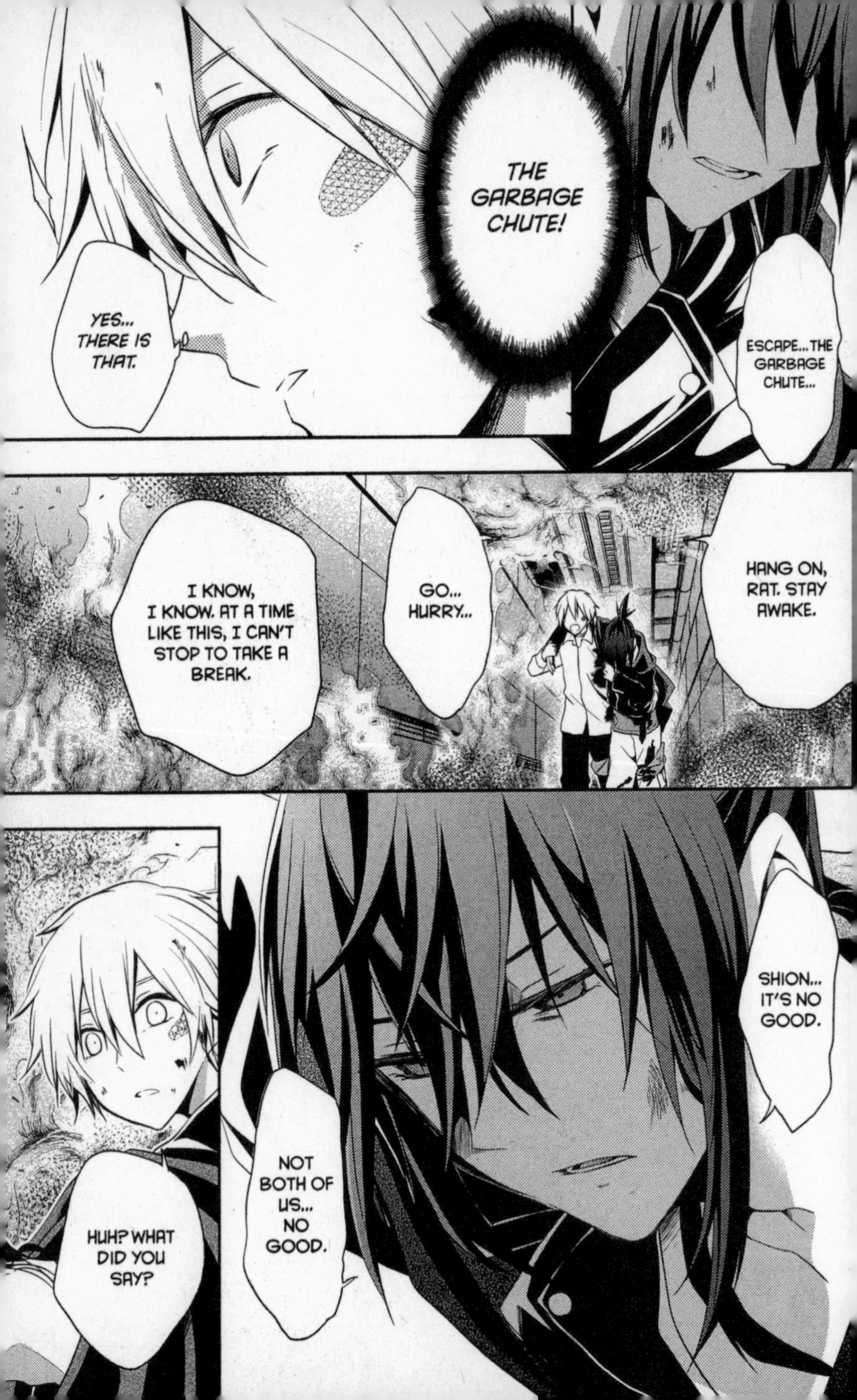
ESCAPE...THE GARBAGE CHUTE...
THE GARBAGE CHUTE!
YES... THERE IS THAT.
HANG ON, RAT. STAY AWAKE.
GO... HURRY...
I KNOW, I KNOW. AT A TIME LIKE THIS, I CAN'T STOP TO TAKE A BREAK.
SHION... IT'S NO GOOD.
NOT BOTH OF US... NO GOOD.
HUH? WHAT DID YOU SAY?

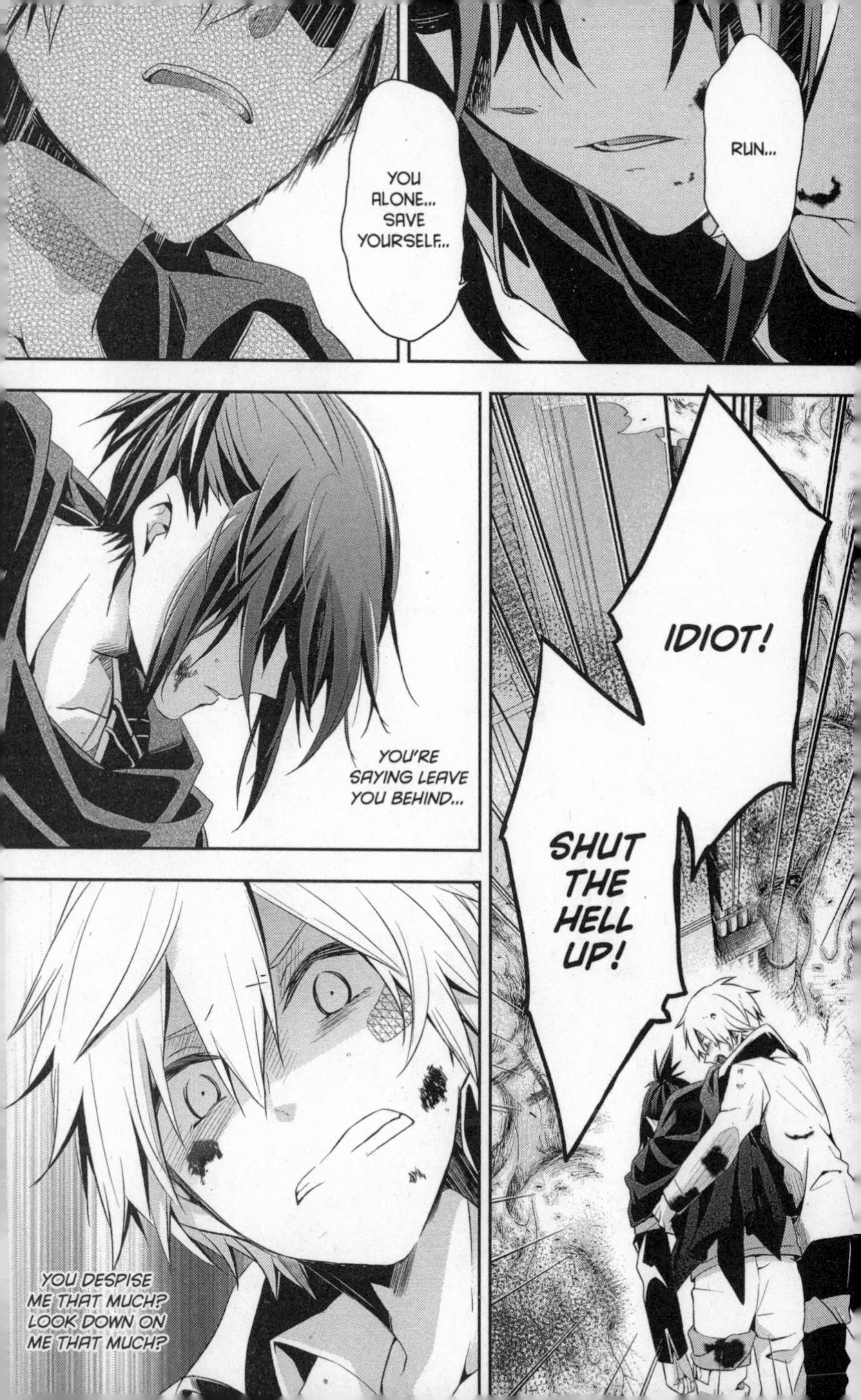
RUN...
YOU ALONE... SAVE YOURSELF...
YOU'RE SAYING LEAVE YOU BEHIND...
YOU DESPISE ME THAT MUCH? LOOK DOWN ON ME THAT MUCH?
IDIOT!
SHUT THE HELL UP!

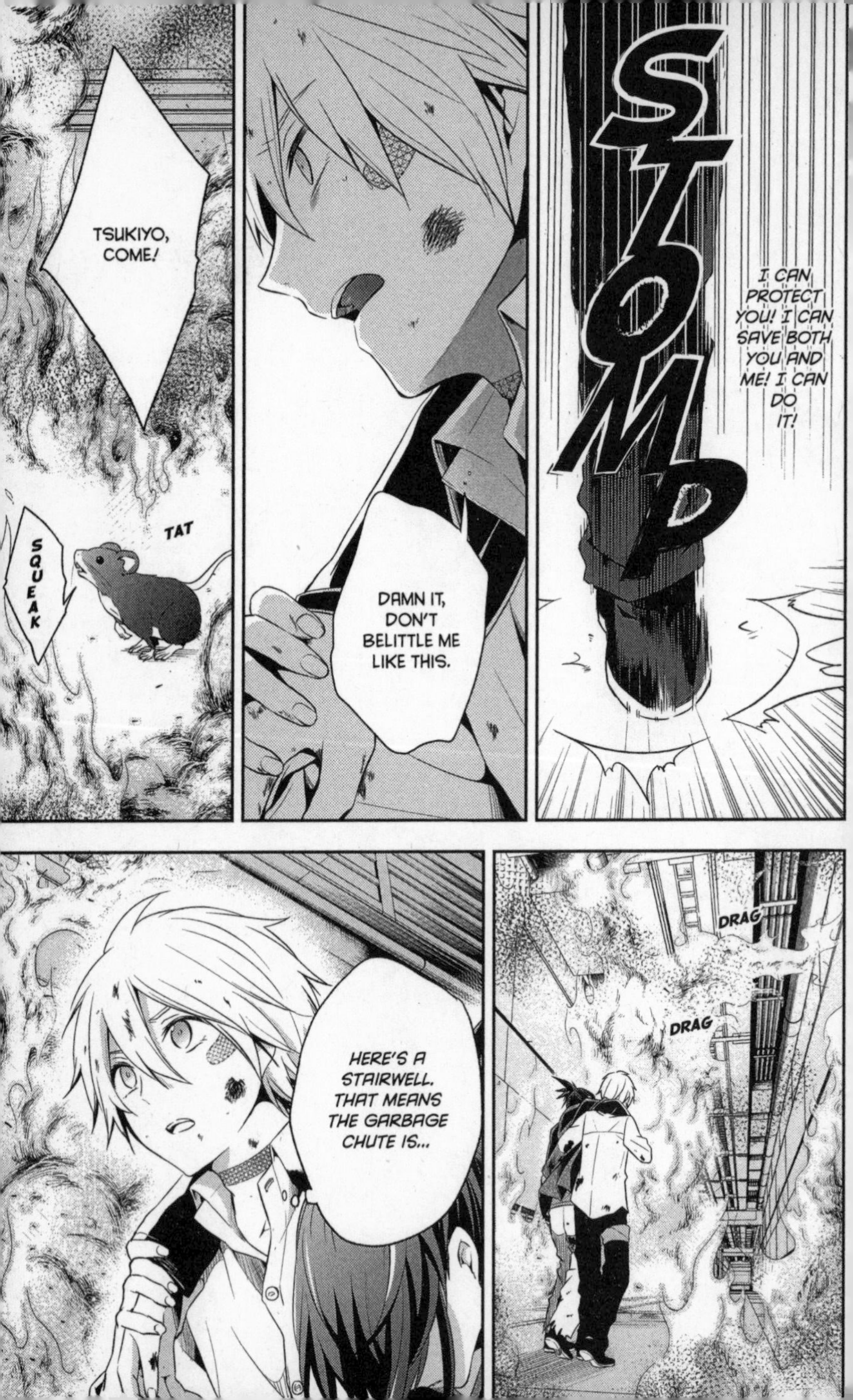
STOMP
I CAN PROTECT YOU! I CAN SAVE BOTH YOU AND ME! I CAN DO IT!
DAMN IT, DON'T BELITTLE ME LIKE THIS.
TSUKIYO, COME!
TAT
SQUEAK
DRAG
DRAG
HERE'S A STAIRWELL. THAT MEANS THE GARBAGE CHUTE IS...

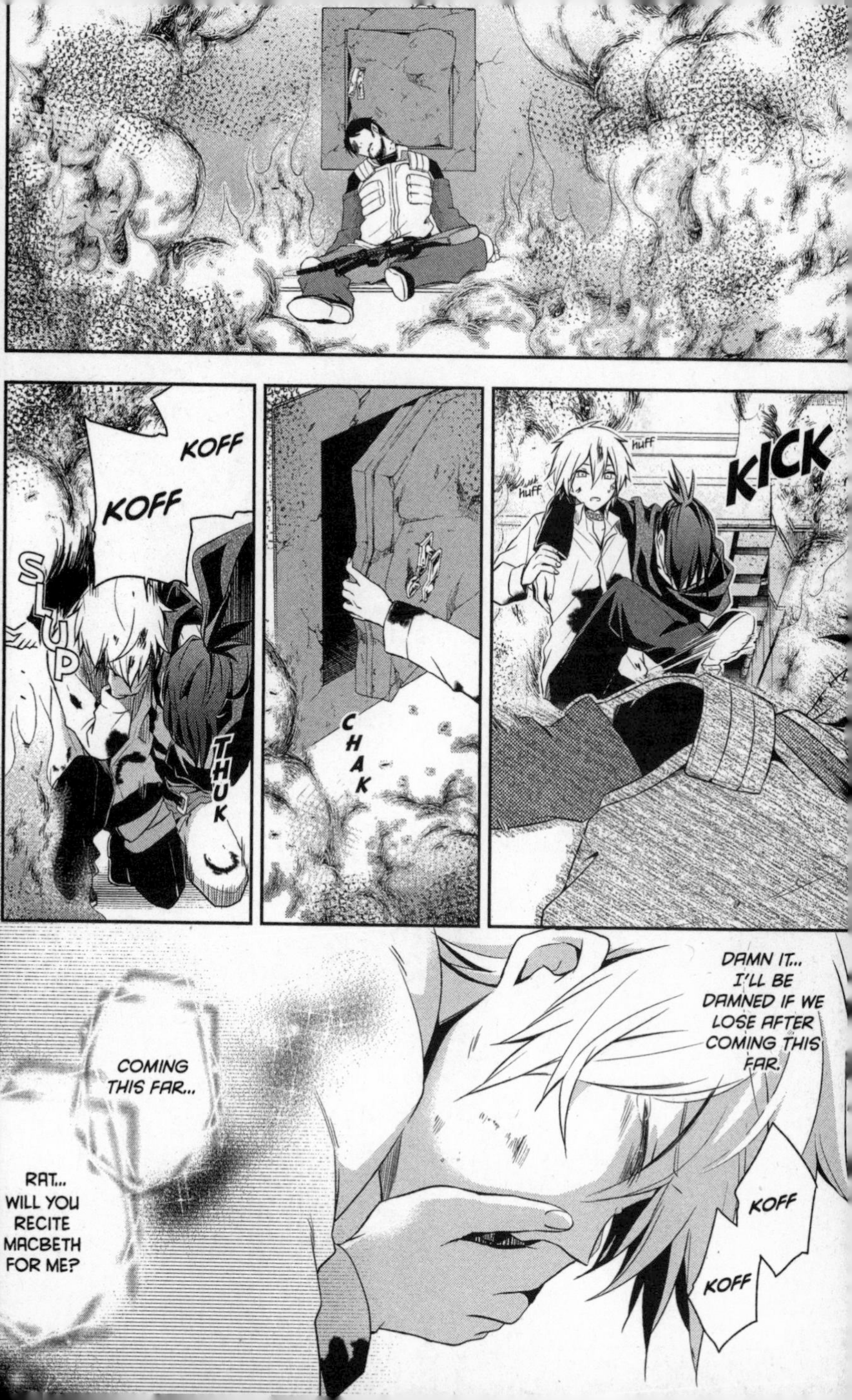
KICK
huff
huff
CHAK
KOFF
KOFF
SLUP
THUK
DAMN IT... I'LL BE DAMNED IF WE LOSE AFTER COMING THIS FAR.
KOFF
KOFF
COMING THIS FAR...
RAT... WILL YOU RECITE MACBETH FOR ME?

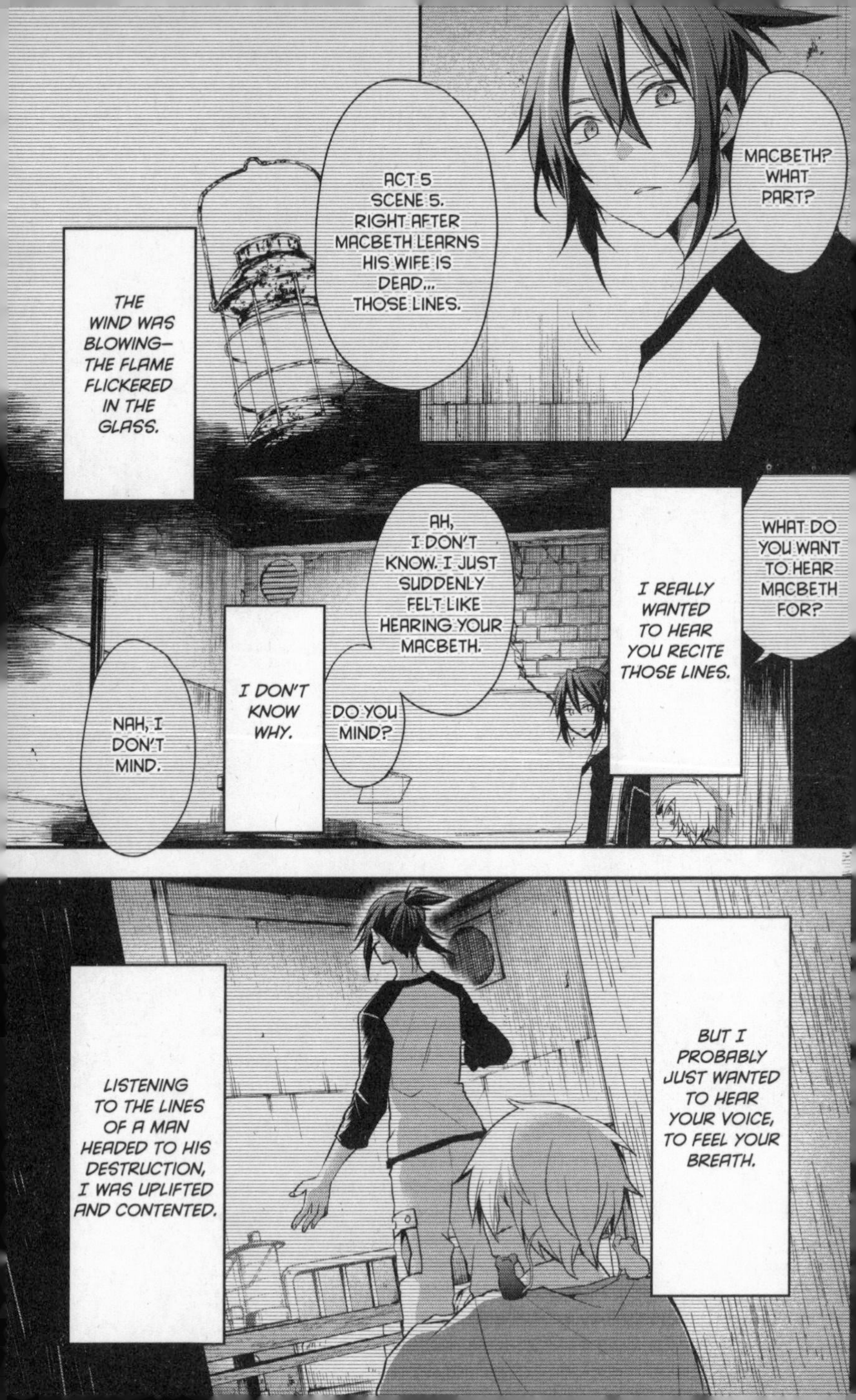
MACBETH? WHAT PART?
ACT 5 SCENE 5. RIGHT AFTER MACBETH LEARNS HIS WIFE IS DEAD... THOSE LINES.
THE WIND WAS BLOWING— THE FLAME FLICKERED IN THE GLASS.
WHAT DO YOU WANT TO HEAR MACBETH FOR?
I REALLY WANTED TO HEAR YOU RECITE THOSE LINES.
AH, I DON'T KNOW. I JUST SUDDENLY FELT LIKE HEARING YOUR MACBETH.
DO YOU MIND?
I DON'T KNOW WHY.
NAH, I DON'T MIND.
BUT I PROBABLY JUST WANTED TO HEAR YOUR VOICE, TO FEEL YOUR BREATH.
LISTENING TO THE LINES OF A MAN HEADED TO HIS DESTRUCTION, I WAS UPLIFTED AND CONTENTED.

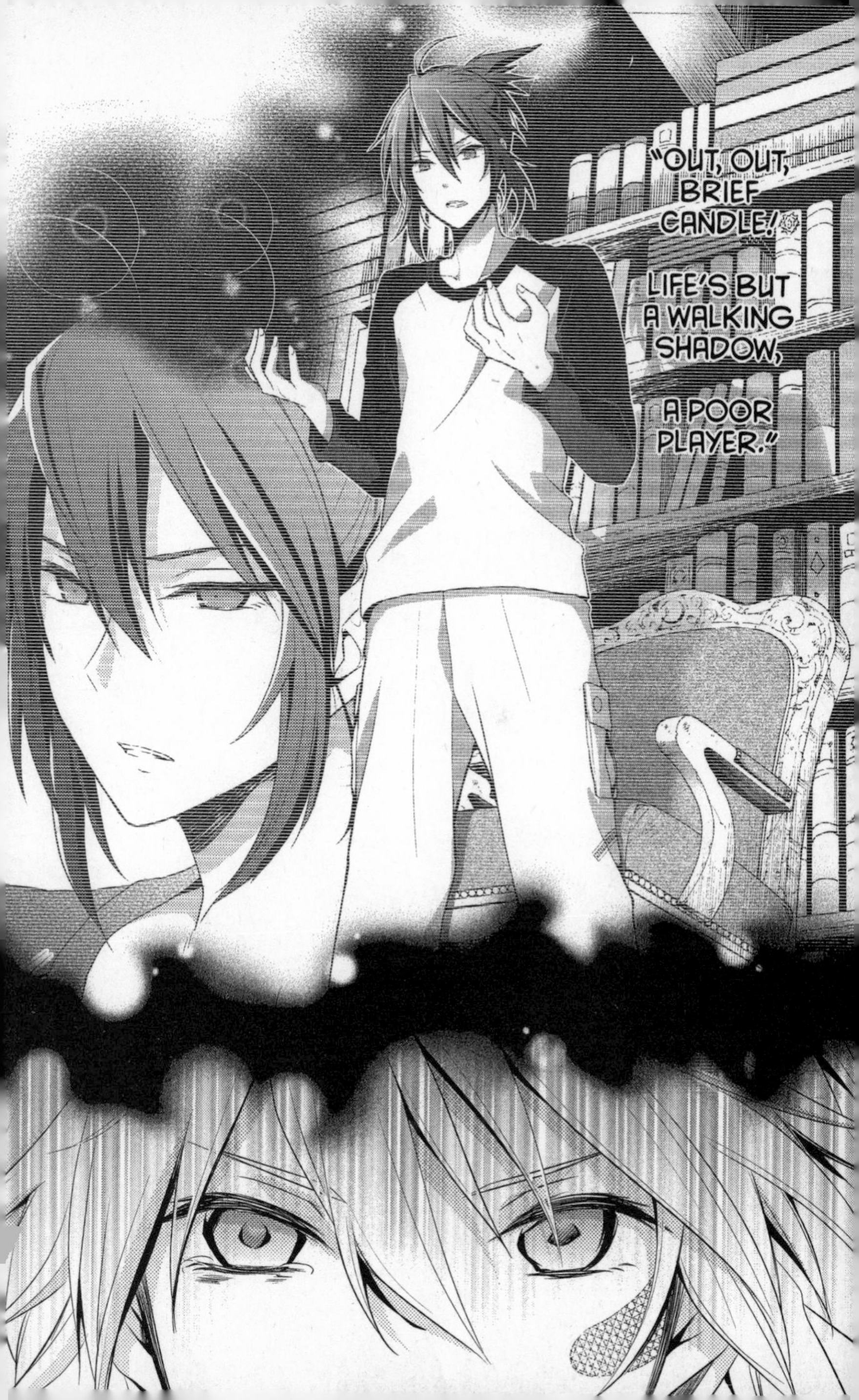
"OUT, OUT, BRIEF CANDLE!
LIFE'S BUT A WALKING SHADOW,
A POOR PLAYER."

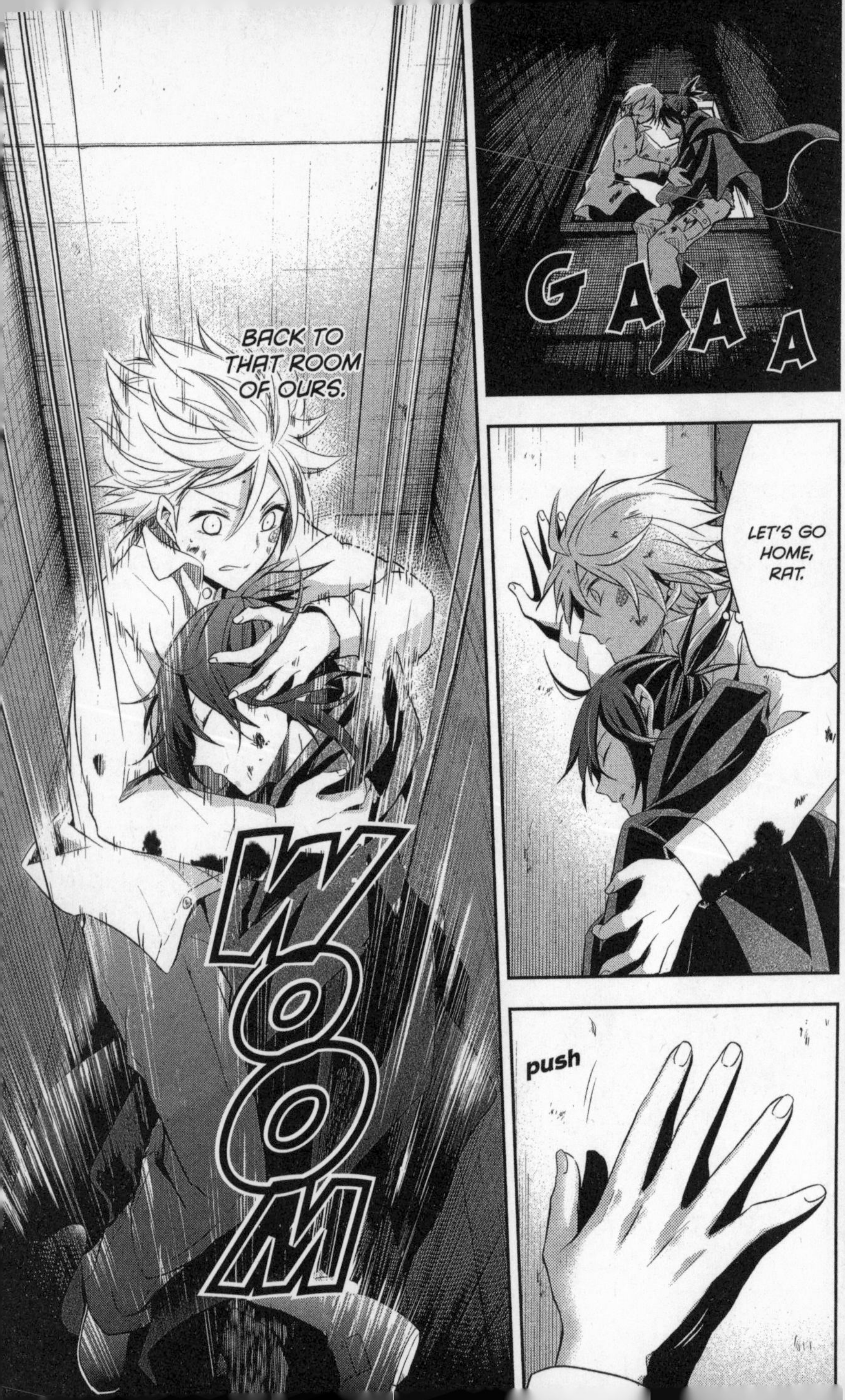
GAAAA
LET'S GO HOME, RAT.
push
BACK TO THAT ROOM OF OURS.
WOOM

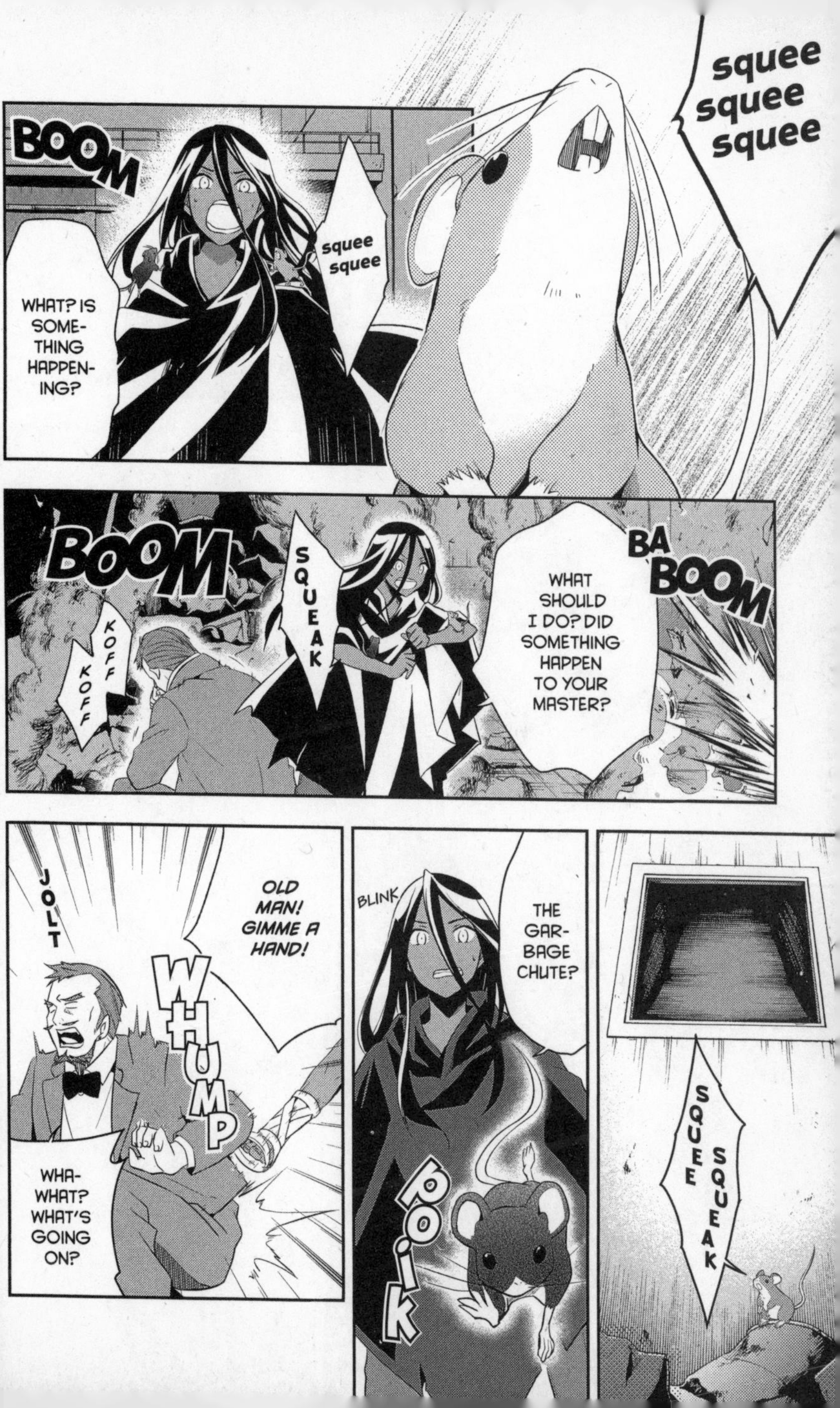
squee squee squee
squee squee
BOOM
WHAT? IS SOME-THING HAPPEN-ING?
BA BOOM
WHAT SHOULD I DO? DID SOMETHING HAPPEN TO YOUR MASTER?
SQUEAK
BOOM
KOFF KOFF
SQUEE SQUEAK
THE GAR-BAGE CHUTE?
BLINK
POIK
OLD MAN! GIMME A HAND!
JOLT
WHUMP
WHA-WHAT? WHAT'S GOING ON?

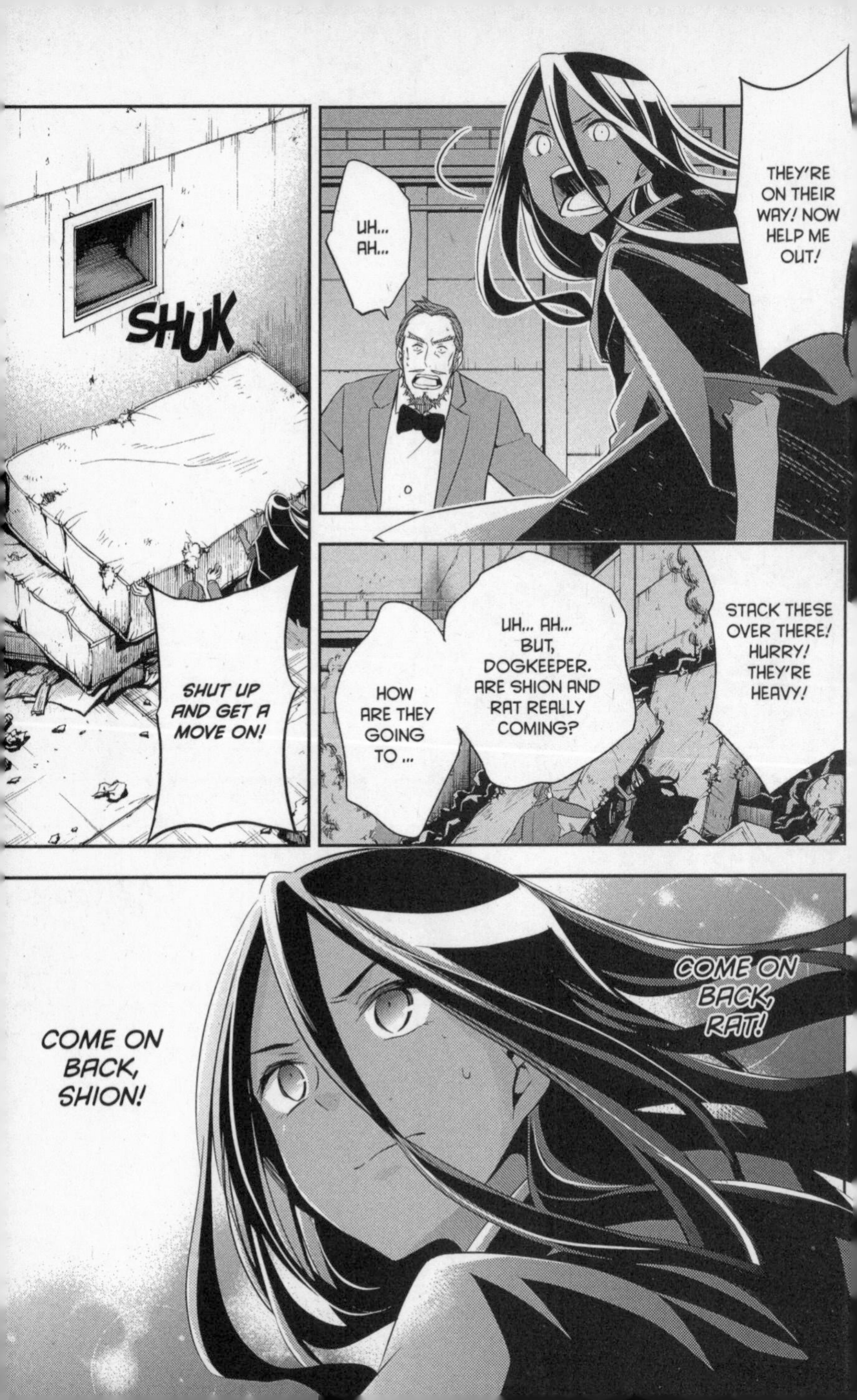
THEY'RE ON THEIR WAY! NOW HELP ME OUT!
UH... AH...
SHUK
STACK THESE OVER THERE! HURRY! THEY'RE HEAVY!
UH... AH... BUT, DOGKEEPER. ARE SHION AND RAT REALLY COMING?
HOW ARE THEY GOING TO ...
SHUT UP AND GET A MOVE ON!
COME ON BACK, RAT!
COME ON BACK, SHION!

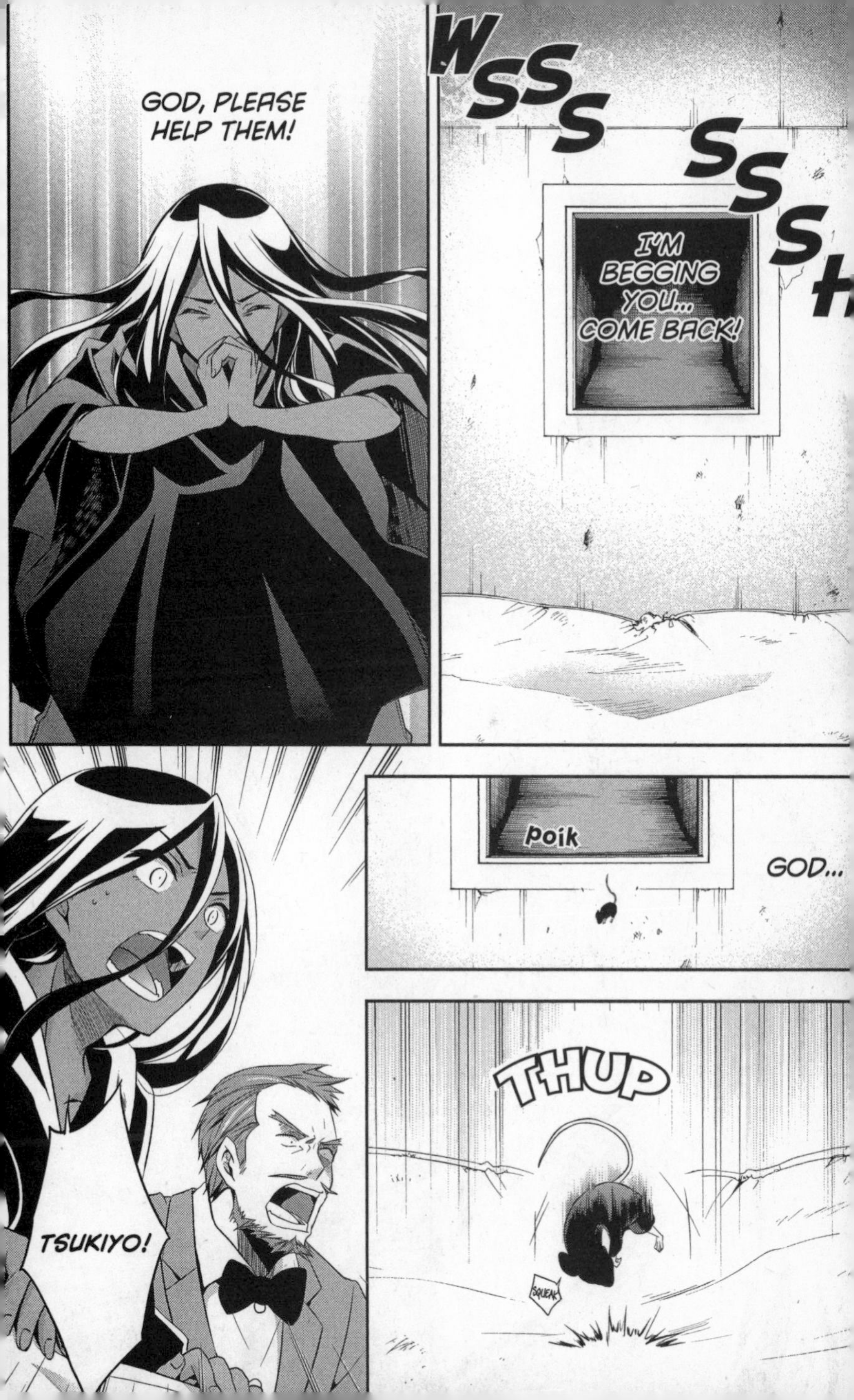
WSSS
SSSH
I'M BEGGING YOU... COME BACK!
GOD, PLEASE HELP THEM!
poik
GOD...
THUP
SQUEAK
TSUKIYO!

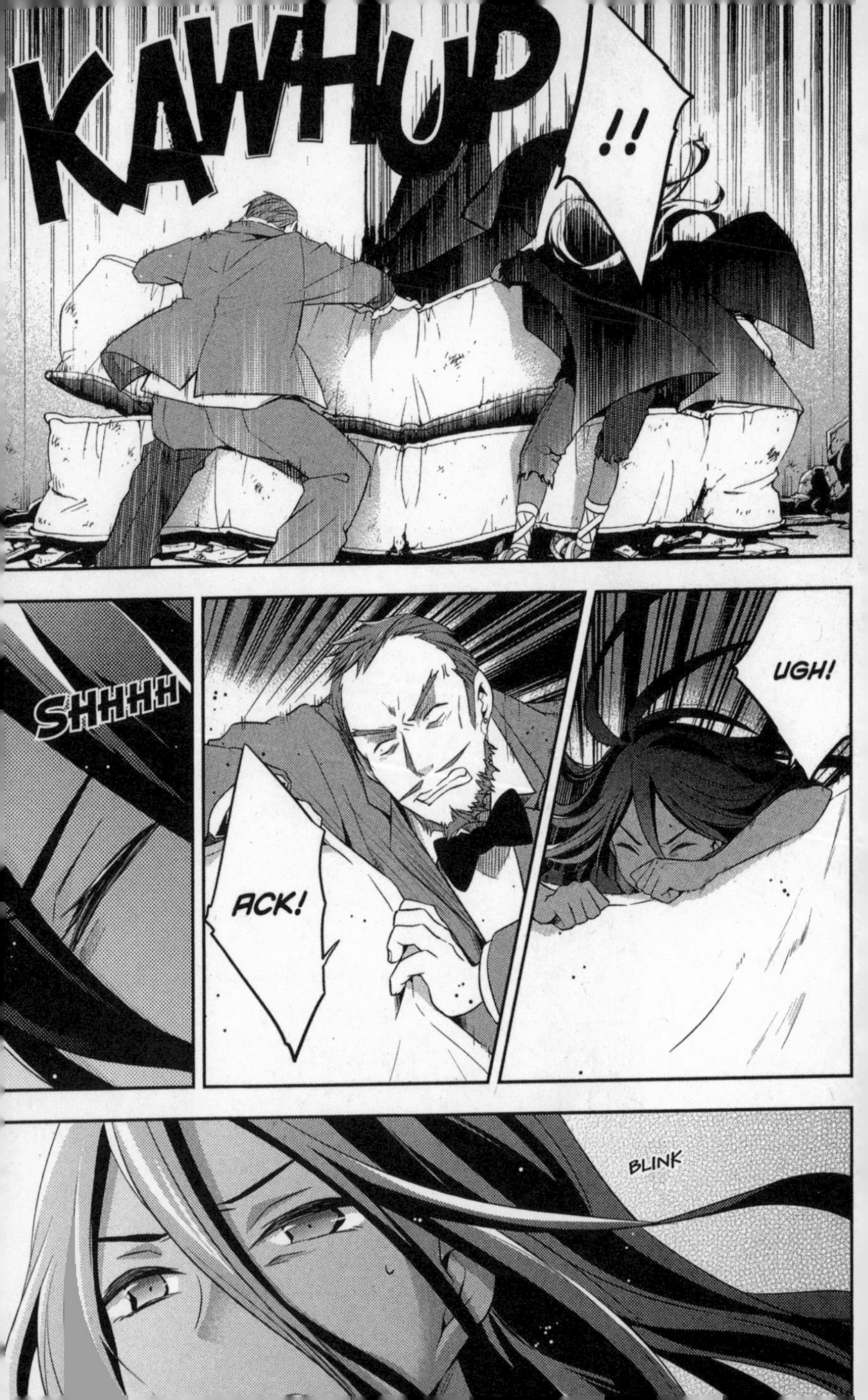
KAWHUP
!!
UGH!
ACK!
SHHHH
BLINK

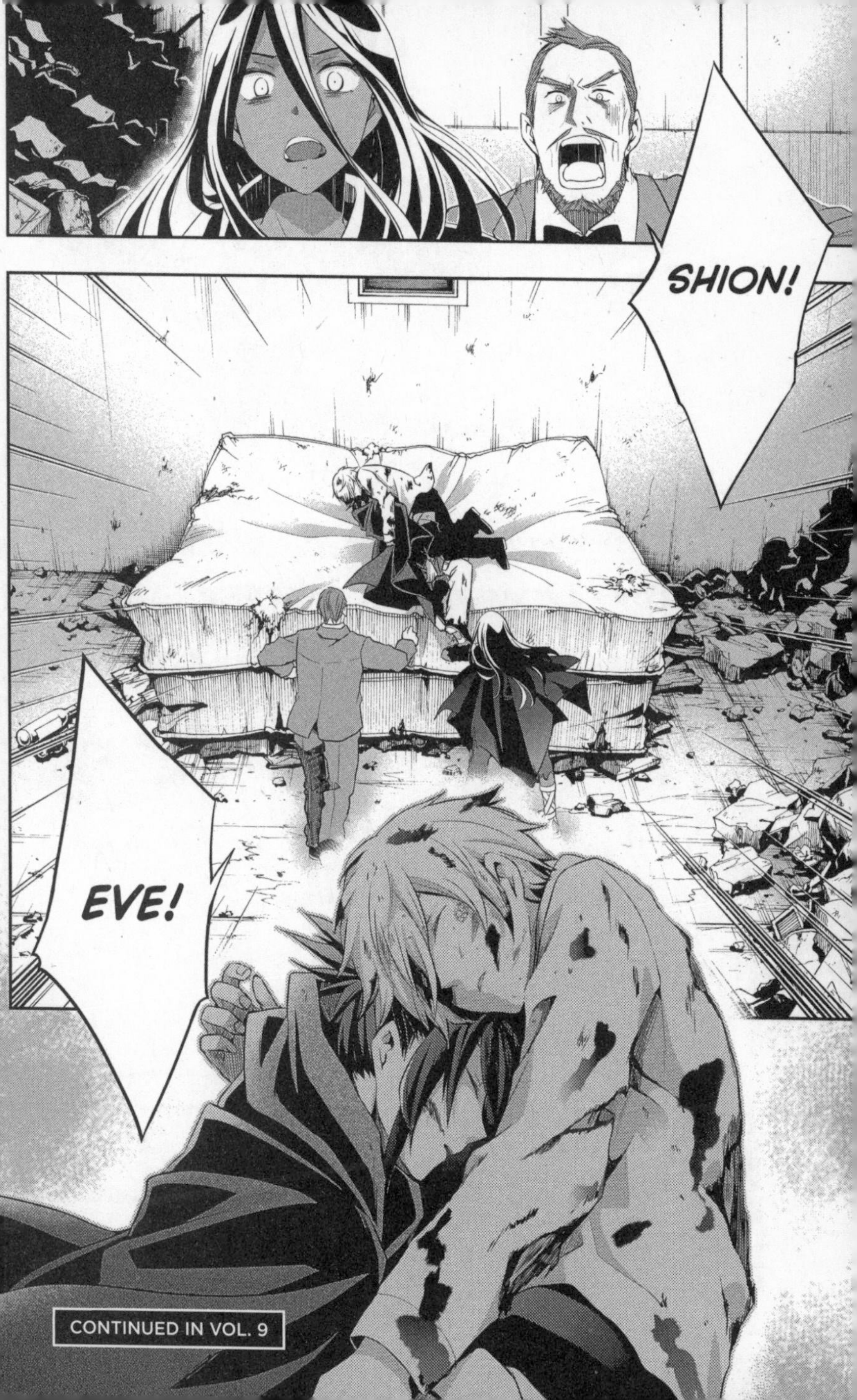
SHION!
EVE!
CONTINUED IN VOL. 9

NO.6

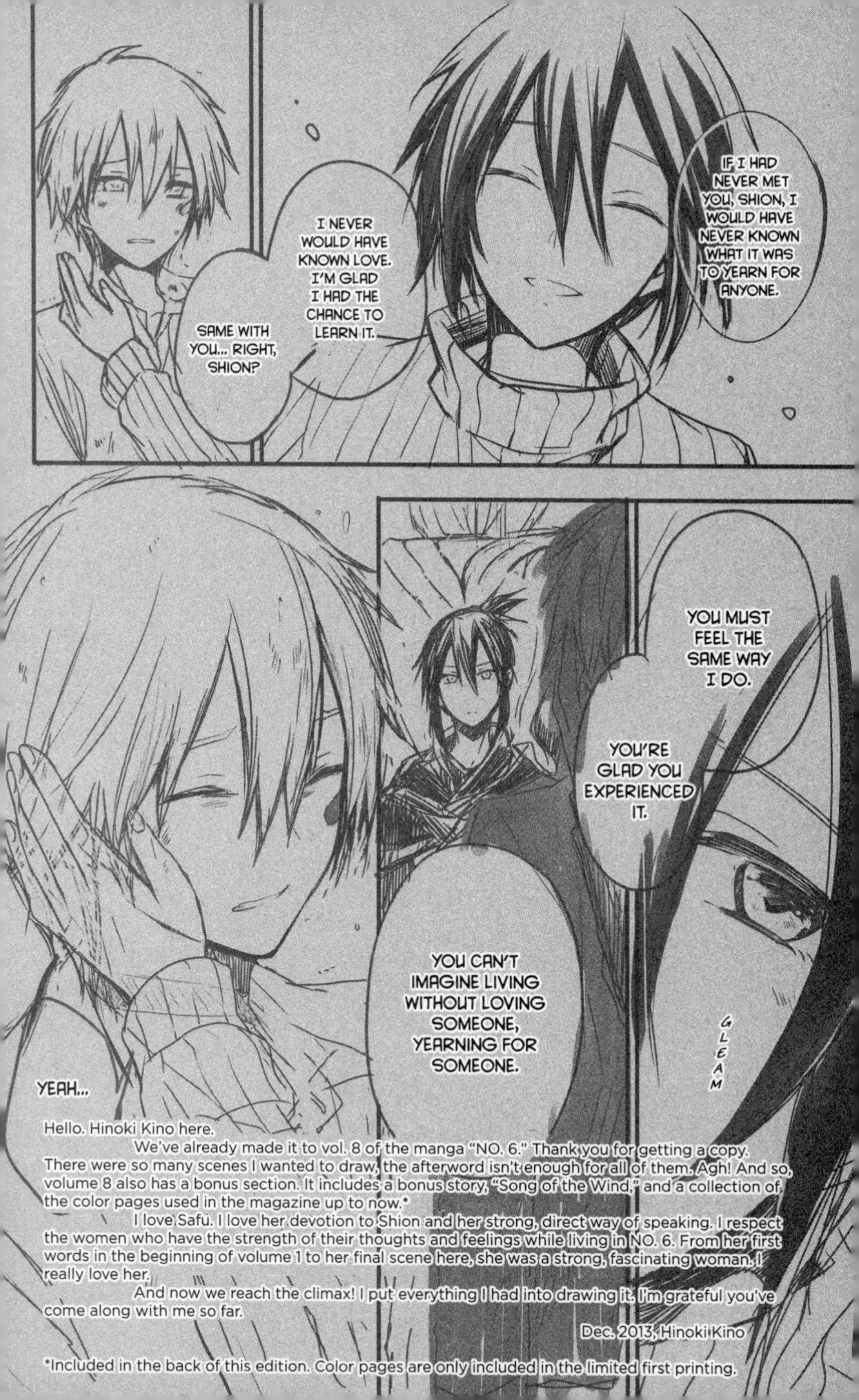
IF I HAD NEVER MET YOU, SHION, I WOULD HAVE NEVER KNOWN WHAT IT WAS TO YEARN FOR ANYONE.
I NEVER WOULD HAVE KNOWN LOVE. I'M GLAD I HAD THE CHANCE TO LEARN IT.
SAME WITH YOU... RIGHT, SHION?
YOU MUST FEEL THE SAME WAY I DO.
YOU'RE GLAD YOU EXPERIENCED IT.
GLEAM
YOU CAN'T IMAGINE LIVING WITHOUT LOVING SOMEONE, YEARNING FOR SOMEONE.
YEAH...

Hello. Hinoki Kino here.

We've already made it to vol. 8 of the manga "NO. 6." Thank you for getting a copy. There were so many scenes I wanted to draw, the afterword isn't enough for all of them. Agh! And so, volume 8 also has a bonus section. It includes a bonus story, "Song of the Wind," and a collection of the color pages used in the magazine up to now.*

I love Safu. I love her devotion to Shion and her strong, direct way of speaking. I respect the women who have the strength of their thoughts and feelings while living in NO. 6. From her first words in the beginning of volume 1 to her final scene here, she was a strong, fascinating woman. I really love her.

And now we reach the climax! I put everything I had into drawing it. I'm grateful you've come along with me so far.

Dec. 2013, Hinoki Kino

*Included in the back of this edition. Color pages are only included in the limited first printing.

SPECIAL THANKS!

Ms. Atsuko Asano

Everyone in the Kodansha Aria Editorial Department
Everyone on the NO. 6 Team
Editor K
toi8
Everyone on the anime staff
Everyone at NARTi;S
Ginkyo

* Production Cooperation
Honma
Megi
Matsugi

* Finishing
Tsunocchi

* 3D
Lim Wan-Gu

* Color backgrounds
Mr. dominori

Family (Mom, Dad, siblings, Granny, the dog)

And everyone else who helped out

Also, all you readers!

Thank you all so very much!

THIS IS WHAT MY EDITOR SAID I SHOULD DO.

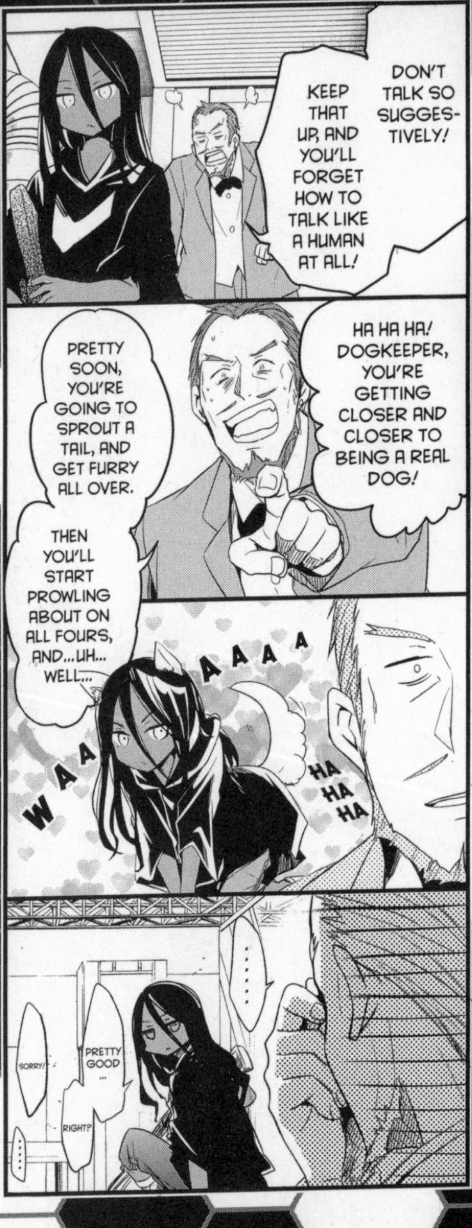

DON'T TALK SO SUGGES-TIVELY!
KEEP THAT UP, AND YOU'LL FORGET HOW TO TALK LIKE A HUMAN AT ALL!
HA HA HA! DOGKEEPER, YOU'RE GETTING CLOSER AND CLOSER TO BEING A REAL DOG!
PRETTY SOON, YOU'RE GOING TO SPROUT A TAIL, AND GET FURRY ALL OVER.
THEN YOU'LL START PROWLING ABOUT ON ALL FOURS, AND...UH... WELL...
AAAA
HA HA HA
WAA
......
PRETTY GOOD ...
SORRY!
RIGHT?
......

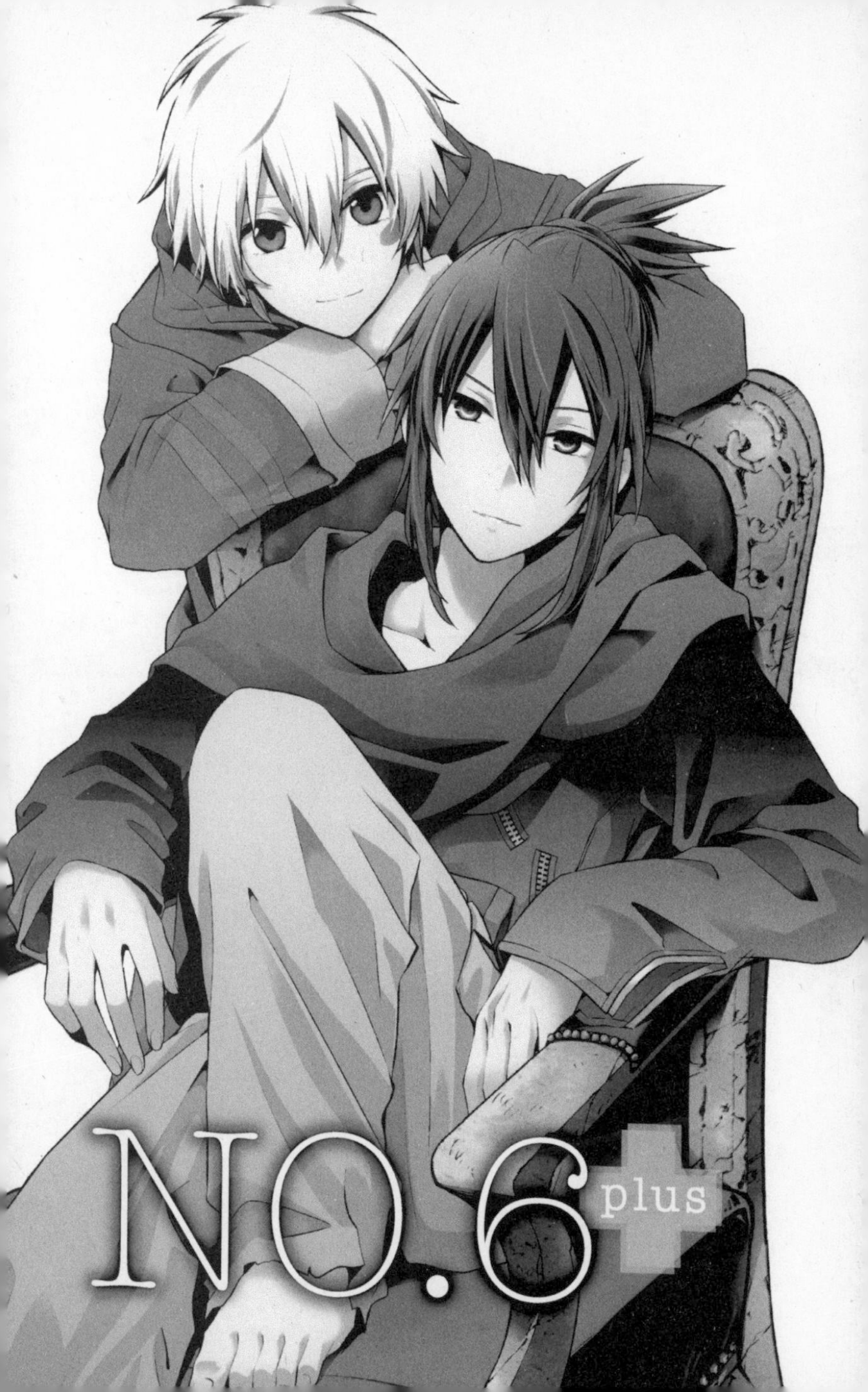
NO.6
plus

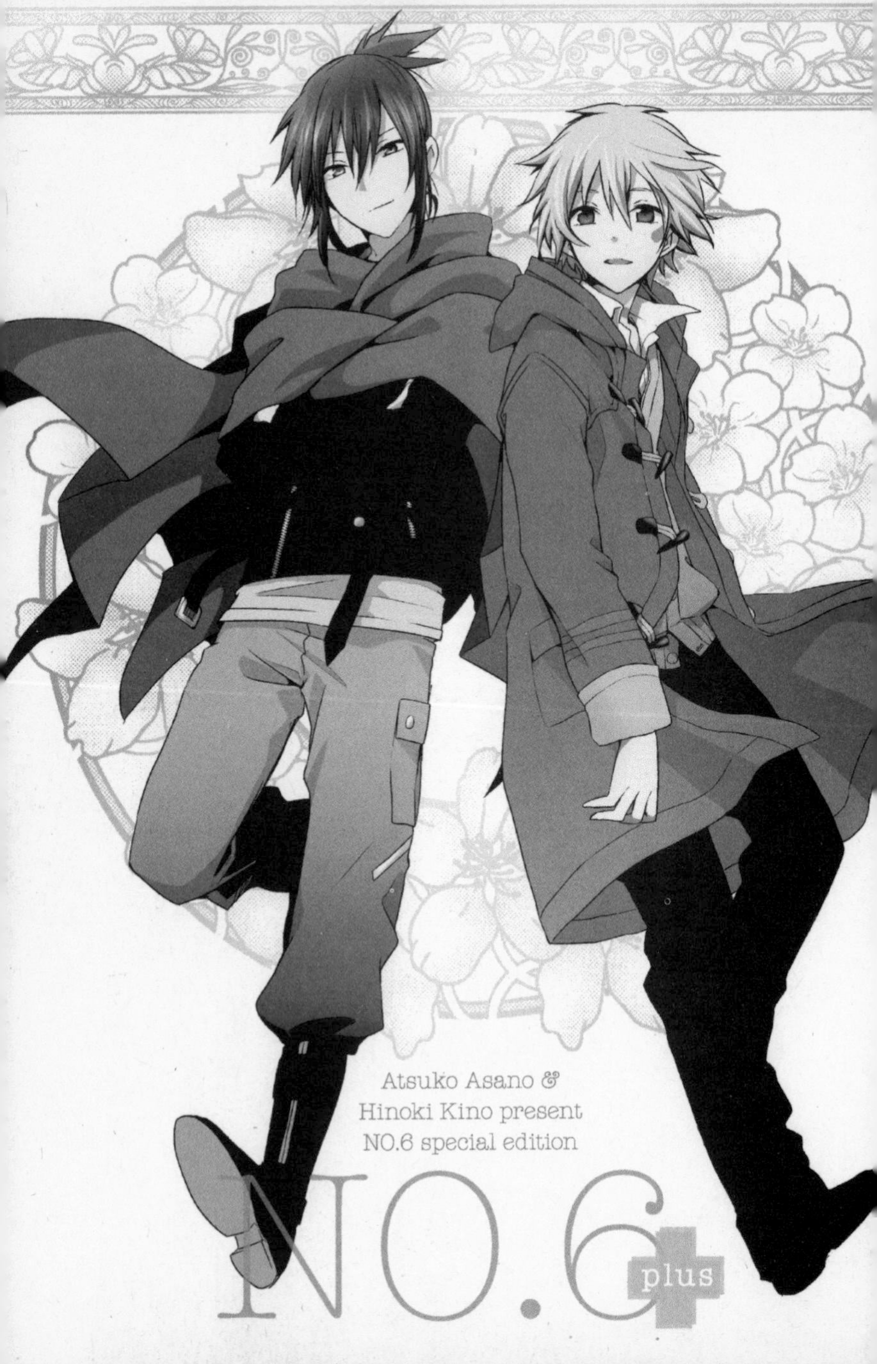
Atsuko Asano &
Hinoki Kino present
NO.6 special edition
NO.6 plus

NO.6 plus

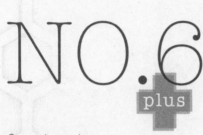

Contents

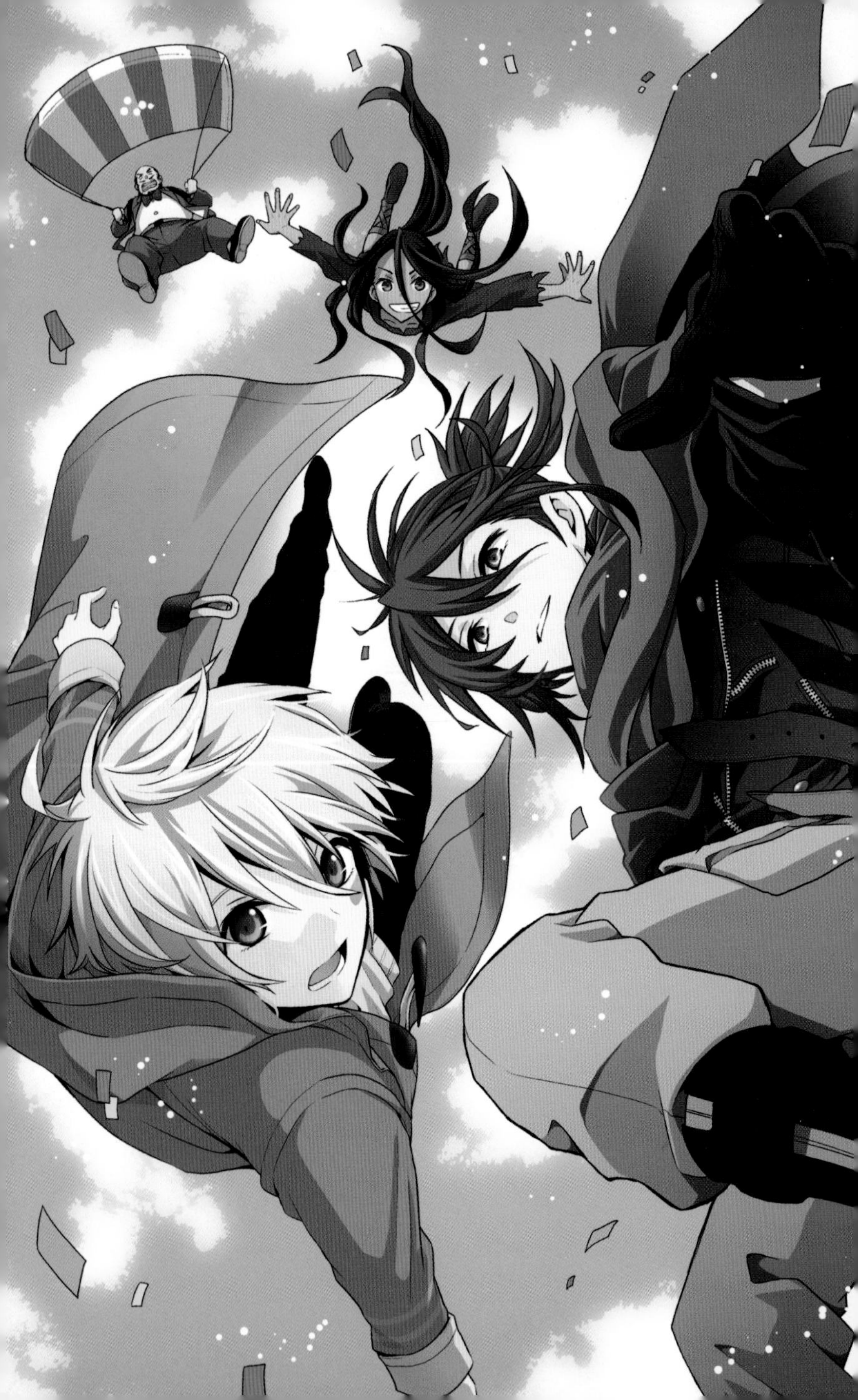

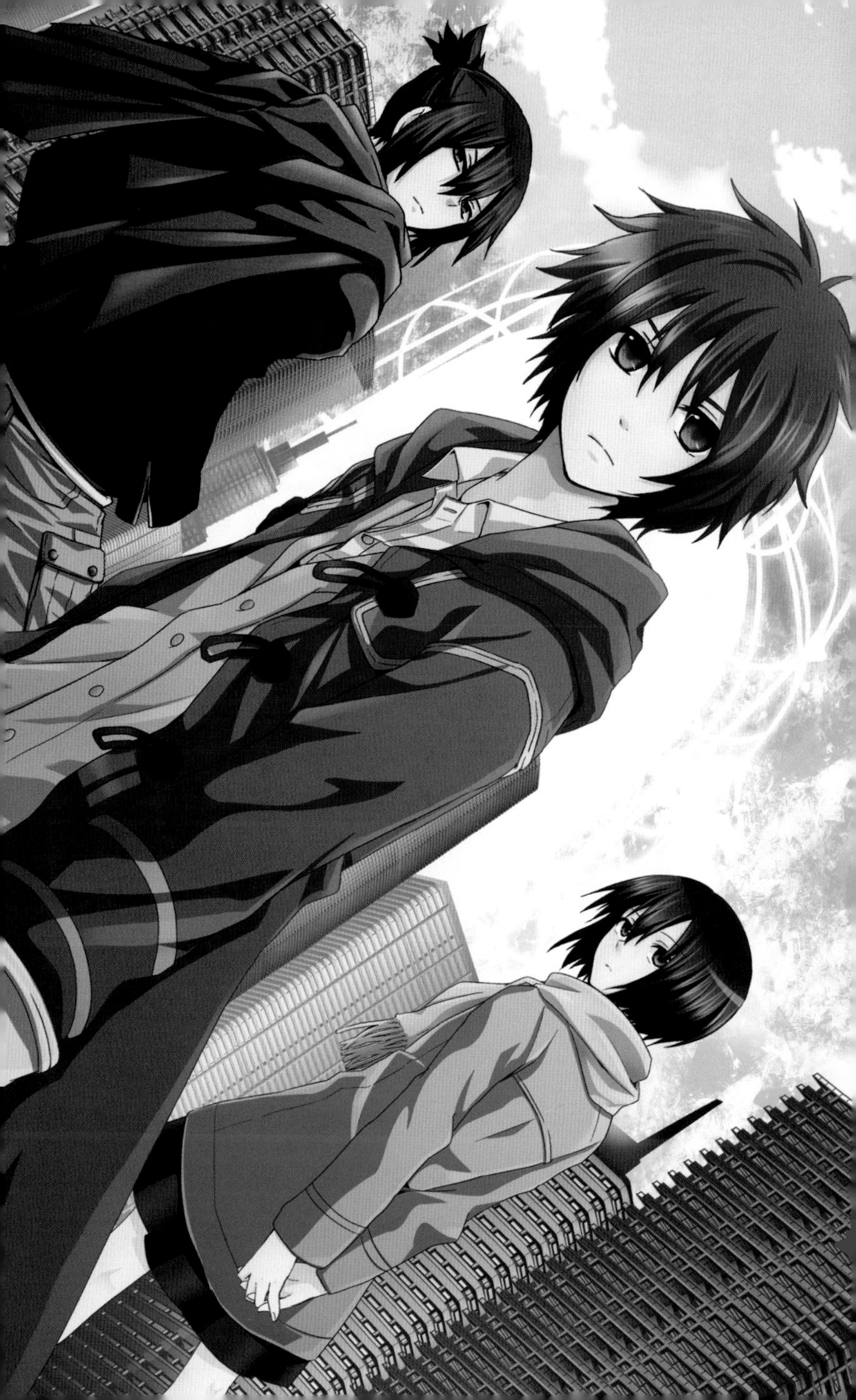

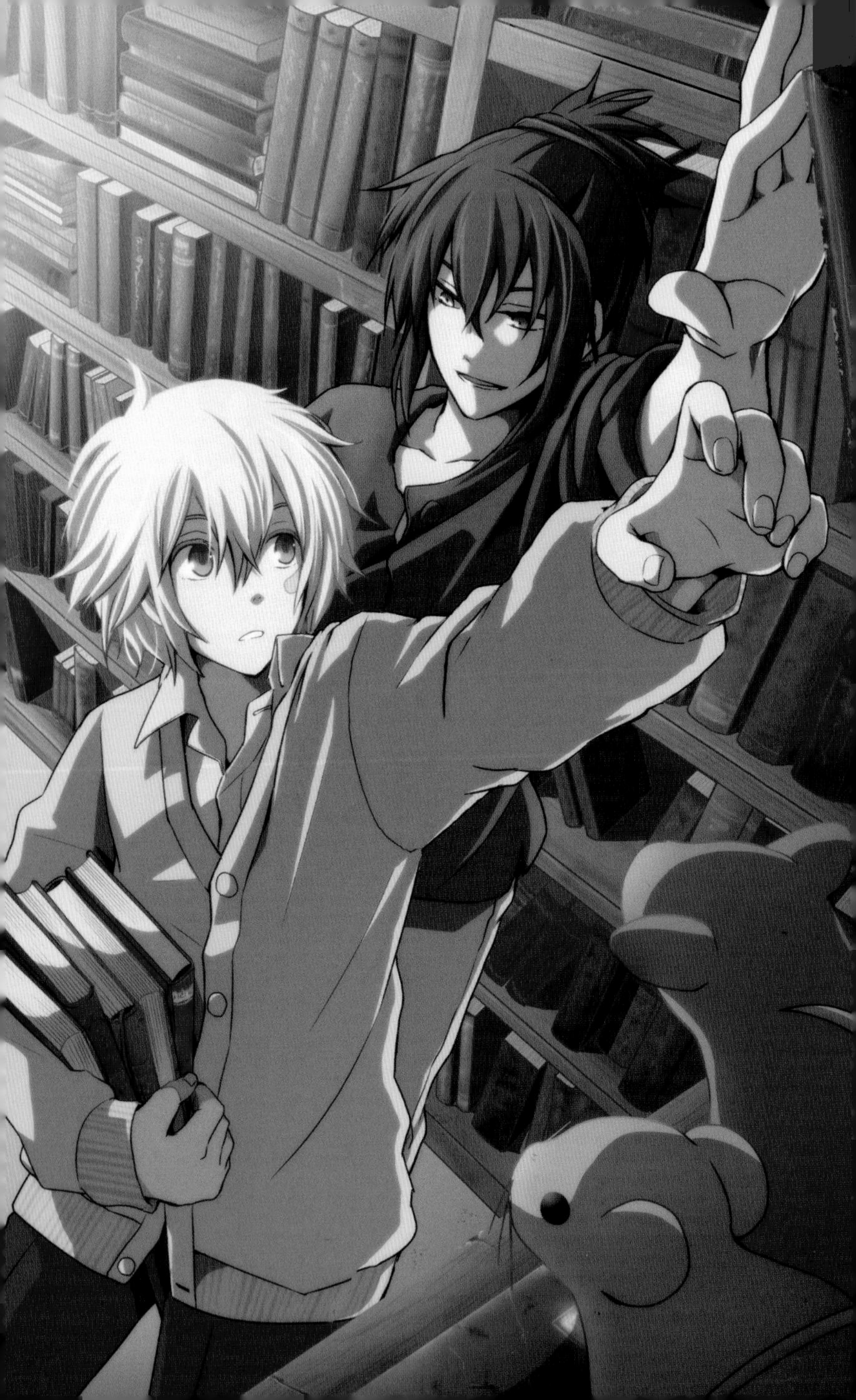

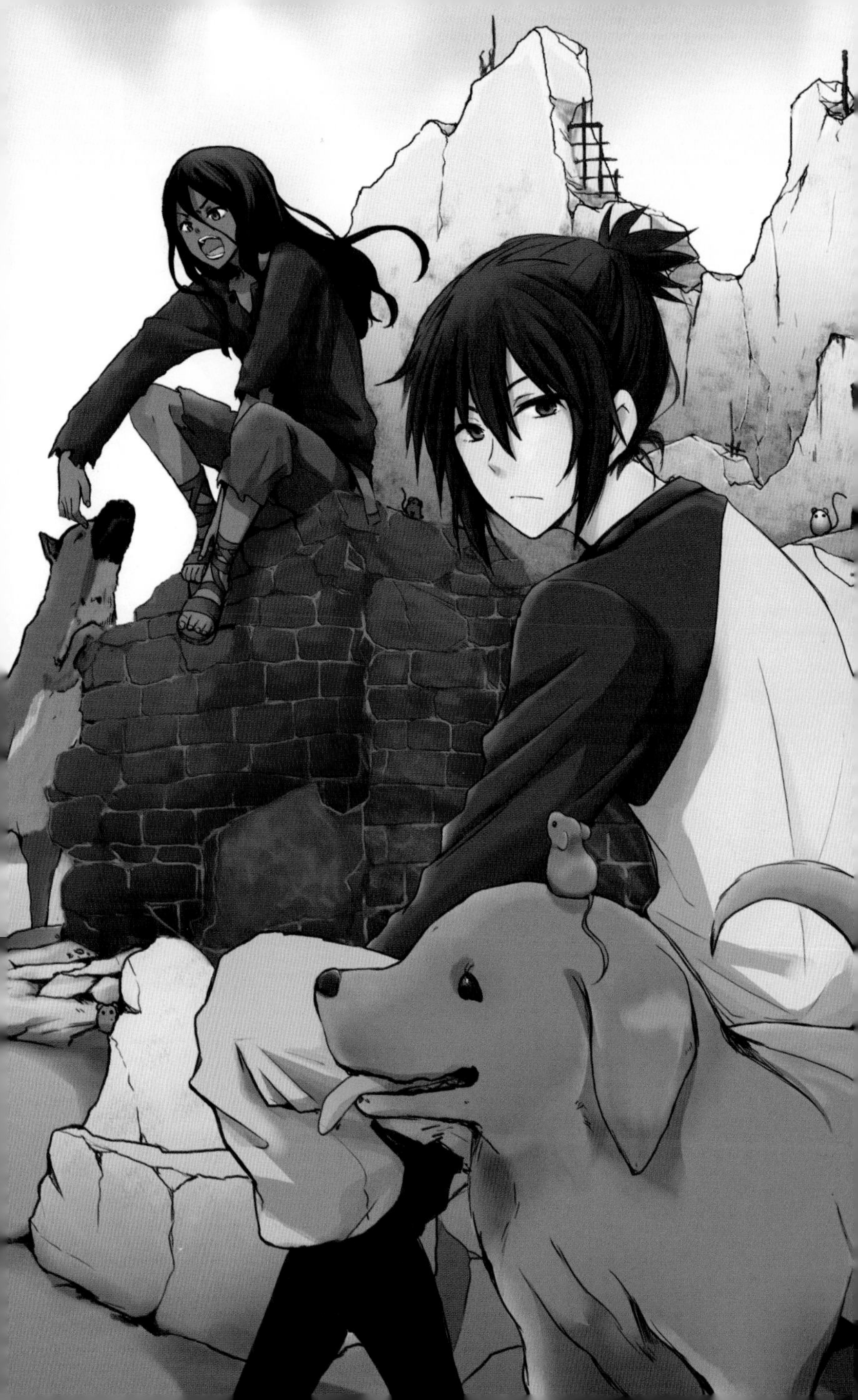

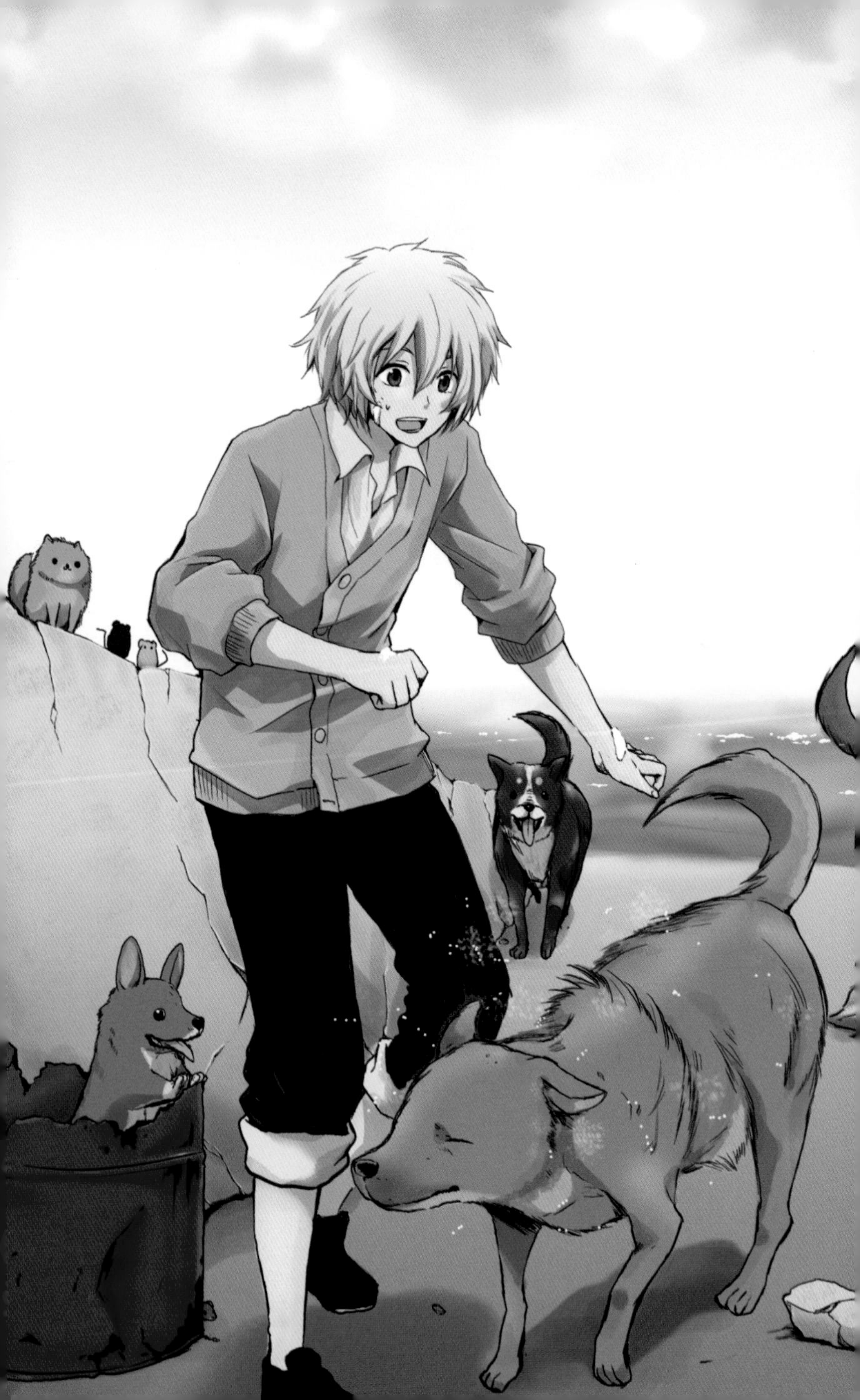

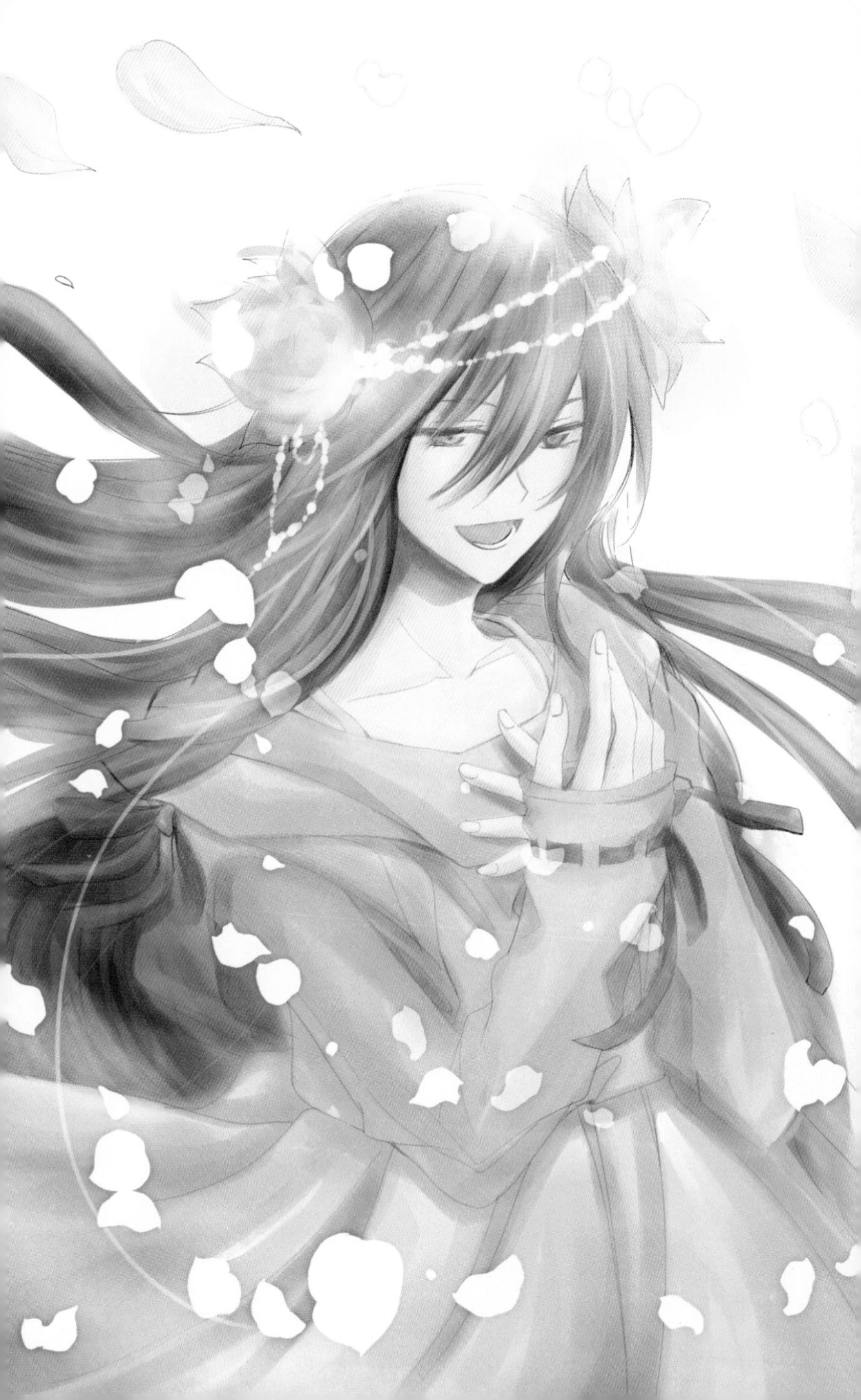

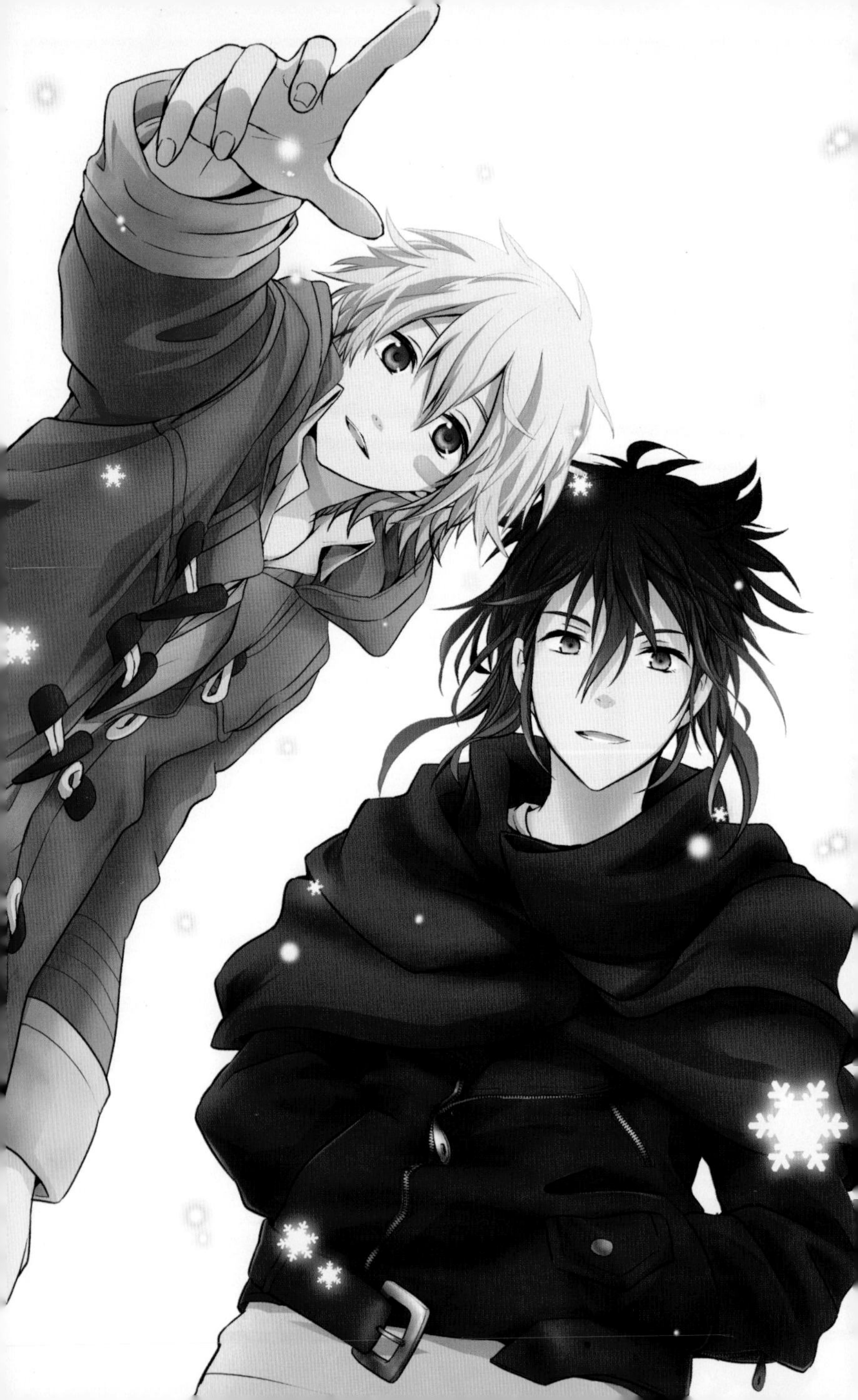

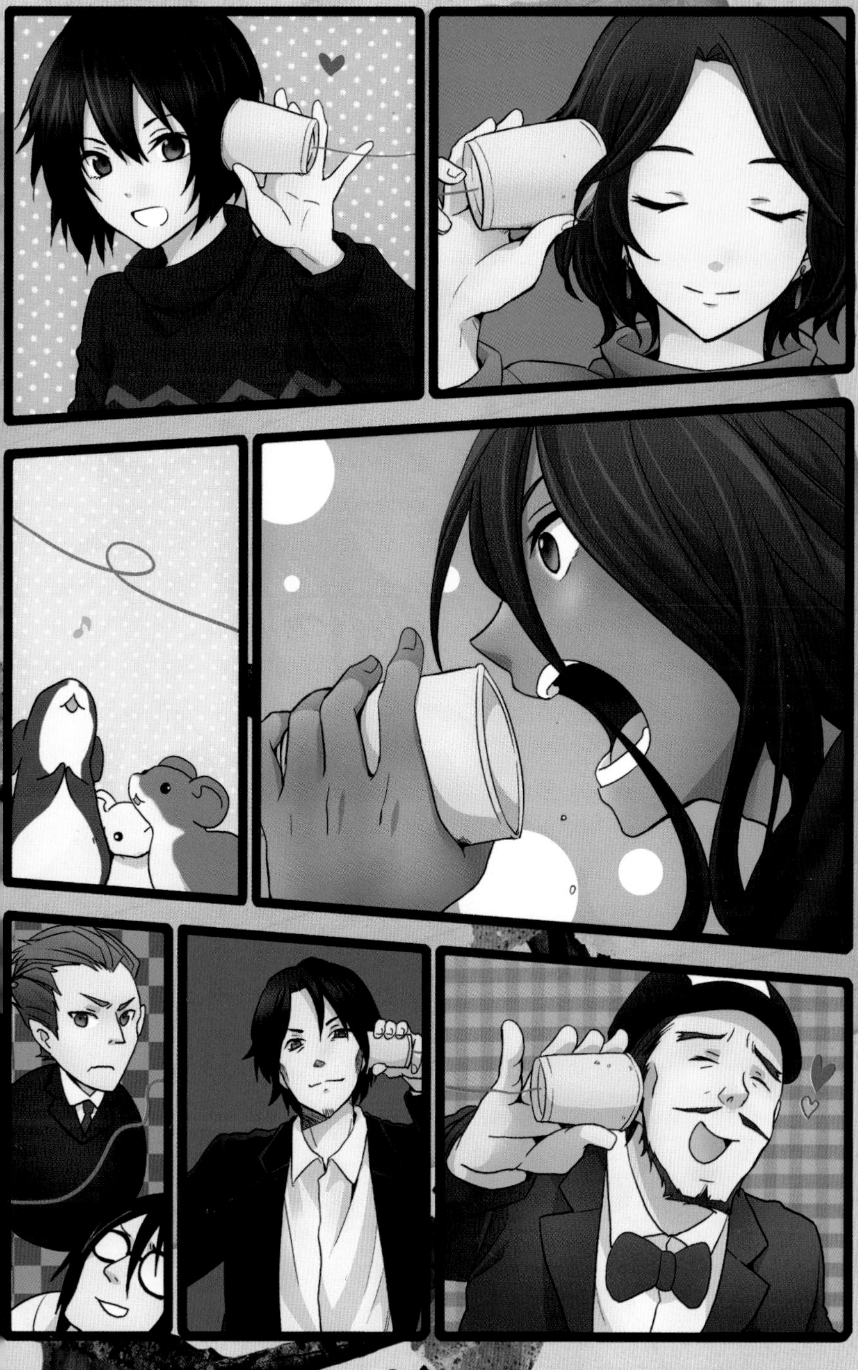

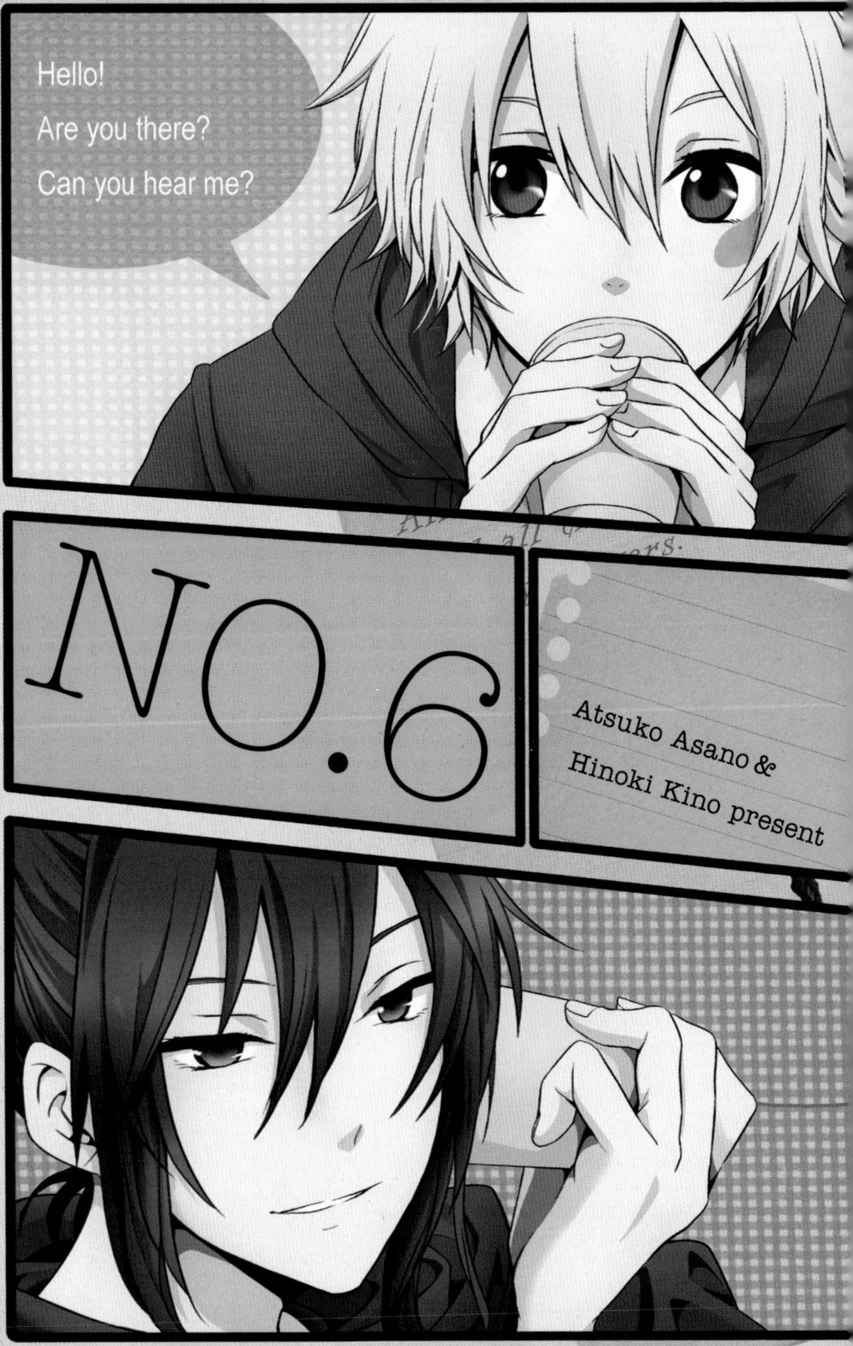
Hello!
Are you there?
Can you hear me?
Atsuko Asano &
Hinoki Kino present
No.6

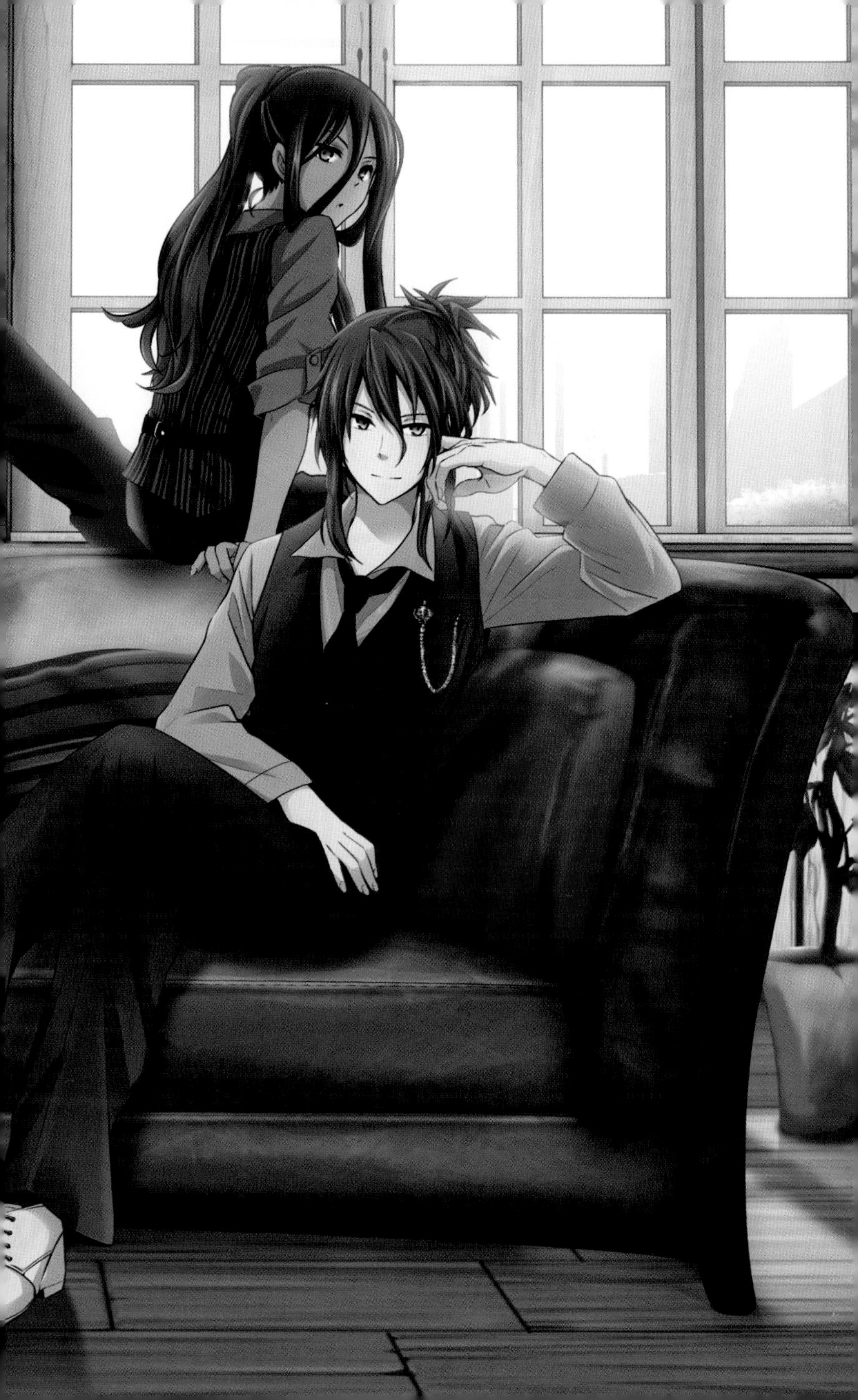

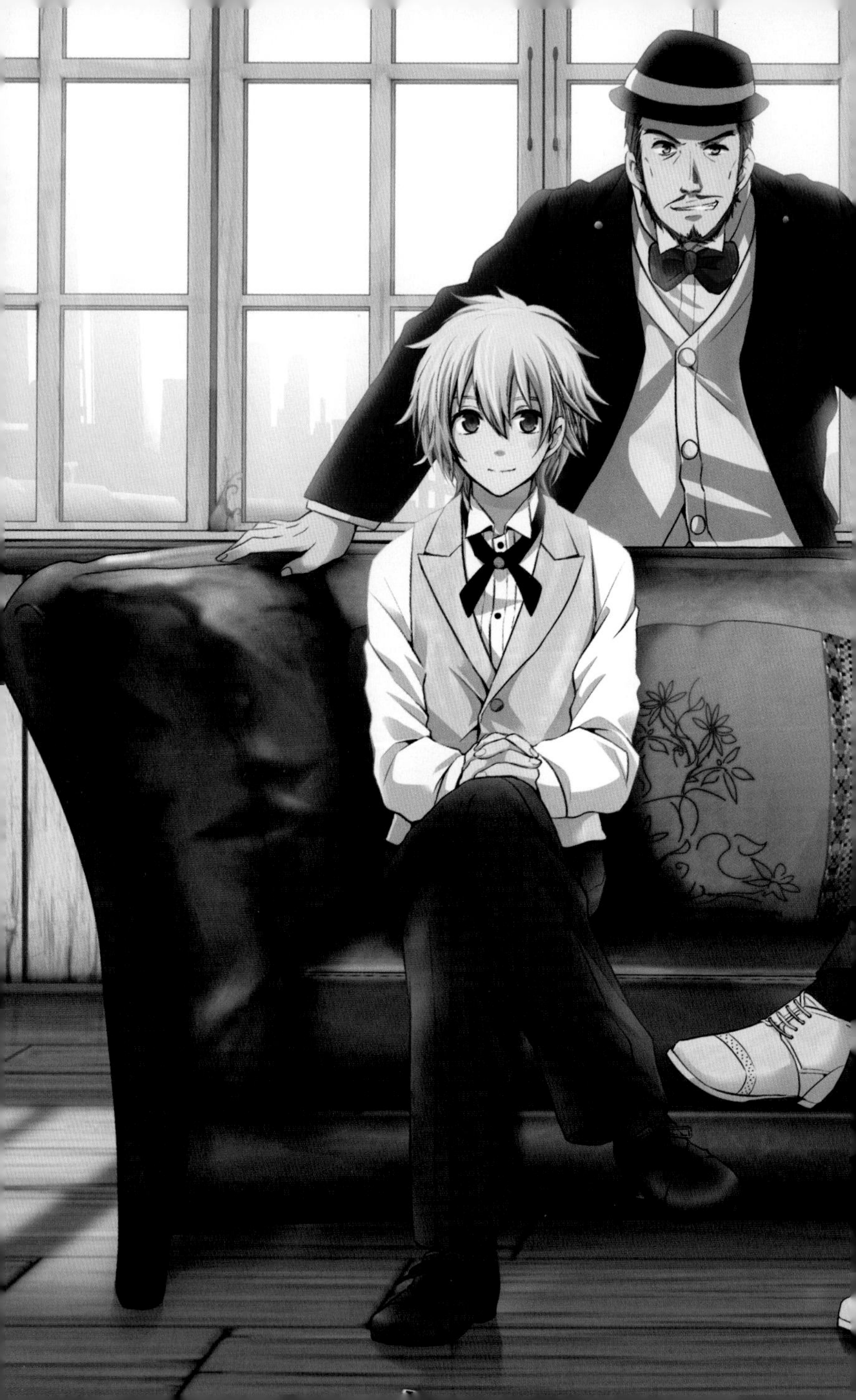

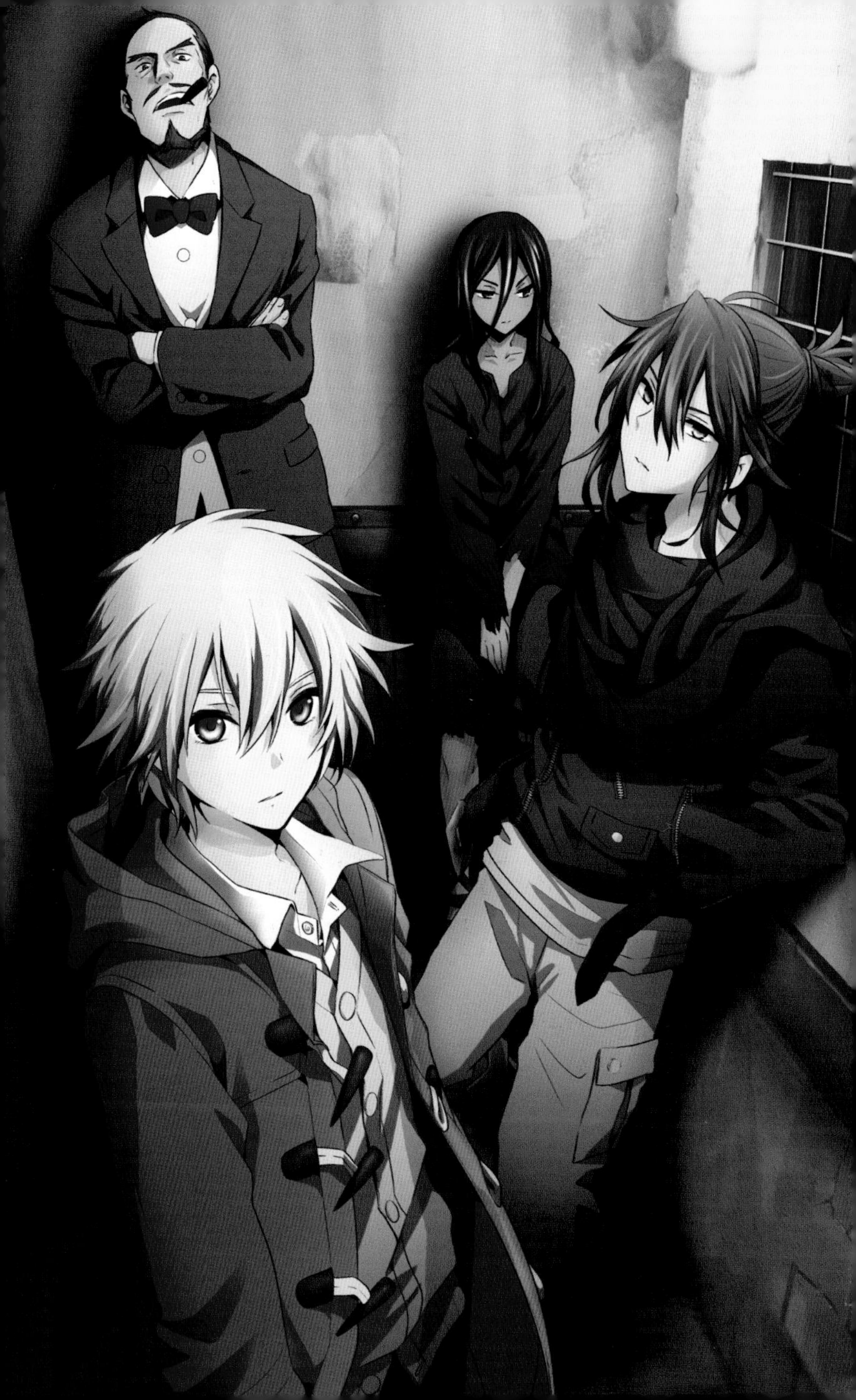

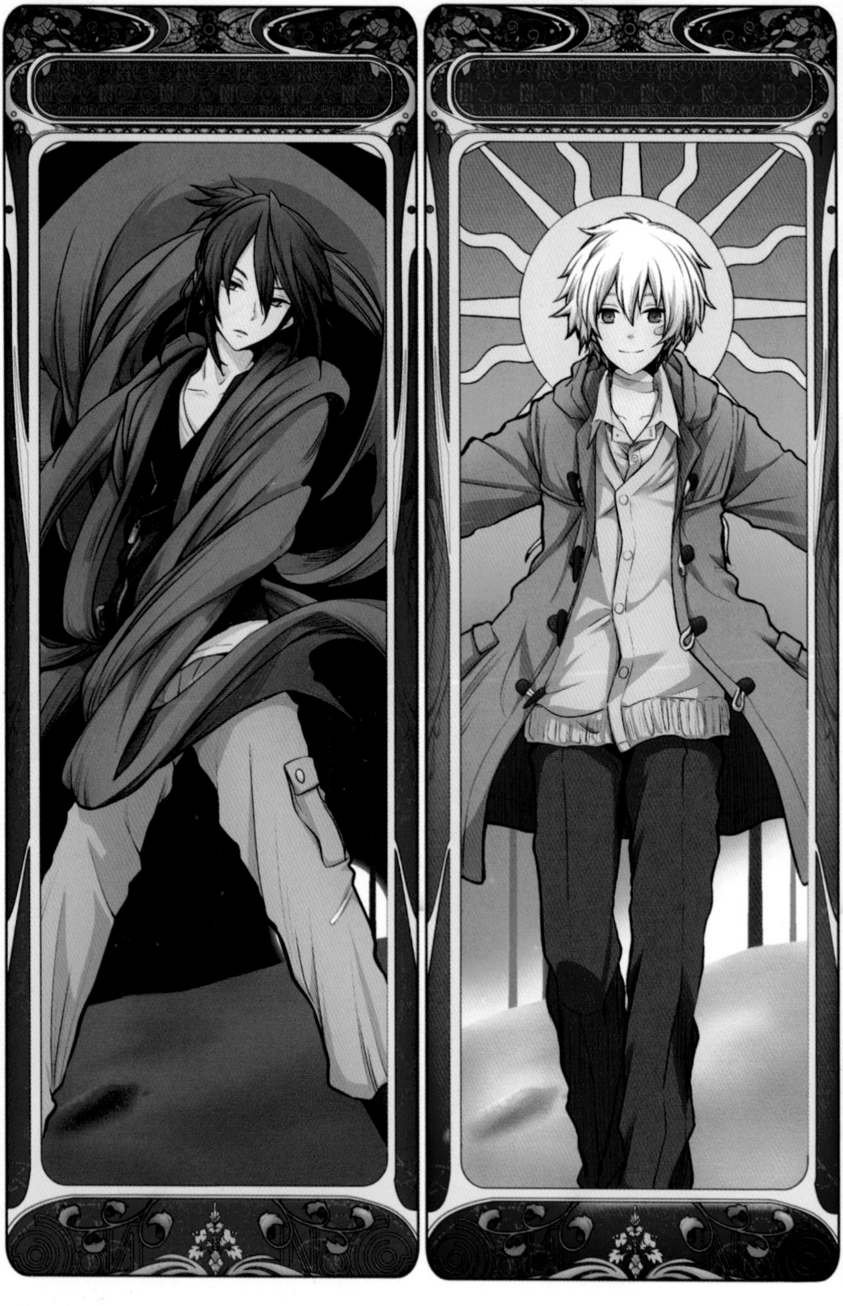

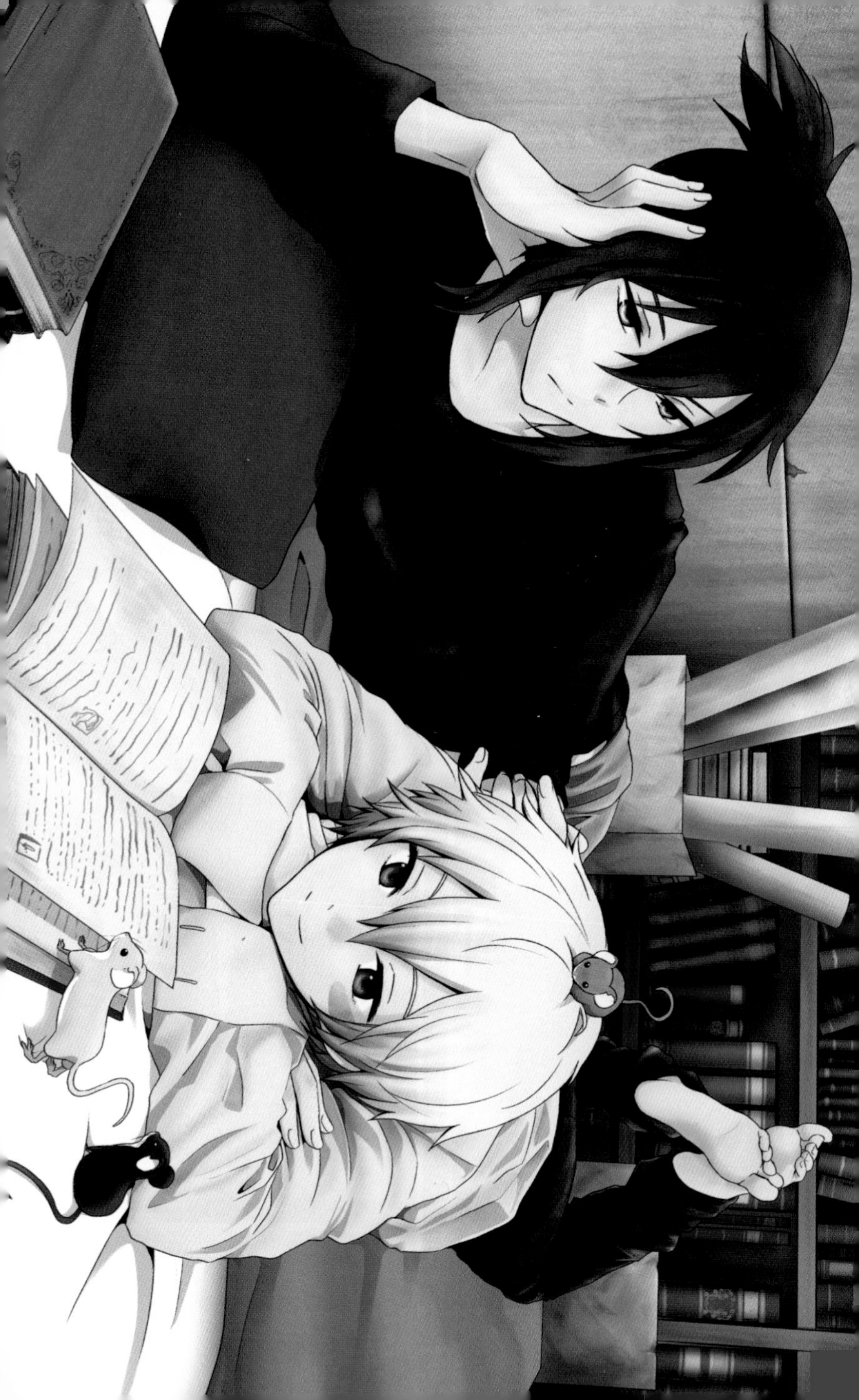

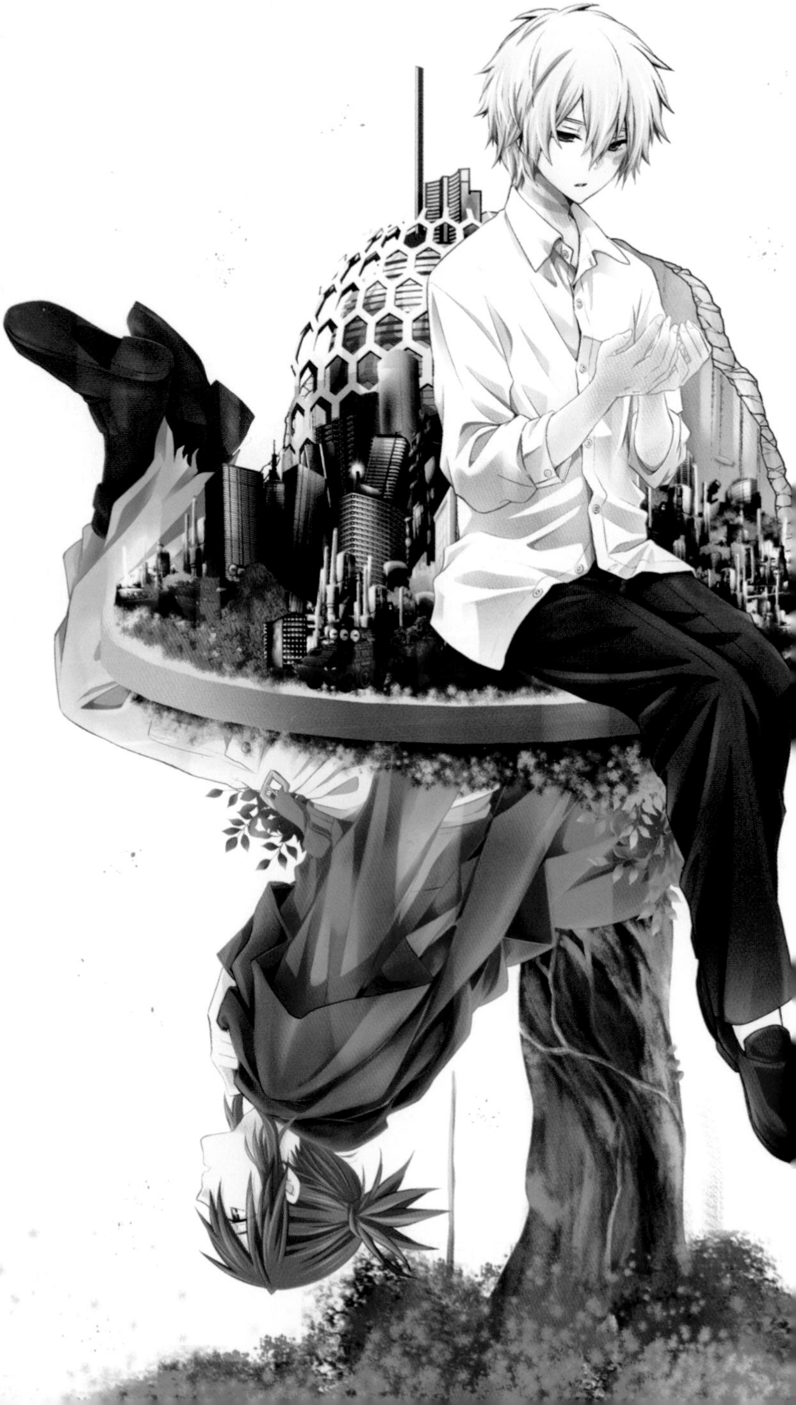

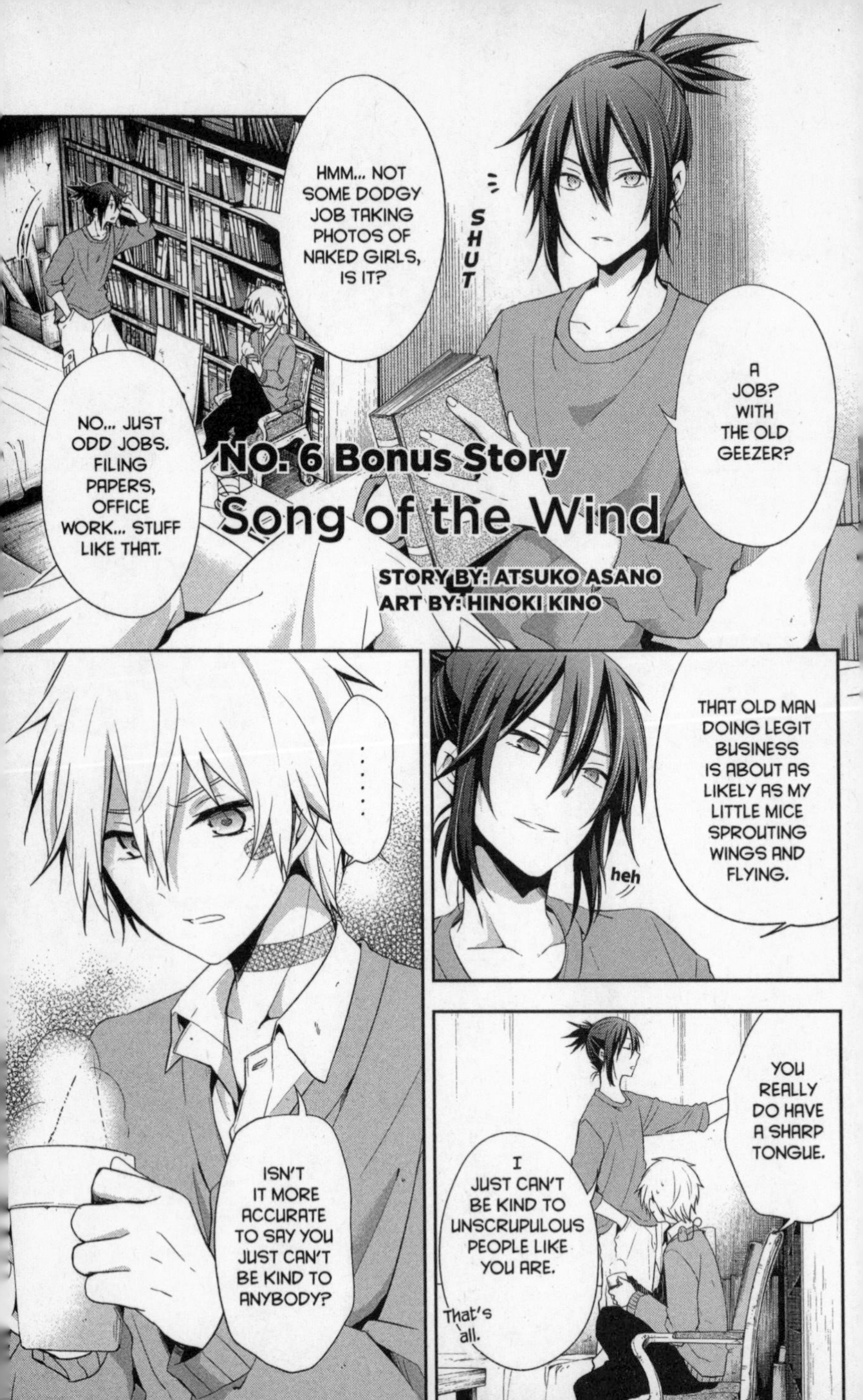
A JOB? WITH THE OLD GEEZER?
SHUT
HMM... NOT SOME DODGY JOB TAKING PHOTOS OF NAKED GIRLS, IS IT?
NO... JUST ODD JOBS. FILING PAPERS, OFFICE WORK... STUFF LIKE THAT.
NO. 6 Bonus Story
Song of the Wind
STORY BY: ATSUKO ASANO
ART BY: HINOKI KINO
THAT OLD MAN DOING LEGIT BUSINESS IS ABOUT AS LIKELY AS MY LITTLE MICE SPROUTING WINGS AND FLYING.
heh
YOU REALLY DO HAVE A SHARP TONGUE.
I JUST CAN'T BE KIND TO UNSCRUPULOUS PEOPLE LIKE YOU ARE.
That's all.
......
ISN'T IT MORE ACCURATE TO SAY YOU JUST CAN'T BE KIND TO ANYBODY?

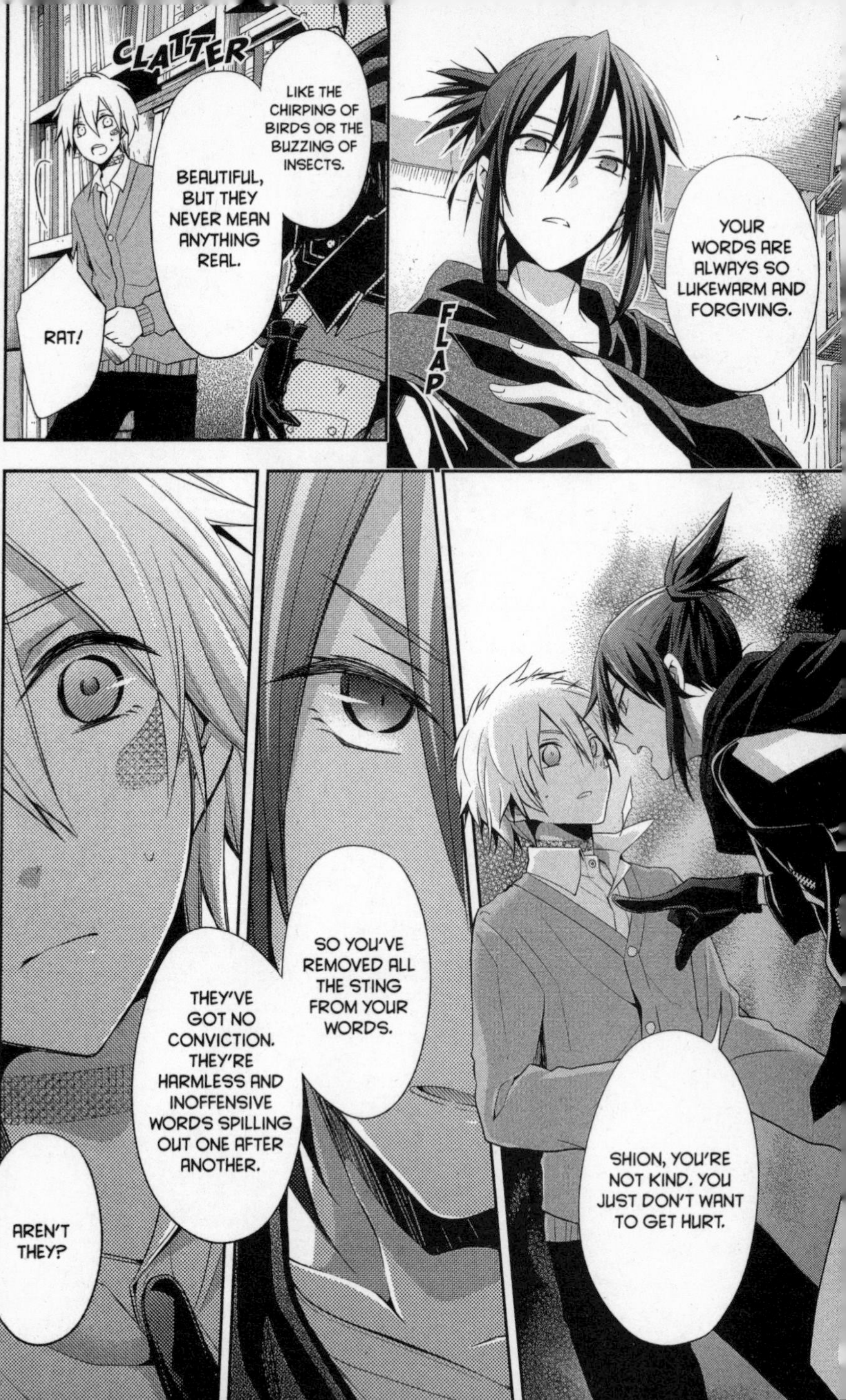

YOUR WORDS ARE ALWAYS SO LUKEWARM AND FORGIVING.
FLAP
LIKE THE CHIRPING OF BIRDS OR THE BUZZING OF INSECTS.
BEAUTIFUL, BUT THEY NEVER MEAN ANYTHING REAL.
CLATTER
RAT!
SHION, YOU'RE NOT KIND. YOU JUST DON'T WANT TO GET HURT.
SO YOU'VE REMOVED ALL THE STING FROM YOUR WORDS.
THEY'VE GOT NO CONVICTION. THEY'RE HARMLESS AND INOFFENSIVE WORDS SPILLING OUT ONE AFTER ANOTHER.
AREN'T THEY?

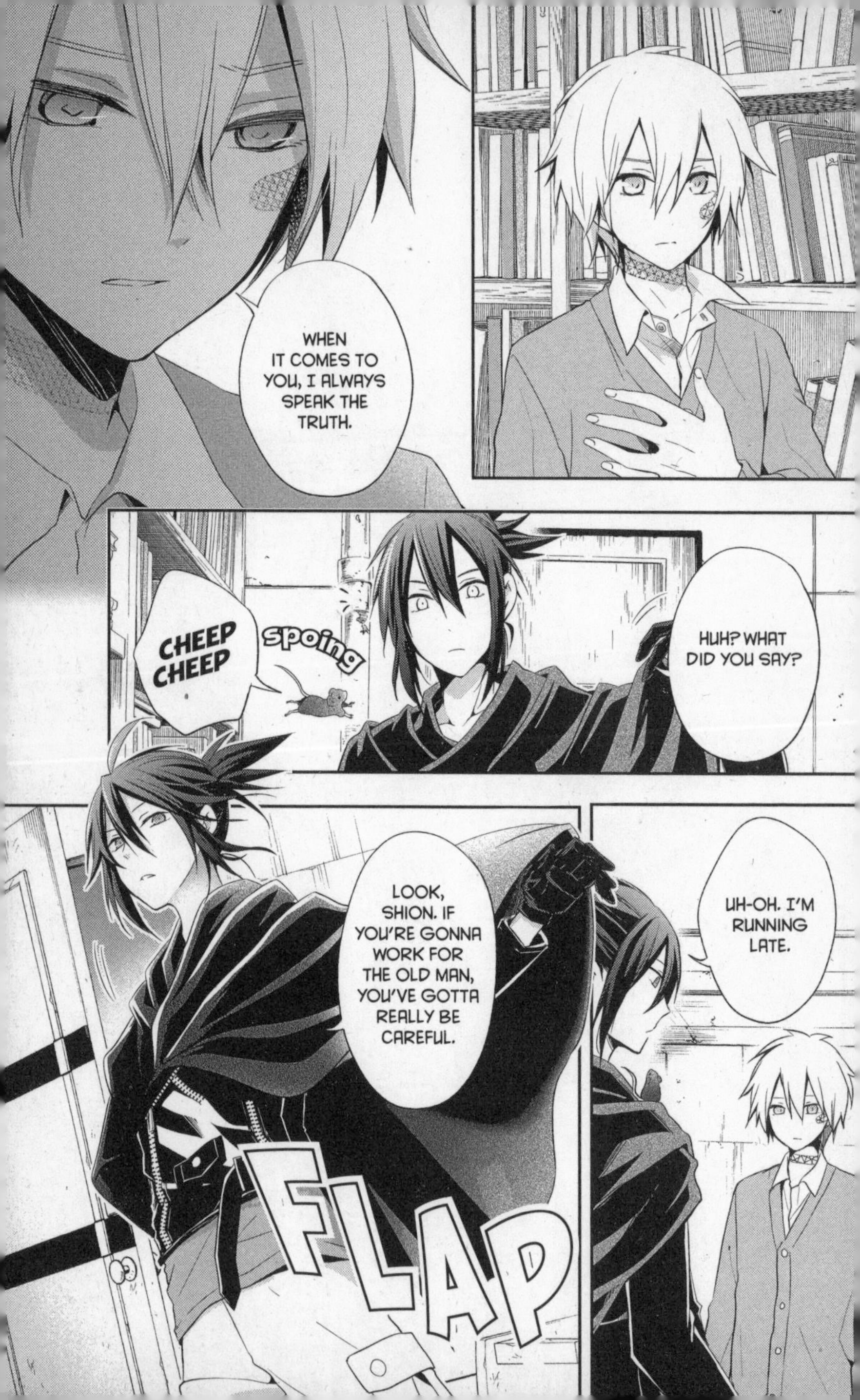
WHEN IT COMES TO YOU, I ALWAYS SPEAK THE TRUTH.
HUH? WHAT DID YOU SAY?
spoing
CHEEP CHEEP
UH-OH. I'M RUNNING LATE.
LOOK, SHION. IF YOU'RE GONNA WORK FOR THE OLD MAN, YOU'VE GOTTA REALLY BE CAREFUL.
FLAP

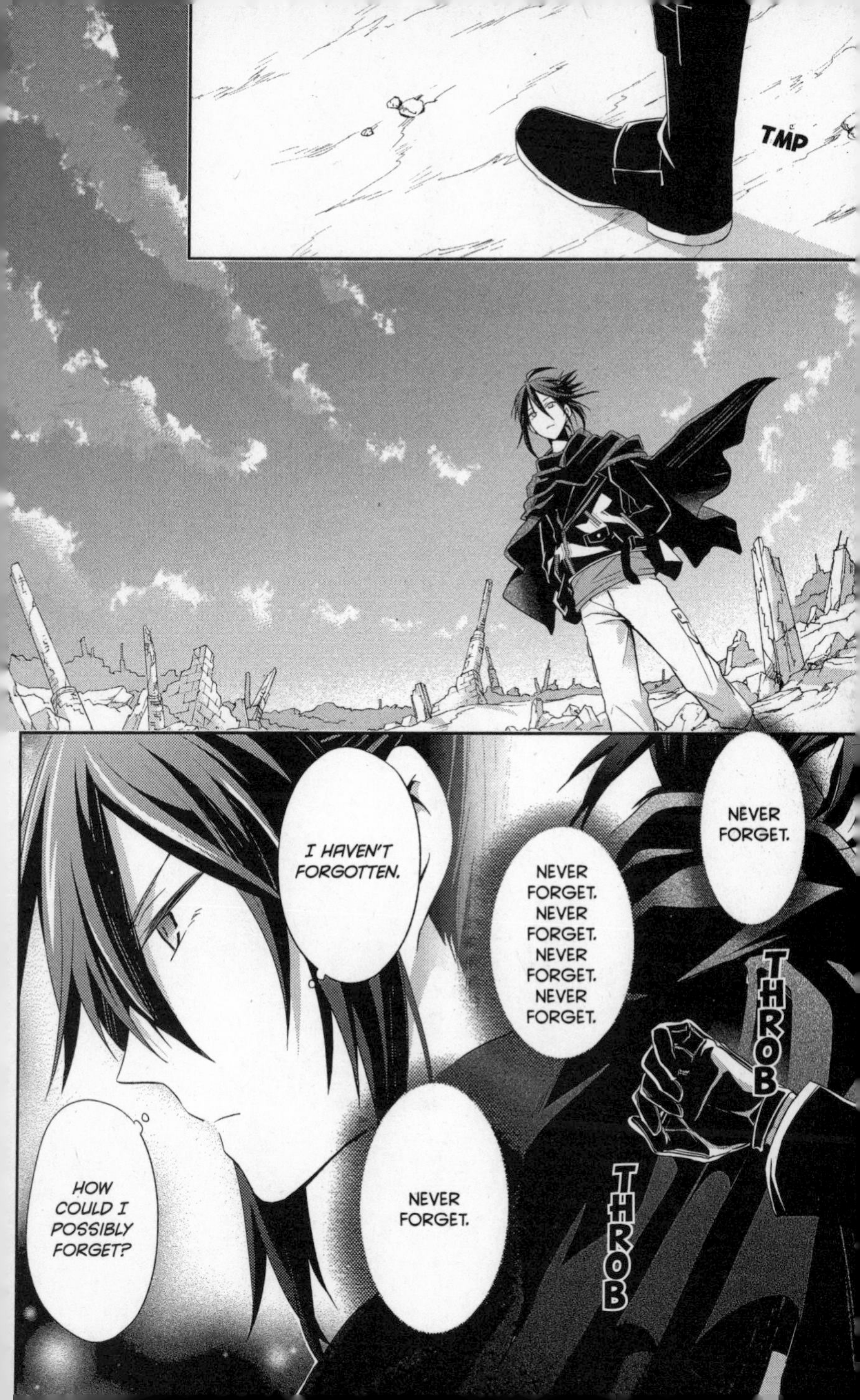
TMP
NEVER FORGET.
NEVER FORGET. NEVER FORGET. NEVER FORGET. NEVER FORGET.
I HAVEN'T FORGOTTEN.
THROB
THROB
NEVER FORGET.
HOW COULD I POSSIBLY FORGET?

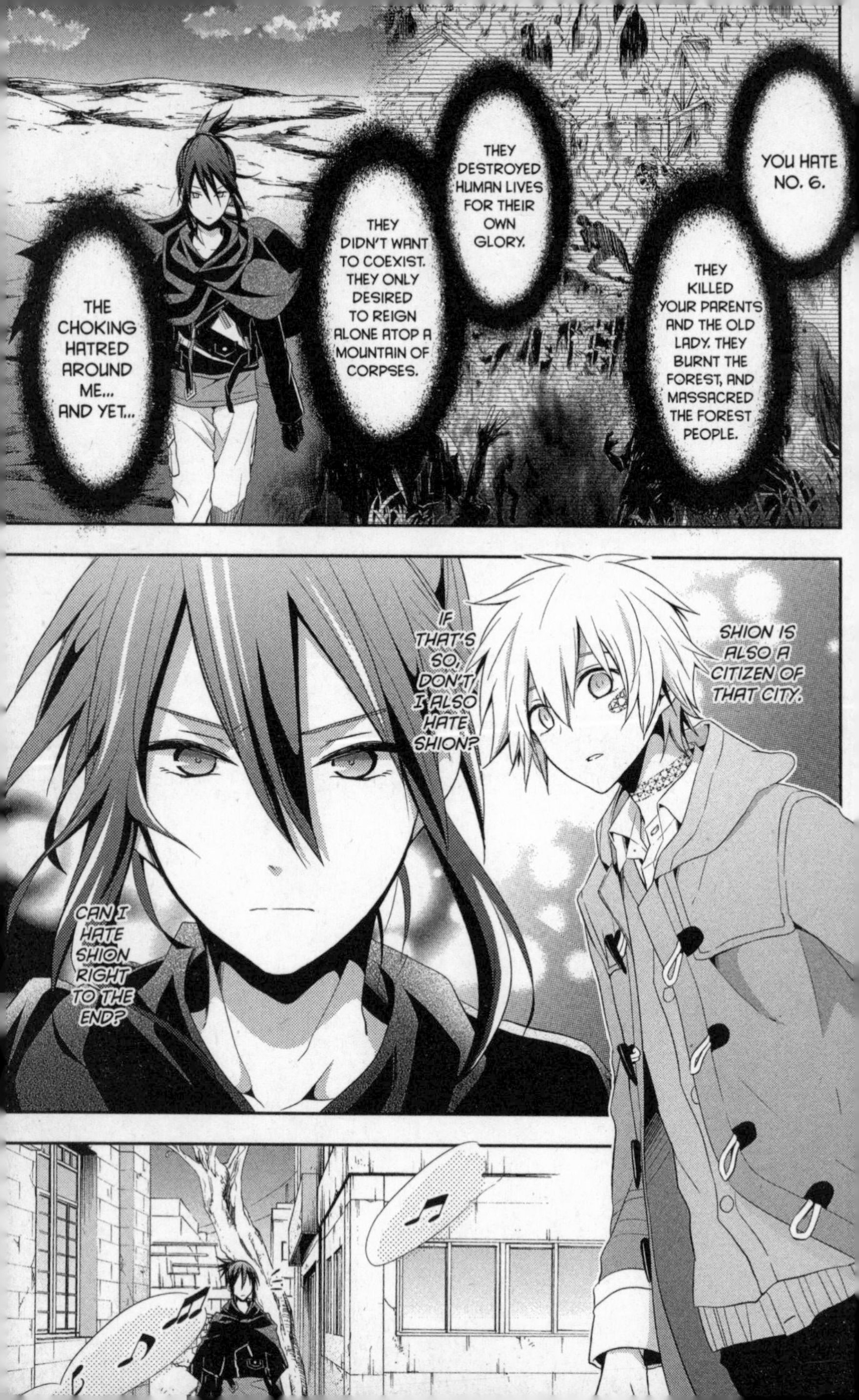
YOU HATE NO. 6.
THEY KILLED YOUR PARENTS AND THE OLD LADY. THEY BURNT THE FOREST, AND MASSACRED THE FOREST PEOPLE.
THEY DESTROYED HUMAN LIVES FOR THEIR OWN GLORY.
THEY DIDN'T WANT TO COEXIST. THEY ONLY DESIRED TO REIGN ALONE ATOP A MOUNTAIN OF CORPSES.
THE CHOKING HATRED AROUND ME... AND YET...
SHION IS ALSO A CITIZEN OF THAT CITY.
IF THAT'S SO, DON'T I ALSO HATE SHION?
CAN I HATE SHION RIGHT TO THE END?

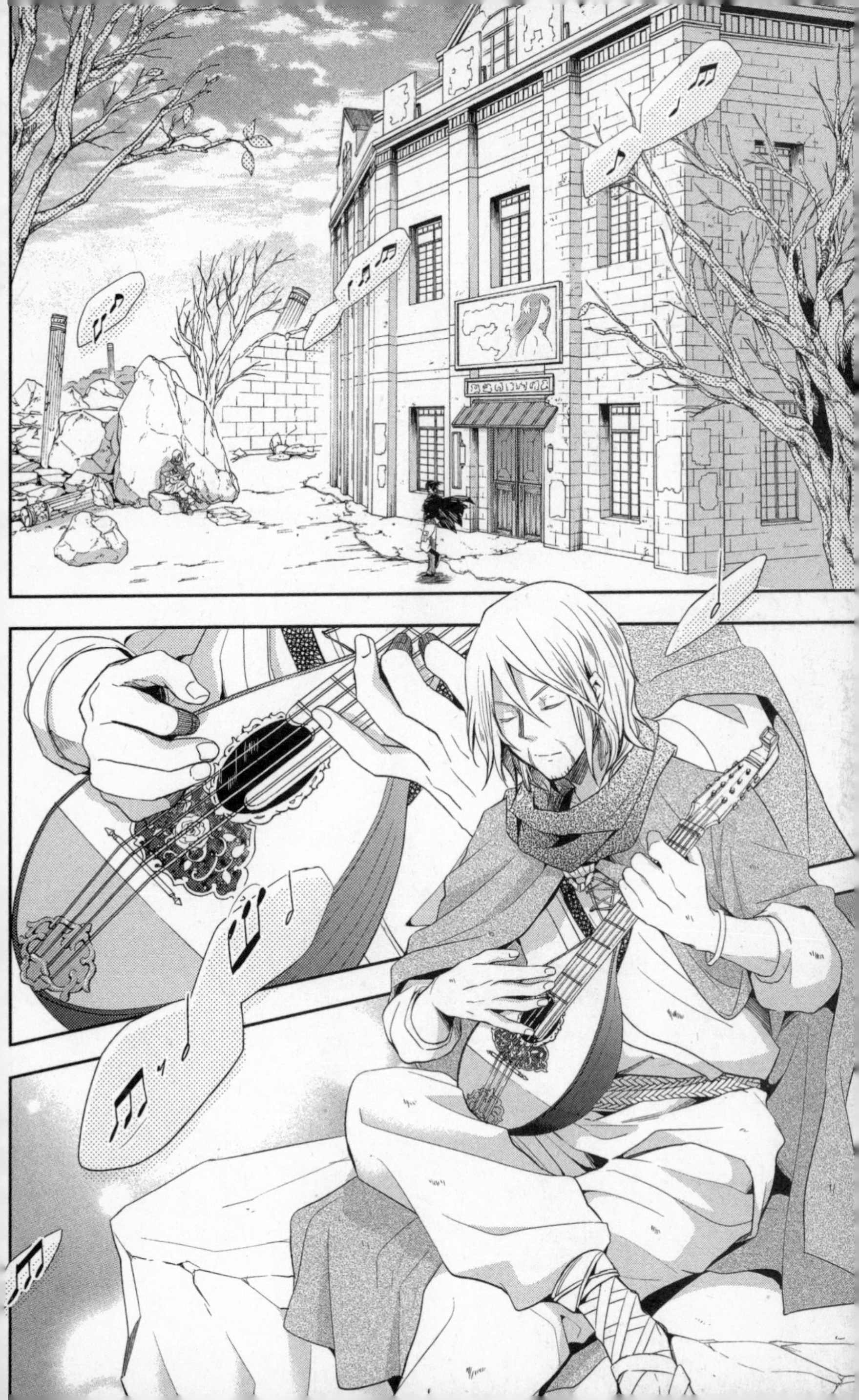

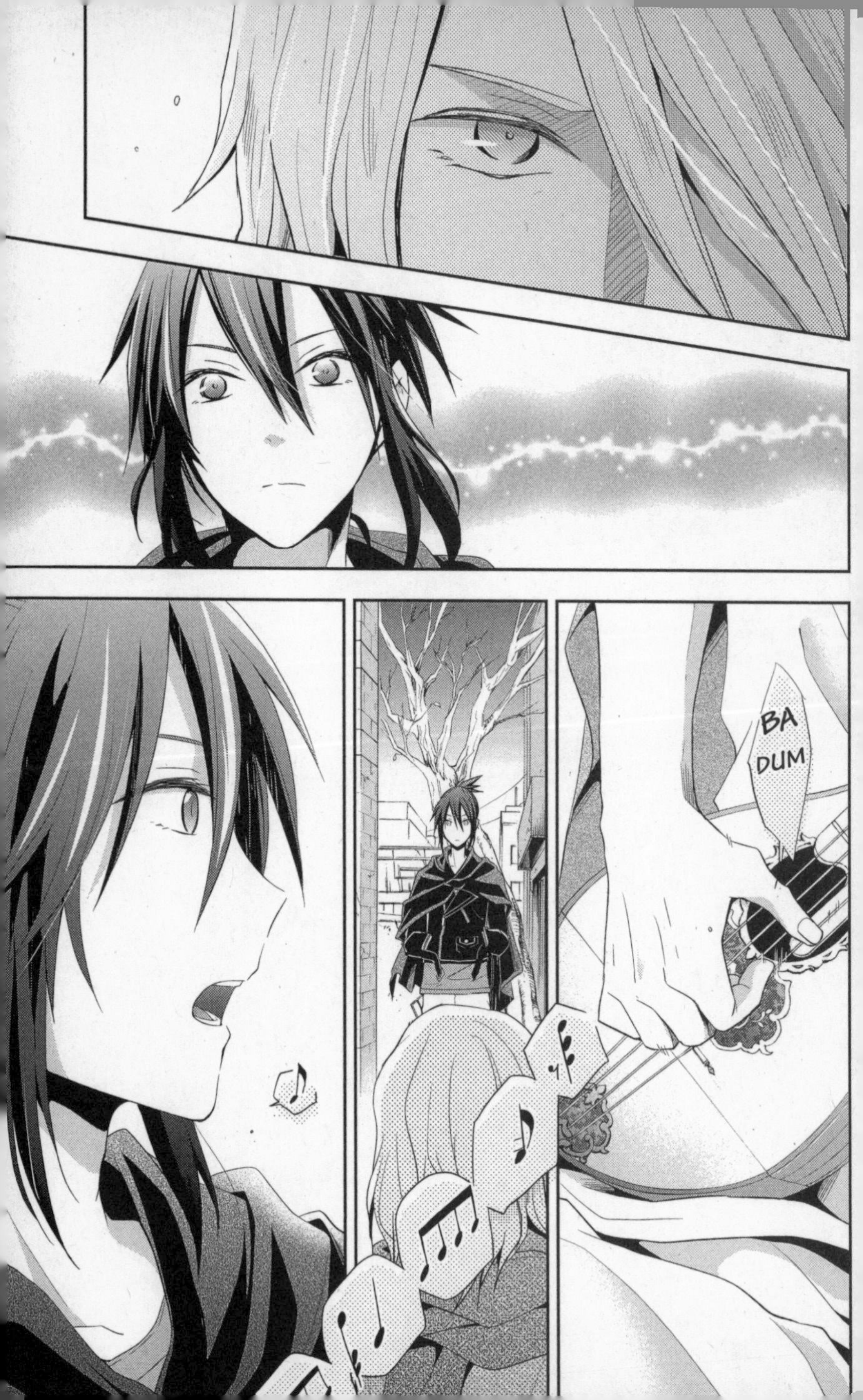
BA DUM

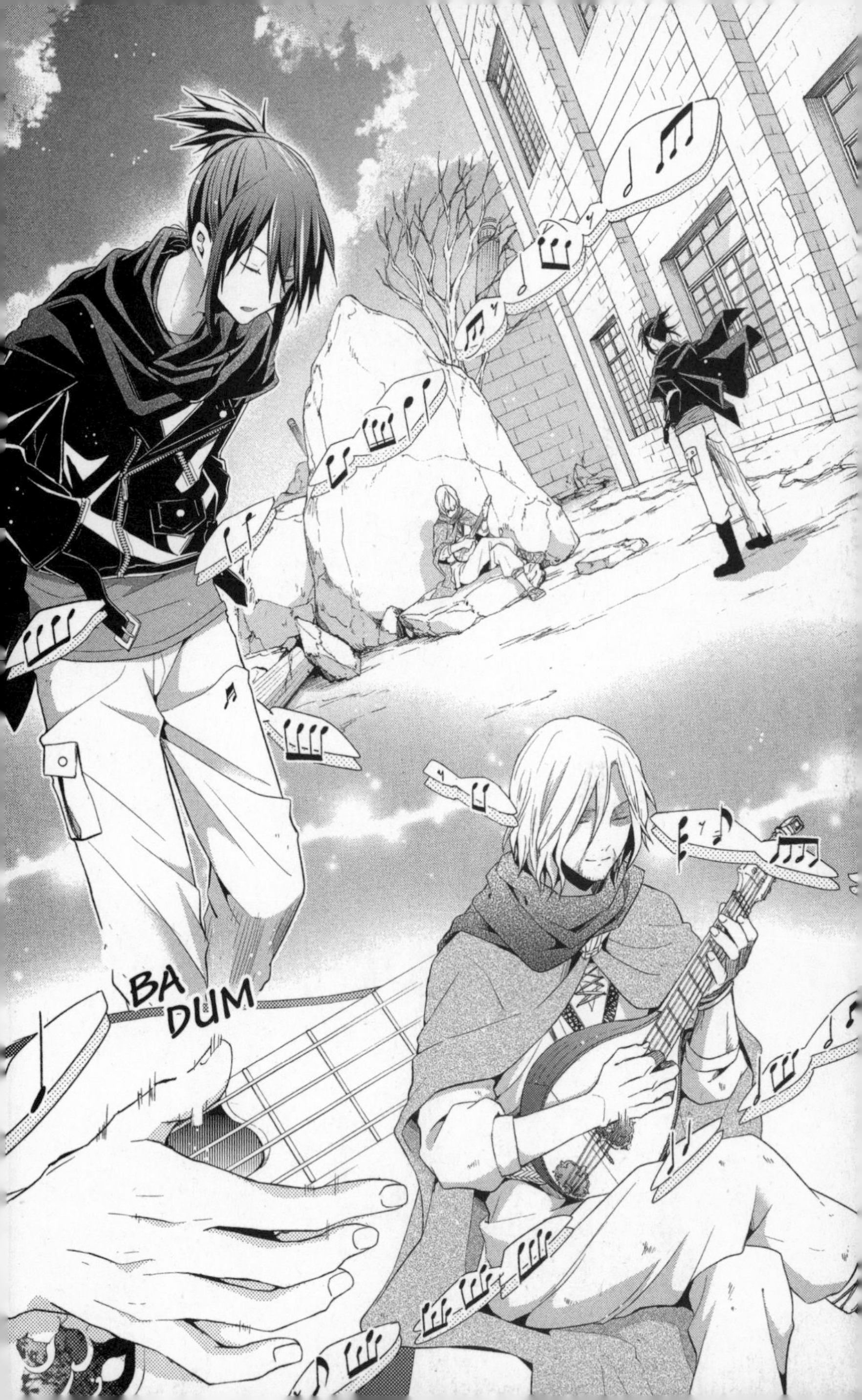
BA DUM

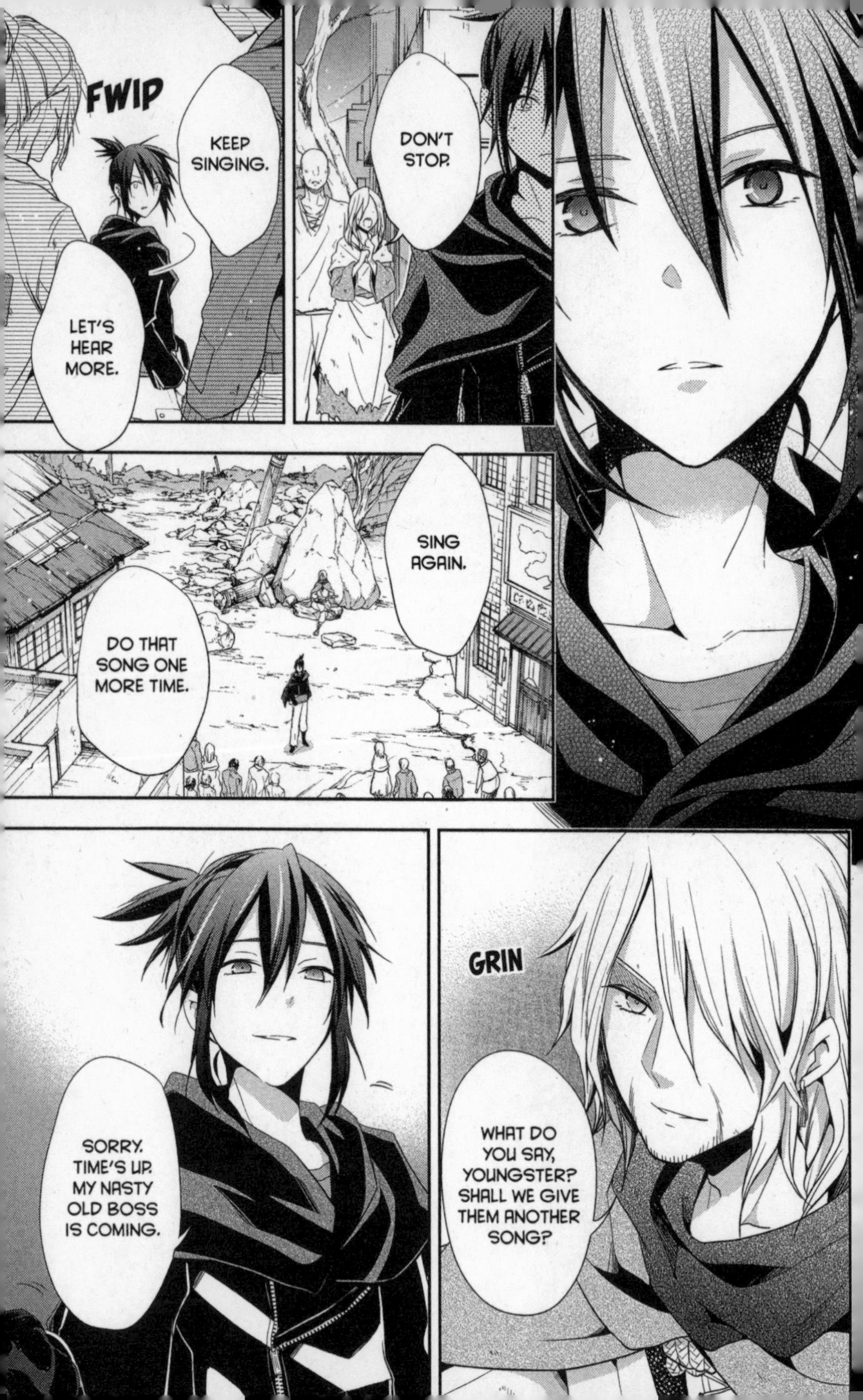
DON'T STOP.
KEEP SINGING.
FWIP
LET'S HEAR MORE.
SING AGAIN.
DO THAT SONG ONE MORE TIME.
GRIN
WHAT DO YOU SAY, YOUNGSTER? SHALL WE GIVE THEM ANOTHER SONG?
SORRY. TIME'S UP. MY NASTY OLD BOSS IS COMING.

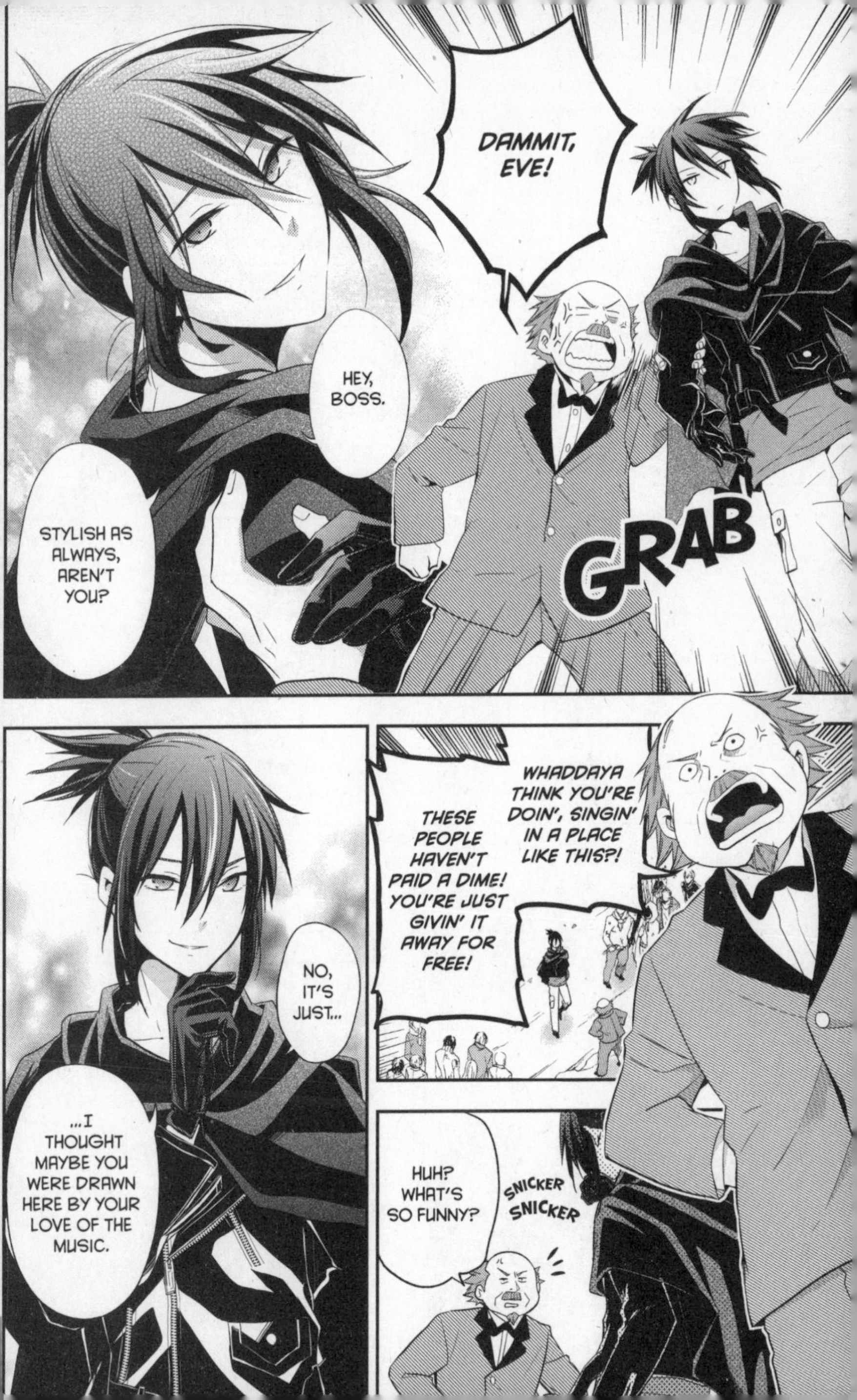
DAMMIT, EVE!
GRAB
HEY, BOSS.
STYLISH AS ALWAYS, AREN'T YOU?
WHADDAYA THINK YOU'RE DOIN', SINGIN' IN A PLACE LIKE THIS?!
THESE PEOPLE HAVEN'T PAID A DIME! YOU'RE JUST GIVIN' IT AWAY FOR FREE!
HUH? WHAT'S SO FUNNY?
SNICKER SNICKER
NO, IT'S JUST...
...I THOUGHT MAYBE YOU WERE DRAWN HERE BY YOUR LOVE OF THE MUSIC.

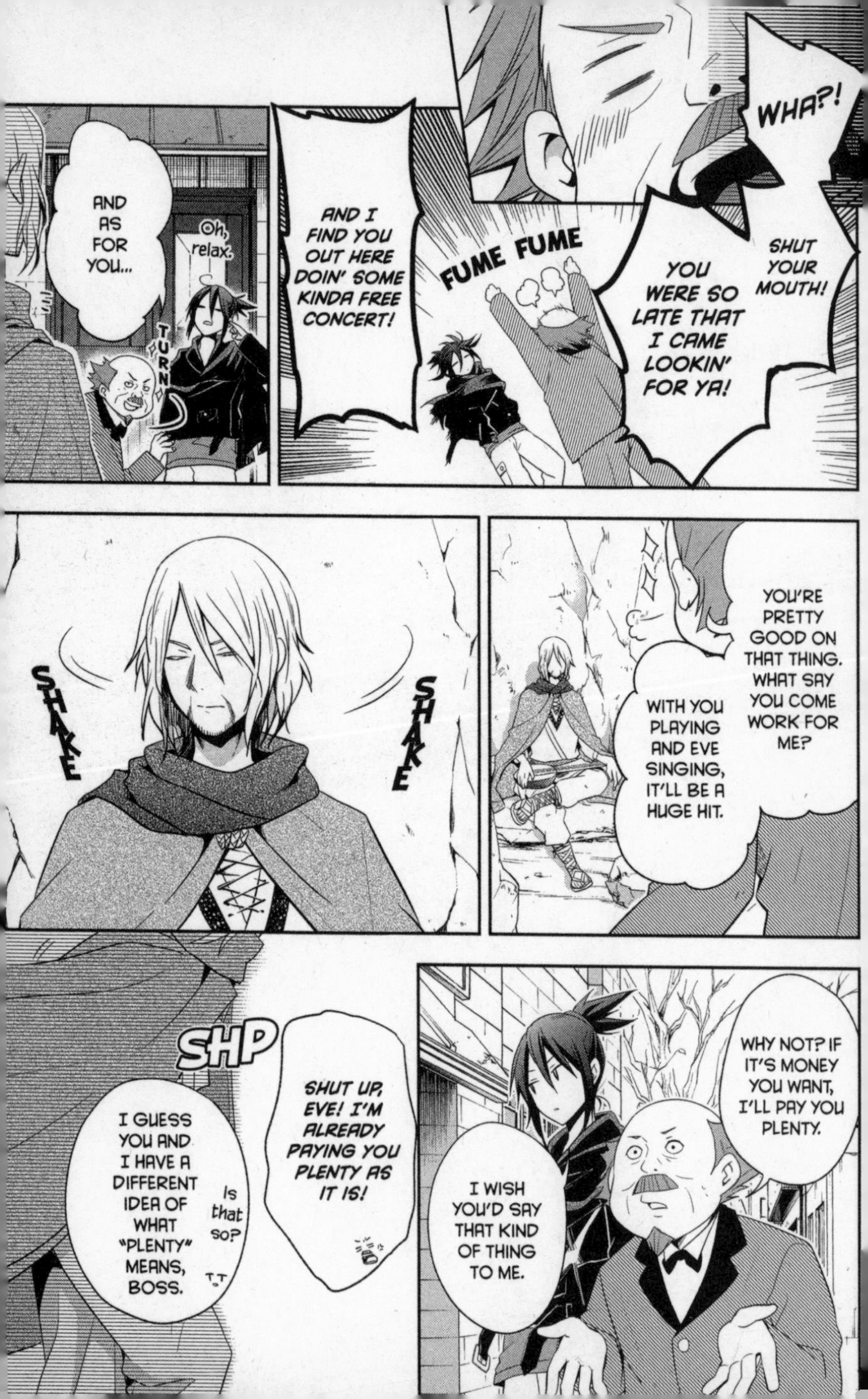
WHA?!
SHUT YOUR MOUTH!
YOU WERE SO LATE THAT I CAME LOOKIN' FOR YA!
FUME FUME
AND I FIND YOU OUT HERE DOIN' SOME KINDA FREE CONCERT!
AND AS FOR YOU...
TURN
Oh, relax.
YOU'RE PRETTY GOOD ON THAT THING. WHAT SAY YOU COME WORK FOR ME?
WITH YOU PLAYING AND EVE SINGING, IT'LL BE A HUGE HIT.
SHAKE
SHAKE
WHY NOT? IF IT'S MONEY YOU WANT, I'LL PAY YOU PLENTY.
I WISH YOU'D SAY THAT KIND OF THING TO ME.
SHUT UP, EVE! I'M ALREADY PAYING YOU PLENTY AS IT IS!
SHP
I GUESS YOU AND I HAVE A DIFFERENT IDEA OF WHAT "PLENTY" MEANS, BOSS.
Is that so?

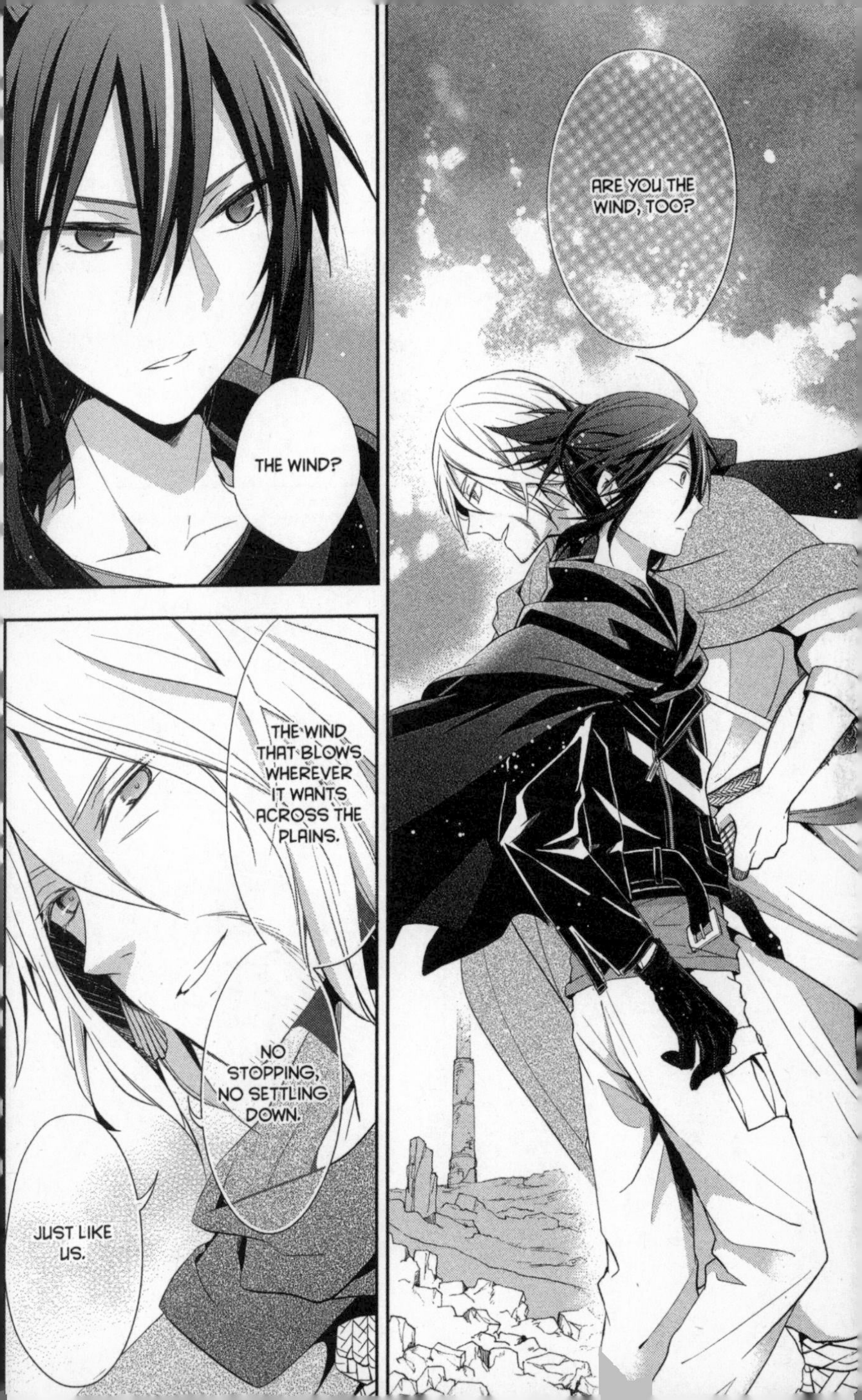
ARE YOU THE WIND, TOO?
THE WIND?
THE WIND THAT BLOWS WHEREVER IT WANTS ACROSS THE PLAINS.
NO STOPPING, NO SETTLING DOWN.
JUST LIKE US.

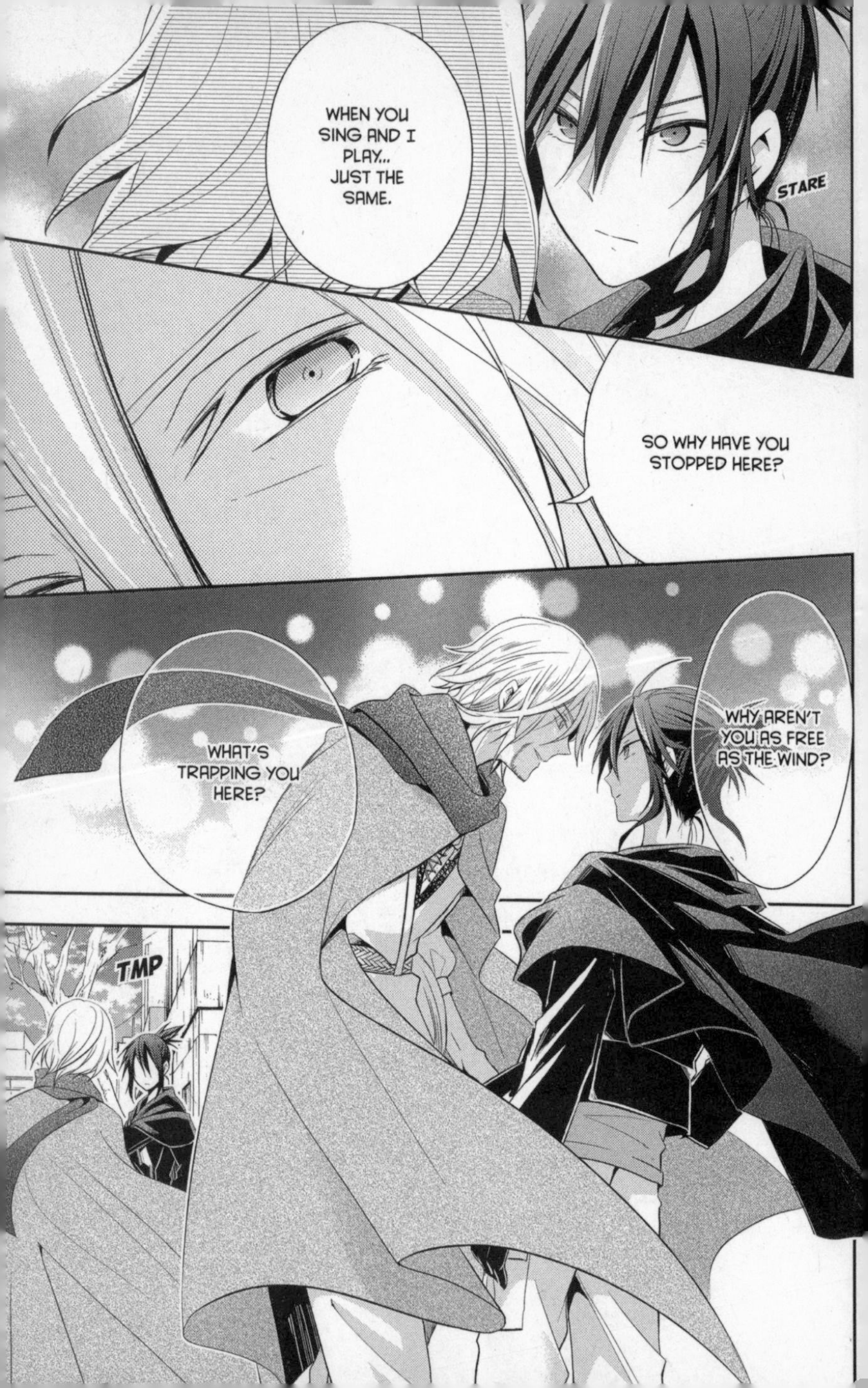
STARE
WHEN YOU SING AND I PLAY... JUST THE SAME.
SO WHY HAVE YOU STOPPED HERE?
WHY AREN'T YOU AS FREE AS THE WIND?
WHAT'S TRAPPING YOU HERE?
TMP

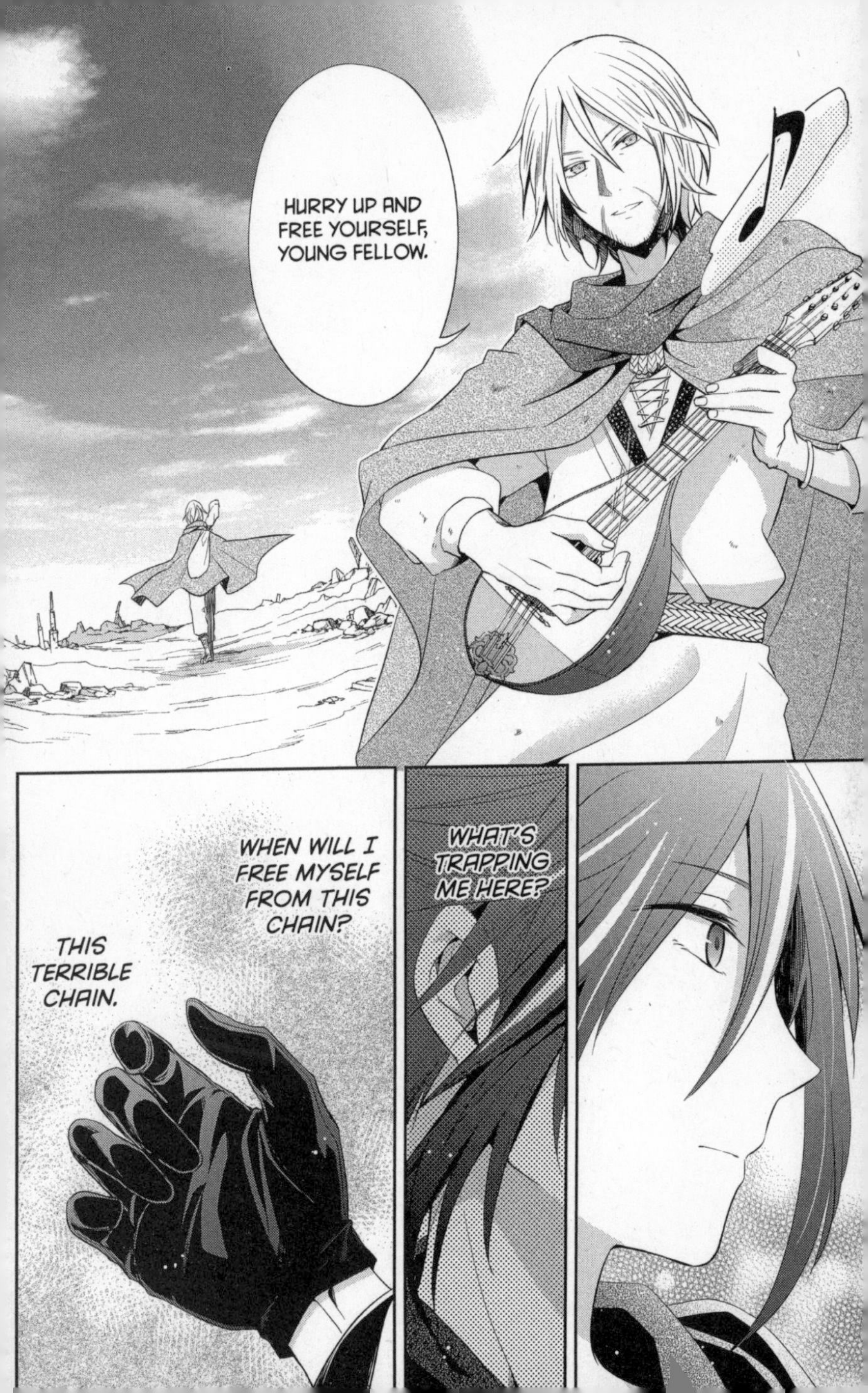
HURRY UP AND FREE YOURSELF, YOUNG FELLOW.
WHAT'S TRAPPING ME HERE?
WHEN WILL I FREE MYSELF FROM THIS CHAIN?
THIS TERRIBLE CHAIN.

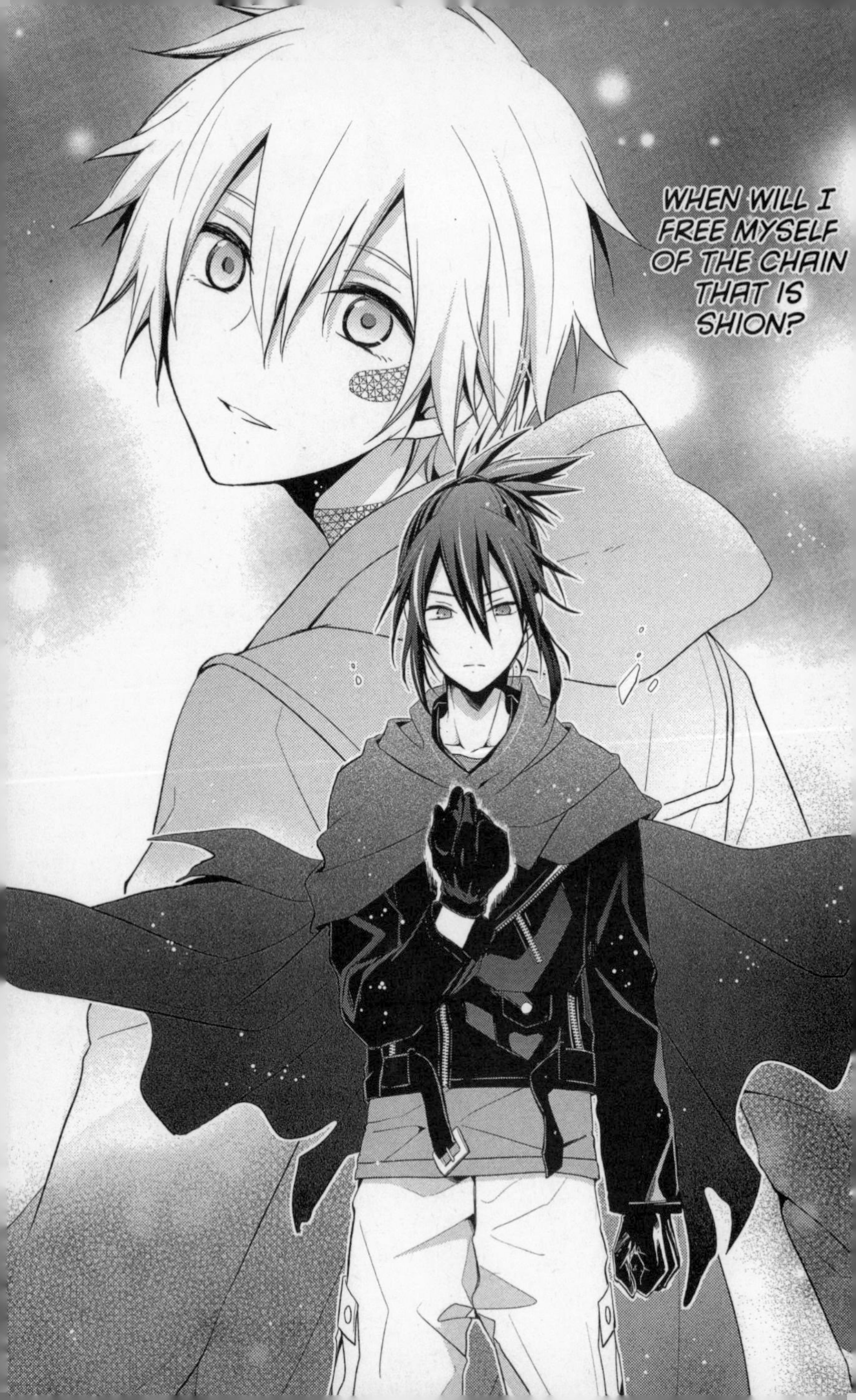
WHEN WILL I FREE MYSELF OF THE CHAIN THAT IS SHION?

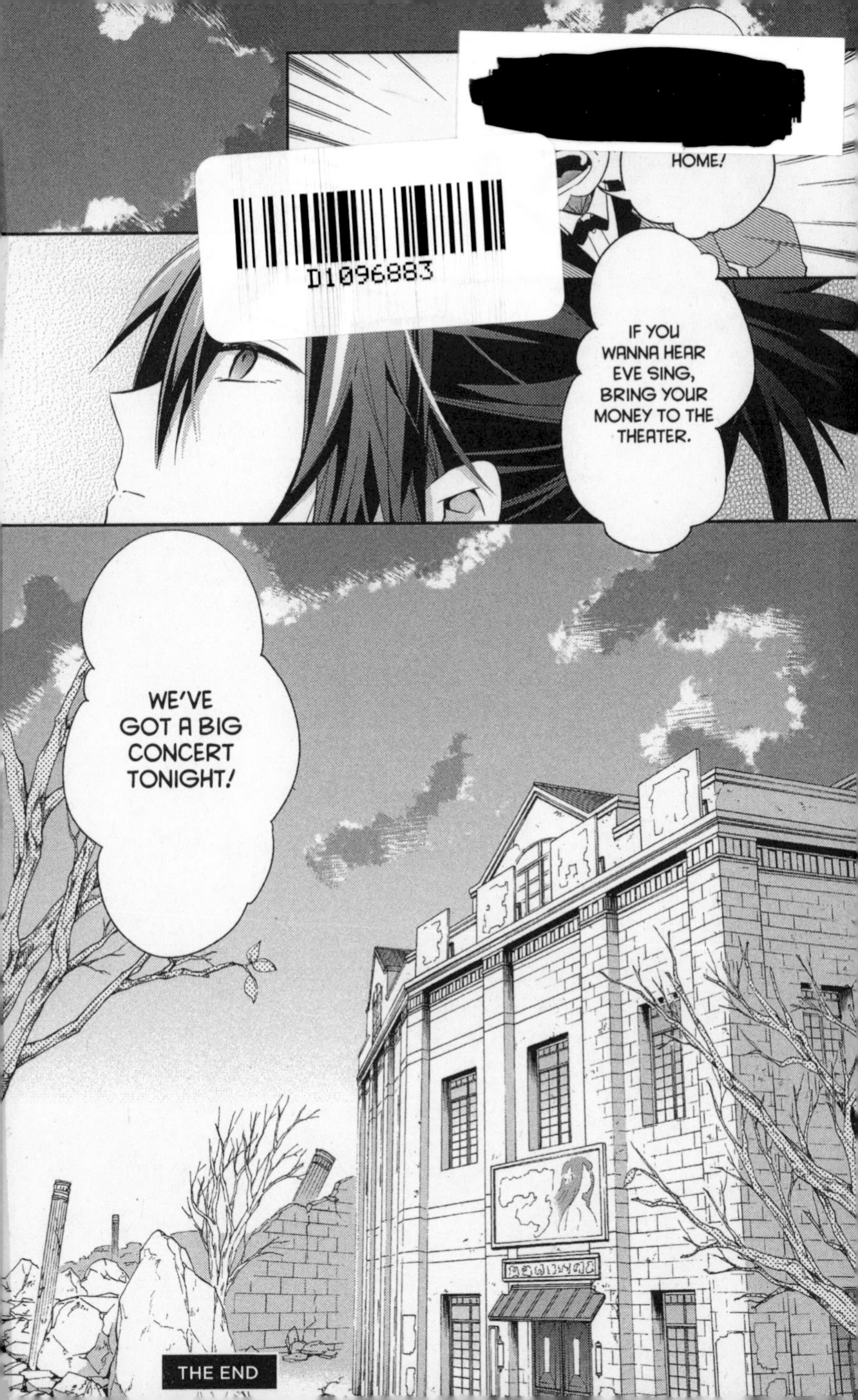
[redacted]
HOME!
IF YOU WANNA HEAR EVE SING, BRING YOUR MONEY TO THE THEATER.
WE'VE GOT A BIG CONCERT TONIGHT!
THE END